INSIGHT GUIDES
POLAND

Contents

THE BEST OF POLAND: TOP ATTRACTIONS

From stunning castles and great lakes to shifting sand dunes and the Chopin Trail, here, at a glance, are Poland's highlights.

△ **Morskie Oko.** The largest and most beautiful lake in the breathtaking Tatras Mountains region. See page 240.

△ **Gdańsk Shipyards.** Spreading along the Mołtawa River, the wonderfully restored waterfront boasts magnificent historic buildings, imposing old cranes, elegant moored tall ships and the pedestranised Granary Island. See page 327.

▽ **Wawel Castle, Kraków.** For centuries this was the seat of power of Polish kings. It towers over Kraków to this day, a symbol not just of the city but of Polish greatness. See page 202.

△ **Łazienki Park.** Poland's greatest public park is home to numerous palaces, and the city's botanical gardens. Half of Warsaw visits on summer Sundays to enjoy free Chopin concerts. See page 164.

△ **Białowieża forest**. Take a walk on the wild side in the Białowieża primeval forest, where you may encounter bisons, lynxes, wolves and numerous bird species. See page 119.

◁ **Słowiński National Park**. The main attraction of this biosphere reserve is its shifting sand dunes, some reaching 40m- (131ft-) high, but there are also deer and wild boars, lakes and desolated beaches to look forward to. See page 325.

▽ **Gniezno Cathedral**. The biggest Gothic church in Poland stands in the centre of what was the first Polish capital. The highlight being a magnificent pair of Romanesque bronzed doors depicting the martyrdom of St. Wojciech. See page 297.

△ **Chopin trail**. Immerse yourself in Fryderyk Chopin's music and learn about the composer's life at several museums across the country, starting with the spectacular Fryderyk Chopin's Museum in Warsaw. See page 186.

△ **Malbork Castle**. The magnificent Gothic fortress is not only a great museum but also a venue of knight tournaments, sound and light shows, and the re-enactment of the castle's siege every July. See page 344.

▽ **Great Mazurian Lakes**. The land of thousands of lakes, hills and dense forests is well suited to water sports, cycling and trekking. See page 357.

THE BEST OF POLAND: EDITOR'S CHOICE

Warsaw and its high-rise skyline, the miraculously preserved Old Town of Kraków, Baltic beaches, chilling memorials and mountain trails... Here at a glance are our recommendations for your trip.

BEST CATHEDRALS AND CHURCHES

Kraków Cathedral. Kraków Cathedral is a Gothic masterpiece, worthy of as much time as you can afford it. Do not miss the Sigismund Chapel or the labyrinthine crypt. See page 203.

St. Mary's Church, Kraków. The lush interior decoration of this 14th-century building was added over the course of the centuries by great artists of the day. Look out for frescoes by Veit Stoss and Jan Metejko. See page 198.

Tyniec Abbey. Sitting imposingly on the banks of the Vistula, the Benedictine Abbey at Tyniec plays host to a series of summer organ concerts. See page 209.

Church of the Blessed Virgin Mary, Starogard Szczeciński. This 13th-century pearl of Gothic architecture boasts a splendid rib vaulted nave. See page 320.

Sękowa Church, near Gorlice. This Unesco Heritage Site is one of the finest examples of wooden architecture in Poland. See page 218.

Church of St Mary Magdalene, Wrocław. Famed for its Romanesque sandstone portal, which dates from the 12th century, St Mary's is a triple-naved red-brick church with flying buttresses. See page 266.

The sumptuous carved altarpiece by master craftsman Veit Stoss at St Mary's Church, Kraków.

The infamous Nazi death camp, Auschwitz, is now a Unesco World Heritage Site and museum.

JEWISH HISTORY AND CULTURE

Museum of the History of Polish Jews, Warsaw. Housed in a magnificent building, this state-of-the-art museum tells the fascinating story of the Jewish presence in Poland. See page 159.

Festival of Jewish Culture, Kraków. Get a taste of Jewish culture, music, history and cuisine during the immensely popular festival held in Kazimierz, Kraków's historic Jewish district. See page 205.

Jewish quarter, Tarnów. Take a stroll along Żydowska and Wekslarska streets to admire fabulous 17th- and 18th-century Jewish tenement houses. See page 214.

Old Synagogue, Kraków. Dating from the early 15th century and extended in the 16th, the synagogue's façade is therefore a mix of Gothic and Renaissance styles; inside is the Museum of the History and Culture of Jews in Kraków. See page 206.

Auschwitz. Now a place of pilgrimage and remembrance for Jews, Roma and any number of nationalities who suffered here, modern-day Auschwitz is a solemn yet compelling place that should be visited by all. See page 253.

BEST MUSEUMS

The coalmine shafts of the Silesian Museum in Katowice.

Warsaw Rising Museum. Learn about the city's grimmest hour and its heroic men at this state-of-the-art venue. See page 147.

Silesian Museum, Katowice. A must-see if only for its new, futuristic building with adapted historic coalmine shafts. See page 248.

Interactive Museum of the Teutonic State, Działdowo. This museum presents in a highly entertaining way the rise and fall of the mighty Teutonic Order. See page 360.

Art Museum, Łódź. The richest collection of Polish modern art is spread over three splendid locations in wonderfully converted historic buildings. See page 179.

Museum of Contemporary Art (MOCAK), Kraków. Another old factory successfully repurposed as an art gallery, housing some of the best works from contemporary Polish and international artists. See page 207.

Gdańsk Maritime Museum. Admire the Gdańsk Crane (Żuraw Gdański), used since the 15th century to raise the masts of the tall ships that docked in the harbour. See page 333.

Gothic Kwidzyn Castle.

BEST PALACES AND CASTLES

Wilanów Palace. Summer residence of Jan III Sobieski, Wilanów dates from 1679 and is the finest Baroque building in Poland. See page 161.

Łańcut Castle. This former Lubomirski family residence boasts fine architecture as well as a classical music spring festival. See page 217.

Krzyżtopór Castle. The partly-ruined former aristocratic palace is breathtaking for its awesome proportions alone. See page 221.

Książ Palace. Perched on a majestic rock cliff surrounded by thick forest, the 'Pearl of Lower Silesia' is the third largest castle in Poland. See page 275.

Rogalin Palace. Situated on the Warta River amid beautiful parkland dotted with ancient oaks, Rogalin is a masterpiece of 18th-century Polish Baroque architecture. See page 296.

Kwidzyn Castle. The highlights of this former Gothic fortress are its sewer tower and adjacent cathedral housing the tombs of the Teutonic Order Grand Masters. See page 345.

THE GREAT OUTDOORS

Tatra Mountains. With their spectacular peaks, the Tatras are a mountaineer's paradise and a haven for wildlife, including rare eagles. There are also excellent trails for hikers. See page 240.

Biebrzański National Park. An eldorado for ornithologists and bird-watchers, the swamps and pit bogs of the Biebrza River are one of Europe's wildest areas. See page 176.

Pieniny Mountains. A raft ride on the River Dunajec, which winds through the dramatically beautiful Pieniny gorges, is one of the most popular tourist attractions in Poland. See page 235.

Bory Tucholskie. Overgrown with pine woods, cut across by river valleys and dotted with lakes, Bory Tucholskie forest is Poland's hidden gem. See page 343.

Karkonosze Mountains. Straddling the Polish-Czech border, the Karkonosze offer great hiking opportunities and some of the most majestic waterfalls in Europe. See page 277.

The Tatra Mountains in winter.

Every hour on the hour a trumpeter plays the "hejnał" from St Mary's Church tower in Kraków.

Folkloric dancing, Rydlówka Museum, Kraków.

Concert in the ornate St Anna's Church in Warsaw.

THE APPEAL OF POLAND

Often caught between the geopolitical forces of east and west, Poland has mastered the subtle arts of survival.

Farmer at work.

For more than a millennium, Poland has played a vital role in European history. The country's position in the heart of Europe has always made it a bridge between the two great cultures on its eastern and western flanks. The resulting diversity of influences has helped to shape the mentality of the people, who are tolerant of differing opinions and ways of life, yet open-minded about new ideas and hospitable towards strangers.

Neither oppression nor the centuries of brutal violence perpetrated by neighbouring countries have succeeded in stifling Poland's liberal spirit. Even during times of upheaval, when the country was obliterated from the map of Europe, the safeguarding of national culture, the recollection of a glorious past, Christian-humanistic traditions and solidarity remained at the forefront of the collective memory. These values still abound, and in such a climate there has never been room for any one 'truth' or a monopoly of any one doctrine. The Poles have never allowed their liberty to be curtailed.

Handpainted Easter eggs.

Poland has so much to offer – seaside resorts by the Baltic, hillwalking in the High Tatra Mountains, canoeing on the rivers and lakes of Mazuria, strolling through the Old Town in the historic city of Gdańsk, touring the monuments in Kraków or enjoying a beer in Old Market Square in Warsaw, the nation's capital. In recent years, Poland's appeal as a holiday destination has grown, as the range of accommodation has improved. Now the choice runs from luxury hotel with swimming pool and fitness suite to rooms in a private house, living with a Polish family, to camping by a lake.

If you are looking for some adventurous outdoor activities, then Poland is just the place. You can explore the countryside on foot, by bike, on horseback or by boat. Hunters and anglers have also discovered the special attractions that Poland can offer. If wildlife is one of your passions, then there is a good chance that you will catch a glimpse of some unusual species. Storks, for example, are very much in evidence in Mazuria, while rare species include bison, elk and tarpan, a kind of wild horse once thought to be extinct.

As well as these natural treasures, Poland possesses some imposing buildings: the Teutonic Knights' castle at Malbork or the magnificent complex on the Wawel in Kraków. Last but not least, the Old Town in Warsaw and the heart of ancient Gdańsk have been rebuilt to their former splendour.

THE POLISH PEOPLE

Despite centuries of foreign rule, the Polish people
have maintained a strong identity and welcome
visitors with lavish hospitality.

Polish-British historian Norman Davies hit the nail on the head when he wrote that 'for far longer than anyone living can remember Polish history has been marked by disaster'. But despite partitions, failed insurgencies, international complots, World War II atrocities and utopic post-war Communist policies, the Polish people showed astonishing resilience, courage and ability to overcome all odds. The emergence of the Solidarity movement, followed by the collapse of Communism and later membership of the EU all put Poland in the fast lane towards modernisation, which in turn has had an enormous impact on Polish society.

The Polish character

The old saying goes that where there are two Poles there are three opinions. Indeed, Polish love to discuss things, argue and even quarrel with each other over minor as well as fundamental matters. History and politics may feature heavily at Polish gatherings – and therefore

Cracovian waitress.

> *Sympathy from the Germans towards the Poles emerged after the imposition of military rule at the end of 1981, when the West Germans sent millions of aid packages to the crippled country.*

at least some basic historic knowledge is needed to follow most conversations. However, being very hospitable, Poles would gladly change the subject if politely reminded that the intricacies of the national political scene do not necessarily hold much interest for their guests.

Another strange Polish habit, perhaps ingrained in the national psyche by years of misery and misfortune, is the constant complaining about virtually everything, be it weather (for some it is always too hot, for others too cold or too rainy), work, family, health problems, ungrateful friends, the country going to the dogs or just a bus arriving two minutes late. This is particularly evident among the older generation, which also tends to have a more pessimistic mindset – miserly pensions being one of the reasons. The Poles' discontent may be surprising or even shocking to foreigners, particularly considering the country's recent successes and robust economy (the average annual growth in the last decade slightly exceeded 4 percent). This vice, however, is strictly confined to the Poles – on no account try to beat them at their own game, particularly by criticising their homeland, as they can get very touchy. Jokes on Poles and their national character will most certainly fall on deaf ears, too.

Otherwise Poles are wonderful companions eager to share anything with their new acquaintances and make them feel at home. As they say in Poland 'a guest in the house, God in the house'. This usually translates into a lavish welcome and farewell parties with great quantities of food and alcohol. Refusal is not an option – it would be considered rude and put hosts in an awkward position.

Young Poland

The last two decades or so have seen dramatic changes in the once traditionally rural Polish society. Today, there are more people living in the cities (59.4 percent, according to the 2011 census), with thousands of young people eager to leave the countryside in search of a better life. In 2011 alone some 21,000 people move to Warsaw for better job opportunities and higher salaries. This, along with the ongoing modernisation and Westernisation of the country, resulted in a radical change of lifestyles and attitudes, particularly among young

Student bar in trendy Kazimierz, Kraków.

Over the centuries, big-heartedness, generosity and legendary prowess in battle have made Poles a much sought after ally and a fearsome enemy. But bravery – or bravado – can have its downside, as the frightening number of road accidents attests. Despite new motorways, severe fines and educational campaigns, driving in Poland may still prove a terrifying experience for an outsider. Speeding, cutting in, and risky overtaking on narrow roads and lanes remain as popular as ever. The government has reacted by installing more and more speed cameras in big cities and along the main routes; this is likely to improve the situation, but for the time being, regrettably, Poland's roads remain among the most deadly in the EU.

Poles. The once obligatory Sunday family dinners have not become a thing of the past, but they are no longer as common as they used to be. The hectic pace of life in cities like Warsaw encourages new patterns of behaviour. A few decades ago, the streets of Polish cities would have been virtually deserted at 9 or 10pm. Now, no matter if it is a normal working day or a weekend, they are full of stylishly dressed bar-hopping young people, drinking and chatting until the small hours. Going out at night in a group of friends has become a ritual for a growing number of city dwellers, whereas parties in private homes, particularly popular with the older generation and known as *domówki*, have lost much of their appeal.

In general, young Poles are well educated, outgoing and know at least a bit of English, so breaking the ice is not a problem. Moreover, they haven't inherited the inferiority complex of their parents, who were all too often in awe of anything from Western Europe. As in any country, young Poles often express radical opinions and brim with enthusiasm for new, shiny things, whether it's the newest smartphone or a recently created political party. It's therefore a great shame that so many of them leave Poland for the UK, the Netherlands, Germany or Belgium, stripping the country of its most valuable asset.

standards. Compulsory education starts from age 6 and ends at 18, comprising of six years of primary school and then three years of secondary school (*gymnasium*) followed by either three years at sixth form/high school (*lyceum*), four years at technical school (*technikum*) or three years of vocational school. Besides public (state) schools run by the government and free of charge, a rising number of children in large cities attend either private or association schools with tuition fees. Many experts eagerly admit that Poland currently has one of the most effective educational systems in the world.

Child in Gubałowka.

Traditions are important.

This trend accelerated after Poland joined the EU in 2004, when many young Poles left to work in Western Europe, mainly in the UK and Ireland. It is estimated that some 650,000 Poles work and live in the UK alone – and Polish is now the second most spoken language in England. With unemployment in Poland still hovering at almost 14 percent (reaching 26 percent among the youth) these young migrants are unlikely to return to their homeland anytime soon.

The power of knowledge

The education system in Poland has been completely revamped following the fall of Communism to come in line with the modern Western

LAND OF TOLERANCE

In the Middle Ages Poland had a far less brutal history than many other European countries. When Polish Jews were obtaining their Statute of Jewish Liberties at Kalisz in 1264, the rest of Europe was engulfed in religious wars. Monks from all over Europe came here to practise their religion; the Convent of Cistercian Brothers had a tremendous input into the growth of Poland's wealth. From countries torn by religious wars and reformation, waves of Huguenots, Protestants, Jews, Hussites and members of the Orthodox church all came to Poland, where they lived in unison under the watchful eye of the Polish rulers.

Polish universities though are far behind their international competitors with the best two: the University of Warsaw and Kraków's Jagiellonian University finding themselves at 419th and 479th place respectively in the 2014 world ranking. Nevertheless, young Polish students, particularly those studying computing, are in great demand, quickly recruited by the biggest international companies. Polish programmers excel in prestigious international competitions including the world championships 'Hello World Open 2014', Pandacodium Topcoder and many others.

can provide for me and my children.' In a way, her words epitomise the attitude of many Polish women who have fought hard for survival and emancipation.

Recent years have seen a rise of feminism in Poland, with gender studies gaining some popularity – or notoriety as the right-wing commentators would have it – and prominent women urging politicians of the mainstream parties to introduce parity. They scored a minor success in 2014 when parties had to include at least 35 percent of women on their lists during elections to the European Parliament. Further-

Young women in Poland are usually better educated than men.

Women in Poland

Women have always played an important role in the Polish society. Whenever men went to war or took part in yet another rebellion against foreign oppressors or were sent to Russian labour camps in the Far East, wives and mothers had to take care of families, houses and businesses left behind. As a result, they have become ferociously independent and resilient as well as ready to deal with any difficulties fate might throw at them. When offered a pension by the French government after her husband died, the then 40-year-old Marie Skłodowska-Curie, a Polish-born physician and the first woman to receive a Nobel Prize, responded, 'I will not accept any pension. I'm still young and

more, some well-educated and eloquent activists such as Professor Magdalena Środa or Dr Agnieszka Graff have beome household names, often appearing as commentators on popular TV shows and in other media.

Although the glass ceiling is still in place and Polish women earn less than men in similar positions, there are many examples of brilliant entrepreneurs who have made astonishing professional careers (Irena Eris, Wanda Rapaczyńska, Henryka Bochniarz to name just a few) trailblazing the path for thousand others. As a matter of fact, young women in Poland are usually better educated than men, adjust quicker to the changing professional environment, and have more determination to succeed and achieve professional fulfillment. The social impact of this has translated into fewer marriages – in 2013 their number fell to the lowest level since 1945 – and an alarmingly low birth rate (1.26), one of the lowest in the world.

Multicultural Poland

The Second Republic of Poland (1918–39) was a multinational state: out of 35 million inhabitants, only 24 million were of Polish origin. After the Poles came the Ukrainians, of whom there were an estimated five to seven million. They were followed by the Jews, who numbered 3.3

decided to distribute the remaining 200,000 Ukrainians over the whole country. In practice, however, they were resettled in the part of the country that had formerly been eastern Germany, since it was the only area where there were still unoccupied farms, abandoned by the Germans. The administrative regions of Wrocław, Szczecin, Koszalin and Olsztyn are now the main centres of the Ukrainian population in Poland.

Today there are around 50,000 Ukrainians living in Poland but every year thousands more arrive to work, mostly illegally, as cleaners, babysitters and construction workers, or to

Elderly couple enjoying a drink in Zakopane.

million, the Byelorussians, with 1.5 million, and a total of 500,000 Lithuanians and Germans.

The new post-war Poland within the borders established at the conferences of Yalta and Potsdam was to be an ethnically homogeneous state free from conflict between different nationalities. Its borders were pushed westwards and the non-Polish inhabitants inside these new boundaries were to be resettled.

Nevertheless, some 700,000 Ukrainians remained in Poland. Most moved to the Ukrainian Socialist Soviet Republic, but many refused to leave their homeland. In southeast Poland, a war broke out between the Polish government forces and the nationalist UPA (Ukrainian Insurrectionary Army). In 1947, the Polish authorities

study at Polish universities, mainly in Przemyśl, a city across the border from Lviv. Poland was the first country in the world to recognise independent Ukraine in 1991 and has continued to support its road to democracy and full integration into the European Union.

The several thousand Lithuanians who lived around Suwałki on the Lithuanian border were left more or less alone after World War II. After 1989, they had their rights fully restored, and today the Lithuanian language is taught at several schools in the Sejny and Puńsk areas. In the latter, Lithuanians make up more than 74 percent of the population. However, Polish-Lithuanian relations remain tense as, despite promises made by several Lithuanian leaders, Polish schools in

Lithuania remain underfunded and Poles must have their names 'Lithuanianised' in all official documents. Lithuanian authorities also oppose the Polish spelling of street names in towns and villages where Poles outnumber Lithuanians.

Over 200,000 Byelarusians were still in Poland after the war, of whom 36,000 were forcefully resettled. Those who remained in the country lived in concentrated groups in their home villages and towns in the area of Białystok, Bielsk Podlaski and Hajnówka.

The country's 300,000-strong German minority is the only one with a political representation

streets and towns in the region are bilingual. Religious festivals such as the sea pilgrimage of the Kashubian fishermen to Puck in June have become popular tourist attractions. Upper Silesia has witnessed a similar revival. Founded in 1990, the Silesian Autonomy Movement (RAŚ) (see page 253) works tirelessly to reclaim local identity, traditions and history, along with calls for the entire region to become autonomous. It even tried to have a separate Silesian nationality officially recognised by Poland, but its motion to the Human Rights Court in Strasbourg was eventually rejected.

Folkloric band in Kamień Pomorski.

in the Polish Sejm (parliament). Most live in the Opolskie region, with much smaller concentrations in Mazuria and Warmia. The signing of the German-Polish Co-operation Treaty in 1991 consolidated the rights of the German minority in Poland. On Annaberg (Góra św. Anny), a mountain that is considered holy by Poles and Germans, mass is now also read in German; it is perfectly legal to attend German classes and new music ensembles and choirs have been funded.

The last quarter of the 20th century saw a minority revival with Kashubians in the north and Silesians in the south of the country being particularly keen on reclaiming their traditions and language. Today, Kashubian is again being thought at schools, and the names of the

There is also a much smaller minority of Polish Tatars, around 2,000 people, inhabiting the Podlaskie region. Their ancestors usually served in Tatar units in the Polish or Lithuanian army and were granted land and privileges for their service. They still conserve their Muslim faith and rituals. Two mosques in Bohoniki and Kruszyniany have been classified as National Heritage sites. The local families run hostels for tourists, where they prepare delicious Tatar dishes.

Cost of living

Poland is no longer a cheap country, especially for those making a living there. However, tourists from affluent Western countries will find excellent Polish restaurants to be substantially cheaper than at home. A three-course meal for two in a mid-range restaurant in Warsaw will cost about 110 zł and is likely to be even less expensive in the countryside and smaller cities. Prices of basic products, such as dairy, meat and bread, have been on the rise for the last few years, but are still significantly lower compared to the West and their quality is excellent (seek out maturing Polish cheeses, such as Rubin, or regional ones like Koryciński, a flagship dairy product of the Podlaskie region). Cigarettes and alcohol are also among the cheapest in the EU.

Clothes, electronic devices and luxury products sold in Polish department stores tend to be more expensive than in Western countries, particularly when compared to the average salary in Poland (the fifth lowest in the EU). A cup of coffee in one of the international chains will cost as much as in London or Paris. Efficient public transport, particularly in Warsaw, isn't as cheap as it used to be, with a single one-way ticket for metro/bus/tram costing 4.40 zł (more than €1). The capital is by far the most expensive place to live in Poland.

Children after church mass.

THE LANGUAGE CHALLENGE

Like most other European languages, Polish has its origin in Sanskrit and is part of the Indo-European group. It is one of 14 Slavic languages. Though it is a phonetic language, with five genders, seven cases and a very difficult pronunciation, the Polish language is said to be among the hardest to learn. It is even difficult for Poles themselves. According to experts, fluency in Polish is reached at the age of 16 (compared to 12 for native English speakers).

Another peculiarity, just like the courteous kissing of women's hands (still a common practice among older men), is the fact that Polish use formal titles Pan/Pani (Sir, Lady) when addressing each other. A 'you' form is accepted only among relatives, close friends and children as well as among young people. Sometimes it may have unintended humorous undertones, such as when a foreigner overhears a phrase like 'Jest Pan kretynem' ('Sir, you are a moron').

The first complete sentence written down in Polish, found in *Księga Henrykowska* (The Book of Henryków) and dating back to 1270, had nothing to do with calling people names: a husband says to his wife: 'Daj, ać ja pobruszę, a ty poczywaj' which loosely translates into 'You rest, and I will grind'. An early sign of the women's emancipation movement in Poland.

VARSOVIA.

VIS

MILES POLONVS NOBILES PO LONIAE

VLA FLV VIVS

DECISIVE DATES

6th century AD
The Slavonic tribe Polanie appears on the Warta river. Related tribes occupy the Vistula basin.

966
The Polish court adopts Christianity. Count Mieszko unifies Polanie and neighbouring tribes.

1000
The first Polish church province is established in Gniezno.

1025
Bolesław I Chrobry is crowned King of Poland.

1226
Duke Konrad of Mazovia and the Teutonic Order of Knights repel the Prussians. The knights establish their own state in the eastern Baltic.

1241
The Mongols raze Kraków and invade Silesia.

1320
Duke Władysław I Łokietek is crowned king of Poland, having partly reunified the country.

1333–1370
King Kazimierz III Wielki consolidates the Polish territory and expands it eastwards.

1386
Queen Jadwiga of Poland marries the Lithuanian Grand Duke Jagiełło, initiating the union of Poland and Lithuania.

1410
Defeat of the Teutonic Order of Knights at Grunwald.

1466
Second Peace of Toruń: the Teutonic Knights recognise the sovereignty of the Polish kings and cede territory to Poland.

1525
The 'Knights' State' becomes the Duchy of Prussia, a fiefdom of the Polish crown, under Duke Albrecht of Hohenzollern.

1543
Copernicus publishes his book *De Revolutionibus Orbium Coelestium* on planetary motion.

1552
An Imperial Council grants the right to religious freedom.

1569
Under the Union of Lublin, Poland and Lithuania are united to form 'an inseparable whole'.

1572
Zygmund August's death brings an end to the Jagiellon dynasty.

1648–54
Rebellion of the Dnieper Cossacks under Bohdan Chmielnicki (Khmelnytsky) brings an army of Cossacks and Tartars up to the banks of Vistula.

1655–60
A Swedish invasion drives the King Jan Kazimierz into exile. The Swedes are eventually expelled but the peace treaty of Oliwa ends Polish domination in northeast Europe.

1683
King John III of Poland (Jan Sobieski) is given the credit for expelling the Turks from Vienna.

The partition of Poland in 1772.

1772
The First Partition of Poland.

1791
King Stanisław II, head of a Polish reform movement, proclaims a liberal constitution.

1795
In the Third Partition, Austria, Prussia and Russia occupy Poland despite fierce resistance.

1830–32
The November uprising against Russia is crushed.

1863–64
The January rising against tsarist rule ends with the execution of its leaders and deportations to Siberia.

1918
Following World War I an independent Polish state is declared on 7 October. Józef Piłsudski assumes military and political control.

1920
Under Piłsudski, Poland stops the advance of the Red Army at the Vistula and occupies part of the Ukraine and Lithuania. Under the Treaty of Versailles, Gdańsk becomes a 'Free City'.

1939
On 1 September World War II starts with the German assault on the Polish garrison on the Westerplatte off Gdańsk. On 17 September, the Soviet Union attacks eastern areas of Poland. Hitler and Stalin then divide the country.

1944
The Warsaw rising is led by the Polish *Armia Krajowa* (Home Army), backed by the government-in-exile in London.

1945
The 'Lublin Committee' proclaims itself the provisional government. The communists suppress all opposition and the Soviet economic system is introduced. At the Yalta and Potsdam conferences Poland's territory is extended westwards. In the east large territories fall to the Soviet Union.

1955
Founding of the 'Warsaw Pact' and 'Treaty of Friendship, Co-operation and Mutual Assistance' with the Soviet Union and other Eastern bloc states in reply to the founding of NATO.

1970
The Federal Republic of Germany and Poland sign a treaty restoring normal relations; 41 protesting workers are shot dead in Gdańsk.

1978
Archbishop of Kraków Karol Wojtyła becomes Pope John Paul II.

1980
Strikes in Gdańsk spread country-wide. Formation of independent trades union 'Solidarność' or Solidarity.

1981
General Jaruzelski declares martial law in December. The opposition goes underground.

1983
Lech Wałęsa is awarded the Nobel Peace Prize.

1989
The communist leadership agrees to share power with the opposition headed by Lech Wałęsa. First partly free elections. Solidarity candidate Tadeusz Mazowiecki becomes leader of the new government.

1990
Following unification, Germany formally recognises Poland's western border. Lech Wałęsa wins the presidential elections.

1993
Last Soviet troops leave Poland.

1995
Alexander Kwaśniewski replaces Wałęsa as president.

1997
Solidarity Electoral Action (AWS), the political wing of Solidarity, wins the general election. Jerzy Buzek becomes prime minister and introduces a new constitution.

1999
Poland joins NATO.

2004
Poland joins the EU.

2005
Right-wing Lech Kaczyński is voted president after defeating Civic Platform's Donald Tusk. Kaczyński's Law and Justice party wins parliamentary elections and his twin brother Jarosław is named prime minister. Pope John Paul II dies.

2007
Jarosław Kaczyński's unpopular government is forced to resign, prompting a general election. The Civic Platform is returned as the largest party, and Tusk is named prime minister.

2010
President Lech Kaczyński and his wife die along with 94 other passengers when Polish plane Tu-154 crashes on Russian soil. The handling of the investigation by the Civic Platform government triggers bitter divisions within Polish society and political elite. Bronisław Komorowski is elected president.

2012
Euro 2012 football championships in Poland and Ukraine.

2014
PM Donald Tusk is voted President of the European Council.

President Lech Kaczyński is laid to rest.

A GLORIOUS PAST

During this period of history the newly formed
Polish nation consolidated its power and took
on much of its present-day territorial form.

The vast plain between the Odra and Vistula rivers, which flow from the Carpathian and the Sudeten mountains as far the Baltic Sea, has been at the interface between two great cultures ever since the Stone Age. After a period of Celtic influences, west Slavic tribes settled here. They had already mastered the skills of iron making and had nurtured good relations with the countries of southern Europe.

The Ślężanie, the Mazowszanie, the Pomorzanie and the Wiślanie – the tribes who inhabited the area we now know as Silesia (in the southwest), Pomerania (in the north) and Mazovia (the region around Warsaw) – combined to form a defensive pact. To protect their settlements, which quickly developed into centres of craftsmanship and trade, they surrounded them with strong defensive walls.

The early state

The ruler Mieszko I, a member of the Piast dynasty, united the Polanie tribe of the Warta Valley with other groups that were linguistically and culturally related. The land occupied by these tribes was bordered to the south and west by Christian states that were closely tied to Rome. In order to project his state onto the European stage, Mieszko was subsequently baptised, together with his subjects. He married the Czech princess Dobrava, thereby securing the southern borders of his territory. Mieszko's son, Bolesław I Chrobry (the Brave), established an independent, ecclesiastical administration which – enlightened yet rigidly centralised – set about integrating the component parts of the state.

In AD 1000, the Holy Roman Emperor Otto III was received with great pomp at Gniezno, the then capital of Poland. When Chrobry took over

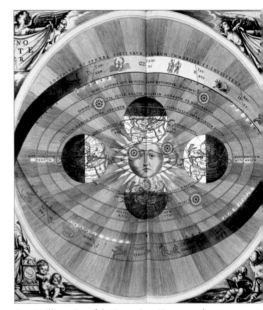

A 1761 illustration of the Copernican (Sun-centred) system of the Universe.

the Bohemian throne in 1003, it brought him into conflict with Otto's successor – Heinrich II, who invaded Poland on several occasions. The protracted war ended with the peace treaty of Bautzen (Budziszyn) in 1018, which established Polish control in Lausitz (Łużyce), west of the River Oder. (History repeated itself just under 1,000 years later, when a German invasion of Poland culminated in a similar conclusion.)

The proud victor was not content with stopping there. He wanted to expand eastwards too – in the name of Christianity. Bolesław annexed Ruthenia (present-day Ukraine) with its capital of Kiev to Poland. In 1025 he was rewarded by the Pope, who presented him with the royal insignia. Poland had become a fully-fledged member of the Christian community of states.

The Piast dynasty

Throughout his lifetime Bolesław III Krzywousty (the wry-mouthed) tightened the bonds between Pomerania and the Polish state, but in his will he divided the country among his four sons. Soon the brothers and their successors were engaged in unseemly disputes over royal titles, leadership claims and commercial advantages. The centre of political life moved from Wielkopolska (Great Poland) to Małopolska

The Polanie tribe, who lived in the Warta valley not far from Poznań, were the peoples who gave Poland its name.

century. It was during this time that Wrocław, Kraków and Poznań decided to adopt the Magdeburg municipal law, which afforded good conditions for economic development.

In the north, Poland bordered with Prussian pagan tribes. They resisted all previous Polish missionary attempts and were particularly dan-

Ivory diptych depicting scenes from the life of Christ, 14th century.

(Little Poland) in the southeast. Its capital, Kraków, lay in a favourable position on the trade route from Regensburg and Vienna to Kiev and Byzantium.

Immigrants soon arrived in great numbers from northern Germany and the Netherlands. Thousands of Jews, persecuted elsewhere in Europe, sought refuge in a part of the continent that had by then become renowned for religious tolerance. They did not arrive empty-handed, but brought new tools and new ways of doing business. Before long, Kraków was enjoying a period of unrivalled commercial prosperity and cultural richness. Nor was the development of the Polish state seriously impeded by the Mongol invasions of the 13th

gerous to Mazovia. In 1226, Duke Konrad of Mazovia, who bore the brunt of their constant raids, invited the German Order of Teutonic Knights to assist him. The Order had just been expelled from the Holy Land after the failure of the last crusade and was ready to take any employment. The Order carried out the task by wiping out the Prussians and establishing a state of their own in the conquered land, but this soon began to threaten Poland. In 1308 it took over Gdańsk and massacred its population. Between 1327 and 1333 its wars laid waste to large parts of Wielkopolska.

Nevertheless, the old Piast dynasty managed to uphold the idea of a united Polish state during two centuries of feudal dismemberment. By the end of the 12th century, the kingdom consolidated itself again. The difficult task was successfully concluded when in 1320 Władysław Łokietek was crowned in Kraków as an undisputed king of a united kingdom.

The restored *Corona Regni Poloniae* received a modern constitution and a stable currency during the reign of his son Kazimierz III Wielki (Casimir the Great). It was said that he had found Poland built in wood, and left it built in stone. During Kazimierz's reign (1333–70) the full 'polonisation' of Małopolska was finally completed.

the kingdom was united with the Grand Duchy of Lithuania. The new ruler, the Grand Duke of Lithuania, Władysław Jagiełło, and his subjects converted to Christianity and Jagiełło married the Polish queen Jadwiga d'Anjou. The immediate reason for this union was the continuing threat posed by the German Order of Teutonic Knights. Despite the spectacular victory of the union's army at Grunwald in 1410, the military power of the Order was not broken until the 1454–66 war. From then on Gdańsk was to have the special status of a free city state ruled by the kings of Poland.

The Grand Duke of Lithuania, Władysław Jagiełło, and his Polish queen Jadwiga d'Anjou.

The most important development, however, was that of establishing the Polish identity as firmly belonging to the western European civilisation. As the last Piast king, Kazimierz may have achieved much on the domestic front, but was less successful from a military point of view. He had a dense network of fortified castles built throughout the country, but the expansion to the eastern territories left other areas of the kingdom vulnerable and resulted in the loss of the whole of Silesia.

The Jagiellons

After the death of the last Piast king, the Polish throne fell to the Hungarian line of the royal family of d'Anjou. Soon afterwards, however,

NICHOLAS COPERNICUS

Mikołaj Kopernik (Nicholas Copernicus) was born in Toruń in 1473. In 1491 he enrolled at the Jagiellonian University in Kraków, and studied in Italy before becoming a priest. However, in true Renaissance fashion, his interests far exceeded the narrow confines of the church and he became interested in astronomy. While canon of Frombork he constructed an observatory and from here discovered that it was the sun at the centre of the universe, not the Earth as previously thought. He published his findings as *De Revolutionibus Orbium Coelestium* in 1543 but died later that year. The treatise was later banned by the Pope.

> *The Renaissance period was influential in Poland, largely because of Polish connections with Italy. Many Italianate buildings survive in Polish towns and cities.*

The new king, Kazimierz Jagiellończyk (1445–92) became known as the 'Father of Europe' Of his 11 children, one son became a cardinal, four became kings, one was canonised and the three daughters were married off to become the mothers of the heirs of some of the

once more enjoyed a cultural and political boom, known in history as the 'Golden Age of Poland'. The Polish language became the *lingua franca* of the eastern European nobility, and Polish, Lithuanian and Ruthenian gentry, quite used to the cohabitation of people of different denominations, readily accepted the revolutionary teachings of Luther and Calvin.

At the time of the Reformation, the Teutonic Order of Knights was also secularised. In effect, this meant it was subjugated to the secular administration of the Hohenzollern dynasty of Germany, which supported the Lutheran doc-

The Union of Lublin, 1569.

greatest dynasties in western Europe. Nevertheless, Jagiellończyk and his successors did not manage to convert these exceedingly favourable family connections into real political power. This was primarily due to the very strong economic position of the nobility, which, as a reward for its participation in wars, was granted numerous and far-reaching privileges.

Around 1500, the population of the multinational, multi-faith Polish-Lithuanian Commonwealth stood at around 7.5 million in an area of about 1.1 million sq km (425,000 sq miles). Ethnic Poles made up only about 50 percent of the total population. However, during the reign of the last Jagiellons – Zygmunt Stary (1506–48) and Zygmunt August (1548–72) – the country

trines and was closely aligned with the house of Brandenburg.

Even though religious wars were raging in the west, the traditional and reformed religious denominations continued to live amicably in the territory ruled by the Polish crown. Religious tolerance was a central element of the 'golden period of liberty', as the Polish state ideology was known at the time.

In 1569 the union of the Polish crown with Lithuania was renewed as the Union of Lublin and a 'Republic of Two Nations' was proclaimed.

An elective monarchy

In the mid-16th century, political and economic life had been characterised by the growing power of the Lithuanian and Ruthenian aristocratic families. Their huge estates in the east afforded them economic independence and enabled them to rise to the highest official posts. There they pursued solely their own interests, without any consideration of matters of state. At the same time, powerful and aggressive forces developed within the adjoining states: in the west the Habsburgs; in the southeast Turkey, with its ambitions to conquer the continent; Moscow under the rule of Ivan the Terrible in the east; Sweden in the north.

Jan Kazimierz, ruled Poland until 1668, but the country's economy continued to decline.

In the 17th century, the Polish political system became fully established. Kings of Poland were elected for life. Although the electorate was limited to the gentry, they formed more than 20 percent of the population, comprising not only large landowners and numerous owners of one to three villages, but also (by far the largest group) those possessing a homestead with a few acres of arable land, which they tilled themselves. Their financial status may have been as low as that of an average peasant, but their social

The siege of Pskov by King Stefan Batory in 1581.

When the Jagiellon dynasty came to an end, the *Sejm*, the Polish parliament, introduced an elective monarchy. However, Henri de Valois, the first king to be elected (in 1573) decided to return to France to rule there as King Henry III. The next king, Stefan Batory, Duke of Transylvania (1576–86) was a superb military strategist, but constantly had to struggle to find sufficient funds to wage war: the powerful nobility evaded all state taxes and the war treasury was bankrupt. In spite of all this, he won the war with Russia and consolidated Poland's position in the east of Europe by annexing Livonia.

In 1587 a member of the Swedish Vasa dynasty was elected King of Poland. Zygmunt III Wasa and his successors, Władysław IV and

standing was as high as any magnate with thousands of peasants working his estate.

In effect, the size of the electorate in Poland in the 17th century was unequalled in the rest of Europe until the second half of the 19th century. New members of parliament were elected by local county assemblies (*Sejmiki*), and, with numbers varying between 65 and 75, these special sessions were, in fact, congresses of the county gentry. Their role was not limited to the election of members of parliament. Their main political task was to discuss, approve or veto any new government measures and legislation. The elected members were then issued with instructions on how to vote in parliament. In this way members of parliament truly represented the general electorate. The powers of local assemblies were considerable: they could impose their own local taxes or even raise their own county troops. The system was not only well established, but worked as efficiently as only parliamentary systems can. It was a supreme exponent of the 'golden liberty of Poland', the pride of every Pole and, without doubt, the only system of its kind in Europe.

The system was based on the representation of local interests, which strongly resembled a federation, and more than any other

by the government. The principle of *liberum veto* (veto of the free) was born, with disastrous consequences.

Whatever merits or demerits of the system, its direction was diametrically opposite to the rest of Europe. The political systems of the West were steadily moving towards strengthening the power of central authorities, until what became known as 'absolutist monarchies' were established. Whether they called themselves 'enlightened' or not, any form of absolute power in the hands of central government was totally alien to the spirit of Poland. In this

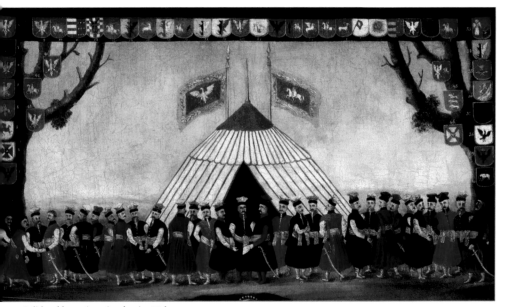

Polish noblemen in regional attire, 16th century.

demanded the universal acceptance of laws by all component parties. Consequently, it was argued that only total unanimity of all members could be just to all. This ideal was often reached after many long debates, but unfortunately it became a parliamentary tradition that, in turn, developed into a principle. Worse consequences followed. In 1652 a member of parliament protested against some matters under discussion and left the House. A baffled speaker suspended the session, and such was the enormous power of the parliamentary precedent that henceforward, one member vetoing the proceedings could cause suspension of the session, thus nullifying all laws proposed for that session

respect, the gap between Poland and the rest of Europe was growing.

Terror of the Turks

The Polish parliament was parsimonious in their expenditure on armed forces and each Commander-in-Chief, or Grand Hetman of the Republic had to fight hard to defend his army estimates and was lucky to get half the money he needed. Consequently, the aim was to command a small but extremely efficient force. The peace establishment of the armed forces never exceeded 20,000, grouped exclusively in the Ukraine (Ukraina meaning 'borderland') under the name of a Mobile Defence Force. Mobile they had to be to meet the annual raids of Tartars, Cossacks and later Ottoman Turks. The war establishment also comprised foreign mercenary troops or, in the last resort, a General Levy of all the gentry, raised under the banners of their own counties.

The army compensated its numerical weakness by its high combat effectiveness, which allowed Poland to emerge victorious from numerous wars of the 17th century. It scored resounding victories over the Russians, Turks, Cossacks, Tartars and even over the large and efficient armies of Sweden. It also produced outstanding commanders. One of them, Grand Hetman Jan Sobieski, was rewarded for his victories

decisive battles of the world – had the Turks been victorious, it is possible that Islam would have become the ruling religion of Europe. After preliminary artillery fire and infantry skirmishes, Sobieski unleashed the charge of his dreaded, winged hussars. The charge broke through the Turkish lines and in a matter of two hours, the Turkish army was annihilated. Its commander fled the field and the green standard of the Prophet fell into Polish hands. As a trophy, it was sent to Rome. The Turkish might was broken and it ceased to present a threat to European civilisation.

Jan Sobieski at the siege of Vienna, 1683.

with the royal crown of Poland, as King John III.

During the 17th century, the Ottoman Empire was steadily enlarging its Balkan possessions, aiming at the conquest of Europe. After suffering serious reverses in wars against Poland, the Turks changed their strategic direction and aimed at the very heart of Europe. After defeating the field army of the German Empire, they laid siege to Vienna. With a force of some 140,000 men, they were masters of the situation and in the summer of 1683 Vienna was in dire straits. Envoys sent by the Austrian emperor to Sobieski begged him to rescue the city and the empire. Sobieski, already known throughout Europe as the 'Terror of the Turks', sent 29,000 men to Vienna. There, on 12 September 1683, was fought one of the most

A CONGENIAL RACE

The *Description of Poland*, Oxford 1733, has this to say about the 'Disposition of the Inhabitants': 'The Polandres are generally of good complexion. Flaxen-hair'd, and tall of stature. The men… corpulent and personable. The women slender and beautiful…. They are naturally open-hearted and candid, more apt to be deceived than to deceive; not so easily provoked as appea'd; neither arrogant, nor obstinate; but very tractable if they be gently managed. They are chiefly led by example;… inclined to civility and hospitality, especially to strangers; whose customs and manners they are forward to imitate…'

DEPENDENCY AND DIVISION

Poland's decline during the 18th century lead to its third partition in 1795. An independent Polish state didn't exist again until 1918.

Poland emerged victorious from the 17th century wars but was economically ruined. Large tracts of land were laid waste. The treasury was empty; the people were exhausted, both materially and spiritually. Polish links with Saxony had always been very close and it seemed propitious to elect a Saxon king on the death of the great Jan Sobieski, John III. Augustus II the Strong, of the House of Wettins, was duly elected King of Poland in 1697.

Russia's dominance

Unfortunately, Augustus II was an adherent of absolutist ideas and his main endeavour was directed towards strengthening his personal power in Poland. He also sought to use the military power of the Republic primarily in promoting the interests of Saxony. To this end, he embroiled Poland in the disastrous second Northern War, which lasted for 20 years and turned the country into a battleground for the armies of Saxony, Russia, Prussia and Sweden. In 1704, under pressure from King Charles XII of Sweden, the exasperated gentry revolted and dethroned Augustus II, electing in his place a Pole, Stanisław Leszczyński. This gave rise to further disturbances, and neighbouring powers had the opportunity to intervene in support of either king. This war, in which the Poles were most unwilling participants, brought about devastation on a vast scale and reduced the country to total penury. Army discipline, which only played a marginal role in the war, disintegrated.

As a result of war, Russia emerged as the dominant power. The parliamentary session held in Warsaw in 1717 bore the full imprint of its new might. Called the 'silent' session because no member was allowed to speak, it marked the beginning of Russian rule over Poland, under

Stanisław Poniatowski, the last king of Poland.

the guise of protecting the old liberties of the Republic. Under Russian pressure, all gentry privileges were confirmed and even extended. It was Russia that officially became the guarantor of the 'golden liberty' of the Poles and any true or imaginary infringement would give it a pretext for military intervention. The total strength of the army was permanently fixed at 24,000, a ridiculous figure in comparison to standing armies of more than 200,000 each of Russia, Austria and Prussia.

Under these prevailing conditions, effective governing of the state was impossible for the king or any other body. With the rapid disintegration of its domestic market and lack of organised foreign trade relations, the state had

The world's first Order for Bravery for all ranks in the field was the Order Viruti Militari (for Military Virtue), instituted by Stanisław August during the 1792 war with Russia.

been heading for bankruptcy since the beginning of the century. Like the sword of Damocles, the threatening coalition of neighbouring states was hanging over Poland.

In 1764, Stanisław August of the Poniatowski family was elected king. He has been brought up

Poland. The confederation's struggle lasted for four years and effectively put a stop to economic revival and turned the country once more into a battlefield. Eventually, Russian military might prevailed and confederates were crushed.

The partition of Poland

The events served as a pretext for a Russian diplomatic initiative to partition Poland between the three powers: Russia, Austria and Prussia. In 1772 these powers annexed large parts of the state of Poland: Prussia gained 36,300 sq km (13,900 sq miles) Austria 81,900 sq km (31,623

Jan Matejko's painting portraying the 1773 partition of Poland.

in the spirit of French enlightenment and he did his best to revitalise the state. His endeavours at reform and in inspiring a cultural movement that had a decidedly national character received much support from the intellectuals and the gentry. First successes were soon apparent: some form of discipline returned to parliament and the tax system was reformed. But the new custom offices, which were to provide the treasury with additional income, were prevented from functioning through intervention from Berlin. In 1768, in the town of Bar (in present-day Ukraine) a patriotic confederation was formed chiefly by conservative elements, directed against Russian dominance. It formed its own army, which attacked Russian garrisons in

sq miles) and Russia 93,000 sq km (35,908sq miles). This annexation by the coalition of three powers became known as the First Partition of Poland. The Republic had no means of defending itself against the onslaught, but it was immediately realised that in order to survive, comprehensive reforms were imperative and the king became the leading spirit of far-reaching changes in political and social fields. A strong government was set up comprising, among other bodies, the Ministry of Education, the first ministry of its kind in the world, preceding other European states by almost a century.

The session of parliament that began in 1788 lasted for four years and reformed the political system of Poland. When the session ended, the country had acquired the most modern framework of political law in Europe, including that of revolutionary France.

This was embodied in the new constitution of 3 May, 1791, which granted more power to all citizens, allowed greater autonomy to towns and gave full legal protection to the peasant class. 'The Great Sejm', as the session was called, fixed the number of the standing army at 100,000 men. Again, it was Stanisław August who led the reform. The influence of his intellect was felt in all spheres of social and cultural life.

One was Tadeusz Kościuszko, who had already distinguished himself during the United States' War of Independence. The other general was Prince Józef Poniatowski, nephew of the king: when in the king's view the war became hopeless, he ordered capitulation and submitted to humiliating conditions by the victors.

There followed the Second Partition of Poland. But even the small part of the country nominally left free was occupied by Russia, with strong garrisons in all towns. They were there primarily to supervise the total disbandment of the Polish army, but the army, though

Tadeusz Kościuszko, one the 500 złoty banknote.

Kościuszko and the peasants

Russia took these manifestations of Poland's revival as a serious threat. Empress Catherine II decided to take immediate action. First she mobilised her own adherents who belonged to the most conservative elements in Poland. On her orders, they formed a Confederation in Targowica and declared the Constitution null and void. Following this they requested Russian military intervention, which the Tsarina was only too eager to grant. The Russian army invaded Poland. The invasion was staunchly resisted by the army, which was still far from the numerical strength as fixed by the Great *Sejm*. The war lasted several months, during which two generals became known throughout Europe.

beaten in the field, retained its high morale. Its officers, supported by large numbers of citizens, requested General Kościuszko to lead them in a new, full-scale war. He promptly agreed, and in March 1794 he stood in the old marketplace in Kraków and proclaimed a national insurrection against the invaders. This scene, immortalised in contemporary prints and subsequent paintings, is known to every child in Poland – it is a part of national consciousness.

Being short of arms and ammunition, Kościuszko called upon volunteers from villages in the Kraków district; they eagerly answered his call. Their weapons were scythes, fixed vertically to shafts. With a few battalions of regular troops, squadrons of cavalry and a battalion of Kraków scythemen, Kościuszko marched to meet the Russian Army Corps. They met head on near the village of Racławice. The battle took the usual shape of the times, opening with the artillery bombardment and infantry on both sides trying to seize commanding positions. At midday, Kościuszko personally led the attack with his scythemen against a strong battery of Russian guns. The attack was delivered in the only way known to this improvised infantry: at the double and in loose column. The gunners had time for one salvo only, after which they met their deaths from terrible

Fighter during the Warsaw Uprising.

weapons in the hands of the scythemen. The Russian line broke and soon the whole corps was in full flight.

News of victory, the first since the relief of Vienna, was greeted throughout the country with enthusiasm. However, soon afterwards, the uprising was crushed by the Russians, which led to the Third Partition of the country, finally blotting out Poland from the map of Europe.

The Napoleonic era

When the last shots of the war were fired in Poland, the name of General Bonaparte was beginning to be well known in Europe. This young general of the French revolutionary army was fighting one of the enemies of Poland in Italy, the Austrians, and he had already had several astonishing successes against them.

One of the first Poles to arrive in Italy was a general who had distinguished himself during the Insurrection. His name was Jan Dąbrowski. His plan, speedily agreed by Bonaparte and the French government, was to form a Polish Army as a force allied to the French Republic. Polish Legions in Italy – as they were called – relied on the Austrians to supply them with men. Sure enough, thousands of Poles who had been pressed into the Austrian army soon filled the ranks of the Legions, in addition to thousands of other volunteers escaping from occupied Poland. The Legions fought with distinction not only against the Austrians, but also against the Russians who invaded Italy to assist the hard-pressed Imperial Austrian Army. The Russians were led by the man known as

1794 UPRISING AND MASSACRE

While Kościuszko and his men were fighting in the field, the citizens of Warsaw rose against the Russian garrison and expelled it after murderous street battles. The same happened in Wilno. Prussia sent its army to assist the hard-pressed Russians and both armies laid siege to Warsaw. After a few unsuccessful attempts at storming the city, they had to abandon the siege.

So far the uprising was victorious, but in October 1794, Kościuszko personally took command of a division with the intention of intercepting the Russians at the crossing of the Vistula at Maciejowice. Faulty intelligence caused him to meet an enemy double in numbers to his own army. Wounded, Kościuszko fell

into Russian hands and, now leaderless, the Polish army suffered reverses. A new Russian army, commanded by General Suvoroff, approached Warsaw. The right bank suburb of Praga was hastily fortified and defended by General Jasinski, the liberator of Wilno. The Russians overwhelmed the defenders by sheer numbers and butchered the civilian population. They murdered every man, woman and child in an orgy of killing which lasted throughout the day and following night.

The massacre of Warsaw's civilian population, unheard of in Europe since the Tartar invasions, shook the entire civilised world.

The 'Song of the Legions of Italy', in the rhythm of the mazurka, declared 'Poland shall not die as long as we live'. The song was sung in occupied Poland and was soon elevated to national anthem.

the 'butcher of Warsaw' – Field-Marshall Alexander Suvorov.

For the rest of the Napoleonic period, Poles fought alongside the French army in all its campaigns. Their hopes were dashed, though, when

Unsettled century

The Congress of Vienna, which ended the Napoleonic wars, reconstituted a small Polish state, more or less within the frontiers of the former Duchy of Warsaw. It was a constitutional monarchy, with the Tsar of Russia as its king. The Poles used a few liberties that were afforded them by the Congress of Vienna to help carry out the variety of tasks specified in the Constitution of 3 May 1791.

In 1816, a university was founded in Warsaw, which soon became a decisive factor in the promotion of scientific and cultural contacts with

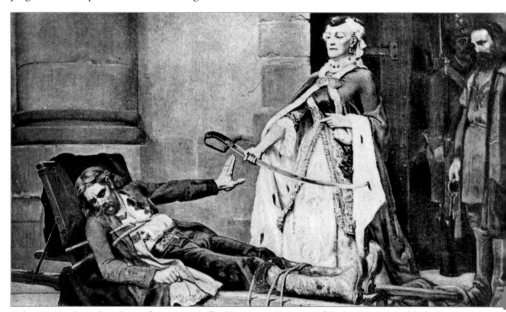

Tadeusz Kościuszko, tied to a litter, refusing a sword offered by Empress Catherine II following his unsuccessful rebellion.

after the defeat of Prussia and Russia, Poland was not allowed to be rebuilt but only to form a small state called the Duchy of Warsaw.

Nevertheless it was a good foundation for the state that was to arise after the defeat of Russia in the 'Second Polish War', which began in 1812. The Polish army, commanded by Prince Józef Poniatowski, marched to the campaign full of enthusiasm and hope. Unfortunately, the campaign ended in a disastrous retreat of the Grand Army and with this ended all hopes of the resurrection of the Polish Republic. But the army remained true to its allies. During the 'Battle of Nations', at Leipzig in October 1813, Prince Józef, by then Marshall of France, fell commanding the rear guard of the army.

other academic centres in Europe. Russia did not yet have a single university. The idea of a national revival was also evident in the establishment of an independent, domestic industry and the administration structures of a modern state.

However, there were frequent conflicts with Russia's stifling bureaucracy. The sharpest conflicts were those in the army whose Commander-in-Chief, Grand Duke Constantine, was brother of the tsar. The prince attempted to introduce Russian forms of discipline into the Polish army, built on principles of military honour and patriotic duty. He had failed to introduce corporal punishment, but he interfered personally with the minutiae of army routine, driving both officers and men to distraction.

This resulted in several cases of suicide among the officers each year. Secret, patriotic associations sprang up everywhere, particularly in the army. The conflicts were growing and finally they erupted in a national uprising in November 1830. The Russians replied with a general offensive, which was broken at the gates of Warsaw, and for almost a year the Poles were victorious in every engagement. However, Russia's overwhelming superiority in numbers began to be felt and this, coupled with strategic errors by the Polish High Command, brought them back to Warsaw.

The Battle of Ostroleka on 26 May 1831.

In October 1831, Warsaw fell after a short siege and Poland, once again, disappeared from the map of Europe. One of the positive effects of the resultant new wave of emigrants was admiration in western Europe for the freedom fight in Poland. In the European revolution year of 1848, Poles sought to re-establish their national sovereignty, but were unsuccessful, as were all other revolutionary movements.

Thirty years later, new generations of Poles again took up the armed struggle for freedom. In 1863, circumstances were far less favourable than those in 1830. The armed uprising was prepared after years of secretly gathering arms and of secret training in their use. Secondly, the Russian terror and the vigilance of the secret police made the preparations risky and difficult. The date of the uprising, in January 1863, was necessitated by the Russian plan to draft most of the young men into the Russian army for 20 years' service from which very few returned alive. In spite of adverse circumstances, the January 1863 uprising lasted longer than the preceding ones. The insurgents continued fighting, even when members of the national government in Warsaw were captured and executed. Without central direction, the guerrilla type of operations lasted well into 1865, with Lithuanian groups being the most effective. A wave of terror followed the end of the uprising. The Russian governor of Wilno, Mikhail Muraviev, gained for himself special distinction by being known as "Muraviev the Hangman".

World War I

It was in the Austrian-occupied part of Poland, with centres in Lwów and Kraków, that the first Polish military organisation since the 1863 uprising was born, allowed by the authorities under the guise of a voluntary rifle association. It was a paramilitary organisation, but its secret work was aimed at the training of officers and men for the future army of the independent Poland. The man who organised and subsequently commanded all 'Riflemen' was Józef Piłsudski, born in Lithuania and an ex-convict in Siberia, where he had served a sentence for anti-Russian activities (see page 47).

When war, which everyone in Poland expected, broke out in the summer 1914, he led his riflemen across the line of partition to fight the Russians. When, as a result of German victories in 1916, most of Poland was cleared of Russian armies, Piłsudski launched a new, secret Polish Military Organisation, to which he transferred his best officers. They were to command the forces destined to liberate Poland when Germany and Austria were next beaten by the western Allies. For his refusal to co-operate with the Austro-German authorities, Piłsudski was arrested and imprisoned in the fortress of Magdeburg for the rest of the war.

Meanwhile, in 1917, the US president Woodrow Wilson included an independent Poland as one of the US war aims. With the disintegration of Austria first, members of the Polish Military Organisation took to arms. Sharp fighting started first in Lwów, which the Ukrainians, armed by the Austrians, tried to seize.

POLISH ARMY - 1ST WORLD WAR

RSHAL PILSUDSKI'S
GIONS, ARTILLERY
OFFICER

1ST LANCERS
1ST EASTERN CORPS
SERGEANT

POLISH ARMY IN FRANCE
GEN. HALLER'S ARMY
RIFLEMAN

Józef Piłsudski led the Second Republic to independence.

REBIRTH: THE SECOND REPUBLIC

The inter-war years were marked by the re-establishment and expansion of the Polish state under the authoritarian leadership of Józef Piłsudski.

In 1918 the banners of rebellion fluttered over the debris of the dynastic empires throughout Europe. Liberty was writ large – larger than it had ever been after 1848 and before 1989.

Now regionally organised, in November 1918 the Poles disarmed the Germans and Austrians, whose leadership had been overthrown and who were too exhausted even to consider a continuation of hostilities. In Poznań weapons for a Polish rebellion were collected. A national government, free from all Bolshevik ambition, was established in Lublin and in Lwów fervently patriotic high school pupils fought street battles with the Ukrainians, who had also started an uprising.

On 7 October 1918, the Regency Council met in Warsaw and proclaimed the Independence of Poland. On 10 November, released from prison, Piłsudski arrived in Warsaw. The Regency Council relinquished its power into his hands, with the title of 'Naczelnik', first given to Kościuszko. This made him a virtual dictator. On 11 November 1918 Independence was officially proclaimed and world governments were accordingly notified. The reborn Republic of Poland had no frontiers, no army and no treasury, but universal enthusiasm and the well-known organisational abilities of the Poles remedied many shortcomings. Time was short, with a new danger looming across the temporary demarcation lines in the east.

The Red threat

Hard on the heels of the retreating German army came a new enemy: the Red Army. It represented a new force in world politics – that of the Communist revolution – with its aim to spread its preaching throughout Europe and to create one universal 'State of Workers and

Bowing before Polonia, by J. Malczewski.

Peasants'. Piłsudski, by then Head of State and Commander-in Chief with the rank of Marshal of Poland, realised the imminent danger. Piłsudski was a patriot through and through, but neither in the Polish nor the Lithuanian tradition. His lodestar was the Jagiellonian idea of creating a strong political and military structure, capable of forming a strong barrier against any aggression from the east. In modern terms, he was a federalist on the old Polish principle of the 'Free Union of the Free People'.

For centuries, the vast lands of the Ukraine, originally populated by nomads from the east, had been the grain store for Poland, and later for the ever more powerful Russian Empire. Piłsudski supported the Ukrainian nationalists and, together with allied Ukrainian forces commanded by Ataman Petlura, the Polish army marched into the capital city of Kiev. However, the bulk of the Ukrainian population did not support their new government with sufficient strength. While Polish lines were extended, the Red Army launched a major offensive in the north. Under the command of General Tukhachevsky, the Red Army broke through the thinly held Polish front and marched west. The aim of the offensive was to turn Leon Trotsky's command into reality. 'Over the corpse of bourgeois Poland' they were to march into Berlin –

> In 1919 the acclaimed concert pianist, Ignacy Jan Paderewski, became Poland's second prime minister. He later lived in the United States.

But Marshal Piłsudski was not idle. To the southeast of Warsaw he concentrated a group of armies that he decided to command in person. On 16 August 1920 Piłsudski struck due northeast. His attack drove a wedge between the Russian forces and cut Tuhatchevski's lines

Lwów was a centre for politics and the arts.

in socialist hands at the time – to add impetus to the expected Red world revolution.

Under this concentrated offensive, the Polish army retreated. Slowly, one after another, the intended lines of defence were broken. In the south, the dreaded cavalry army, led by Budyonny, spread havoc and panic; in the north, the relentless pressure of the main Russian force, led by Tukhachevsky, turned an organised retreat into headlong flight. This group of armies had outflanked Warsaw defences from the north, cutting off the lines of supply from Gdańsk and crossing the Vistula at Płock. Seemingly, there was nothing to stop the Red Army from its conquest of Europe, over the dead body of Poland.

of communications, and their centre gave way. With the Polish offensive pressing on, the whole right wing of the Russian army was annihilated.

A general rout of the Red Army followed. Marshal Tukhachevsky wrote: 'There is not the slightest doubt that, had we been victorious on the Vistula, the revolution would have set light to the entire continent of Europe.' The British ambassador in Warsaw, Lord D'Abernon, set down his judgement, as follows: 'The history of contemporary civilisation knows no event of greater importance than the Battle of Warsaw.'

Major General J.F.C. Fuller, in his work *The Battle of Warsaw* (1920), concurred with this opinion: 'It should be the task of political writers to explain to European opinion that Poland saved Europe in 1920, and that it is necessary to keep Poland powerful and in harmonious relations with western European civilisation, for Poland is the barrier to the everlasting peril of an Asiatic invasion... by shielding Central Europe from the full blast of Marxist contagion, the Battle of Warsaw set back the Bolshevik clock.'

A new democracy

In 1921 a general political consensus resulted in the acceptance of a democratic constitution, based on the French model. After the election victory of the right-wing National Democrats

in 1922, Gabriel Narutowicz became the first president of the new republic, elected with votes by the left, centre and national minority parties. Piłsudski was compelled to tender his resignation. Narutowicz did not last long: he was assassinated some days later. When Sikorski became prime minister, a new president, Stanisław Wojciechowski, was elected and eventually a degree of stability was once more restored to the political scene.

Although the parliamentary constitution protected the fledgling democracy from the monopolistic claims of the central executive, it

First Cavalry Army leaving for the Polish front line, 1920.

POLAND'S MILITARY HERO

Józef Piłsudski (1867–1935), born in Lithuania into a noble but impoverished Polish family, began his career as a revolutionary. But as far as his political inclination was concerned, he was a pragmatist. Throughout the last 10 years of his life he had a formative influence on the power structure of the state. In theory the structure of the democratic order remained untouched. In practice, however, fervent Piłsudski supporters held all the key positions in the army and the administration. A loyal élite was forged from the group of erstwhile soldiers who had fought for independence under his command. A large portion of the intelligentsia was employed in the state administration. Also, the

influence of the aristocracy, who for centuries had owned the landed estates, increased. The socialists in turn – initially supporters of Piłsudski – soon lost any illusions they may have had and joined the opposition. The undoubted charisma of the Marshal was cleverly marketed and his political premises were popularised. The equality of all religious denominations – specified in the constitution – was retained due to his political dexterity. His savoir-vivre, his adherence to the traditions of the Polish multinational state, his preference for horses, sabres and swords; all this fused in the eyes of his countrymen to make him the embodiment of a popular hero.

had insufficient control to afford total political freedom. The coalition governments of the 1920s worked in an atmosphere of mutual distrust and disunity. Their attempt to turn high-flying modernisation plans into reality did not really get off the ground – not surprising, considering the vast number of problems the country faced.

Currency reform ultimately proved advantageous, but it entailed an unpopular limitation of social rights. As was the case in other European states, this in turn encouraged radical political groupings to begin to question the legitimacy and leadership mandate of parliament.

Piłsudski's paternalistic leadership ideal was underscored by a cult of strict bureaucracy and the reliance on the obedient and loyal citizen. The encouragement of such characteristics in the national consciousness was not only designed to guarantee survival for a nation wedged between 'traditional enemies', but also to enable Poland in the long run to play a mediating role between the so-called 'wild east' and the 'civilised west'. With the creation of a Non-Partisan Bloc for Cooperation with the Government, parliament was left with only a very few legislative functions.

The Polish parliament on the eve of war in 1939.

Only within the army did a strong, supraregional link to the new, united state emerge. In the spring of 1926, the economic conditions worsened with increased inflation and unemployment. In May, the new centre-right government of Wincenty Witos met strong opposition from the socialists and from Piłsudski, who was also deeply dissatisfied with the existing structure of the high military command. On May 12 Piłsudski decided to lead his loyal military units into Warsaw. After several days of street battles the coup succeeded and Piłsudski once again managed to gain total control. A new political strategy of restructuring, which went under the name of 'Sanacja' ('Recovery'), was introduced.

Using an impending coup as a pretext, legal proceedings were instigated against the socialist deputies. The judiciary managed to save face by remaining independent and passing purely symbolic sentences, but nevertheless the young democracy lost much of its credibility.

Piłsudski not only sanctioned this development, he even consented to the new, restrictive constitution during his final hours on his deathbed. Upon his death in 1935, he left a vacuum that was filled by the somewhat weaker General Edward Rydz-Śmigly.

Racial tensions

The only significant opposition against the Piłsudski clan came from the National

Democracy Party. Particularly in rural areas, this movement was inseparably linked with the Roman Catholic hierarchy. It propagated the concept that people had a natural right to their land, language and traditions. Roman Dmowski, the chief ideologist and strategist of this movement at that time, deemed the search for an ultimate solution to the nationality conflicts the most important task of any political agenda. The various peoples were to be settled on their own respective territories and a system of peaceful co-existence established. The movement also called for racial purity.

extreme right of these groups, fascist tendencies became evident. Violence against minority groups was no longer an isolated occurrence.

Economic struggles

In the period between the two world wars, Poland had become a relatively homogeneous economic unit. But radical change had been needed to enable this to happen. Provinces that for centuries had been characterised by totally diverse influences had to be economically integrated, and a combination of radically different cultural elements within Polish society had

A demonstration in America against the oppression of Jews in Poland, circa 1930.

The Jewish community, who made up more than eight percent of the population, were the prime target of attack. But in addition, loyal, often non-denominational citizens whose families may have been 'polonised' for centuries, became the victims of these persecutions. The main pretext for the attacks were the utopian-socialist ideas propagated by prominent members of the Jewish intellectual scene.

When in the late 1930s the feeling of external threat increased, it soon became clear that Poland lacked anyone of the calibre of Piłsudski; the kind of figure required to maintain the integrity of the state. Nationalism grew apace and the government became ever more aligned with the National Democratic Party. On the

THE IDEA OF A STATE

In 1921 the idea of a state was a modern concept for Poles. The aim was to create a democratic political system, which withstood the efforts of the church to raise Catholicism to a state religion. Liberation from patriotic obligations was endemic in intellectual circles and there appeared to be a cultural renaissance. Through contact with the west, the belief that Poland was, once again, a member of the European family was strengthened. The cinema became the main attraction in large cities and small theatres in Warsaw flourished. The nightlife in large cities was on a par with any that may have been offered in Paris or London.

to be assimilated: the efficient 'Prussian-style' industrial machine; an easy-going 'Austrian' Bohemian way of life; 'Russian' dynamism – all had to be brought under one roof. This process of assimilation, particularly with regard to legislation and infrastructure, took time to achieve. A port was built in Gdynia and linked to industrialised Silesia by miles of railway track. Nevertheless, even during the years of economic growth there was a dearth of funds to enable independent Polish investment. Heavy industry, for example, remained controlled by France and Germany.

Anti-Prussian poster.

At this time, the annual capital transfer to foreign banks was five times higher than any investments made at home. Moreover, the primitive banking system levied the highest interest rates in Europe; the prime lending rate was three times higher than in the United Kingdom or in Switzerland. Even in 1939 it was still not possible to regain pre-World War I levels of industrial production.

Almost 65 percent of the population lived tied to the land in rural areas. With the exception of Greater Poland and Pomerania, the agricultural structure remained backward without modern machinery or outside investment. Seven-tenths of the rural population was only marginally involved in the circulation of goods and currency. As well as this sluggish pace of industrialisation, a catastrophically high birth rate caused a drastic decline in the overall standard of living and triggered a fresh wave of emigration. During the time leading up to the Great Depression (1926–30) approximately 200,000 people left Poland annually to start a new life somewhere else, with the United States being a popular destination. In subsequent years, overpopulation led to further subdivision of rural estates and thus to lower revenues for those who made their living from the soil. The rural population, which was largely illiterate and highly indebted to provincial usurers, remained in a suffering, seemingly divinely ordained state of lethargy.

Controlling eastern Europe

In the 1930s Poland's foreign policy situation deteriorated rapidly. Stuck in the doldrums of the world economic crisis of 1929, the country's plans for rapid modernisation and social improvements collapsed. After 1935, the government was having to rely even more strongly on the traditional forces of the army and the landed gentry, and passed a new, far more authoritarian, constitution.

In Warsaw the popular slogan of a 'superpower Poland' found favour among the masses. Despite all endeavours to achieve a national consensus, in this tense situation there was far too little freedom of movement for such a conflict to be resolved. As far as the propagandists were concerned, the Polish 'superpower' should, with the assistance of its culture, influence the whole of central and eastern Europe and, at the same time, form a military protection wall to the east.

An alliance with Berlin or Moscow was out of the question, but when Hitler occupied Bohemia and Moravia after the Munich agreement, Marshal Edward Rydz-Śmigły, in turn, gave orders to reclaim part of the territory of Polish Silesia which Czechoslovakia had annexed in 1920.

In this optimistic atmosphere, a young generation of Poles waited for a solution to the mystery of independence. On 11 November 1939, it intended to celebrate its 21st birthday, together with the republic. But, as it happened, matters were to turn out very differently. Another power sought to find its *lebensraum* (living space) in the east.

Lviv and Vilnius

The reunification of Germany in 1990 brought about a renunciation of the former East German territories. Meanwhile Poland has gained a secure western border.

Millions of new Polish citizens in Wrocław, Malbork and Szczecin are guaranteed a right to their homeland. Many of these people had had to leave their homes either as part of the resettlement policies within the Polish state or when they were expelled from the former Polish eastern territories, now part of Lithuania, Russia and the Ukraine. Luckily, nobody in Poland today has any intention of reclaiming these territories. Instead, it is becoming apparent that only through intercultural exchange will there be common access to regions characterised by centuries of shared cultural history.

This point is clearly demonstrated by the former Polish cities Vilnius (Wilno) and Lviv (Lwów), with their rich multi-cultural traditions. In free Poland during the inter-war years both cities developed into centres of intellectual life. Regaining them had been a considerable task for the young Poland. Although largely inhabited by Poles, Vilnius was regarded by the Lithuanian republic as its true capital, and Lviv, also with a Polish majority, had to be defended against claims from the Ukraine.

Poland's melting pot

Lviv was founded in the mid-13th century by the son of Prince Daniil of Galicia, who built a fort on the site of the present-day town. In the years of Polish partition, Lwów became an important city: it was located at the junction of major trade routes and its population was made up of a variety of cultures and nationalities.

In the 19th century, trade, transport and industry developed rapidly and in 1894 an electric tram system was in operation. Science and literature were allowed to flourish and the university produced great humanists. The town also became a meeting place for Ukrainians, Poles and Jews and prominent cultural and political leaders lived here towards the end of the 19th century, including Ivan Franko and Mykhailo Hrushevsky. The mathematics department of Lwów University, founded by Stefan Banach and Hugo Steinhaus, was once the leading institute of its kind in the world. It was in Lviv that Rudolf Weigl

developed the vaccine against typhoid. The theatre was deemed one of the best in the country and two legendary Polish actors, Leon Schiller and Wilam Horzyca, were members of its company.

The city of poets

Vilnius, now capital of Lithuania, is one of the country's oldest cities, founded in 1323 by Gediminas, a Lithuanian duke. After a short war the former capital of the Grand Duchy of Lithuania was returned to Poland in 1922. Interaction between these two cultures determined the stature of this city. Piłsudski was a descendant of Lithuanian dukes; Adam

St Anne's Church in Vilnius.

Mickiewicz, the Polish national poet, began his epic poem Pan Tadeusz with the exclamation: 'Lithuania, my fatherland!' The literary tradition was further developed by Czesław Miłosz, who was awarded the Nobel Prize for Literature in 1980. Antoni Gołubiew and Paweł Jasienica were also active in Vilnius during the inter-war years. Stanisław Mackiewicz, prime minister of the government-in-exile after World War II period, began his political career in the city.

Both Lviv and Vilnius retain evidence of this multicultural diversity. In Vilnius the Górny Zamek Giedymina, the Church of St Casimir and St Anne's Church characterise the landscape. In Lviv there are Armenian, Greek Orthodox and Roman Catholic cathedrals and it was the only city in Poland to be the seat of three archbishops.

Polish Air Force propaganda poster, 1939.

WORLD WAR II AND ITS AFTERMATH

When Germany invaded Poland in 1939 it set off a catastrophic chain of events that were to change the world – and totally transform Poland.

I n autumn 1938, the German Reich under Adolf Hitler summarily confronted Poland with a number of political demands, including the return of the 'free city' of Gdańsk, access via a motorway to East Prussia across the so-called Polish corridor and a realignment of Polish foreign policy towards the Third Reich, namely signing up to the Anti-Comintern Pact.

Neither Great Britain nor France made any attempt to halt the growing expansion of the Third Reich to the east. The only obstruction to Hitler's plans was uncertainty about how the Soviet Union would react to these claims.

In fact, after Hitler's troops invaded Czechoslovakia in March 1939, the Soviet Union agreed to collaborate with the 'Greater German Reich'. In response, Great Britain and France concluded a treaty with Poland, assuring each other of mutual military assistance in case of a German attack on any one of the countries. It entailed a huge risk of world war.

Defeat and partition

On 23 August 1939, Germany and the Soviet Union concluded a 'non-aggression pact'. In an additional, secret protocol both countries specified their territorial claims against Poland: Eastern Poland was assigned to the Soviet Union, while the remainder – the whole of the western and central territories – was to come under Hitler's control.

In the late evening of 31 August 1939, the Soviet parliament ratified the Hitler–Stalin pact; only a few hours later, without making any declaration of war, the German Wehrmacht marched into Poland, the first country to offer military resistance to Nazi aggression.

Polish troops were mobilised in a matter of hours, but the unprepared soldiers faced a

German victory parade in Warsaw attended by Hitler, 5th October 1939.

German army that was both numerically and technically superior. Attempts to resist the German advance in the north, west and south, over a front some 1,600 km (990 miles) in length, were in vain. A popular myth has grown up that the Polish cavalry charged German tanks. What really happened was that detachments of mounted infantry and cavalry met German panzer divisions. The cavalry, whose duty it was to charge the infantry following behind the tanks, naturally had to gallop towards oncoming armour in order to attempt this objective.

By the terms of their mutual defence pacts with Poland, Britain and France were duty-bound to immediately declare war on

Germany, but they were procrastinating. Only on the third day of the invasion, 3 September 1939, did they make their declarations official. According to additional military clauses of the pact, Britain was to start a bombing offensive on Germany without delay, while France was to attack Germany 'with the bulk of her forces' by 15 September. Neither obligation was kept.

Cut off from the rest of the country by the Russian invasion, the Polish government crossed the frontier of allied Romania to carry on the war from abroad. However, instead of being given the opportunity to travel to France,

The Polish soldiers who trained with the British Royal Air Force were later to win great fame at the Battle of Britain.

Polish army in exile

The remnants of the Polish army, which crossed the Romanian and Hungarian frontiers, were put in internment camps, but mass escapes from these began almost immediately. Their target was France, where in October 1939 a new government of Poland was formed,

Home Army soldier during the 1944 Warsaw Uprising.

the Romanians interned the allied government of Poland. Nevertheless, the armed forces continued to fight. Warsaw capitulated only after the last rounds of ammunition were fired and the city itself was turned to rubble under air and artillery bombardment. The last group, surrounded by Germans and Russians, gave up the unequal contest on 5 October. As the post-war testimonies of German generals make plain, the war could have ended in 1939 because almost the entire German army and practically the entire air force were thrown against Poland, leaving only an insignificant screen in the west. Had the Western allies intervened, as they were obliged to do by treaty, Germany would certainly have been crushed.

headed by General Władysław Sikorski. A new army was also being organised there. Part of the Polish Air Force personnel was directed to England, where they began training on the British aircraft. Another strong group of Polish Forces formed in Syria, then a French protectorate. By the spring of 1940, Polish Forces gathered in France had already reached the 100,000 mark.

The first Polish group to go into action against Germany was the so-called 'Podhale Brigade', which formed part of the allied expeditionary force in Norway. Some units of the Polish navy had been in constant action already under the tactical command of the Royal Navy. It was the submarine *Orzeł*, which, after her epic escape from the Baltic, torpedoed a German troop transport, thus first signalling their invasion of Norway.

Two Polish infantry divisions and one armoured brigade also fought side by side with the allies to the bitter end during the French campaign of 1940. The remnants of the army were then evacuated to Great Britain.

The Home Army

While Warsaw was still under siege in 1939, the first steps were taken to create an underground army. It was to this end that General German police, which were kept on constant alert by the activities of partisan detachments.

By 1944, the Home Army numbered 350,000 men in active formations – by far the largest and the most effective underground army in Europe. They were armed with what they had taken from Germans and also by a continuous stream of supplies delivered by air from Britain, mostly by the Polish air crews. Towards the end of 1943, the blowing up of bridges and rail tracks disrupted German supply lines with the Russian front to such an extent that it had begun to play a substantial part in their defeat.

Home Army getting ready for their patrol.

Tokarzewski-Karaszewicz was appointed its Commander-in-Chief and given appropriate staff, with such funds as were available. This Organisation formed the basis of the future Home Army (Armia Krajowa or AK), which incorporated a great many clandestine groups, formed spontaneously all over Poland. The Home Army formed an integral part of the Polish Forces, subordinate to the government, first in France, later in Great Britain.

As part of the Armed Forces of Poland, the Home Army carried out the war against Germany, as distinct from what is called 'the resistance', in which almost every Polish man and woman took part. The primary targets of the Home Army were the German forces and

UNDERGROUND RESISTANCE

Among civilians there was a great deal of activity under German Occupation. The Poles were not allowed to receive higher education but were to remain on a barely literate level to provide cheap labour. The vast Organisation of the 'Underground State' clandestinely arranged for young Poles to obtain diplomas and university education. An underground administration and press continued; there was even a police force, law courts and a theatre. It was to the nameless authorities of this State that Poles owed their allegiance, at the risk of death or concentration camps.

Finally, the Home Army power revealed itself in full force in its attempt to liberate the capital city of Poland, Warsaw.

During the last week of September, a treaty was concluded between the Soviet Union and the German Reich and German and Soviet soldiers fraternised on Polish soil. In the subsequent months, the German Wehrmacht occupied Denmark and Norway and conquered France. The Soviet Union occupied the Baltic states and eventually large areas of Finland and Romania too.

Once the Polish campaign had come to an

Map showing the major concentration camps in Poland in 1942.

end, West Prussia, Greater Poland and Upper Silesia were swallowed up by the German Reich. After various unsuccessful attempts to establish a puppet state, Germany declared the rest of occupied Poland a 'General Government' with its administrative seat located in Kraków. Its powers were limitless, its subjects stateless.

Hitler's reign of terror

Hitler exploited for his own ends the anti-Semitism that had long been latent throughout Europe. With the help of chauvinistic propaganda, the party apparatus and its organisations – above all the Waffen SS and the Gestapo – he ruthlessly applied his theories concerning racial purity. The final victory would give the German 'master race' *lebensraum* a territory that stretched as far as the Urals. This aim was to be achieved in accordance with a 'legal punishment system', which could be interpreted

> Craftsmen and labourers were deported to do forced labour in the Reich. Artists, scientists and priests were taken into 'protective custody', often a synonym for concentration camps.

so broadly that in the occupied areas the decisions of an SS commander could never be challenged.

In accordance with the guidelines of the propaganda ministry, Poles were regarded as *untermenschen* – a sub-human species. The final aim of national socialist policy was the destruction of the Polish people, their expulsion or 'germanisation', the extermination of Jews and gypsies as well as the settlement of Germans in the newly 'liberated' areas. Any racial group that was deported from the provinces within the German Reich in the course of the ethnic cleansing process was to be concentrated in the General Government. The racially pure were to be resettled in the new provinces, and the 'inferior races' dispatched to Kraków, where they would face an uncertain fate.

Anyone who attempted to resist had to reckon with brutal retaliation. Mass executions were the order of the day. In 1940 the Germans established a number of camps on Polish territory (see page 62), which, in January 1942, were semi-officially refashioned and enlarged to function as extermination camps. People deported to these camps were officially described as 'vermin'. Before being killed, they were abused as slave workers and used for medical experiments. From 1942 onwards the prisoners of these camps were killed by poison gas and the corpses incinerated. Of more than five million people interned in Polish concentration camps, more than 3.5 million were killed – three million of those as a consequence of the *endlösung* (Final Solution) policy that had been planned for the Jews.

In conjunction with the executions in the camps, there was also the *Aktion Reinhard*, which simply meant that those who had been condemned to death were first relieved of any valuables they may have had. In the fiscal year 1943–44 this brought the Deutsche Reichsbank an incredible net profit totalling over 100 million Reichsmarks.

The military and political collapse of Poland was a severe shock for the Polish people and it forced them into a painful reappraisal of their situation. Terror, torture, death and starvation, and the suppression of any independence movements further intensified the general feeling of hopelessness. Corruption and human rights abuses were rife.

designated as 'western Ukraine' and 'western Belorussia.' After a manipulated 'referendum' on 1 and 2 November both were incorporated into the two Soviet republics.

In February 1940 the deportation of Polish citizens to Kazakhstan, to the Russian Arctic and to Siberia commenced. Stalin was of the opinion that it was possible to expel anyone or anything: the nation from its identity and its land, the family from home and hearth. His aim was that ultimately people would lose their self-esteem and all sense of personal identity.

Jews on a Warsaw street awaiting deportation to the concentration camps.

Soviet control

In tandem with the German terrorising campaign, the Soviet Union set about the annexation of occupied East Poland and began with the 'russification' of its newly won territory. This was personally undertaken by the head of the Communist Party in the Ukraine at the time, Nikita Khrushchev, who later, on Stalin's death, became the first Secretary of the Soviet Communist Party. In Moscow, Stalin propagated the occupation of Poland as an 'act of liberation from the capitalist system by a fraternal nation.' A precise census was carried out, and subsequently the Soviet administration foisted Soviet passports on every east Polish citizen. The occupied regions were

MASS DEPORTATIONS

One Stalinist method that was especially successful was the expulsion of whole sections of the Polish population from their homelands. State officials, judges and foresters were the first to be deported. Eventually whole families, merchants, members of the self-employed classes, professors and teachers followed. In one year almost 1.65 million Polish citizens were deported in cattle wagons, many of them refugees who had recently arrived from central and eastern Poland. A large percentage were taken to hard-labour camps for 're-education'. By 1942 more than half of the people who had been deported were dead.

Stalin's method of control was based on rather different premises from Hitler's reign of terror. He believed that in the end his victims would surrender to a system in which they were forced to do slave labour and were pressured day and night by functionaries or police.

Sikorski versus the Communists

The Polish government-in-exile under General Sikorski was not just involved in military matters, but was also active politically. As early as 20 December 1939 and despite the harsh realities of the situation, it was calling for the liberation

the Polish Forces, which subsequently landed in Italy. The Corps, commanded by General Władysław Anders, played a prominent part in the Italian campaign. Its successes included breaking through 'Hitler's Line', with its key position at Monte Cassino, one of the great battles of World War II.

Meanwhile in Russia, the Germans discovered the mass graves of Polish officers, murdered on Stalin's orders. They were the bodies in Katyń of officers unaccounted for during the formation of the army in the USSR. Understandably, German propaganda was making

A cabinet meeting of the Polish government-in-exile, presided by General Sikorski.

of Poland from enemy occupation, pleading for boundaries that would guarantee Polish security. When Hitler attacked the Soviet Union in June 1941, Sikorski, met with Stalin and was granted the concession that a number of Poles who had been deported to Soviet camps should be released in order to set up a Polish army. Stalin was even prepared to annul the earlier pact with Hitler concerning the partition of Poland, but he peremptorily rejected the Polish demand to be allowed to re-establish its pre-World War I border.

Eventually, about 100,000 soldiers, women and children were safely evacuated to the Middle East via Iran. Men, armed and equipped by the British, formed the Second Army Corps of

the best possible use of the discovery. To put an end to it, the Polish Government proposed that a neutral Red Cross commission should investigate the matter. This proposal was met with a furious Russian reaction. They accused the Polish Government of siding with the Germans and, using it as a pretext, the Soviet Union broke off diplomatic relations with Poland.

At the time Stalin was totally convinced of his victory over Germany and he believed that the Soviet expansion to the west would obliterate any memory of Katyń. He even had the temerity to invite Polish Communists to Moscow. Just a few years previously many of them had barely escaped the execution that Stalin had ordered for all members of the Polish Communist Party.

(In 1938 the Polish Communist Party, at the time illegal, had been disbanded because of a 'betrayal of the world revolution'; the party had collaborated with the Socialist Party and the Peasant Party in Poland. Some 5,000 comrades invited to the Soviet Union were murdered on Stalin's orders).

Those members of the Polish Communist Party who had formed a pro-Soviet wing in the years before 1939 – Bierut, Minc, Ochab, Gomułka and others – now made it clear that they were ready to co-operate with Moscow. In March 1943, they combined to establish the

> At the Tehran Conference in November 1943 Stalin made it clear to Britain and the US that most of post-war Poland would become part of the Soviet Union.

Union of Polish Patriots and, as far as Stalin was concerned, were the 'true representatives of the Polish people'. In autumn 1943, the newly organised Polish divisions fought side by side with the Soviet army at the Eastern front. As a sign of their identity, these soldiers wore the Piast eagle – without the crown – on their helmets.

Government-in-exile isolated

While fighting was continuing on various fronts around Poland, tough negotiations on the borders for the future of the Polish state were continuing at a diplomatic level. Various differing views existed at that time regarding mainly the eastern border. The government-in-exile was looking towards the restitution of the 1921 borders and the return of the areas annexed by the Soviet Union; while the pro-Soviet Poles, on the other hand, now preferred the so-called Stalin Compensation Plan. Within the guidelines of this plan, in return for shifting the western border to the Oder–Neisse line, the Poles would give up claims to the eastern regions and Polish territory would, in addition, include Gdańsk and southern East Prussia.

The Allied forces found these ongoing disputes increasingly embarrassing, as the demands of the Polish government-in-exile conflicted with those of their military alliance with the Soviet Union. By the autumn of 1943, the

government-in-exile found itself dangerously out on a limb.

The Warsaw Uprising

In January 1944, the Soviet army had reached the pre-war frontiers of Poland. After the death of General Sikorski in an air crash in Gibraltar on 4 July 1943, Stanisław Mikołajczyk became the Prime Minister. He instructed the Home Army command to liberate parts of Poland from the Germans before the Red Army arrived and to co-operate with the Russians afterwards.

The plan worked well in the Vilno district,

Władysław Sikorski, commander of the Polish army and prime minister of the government-in-exile during World War II.

which was liberated by the Home Army division. However, when according to government instructions, the division made contact with the Russians to plan future co-operation, the officers were immediately imprisoned and their units disarmed. But there still remained the slight chance to liberate the capital city of Poland, Warsaw, before the arrival of the Red Army and thus make it the true seat of government of Poland.

With this in view, on 1 August 1944, the Home Army attacked the German garrison in Warsaw. Eventually, considerable forces of the German 9th Army had to be diverted into the battle for Warsaw. It lasted for 63 days, with the

Russian Army impassively observing it from across the River Vistula.

The Home Army needed ammunition most of all, but providing air supplies from Italy and England was difficult over such long distances, in the face of alerted German anti-aircraft defences. The Russians flatly refused to allow allied aircraft to refuel on their territory. So, in spite of the sacrifice of many a brave air-crew, mainly Polish and South African, the uprising slowly died.

When the Home Army capitulated on 2 October 1944, the casualties among the civilian they elevated the committee of the Polish Communists to the government of Poland, with its seat at Lublin.

By the time of the conference in Yalta, in February 1945, Russian troops had already reached this line, thus cleverly presenting Roosevelt and Churchill with a *fait accompli*. According to Russian plans, this shift of Polish frontiers to the west would have been a compensation for the lands of Eastern Poland, invaded in 1939 as a result of the Ribbentropp–Molotov agreement. This plan received a tacit approval from Roosevelt and Churchill,

Monument to the Warsaw Uprising in Warsaw.

population amounted to around 180,000 and 85 per cent of the city was totally destroyed.

However tragic the fate of the city, the uprising had succeeded in halting the Red Army's progress into Europe for at least two months, while it waited for the Germans to eliminate the Poles. Given these two months, it is reasonable to suppose that the Red Army would have met the Western Allies on the Rhine and Germany as a whole, not only its eastern part, would then have become a People's Republic.

Yalta and Potsdam conferences

In mid-December 1944, the Russians decided to fix the western Polish border along the line of the rivers Oder and Neisse. Soon afterwards although the final decisions were postponed until the end of the war. It is certainly notable, however, that the Government of Poland, still residing in exile in London, was not once consulted on matters concerning the frontiers of its country at this time.

As was expected, the Potsdam Conference, which began on 17 July 1945, ended in complete political victory for Soviet Russia. It approved the Soviet solution for the post-war frontiers of Europe and consigned half of its countries into Soviet overlordship. The Western allies, surprisingly, also agreed to the Russian method of settling nationality problems, first used in Poland, where about two million people were forcibly removed from their

> *Enraged by the activities of the Warsaw Uprising, Hitler demanded that the city be razed to the ground, hoping to leave the rubble to the awaiting Red Army.*

homes and sent to labour camps in Russia. In the same way, Germans east of the Oder–Neisse line, were to be resettled in the new People's Republic of Germany. In Churchill's opinion, this was the only way to bring lasting peace to the region.

had no country to return to. In spite of that, the soldiers remained loyal to their allies. In 1947, all units of the Polish forces were concentrated in Great Britain, where they were disbanded on the orders of the British Government. A small percentage of men returned to Poland, but the great majority remained in Great Britain to seek civilian employment and start a new life.

No nation throughout the world was to suffer more than Poland in the machinations of World War II. Although Hitler was clearly defeated, he had decimated the population through his racist policies and ethnic cleans-

A squadron of Polish fighter pilots memorise the day's operations at a British airbase, February 1943.

Polish forces disbanded

In 1945, Polish forces numbered 250,000 men, spread between the army, navy and air force. They had fought on all major fronts of the war, in the air over Great Britain and Germany and on the seas and oceans. The Second Army Corps took part in the African and Italian campaigns, ending the Italian one with the liberation of the city of Bologna.

The First Corps, with its rear echelons in Great Britain, took part in the invasion of the Continent. Its famous armoured division covered itself in glory at Falaise, while the Parachute Brigade fought with distinction at Arnhem. Ever since the conferences in Tehran and Yalta, every soldier knew that he would have

ing by almost 25 percent, many of the victims being among Poland's brightest and most creative pre-war citizens. The cities and landscape were ravaged by war and the evil testaments to Hitler's 'Final Solution' still haunt the country dotted with barren and eerie land that once supported his death camps. Stalin, however, far from being defeated, had gained his original aims, shifting the borders of eastern Europe and infiltrating greater areas with his politics.

Poland lost great cities, rural communities and a strong pre-war sense of national identity, despite participating bravely in a war that had begun in its defence by its Allies. It would take many decades of hardship and political struggle before the Polish nation would regain its former strength.

The Concentration Camps

Poland was ground zero for Nazi Germany's horrific campaign to rid the world of all Jews.

The Russo-German alliance of August 1939, known as the Ribbentrop–Molotov pact, had a double purpose. Its most immediate aim was a joint invasion of Poland, whereas its long-term purpose was the annihilation of the Polish nation. It was put in operation

grew steadily between 1940 and 1945 to accommodate and destroy people of many nationalities. It is calculated that 1.5 million people perished there, mostly Jews from Poland and all over Europe.

It was the only German concentration camp that tattooed identity numbers on prisoner's forearms. However, the number of prisoners thus marked did not exceed 200,000. The rest ended up in gas chambers straight from their trains, without being registered. The first test killing by the gas Cyclon B was carried out in September 1941. After that date, additional gas chambers were constantly constructed. The camp was greatly enlarged by adding new areas

Concentration camp victims.

after the end of the September 1939 campaign on Poland, when the secret police of both aggressors (Gestapo for Germany and NKVD for the Soviet Union) had established friendly co-operation. In the autumn, the Gestapo carried out the first of its mass arrests comprising of people prominent in politics and the arts, who were subsequently murdered or sent to concentration camps to await a slower death.

Auschwitz

To provide for the fast growing number of prisoners, a new concentration camp was set up in Poland, near the town of Oświęcim. It became known under its German name of Auschwitz, as the most dreaded *Vernichtungslager*, or extermination camp, in Europe. It was built to provide a killing ground for Poles, but it

near the village of Brzezinka (German Birkenau). The gas chambers of Birkenau became the central extermination camp, established for the Jews.

On 18th January 1945, the camp was evacuated and 60,000 prisoners were marched on foot in scanty clothing without food and in the depths of the winter to camps in Germany. Most perished before they reached their destination. Another major concentration camp was built in Poland, near Lublin. At least 1 million people (almost all Polish Jews) died in Majdanek and Treblinka – but it was the name Auschwitz that became a symbol of martyrdom for the mass extermination of countless European Jews.

In the Soviet-occupied part of Poland, the NKVD began arrests of the 'enemies of the people'. As in German-occupied Poland, the term embraced people prominent in their professional capacity, with the addition of property owners. In fact, this meant anyone suspicious in the eyes of local NKVD agents, without any reference to their past, social or economic standing. Those arrested were sent to the Soviet equivalents of German concentration camps, the so-called 'labour camps', or gulags, in Siberia, where their chances of survival were minimal. Polish prisoners of war were also sent to gulags, with the exception of officers. Early 1940, the mass deportations of entire families began. Some 1.5 million adults and children were deported to remote parts of Russia, in what is now known as 'ethnic cleansing'.

The Katyń Massacre

The army officers taken prisoners of war during the defence of Poland were imprisoned in three camps: Kozielsk, Ostaszków and Starobielsk. Their total number in these camps amounted to 15,570. As might be expected, the majority were reserve officers, representing many professions, including 800 medical doctors. Over 10,000 of them, along with some 11,000 Polish civilians, were murdered during April 1940, on orders from the Soviet Government. Two years later, the bodies of officers from the Kozielsk camp were accidentally discovered by German army personnel in a wood near the village of Katyń. All had been killed with a single pistol shot to the base of the skull. Goebbels enthusiastically embraced this golden opportunity for German propaganda.

At the time, it was assumed that all 15,000 were killed there, and Katyń Forest became known as a scene of the greatest single war crime committed in modern history. German forensic authorities established the date of the crime as spring 1940. The Soviet government, however, denied any complicity and accused the Germans. It was Germans who were accused during the Nuremberg war crime trials in 1945, but the case against them was dropped for lack of evidence. This didn't stop the allied governments from supporting the Soviet version of events, right down to the end of the Soviet State.

It was only after the collapse of the Soviet Union that the Russian authorities admitted responsibility for the crime and published the relevant orders which originated from the Politburo, the supreme organ of the Soviet Government, presided over by Stalin himself. However, Russia has yet to hand over to Poland the remaining classified documents concerning the Katyń massacre. Only after the Russian admission was it possible to seek the graves of thousands of missing officers who were not buried at Katyń Forest. In all, 15,000 murdered prisoners of war were finally accounted for. Like Auschwitz in German-occupied Poland, so Katyń Forest became a symbol of the martyrdom suffered by the Poles at the hands of the Soviets.

Treblinka

The concentration camp at Treblinka provides one of the most chilling reminders of the Nazi atrocities: the site was strategically well chosen, about 100 km (60 miles) to the northeast of Warsaw, with its rail terminal linked with the international rail network to Russia. At the junction there was a large supply depot for the German advance to the east. It is almost cer-

The site of the crematorium at Treblinka, covered with basalt rocks, is a memorial to indescribable suffering.

tain that the two extermination camps, Treblinka I and II, were built along the demarcation line that the German Reich and Russia had drawn through Poland when they divided the country between them.

The Nazis closed the Treblinka camps in November 1943 and obliterated their bloody traces. Before the closure they had committed 2,400 murders per day. Documents were burned, all possible eyewitnesses were liquidated: the SS literally tried to let grass grow over the horrors they had committed. But their attempts at a cover-up failed – a few dozen eyewitnesses escaped and conveyed the cruel truths about the camps to the rest of the world. In 1964 a commemorative site was inaugurated to do some justice to the human tragedy that this place represents.

Manifest, a depiction of the issuing of the Polish Communist manifesto, by Wojciech Weiss.

THE COMMUNIST STATE

The rise of Stalin at the end of World War II saw the whole of Eastern Europe ruled by the restrictive and often terrifying Communist regime.

When in the summer of 1944 the Soviet army liberated parts of Poland from the German occupying forces, the generals immediately set about installing a Polish Communist administration. That same year the 'July Manifesto' (Manifest Lipcowy) appeared with proposals for a new social and economic order. Slogans urged Poles to welcome plans for agrarian reform, the state ownership of industry and a transformation in society, accompanied by justice and democracy. With the strong support of the Soviet army, Polish Communists began establishing a totalitarian dictatorship along Russian lines.

Communists seize power

The 'revolution from outside' was not accepted passively by the Poles. Units of the Home Army were still active and considerable forces were needed to put them out of action. As Stalin had no faith in the Polish Communists, he wasted no time in putting Soviet secret police in the front line. Their job was to ensure the loyalty of the Polish population to the Soviet Union and to the Communist party. Those who dissented were either executed or imprisoned. In an atmosphere of terror, the Provisional Government of National Unity was set up. Bolesław Bierut became president and Edward Osóbka-Morawski became prime minister.

Open political opposition to the Communists came mainly from the Polish Peasant Party (PSL) with Stanisław Mikołajczyk, the former prime minister of the government-in-exile, as its head. He garnered support mainly from rural communities and intellectuals. Other independent politicians were systematically isolated. Many were put to death.

An example of Socialist Realist art.

For official purposes, the Communists gave the impression that a democratisation process was taking place in post-war Poland. Soviet advisers urged their Polish counterparts to promise the end of poverty and fear, the prospect of a bright future and a fresh new beginning after the harrowing years of German occupation.

On 19 January 1947, the long-promised general elections were held. While foreign observers recorded a 60 percent vote in favour of the PSL, the Communist-led 'Democratic Block' was awarded 394 of the 444 parliamentary seats. There followed a wave of mass arrests among the PSL members and Mikołajczyk fled abroad.

Rebuilding the economy

In 1945, the Polish economy lay in ruins. Although the people found themselves living in a new state with geographically favourable and historically acceptable borders, some six million Poles had lost their lives since 1939. A third of the national wealth had gone and two-thirds of its industrial potential had been destroyed. Those areas in the north and west that had seen the expulsion of some 3.5 million Germans were optimistic about the future, as new arrivals from eastern Polish provinces moved in to take the Germans' places. But here,

> In 1955 Poland became a member of the Warsaw Pact, intended to be the reply to NATO. In 1949 it became a member of COMECON, the Union of Mutual Economic Aid.

The Stalinist era (1948–56)

In 1948 Europe entered the long dark tunnel in its history known as the Cold War. With the blockade of Berlin, the era of Stalinism also began for Poland. In March 1948 the prime minister, Józef Cyrankiewicz, received instruc-

Workers' May Day demonstrations in 1952.

too, the war had left a bitter legacy: the Soviets had dismantled any surviving industrial plants and transported them to Russia.

In 1946 nearly all companies were nationalised. As compensation for Poland's properties abroad, the state received some 200 million dollars. But under pressure from Moscow, Poland was not allowed to take advantage of the Marshall Plan money; the Communists imposed a centralised economy on the country. Private industry and services were abolished in 1947 but, as the new bureaucracy was unable to replace the private sector, the black market flourished. By dint of hard work, the targets set in the 1947 Three-Year Plan were met and Poland quickly reached its pre-war per capita income.

tions from Moscow to establish a governing unity party. This was to include the remnants of the Polish Socialist Party (PPS) and the Polish Workers Party (PPR). The pre-Communist Peasant Faction, the United Peasant Party (ZSL) and the Democratic Faction (SD) were allowed to remain independent but under the auspices of the Communists.

In June 1948, the head of the Polish Communists, Władysław Gomułka, was accused of right-wing nationalist tendencies and spent from 1951 to 1954 in prison. He was in favour of a 'Polish route' to socialism and advocated the maintenance of private property. Some months later, the PPS was incorporated into the Polish United Workers' Party (PZPR). With the approval of Stalin, power passed to the loyal, but incompetent figure of Bolesław Bierut, formerly a member of Comintern.

In December 1948 the congress of the PZPR was formed and Beirut was appointed as first secretary. With the embodiment of the pre-eminent role of the PZPR in the new constitution of 22 July 1952, the last chance to establish a democratic society in Poland passed.

Along with the tyranny of PZPR and its front organisation, the hallmarks of Stalinism in Poland were: the adoption of Marxism-Leninism as an infallible ideology; the amassing of armed forces on a huge scale; centralised economic planning; and concentration on heavy industry. This model was transferred directly from the Soviet Union to all countries of the Eastern bloc and was retained, virtually unchanged, until the end of the 1980s.

Officially the constitution was quite democratic: it guaranteed civil rights and a so-called democratic government elected by parliament with a president and a state's council. The parliament itself, the *Sejm*, was voted in by general election. In reality, however, it was little more than a front. The 'working people in the city and in rural areas', according to the letter of the constitution nothing less than the true rulers of the country, were only helpless victims of the state. The party alone, the Politburo, the first secretary and the privileged élite of the nomenclature, really wielded all the power. In effect, it was a dictatorship of the party over the people.

The conviction of Stalin and his minions that the Soviet bloc was constantly threatened by an invasion from the 'powers of American imperialism' led to the recruitment of an enormous Polish army (400,000 troops). The officers were trained in a Political Military Academy (WAP, founded in 1951).

Top priority was accorded to building up the steel, coal, iron and armaments industries. In order to accommodate the flood of migrant workers from rural areas who were now required to take their places on the production lines, whole new cities and suburbs were built virtually overnight. On the outskirts of Warsaw and in Nowa Huta near Kraków these municipal, architectural monstrosities can still be seen

Propaganda poster praising "Polish-Soviet Friendship", with Stalin alongside Polish President Bolesław Bierut.

in all their ghastliness. The supply of foodstuffs was largely handed over to the newly established PGRS (national farmsteads – the Polish version of the Russian state farms), and its gross inefficiency resulted in disastrous consequences for both productivity and quality.

The system's intention was to fashion a new, socialist man: in effect that meant the abolition of humanitarian ideals. Political terror and repression reached a climax in 1951. Everyday life became a nightmare. All contacts with the outside world were immediately denounced; in bogus trials innocent people were arbitrarily accused of being spies and sentenced to internment or death. There were also

CATHOLIC RESISTANCE

The Roman Catholic Church was one of the few 'organisations' that retained a level of independence against the new Communist regime, but it was generally regarded as a reactionary relic of the pre-war system and priests and laymen alike were openly attacked and constantly threatened with arrest by the governing forces. By 1950 the financial assets of the Church had been confiscated. In 1952, one of the heroes of this frightening era was Cardinal Stefan Wyszyński, the primate of Poland, who was arrested for his 'anti-state' attitudes and was exiled to a monastery where he was kept prisoner for three years.

executions without trial (in 1990 mass graves were found dating from this time). Many people were deported to the Soviet Union and simply vanished without trace. A dense network of informers infiltrated factories and offices, schools and universities.

The propaganda, of course, told a different story. The news was full of stories about the construction of gigantic collective combines, factories and other buildings, and tales of rising work quotas. The ever-increasing number of success stories perpetuated the course that Stalinism had planned for the country. Monu-

in Poland. In December 1954 the despised Ministry of Public Security was disbanded and the censorship laws relaxed. Władysław Gomułka was released from prison. There was no further talk of collectivisation. The political thaw commenced. In June 1956 worker protests in Poznań, which started with the slogan 'bread and liberty', showed that the country needed a new pragmatic party leader whom the people could trust. This man turned out to be Władysław Gomułka. After Khrushchev had assured himself of his loyalty, the Stalinist era came to an end in Poland.

Khrushchev arriving at Warsaw Airport for the 20th anniversary of the Polish Communist government, 25 July 1964.

mental sculptures in the style of socialist realism provided visible proof of the superiority of the new system and its ideology to all who saw them.

And yet in Poland the omnipotence of Stalinism never quite reached the level that it did in other Eastern bloc states. The political trials never developed into a series of propaganda trials. It proved impossible to eradicate the bourgeois and intellectual milieu. The collectivisation of agriculture was carried out slowly and incompletely. Nevertheless, the memory of the Stalinist years was engraved upon the mind of the nation.

Josef Stalin died in March 1953. Within two years the liberalising effect of his death was felt

National Communism (1956–80)

In October 1956 Gomułka managed to free Poland from total control of the Soviet Union, which determined the political life of the nation for the next 25 years. Gomułka was of the opinion that there were 'various ways to socialism' and he managed to prove that Polish Communists could look after the affairs of their country on their own account, without having to take constant instructions from Moscow (Imre Nagy in Hungary was not so lucky).

Gomułka managed to achieve three vital concessions: an independent church, free agriculture and an open political forum. These concessions were designed to be transitional only, until the party had found a firm footing, but matters turned out differently. The Church was stronger than ever before. Within the framework of its self-administration, it continued to run its priest seminars, its own social and intellectual societies and its own university. It thus became the only really independent church in the whole of the Eastern bloc.

Sociologists who adhered to the party doctrine had prophesied that industrialisation and urbanisation would change the cultural patterns of traditional society and would sever the ties between people and church. They couldn't have been more wrong. The Polish Church did not lose its adherents – on the contrary it turned out to be a place of refuge and the driving force behind the Polish opposition. The same kind of fate befell the collectivisation plans of the agricultural programme. Gomułka had no intention of committing the same errors that had led to the death by starvation of millions of people in the Ukraine 30 years previously. More than 70 percent of the arable land thus remained in private hands, while collective farming was only retained in the areas where it had already been introduced (for example on the huge, former German estates in the west of Poland). The experts did not regard

Pope John Paul II with the Polish Communist leader Edward Gierek in 1979.

SOCREALISM

Socialist Realism – socrealism for short – was the form of visual art allowed by the Communist regime. The object was the veneration of the working class and of its self-appointed leaders. In its pure form, it was characterised by an almost photographic realism, a style at odds with the idealism of its message. Typical subjects were workers, happy in their work and communist leaders in heroic poses heralding the utopia to come – aspirations which were far removed from the brutal realities of the day.

The most imposing manifestation of socrealism was in architecture, much of which remains to this day – the Palace of Culture and Science in Warsaw being the supreme example. This gift of the Soviet Union to Communist Poland is a mix of concrete tower block and Baroque decoration. Despite some calls for it to be demolished, the majority of Warsawians believe that the building is now an integral part of the city's history and should therefore remain. Houses along the central Marszałkowska street are decorated with large concrete figures of workers. They lead to Plac Konstytucji (Constitution Square), another icon of socrealism which has shed its past notoriety and is now often praised, particularly by the younger generation.

that as a problem. In time, the small, private farms would disappear of their own accord, as the state had other means of making it plain to the farmers that private industry was not worthwhile. In practice that meant granting privileges to the collective sector and neglecting the private sector, measures that ultimately ended in unmitigated disaster for the whole nation.

Within 40 years the government managed to lead the country to the very brink of starvation. Poland, traditionally an agricultural country, was ruined, despite its fertile soil. The population was plagued with food rationing and queuing outside grocers' shops. Nevertheless, private agriculture survived.

As for demands for pluralism, the leadership accommodated those by licensing several political organisations. However, the fact that these were all united under the one roof of the National Union Front – under the patronage of the party – meant that any ideas of pluralism were pure illusion. It soon became clear that neither Gomułka nor his successor, Edward Gierek, backed as they were by a total lack of any constitutionality, were prepared to adhere to the promised concessions. Civil liberties were

Members of the Solidarity trade union on strike at the Lenin Shipyard in Gdańsk, August 1980.

BREAKING DOWN THE BARRIER OF FEAR

The protests of March 1968 not only mobilised the students, but also the whole intelligentsia. For the first time the names of several dissidents became well known, including Adam Michnik, Jacek Kuroń and Karol Modzelewski.

Unrest in December 1970 in Gdańsk and Szczecin succeeded in moulding a generation of intransigent and embittered workers. Between 1975 and 1976 the changes in the constitution, which resulted in even greater dependency on the Soviet Union, contributed to the organisation of a national dissident group, the Polish League for Independence (PPN) in 1976, by Zdzisław Najder.

In June 1976, when workers in the tractor plant in Ursus and the armaments factory in Radom were punished for their participation in a protest action, intellectuals founded the Workers' Defence Committee (KOR). For the first time intellectuals and workers were unanimous in pursuing a common goal, and from this moment on one could talk of an organised, supranational opposition. The committee worked quite openly (although not legally) as an information and co-ordination centre for the whole country. With the investiture of the cardinal of Kraków, Karol Wojtyła, as Pope in 1978 and his visit to Poland in 1979, the psychological barrier of fear was also destroyed.

severely curtailed. Again and again (1968, 1970, 1976 and 1980) dissent broke out. The slogan of the protesters was 'bread and liberty'. The protests were organised either by labourers or students and intellectuals. They had to be put down forcibly by the government and there were frequent casualties. By this time there could no longer be any doubt that the government had lost the confidence of the Polish people.

The founding of Solidarność

The organised opposition that emerged in 1980 had a long history that had begun with

themselves willing to accept the leading role of the party.

An agreement between the workers and the government was eventually signed on 31 August 1980. As an immediate consequence of this event, representatives of the strike committee from all the provinces of the country formed the national co-ordination committee of the independent, self-administered trade union *Solidarność* known in the west as Solidarity. The 37-year-old Lech Wałęsa was elected chairman. Just a few months later the Farmers' Solidarity (*Solidarność Wiejska*) was permitted as an official organisation.

Crowds welcoming Pope John Paul II in Poznań, 20th June 1983.

the student protests of 1968.

In the summer of 1980 government attempts to implement drastic price increases for foodstuffs and consumer goods caused a wave of public strikes. The epicentre of the protest was in Gdańsk, in the Lenin Shipyard, whose tradition of resistance went back to December 1970, when workers had been killed during protest action. The KOR members were involved right from the start of the political agitation. Included on the list of 21 demands posed by the strike committee were the right to strike, the right to form independent trade unions and the permission to erect a monument for colleagues who had died in the 1970 uprising. In return the workers declared

In the 15 months of its activity Solidarity proved to be a peaceful reform movement which, with its 10 million members, represented a broad section of the whole nation. It could only defend itself with its own ideals.

Martial law

The rise of Solidarity was viewed with great misgivings in the Soviet Union. However, the leaders of the Kremlin rejected the idea of military intervention. Unlike in the case of Czechoslovakia, it was feared that part of the Polish army, supported by the majority of the population, would actively resist the invasion, embroiling the Soviet Union in a war in Europe while the Afghan war was still in progress. In addition, NATO powers did not declare their total indifference (unlike the Soviet invasion of Czechoslovakia). Taking into account the well-proven fighting qualities of the Poles, the risk was too great. Instead, the Head of the Communist Party and the Commander-in-Chief, General Jaruzelski, was ordered to crush Solidarity.

On 13 December 1981, he proclaimed martial law and ordered the army to virtually occupy the country. Solidarity was officially abolished and all its leaders, including Lech Wałęsa, were imprisoned. A wave of repression was put in motion and all remnants of constitutional rights

disappeared. The success of martial law in suppressing Solidarity was, however, very short-lived. Its organisation simply went underground.

The entire population now clearly understood that the time for compromises had come and gone. From then on, the only true political division among Poles became between that of 'us' (which meant every Pole) and 'them' (the Communists in power).

The next few years were characterised by an ever more acute economic crisis. With Solidarity banned, the opposition centred on the Church. It became the only truly independent

Lech Wałęsa at a rally in May 1989.

THE FACE OF SOLIDARITY

Like the TV images of the fall of the Berlin Wall in November 1989, Lech Wałęsa's personality and the Solidarity movement has come to symbolise popular demands for the end of East European communism in the late 1980s.

Awarded the Noble Peace Prize in 1983 for his work on human rights, Wałęsa's political career had humble beginnings. Born in 1943 in Popow, Poland, in the mid-1960s he worked as an electrician in the Lenin Shipyard in Gdańsk. In 1976 he was sacked for anti-government activities but he returned to the shipyard in 1980 to lead a workers' strike demanding, among other things, better working conditions, the

right to form a trades' union and the right to strike. After most of the 21 demands were met, Solidarity began to represent the national consciousness. New members were drawn from across Polish society and within a year and a half more than 10 million people joined the movement.

When Solidarity won a landslide election victory in 1989 it declared 'History has taught us that there is no bread without freedom.' When Wałęsa was elected president in 1990, Solidarity stated 'What we had in mind was not only bread, butter and sausage but also justice, democracy, truth, legality, human dignity, freedom of convictions and the repair of the republic.'

Martial law was only lifted in 1983, triggered by the second visit to his homeland by Pope John Paul II.

institution that could afford protection to anyone requiring it. The Church was at the same time a forum for political discussion, meetings, lectures, tuition and the dissemination of illegal literature, publicity and magazines. For all this, its members often paid a heavy price. Fearless Father Popiełuszko was tortured and murdered by members of the security police in 1984.

Life was, for the majority of the population, now divided into two spheres: the official, legal, everyday routine and the clandestine, illegal underground. The government proved entirely incapable of coping with the political and economic crisis.

Signs of a deep political crisis were also to be seen in Russia. The new leader in power, Mikhail Gorbachev, who came to the Kremlin during 1985, was only too aware of a progressive weakening of the Soviet grip on Poland but was no longer able to strengthen it. The Soviet Union for the first time no longer showed any imperialistic tendencies. An invasion, such as had been feared in December 1981, was therefore no longer a realistic possibility by the latter half of the decade.

The collapse of Communism

After waves of strikes in the spring and autumn of 1988, the Communist Party agreed to share political power. After 'round table' talks were held to discuss basic political, social and economic reforms and an agreement was signed on 5 April 1989, in which party and representatives from the Solidarity movement specified their conditions. These included legalisation of Solidarity, the right to a free press and elected seats in parliament. The path towards democracy had finally been laid.

For the elections, Solidarity founded citizen committees to represent the opposition. Even during the 'round table' talks, the Communist Party had reserved the right to form the government. But in the election of June 1989 the Communists were so soundly thrashed that any attempt to do so would have failed. The Solidarity movement won almost every seat it contested. Ultimately, Tadeusz Mazowiecki

was entrusted with the task of forming the new government. A journalist by profession, he had already acquired authority as the editor-in-chief of the *Tygodnik Solidarność* in 1980–81 and, later, during his imprisonment, he had enjoyed popular esteem. The PZPR dissolved in January 1990 and Polish Communism was on the wane.

The events in Poland led to the collapse of Communism in Europe as a whole. What had begun with a wave of strikes in the spring of 1988 had resulted in general unrest; the Communist party had lost its power and was soon to disappear altogether. Other Eastern bloc coun-

Polish President Bronisław Komorowski and Lech Wałęsa at the inauguration of the European Solidarity Centre in Gdańsk on 31 August 2014, the 34th anniversary of the signing of the August 1980 agreements.

tries were quick to follow the example set by Solidarity and the process became unstoppable. It eventually led to the fall of Communism in the Soviet Union.

Ten years later, in 1999, Poland became a member of NATO. By this act, Poland returned to its 1,000-year-old historical role. In this role, the country provided a shield to Europe, defending it from Tartars, Turks, Cossacks and from invasions of the semi-barbaric Grand Duchy of Muscovy. The shield was broken in the 18th century, with calamitous consequences, not only to Poland, but to many other nations.

A farmer's market in Kazimierz Dolny.

POLAND TODAY

While Poland has swiftly adapted to the free market and economy, many social maladies still linger, with huge gaps between living standards in different parts of the country.

Post-communist investment in Poland did not take long to materialise. While the early years were chaotic to say the least, the sheer size of the Polish market, and of the potential returns, were enough to allay any fears of political instability – and there was plenty of that. Now a member of both NATO and the EU, Poland is a modern parliamentary democracy unrecognisable from the country that had to be dragged quite literally kicking and screaming into the 1990s.

The road to a market economy

At the beginning of the 1990s, visitors to Poland were greeted by a bizarre sight: between the city's three largest department stores (built in the 1970s as symbols of a new attitude towards consumerism) and outside the vast Palace of Culture, thousands of people were out on the streets buying and selling consumer articles of every conceivable kind. People wanted not the goods on the shelves in the shops, but those spread out on the pavements. The atmosphere amid the drab landscape of central Warsaw was more akin to that of an Oriental bazaar.

From cassettes and bananas to ladies' underwear and Lacoste tops, the booty from weekends in Berlin or trips to Turkey – anything that would sell – was spread out on blankets, if not on the ground then on the bonnet of the ubiquitous Polski Fiat 126P. The Poles were doing what they have often had to do at times of crisis: putting into practice the skills of survival, essential during this difficult period of transition to a market economy.

Prices of basic goods were rising faster than wages. In August 1989, the government lifted price restrictions and the price of a kilo of butter rose within a year from 1,000 to an astonishing 10,000 złoty. Poland found itself without

Warsaw is now a major international centre of business.

state support and production plummeted. Unprofitable companies were closed down, and unemployment increased dramatically, putting thousands of people out of work almost overnight and presenting families with severe financial difficulties.

For many, street trading of almost any goods they had access to was the only way of obtaining income to continue to feed their families and pay the rent on their homes.

Root and branch reform

The country has undergone a dramatic transformation within only a few years, as a quick look back at history will reveal. The new government, the first freely elected non-Communist

The Euro 2012 football championship was a huge success for Poland, and showcased a modern country to the world.

leadership in a Warsaw Pact state, took office on 12 September 1989.

The cabinet, consisting of both Communists and democrats, had to face up to some extremely serious problems: the political reorganisation of the state, a revival of democracy and political and social pluralism, armed defences, not to

Daewoo Factory assembly line in Warsaw, 1997.

mention the avoidance of an impending economic collapse. The latter was averted, though at great social cost, thanks to radical 'shock therapy' administered by the finance minister and Deputy PM Leszek Balcerowicz. A fervent supporter of monetarism and fiscal discipline, Balcerowicz was harshly criticised by his adversaries for the disastrous impact this had on the country folk. Their battle cry 'Balcerowicz must go!' rallied all those disgruntled with the harsh realities of the so-called Balcerowicz plan. Nevertheless, the measures introduced by the finance minister, drastic as they were, paved the way for the rapid transformation and growth of the Polish economy. The first elected prime minister, Tadeusz Mazowiecki, took great pride

in the fact that the revolution in Poland had been bloodless, unlike in some other countries of the Soviet block. However, his policy of the 'thick line', which was meant to separate modern Poland from the communist times, has been interpreted by some as leniency towards former communists, and this triggered deep divisions within the post-Solidarity movement.

The first coalition government was quite clear in its goals and plans for reform. It also saw its principal foreign policy goal as making approaches towards integration with the west. It wanted Poland to withdraw from the Soviet-oriented group of Communist nations known as COMECON (Council for Mutual Economic Aid) and the Warsaw Pact and to become an associate member of the EU.

Domestic politics

For many, the victory of the old cadres in the elections of September 1993 was an unexpected and worrying development. As in other former Eastern Bloc states, after four Solidarity-led governments – all of which had difficulty implementing their policies when there were as many as 29 different parties represented in the Sejm – many voters chose to elect the reformed Communists (SLD), the successors to the reviled Communist Party. They increased their number of parliamentary seats from 60 (in 1991) to 171.

There are many reasons why this party became the strongest faction within the *Sejm*. Given the great economic changes, many Poles simply forgot about the political patronage and economic misery over which the Polish Communist Party had presided. Many looked back wistfully to the days of state-guaranteed employment and the harmonious interpersonal relations that they as workers once enjoyed. That September, the last troops of the Russian army, instrumental in bringing the communists to power after World War II, left Poland.

The coalition government of 1995

The government formed in October 1993 by Waldemar Pawlak was an alliance between the Democratic Left Alliance (SLD) and the Polish Peasant Party (PSL). On 1 March 1995, Józef Oleksy, a former senior Communist Party official was elected prime minister after a crisis within the ruling coalition. The dominance of the Communist old guard was further reinforced by the narrow victory in the 1995 presidential elections of Aleksander Kwaśniewski, a former Communist minister (but now no longer affiliated to any party), after a hard-fought battle with the previous president, Lech Wałęsa.

The Polish Peasants' Party, the SLD's coalition partner, a satellite of the ruling Communist party in the pre-1989 era, draws its strength from the fact that 30 percent of the Polish population still live from the land. The new government was able to benefit from the achievements of the previous administration, which between 1989 and 1993 had pointed the country firmly in the direction of democracy and market eco-

in that year's elections. Indeed, it was the newly formed Solidarity Electoral Alliance (AWS; the political wing of the Solidarity Movement) which procured most votes, its ebullient leader Jerzy Buzek becoming prime minister.

Buzek's first task was to oversee the rewriting of Poland's communist-era constitution. The new version made sweeping changes to the way Poland was governed, decentralising the administration, though its ultimate aim of bringing government closer to the population did little more than create new levels of bureaucracy. It also created a new kind of bureaucrat to fill the

The Sejm, Polish Parliament, in session.

nomics. The economy, which by now had virtually freed itself from political interference, had been boosted by a six percent growth in Gross Domestic Product.

In December, Prime Minister Oleksy was accused of spying for Russia and resigned in January 1996. His successor, also a former communist, Włodzimierz Cimoszewicz, continued the mass privatisation programme under which every adult Pole was able to buy a share certificate for 20 złoty in the privatised enterprises. Poland became a member of the OECD.

The government's slow and ineffective response to devastating flooding in Southern and Western Poland in 1997 was the death knell for the coalition, which performed badly

EMIGRATION

The biggest effect of EU membership has been emigration. From Eastern Poland especially, 1 million Poles – mostly young – have emigrated to the rest of the EU since 2004. Over two million have left since 1989. The majority went to the UK and Ireland, which first opened their labour markets to the new EU members. So widespread has emigration been that many Polish regions, particularly in poor parts of the country, have become depopulated and industries now face labour shortages. Another negative consequence of so many departures has been a severe drop in demography. Poland now has one of the lowest fertility rates in the EU.

many vacancies created: in the main, Solidarity members filled these posts. Many Poles began to feel that a new party-state was being created.

Solidarity – whose base had always been in the cities – also made the fatal error of neglecting the countryside.

As quickly as skyscrapers were going up in Warsaw, so living standards were falling for most agricultural workers, who form almost a third of the country's workforce. Solidarity's support collapsed and many of its members deserted for other parties. By 2001, when a general election was held, what was left of the AWS was so

At work in a copper smelting factory in Głogów.

unpopular it failed to win a single seat in parliament. Instead, the former communists (SLD) were returned to office, with the Polish Peasant Party as coalition partner. Kwaśniewski, who had tilled a steady course through the turbulent AWS period, easily won a second term as president. The AWS disbanded a year later, Solidarity becoming once again solely a trade union.

21st-century Poland

Poland entered the 21st century with a single issue on its mind, membership of the EU. Broadly backed by all political parties, the SLD-led coalition set about ensuring that Poland met all of its targets to ensure entry to the EU on schedule in 2004. In order to do so it had to deal

> With the recognition of the Oder–Neisse line – awaited for 45 years – a new chapter has opened in the history of German-Polish relations.

very visibly with high-level corruption, and to set about finally reforming its under-performing agricultural sector. The former proved surprisingly easier than the latter. Nevertheless, the EU was happy to conclude entry negotiations with Poland in 2002, the country duly became a full EU member on May 1st, 2004. On the international scene, the left-wing government based its policy on close – some say too close – ties with the United States. Polish troops were consequently sent to Iraq and also took part in the ISAF, the NATO-led security mission in Afghanistan. According to many international reports, Poland hosted a secret CIA detention centre (black site) in 2002–03, where top Al-Qaeda suspects were held and questioned with the use of 'enhanced interrogation techniques', including mock executions and waterboarding. Despite the fact that many documents seem to confirm the existence of the CIA black site in the north of Poland (at Stare Kiejkuty), the then PM Leszek Miller flatly denies any involvement on the part of his cabinet.

Meanwhile, the economy, fuelled by EU funds, robust export and foreign investments continued to boom. This boom has been most visible in the cities: Warsaw especially, with its increasingly New York-esque skyline, now looks the part as a major international centre of business. In 2005 Kaczyński twins – Lech and Jarosław – took the reigns, Lech as president and Jarosław as prime minister. Their national-conservative mildly eurosceptic government embarked on a mission to eradicate corruption and improve the lot of those who had not benefited from the democratic transformation. It also vowed to rid the country of the former communist security services collaborators. Controversial *lustracja*, or vetting, was introduced to prevent them taking up public posts. As for the economy, the Kaczyński brothers favoured state interventionism and tight control – a newly created Anti-Corruption Bureau (CBA) was instrumental in this respect.

Their Law and Justice Party (PiS) was beset by infighting, however, and Jarosław was forced to resign in 2007. New elections brought the Civic Platform of moderniser Donald Tusk to the fore,

Tusk becoming Poland's youngest prime minister for a generation and the only one so far to hold on to power for two successive terms. His rule saw steady economic growth, even when the rest of Europe succumbed to crisis in 2008, and the tightening of bilateral relations with Germany, fuelled by good personal chemistry between Tusk and Chancellor Angela Merkel. As a result, Poland's position in the EU has been substantially strengthened. Political stability at the top level was further enhanced after PO's candidate Bronisław Komorowski was elected president in 2010 following the tragic death of his predecessor Lech Kaczyński in an air crash near Smolensk (see box). Poland's economy flourished, with its GDP increasing by about 40 percent between 2004 and 2014.

The Euro 2012 football championship co-hosted by Poland and Ukraine gave another impulse to the modernisation of the country, particularly its poor road and railway systems. Motorways and modern stadiums were built, dilapidated railway lines and country lanes upgraded. The championship itself proved to be a boost for Poland's image.

In EU matters, Oxford-educated Polish Foreign Affairs Minister Radosław Sikorski and his Swedish counterpart launched the Eastern Partnership programme, with the aim to bring former Soviet republics in Eastern Europe and Southern Caucasus closer to the EU by fostering democratic reforms and their political stability. Meanwhile, good relations with Germany and a personal friendship with Chancellor Angela Merkel helped catapult PM Donald Tusk to the presidency of the European Council in 2014.

Despite setbacks, Poland has come a long way from being a nearly bankrupt socialist country to a modern free market economy. Obvious problems remain: the poor eastern part of the country has yet to catch up with the more prosperous west and the capital; the public sector is in dire need of structural reforms; and Poland still awaits a home-grown global company offering innovative products. And though certain sectors of society have unquestionably been left behind – senior citizens in particular – today's Poland is truly unrecognisable from the place it was 25 years ago.

A reflection of old and new in Warsaw.

KATYN'S CURSE

On April 10 2010, president Lech Kaczyński, his wife and 94 other passengers, including government, public, army and church officials, took a Tu-154M plane to Smolensk in Russia to take part in the 70th anniversary of the Katyn massacre. The poorly equipped Russian military airfield was deep in thick fog. When approaching the runway, the plane hit the trees and struck the ground killing all passengers on board. A week-long national mourning was announced in Poland. Flags flew at half-mast, and sport events and concerts were called off. Thousands of traumatised Poles wept openly, lit candles and queued for hours to pay their respects to the late president when his body was laid in state at the Presidential Palace. More than 100,000 took part in the memorial service held on April 17 to honour the victims. The bitter irony of this tragic event wasn't lost on the former president Aleksander Kwaśniewski, who called Katyn 'a cursed place'. Although Russian and Polish investigation reports stated pilot's error as the principal cause of the accident, the crash fuelled many conspiracy theories and became a tool in political struggles that left Polish society deeply divided. A short-lived thaw in Polish-Russian relations came to an end when, in their final report on the crash, the Russians failed to acknowledge errors made by controllers at Smolensk airport, and also refused to return the plane wreckage to Poland.

Sheep grazing in the Tatra Mountains.

Setting off for a day's work.

LIFE IN RURAL POLAND

Although the number of farmers has been decreasing over the last decade, still around one fifth of the population works on the land and many people maintain their traditional customs and way of life.

Visitors to Poland are greeted by a fantastic, brightly coloured mosaic of small fields and meadows: the yellow of the rape crop, the ochre-coloured fields of wheat and rye and dark green squares of bushy-topped potatoes. Narrow strips of land are separated from one another, and hardly any of the farmers have more than one diminutive field to till.

The rural landscape

Poland's landscape is one of almost endless greenery, with many shades of forests, woods, fields and meadows. There are six different determined types of landscapes in Poland: the Baltic lowlands, the lake district, the central lowlands, uplands, the sub-Carpathian depression and mountain regions. The central Polish plains are the most agricultural area of the country, with a specific charm of their own. The landscape here is enlivened by isolated hills, dune embankments and the wide valleys of the largest Polish rivers, the Vistula, Oder, Warta and Bug.

Sheep grazing by Lake Czorsztynskie.

Though the influx of EU subsidies after 2004 contributed to a rapid modernisation of rural Poland, the country has nonetheless retained much of its traditional charm. The gap between regions, which had fallen under different foreign rule in the past, has been largely bridged. This said, some substantial differences remain: the west and northwest regions (Wielkopolska, Pomerania, Kashubia) in particular bear the imprint of the German and Prussian presence.

The villages vary in appearance as well. In the west the houses are large, wide and built from stone. In Mazuria they are smaller and sometimes thatched. The eastern provinces still sport thatched wooden cottages but most villagers have moved to more modern, if less esthetically pleasing dwellings. In the mountains houses are built of wood with stone foundations and a pointed roof to deal with heavy snowfalls. Zakopane is famous for its particular wooden architecture and interior decoration.

The economy of Poland's agricultural regions has also altered considerably since the Communist days. The houses are better built and the surrounding areas are far cleaner and well tended by the farmers. Today, large private farms have developed, financed by credit from banks and better equipped with modern machinery.

Folk traditions

Polish village life and old traditions have successfully survived down the years. Catholic traditions and family ties have remained intact and the church is still present at every important occasion: christenings, weddings and funerals. The local church, shop, restaurant and administrative office are the focal points of village life.

Polish country villages are still home to talented embroiderers who continue to copy the designs passed down from their great-grandmothers, folk artists specialising in

> To celebrate Midsummer's Night wreaths of flowers are cast into the Vistula with burning candles on St John's Night (24 June).

of the kind of small stable once found on every Polish farm and considered to be the birthplace of Christ in Polish folk tradition. Each crèche has models of the infant Jesus and Joseph beside each other, together with a group of animals who, according to legend,

Farmstead in the Bieszczady Mountains.

paper cut-out decorations (particularly in the Kurpie region), skilled potters and woodcarvers specialising in mournful religious figures chiselled out of pear or linden trees.

Christmas has its own set of very specific traditions. Hay is placed under the white tablecloth when families eat their Christmas meal (see page 117). Afterwards they predict their health and fortune based on the length and quality of the stalks. On Christmas Eve many country people still follow the tradition of sharing their food and homes with their animals, whom they believe understand what the people say.

Christmas is also associated with the preparation of nativity crèches – miniature models

TRADITIONAL COSTUMES

In regions such as Kashubia, people still wear traditional coloured aprons and headscarves when going to mass or a church fair. Picturesque peasant dress, dances and customs are also still very much alive in Łowicz, the biggest feast of Corpus Christi. In the Tatras villages, men wear low rounded black hats, embroidered cloth jackets, white cloth trousers and mocassins made from one piece of leather, holding a *ciupaga* (walking stick) in one hand with an axe-shaped handle, the shaft decorated with brass studs. The women sport flowery kerchiefs, colourful jackets and aprons, beads round their necks and leather mocassins.

are capable of speaking in human voice once a year on Christmas Eve.

The feast of Christmas has for centuries been the most important in the Polish calendar. One of the old customs is *Jaselka*. A group of youngsters, called *herods*, go from door to door asking for money and in each group there is always one youngster dressed up as a winged angel, one as the Grim Reaper, complete with scythe, and one as the wicked King Herod. Buying off the young actors is said to bring good luck in the New Year.

At Easter, brightly painted eggs are knocked

religious ceremonies, performed in smoky cemeteries among burning candles, resembling pagan rituals.

Town meets country

Social changes in the 20th century have brought the rural population into the towns. This migration has greatly benefited the country as a whole. For individual rural families it brought an improvement in living standards and opened up new opportunities. But this migration was selective – it was the more enterprising individuals, better educated and

Harvesting wheat the traditional way.

against each other as in the English game of conkers. The person whose egg proves most resistant wins the next Easter egg. The tradition of sprinkling people with water is on Easter Monday.

An equally ancient custom is the drowning of the *Marzanna*, an ugly scarecrow figure symbolic of winter, on the first day of spring.

For the Catholic feast of Palm Sunday, commemorating the Biblical account of Christ's entry into Jerusalem on a donkey, symbolic palms are prepared, often several metres high, from dried flowers and coloured paper, to be carried in the procession to church. All Saint's Day has never ceased to be an occasion for emotional demonstrations and patriotic and

with greater aspirations, who moved.

Once in the towns, children from the country often cease to identify with their own village, especially after having made a considerable effort to shed the rural elements of their language, traditions and everyday culture.

However, not all the ties are broken: some rustic traditions and rituals are still common in the big cities. In Katowice, in the mining region of Silesia, for example, the most visible elements are probably the grand costumes worn by the miners on such ceremonial occasions as the veneration of St Barbara, patron saint of all miners, which is universally evident all over the region on her feast day, 4 December. An interesting urban folklore is also maintained in Kraków to commemorate the Tartar invasions in the 13th century by the bugle call at midday from the tower of the Church of St Mary. During Kraków festivals, the Lajkonik, an Orientally-clad rider on a hobbyhorse cavorts round the Market Square.

Country people

Country people in Poland have a highly developed sense of honour. Business agreements in the marketplace are often sealed with a handshake.

farmers often still sit on the benches in front of their homes and tell stories about the mysteries of nearby forests and marshlands.

Poles are fond of a big family occasion, when several dozen members of the family

> *Modern attitudes to sex meet with conflict in rural Poland, where puritanism and intolerance on the part of parents and the priest conflict with risqué images seen in the cinema and on television.*

Ploughing fields in rural Poland.

Poles, be it in the cities or in the remote countryside, generally have a friendly disposition towards their fellow human beings – they raise their hats to greet them and gladly show them the way. Polish men are chivalrous and will let ladies pass through a doorway first.

The Poles as a whole are friendly and hospitable towards foreigners. They laugh and chat naturally, and speak their mind openly without hesitation. Highlanders in particular, combine this friendliness with a hot-blooded temperament. When they take to someone they will do anything for them, but if someone falls foul of them, he would be better to keep his distance. On summer evenings,

can get together and eat and drink for two or three days. These gatherings includes the consumption of large quantities of hard vodka. In fairness, the celebration without vodka would be interpreted as an act of inhospitality, or even a sign of poverty on the part of the host. When weddings take place, Polish tradition dictates that the festivities must last at least three days.

Agrotourism

Whereas for so many years it was the country people who sought out urban life, now some people suffering from the pressures of big city life wish to own a second home in rural villages. Weekends spent in a rural setting have become increasingly popular, but people these days crave a high standard of luxury despite wanting to rest on an actual farm in a typically rural environment.

As a result, Polish agrotourism is becoming increasingly fashionable. A lot of tourists from the West and from urban Poland prefer rural holidays with unspoiled countryside, a beautiful landscape and interesting flora and fauna to marvel at. It also allows long-standing city dwellers to learn about the traditional way of life in the country.

Host families serve as tour guides for visi-

Open-air museums

Every historic region of Poland today has an open-air folk museum, called a *skansen*, in which the tourist can often view within a few acres of land traditional buildings such as a wealthy country manor house made of valuable larch wood, prosperous farm buildings, a poor peasant's hut thatched with straw and a small country chapel. In addition, there may well also be a village inn, watermill and windmill. Inside these buildings are usually authentic wooden, metal or clay implements and utensils and sometimes demonstrations of

Skansens (open-air museums) preserve traditional rural architecture and crafts and can be found all over Poland.

tors, using their local knowledge of the parks and nature reserves, history, culture and historic monuments. Leisure activities on offer include hiking, cycling, horse riding, camping and forest walks. Some farmers also provide their guests with fresh milk, home-made cottage cheese and genuine country broth made from the cockerel that was strutting around the farmyard the day before.

The Federation of Country Tourism (www.agritourism.pl) now publishes a catalogue in several languages entitled "Host Farms", which includes detailed descriptions, photographs and addresses of all associations and the 180 farms nationwide which offer accommodation.

traditional crafts and skills such as thatching and weaving.

Moreover, every region, no matter how small, also has presentations in its local folklore museums – permanent ethnographic exhibitions exist in more than 120 Polish museums.

But despite the popularity of *skansens*, nothing competes with the real thing. A large number of villages in Poland may resemble outdoor museums but are in fact genuine communities, where the wells still creak, pots and jugs are hung on the fences to dry, and on the roofs of many houses storks in their nests prepare their offsprings for a long flight over the seas.

The Wailing Wall at Remu'h Synagogue, Kraków.

THE JEWS

The history of Polish Jewry is one of the most tragic of the last century. Today, the Jewish community is slowly coming to terms with the past and building a future.

According to the earliest reliable records, Jewish exiles arrived from Prague towards the end of the 11th century. For centuries, Jews then converged on Poland from all over Europe, fleeing political or economic persecution in their home countries. However, there were also many who came, not because of any external threats, but because they were drawn by the opportunities in the most tolerant country of the continent. It was not without justification that Poland was known as 'a paradise for the aristocracy, heaven for the Jews and hell for the peasants'.

A safe nation

The Jews called Poland 'Polin' ('po' means 'here' and 'lin' means 'rest') because they felt safe there. Poland's masters needed Jewish traders and craftsmen and their knowledge of commerce. Jews were subject only to the king's own courts or those of his representatives; the murder of a Jew was punishable by death, and even failure to help a Jew who was attacked was punished with a fine. Towns that did not step in quickly enough to quell anti-Jewish riots were also fined, ritual murders could be brought to court, the distribution of anti-Jewish literature was forbidden, and so on.

In 1264, by the decree of the Statute of Jewish Liberties issued in Kalish, the Polish King established a Jewish social class, an unprecedented attitude at that time in Europe, which was engulfed by the Holy Inquisition.

The Jewish Council of Four Lands, founded in 1581, was another political institution unique in Europe. It was responsible for Great Poland, Little Poland, Lithuania and Russia, the four main territories within the Polish-Lithuanian kingdom. It was concerned mainly with internal Jewish affairs and kept in close contact

Holocaust Remembrance Day in Kraków.

with the authorities. The Jews' main occupation was banking, money-lending and financial activity, often leading to conflicts with nobility deprived of the rights of financial operations. But these disagreements were acted on the individual not on an ethnic or religious level.

During the First Republic (1569–1795) there were relatively few anti-Jewish excesses in comparison with the rest of Europe. This is partly explained by the financial status of the state and the pragmatism of the Polish aristocracy: in Poland, there was simply no general hatred of the Jews, and the aristocracy was not inclined to harass the Jewish communities.

In contrast, in the violent uprising of Bohdan Chmielnicki in the Ukraine (1648–57), which was actually directed against the Polish rulers, the Jews were massacred in their thousands as suspected allies of the Poles. The tragedy was repeated during the popular uprising in the Ukraine and Podolia in 1768, when thousands of Polish aristocrats as well as Jews suffered terrible deaths.

The Catholic Church in Poland was ambivalent towards the Jews. While on the one hand they were regarded as 'the chosen people', on the other they were also 'the murderers of Jesus'. The Church accordingly announced that they should not therefore be persecuted, but that

by specific Jewish characteristics. They made major contributions to scientific development and frequently occupied leading positions in medicine, mathematics and astronomy as well as in architecture, painting and goldsmithing.

Jews were industrious and usually worked as craftsmen, merchants, doctors and bankers, seldom as farmers. They were often wealthy. The basic unit of Jewish autonomy was the community, governed by the *kahal*, a body responsible for the judicial system, administration, religion and welfare, where all were responsible for one towards the outside world.

The standard of living was high for most Jewish families before the growth of anti-Semitism.

they should live together in a separate community. This attitude fell upon fertile ground with Polish peasant communities, where Jews ran inns and mills. Peasants, oppressed by the nobility found themselves often indebted to the landowners and their rich Jewish advisors alike. Their animosity towards both grew with the level of oppression.

The unique position of the Jews in Poland is illustrated by the fact that a Jew who had been converted to Catholicism could even be elevated to the nobility.

Wealth and poverty

Because most Jews remained true to their faith, for centuries Polish culture was enriched

During the 17th century, however, the Jews were badly affected by the weakening of Poland because of wars and internal anarchy. Gradually their economic and political situation deteriorated. In 1764 the Polish parliament, the *Sejm*, dissolved the Council of Four Lands for economic reasons, but it did not touch the communities. Although the government was aware that the status of the Jews in Poland was in need of fundamental reform, no changes were made before Poland finally lost its independence. In 1795 some 900,000 Polish Jews automatically became citizens of one of the three occupying countries.

In the 19th century the occupying powers abolished many of the laws that protected the

Jews, but patriotic feelings towards Poland prevailed and they supported the struggle for independence, fighting alongside them in the Kościuszko uprising (1794), the November uprising (1831) and the People's Spring (1848–49).

But as nationalism swept Europe at the turn of the 20th century, the Jewish community turned increasingly to Zionism. The worsening economy, the politics of the occupying powers and growing signs of anti-Semitism led many Jews to emigrate, many to the United States.

The growth of anti-Semitism

During the Second Republic (1918–39), the National Democracy Party, which had strong right-wing leanings, became increasingly radical in its attitudes towards the Jews. The party had placed a high value on the 'national cultural community'. From this perspective, the fact that the Jews used a language similar to that used by Poland's enemies, Germany and Austria was perceived as a threat and an attempt to maintain a separate cultural identity. Also, in a country devastated by wars and partitioning, the financial strength of the Jewish community and the unwillingness of some of its members to invest in the country could be interpreted as deliberate alienation from Poland.

Again, it became fashionable to make the Jews responsible for every social evil. They were accused of Communism, association with the Freemasons, economic parasitism and of an inability to assimilate into Polish society. There were pogroms, harassment at the universities and an economic boycott.

The sections of society that supported Marshal Piłsudski (in power from 1926) did not share these attitudes. Many Jews had fought for the independence of Poland under his leadership and their loyalty to the state was more important to the political realist Piłsudski than their forced assimilation. After his death in 1935, however, his followers' programme gradually grew closer to that of the nationalistic right. Although the state condemned the use of force, various politicians seemed to support an economic boycott of the Jews.

The Zionists had a good relationship with the government of Poland. The left wing of the Zionist movement, under the leadership of Włodzimierz Żabotyński, was even supplied with weapons and money, and offered military training. The first 'Kibbutz' communities were established in Poland.

The Orthodox Jews, represented by the party Agudat Israel, were also on perfectly normal terms with the state administration. The Jewish socialists, on the other hand, acknowledged

Jewish linen weaver in Wąwolnica, circa 1910.

JEWISH SECTS

The Jewish way of life in Poland remained by no means unaffected by the religious and social trends of the times. As well as Sabbatarianism with its strict observance of the Sabbath, there was Frankism, a mystical cabbalistic sect that emerged in Podolia in 1755, and the Haskalah, or Jewish Enlightenment. Hasidism, a popular movement of both a religious and mystic nature based on the cabbala and Judaism, also had its origins in Podolia in the 18th century. Its founder, Baal Schev Tov, was born in Poland, and the movement is still regarded as Polish with its characteristic philosophy, traditional dress, music, dance and warm joy of life.

only one homeland: Poland. Understandably, however, the right-wing rulers did not approve of some of their political programmes, which sympathised with the Soviet programme of Communist ideologies.

Poles and the Holocaust

Of the 3.5 million Polish Jews, only 250,000 survived the war, mostly because they were able to escape from the Nazis. Opinions differ greatly when it comes to evaluating the attitude of the Poles to the Jews and the concentration camps during the Occupation. Nevertheless,

themselves unscrupulously by appropriating Jewish possessions. In what were desperate times, many are known to have handed Jews over to the Nazis in exchange for a kilo of sugar. On July 10, 1941 in the small town of Jedwabne, in today's Podlaskie Voivodship, several hundred Jews were burned alive by the local Poles, probably at the instigation of the German police. A highly controversial book about the massacre, entitled *Neighbours: The Destruction of the Jewish Community in Jedwabne, Poland* and published in 2001 by Jan T. Gross, professor of history at Princeton University, triggered a bitter national debate on

A Holocaust survivor attends the 70th anniversary of the liberation of Auschwitz on 27th January, 2015.

many Poles took the risk of helping Jews. Often, in this changing climate, people even overcame their own pronounced anti-Semitic prejudices. It is known that Jews were hidden and saved from the Nazis by National Democrats. The Christian community was also very much involved in rescue operations, above all the clergy themselves; nunneries were particularly active and saved many Jewish children. An important part was played by the Council for Jewish Assistance, ŻEGOTA, an organisation which the government-in-exile helped finance.

The risks cannot be overstated – helping Jews was punishable by death of not only the 'guilty' but also his family. There were, of course, many cases of denunciation and some Poles enriched

THE JEWISH STETL

The contribution made by Polish Jews to the country's culture and the major part they played in shaping its renaissance is undisputed. The wealth of literature produced by this community is a good example of its cultural involvement. Yet the Polish Jews always retained their cultural independence. It was a separateness that made them vulnerable to racist and religious harassment, a problem nowhere more obvious than in the *stetl*, the Jewish quarter that existed in almost every Polish town. This Jewish world in miniature was one of characteristic architecture and a dense network of cultural relationships and deep-rooted religious tradition.

Polish-Jewish relations during and soon after World War II and inspired Władysław Pasikowski's film *Aftermath* (2012). Although there are no doubts that Poles took part in the killing, the eminent British-Polish historian Professor Norman Davis called the book 'deeply unfair to Poles'. It is

network to bear witness to the terrible crimes committed on their race in the Warsaw Ghetto (see page 158).

Of all the extermination camps in the whole of Poland Auschwitz–Birkenau is the most horrific. Built in 1940 it became one of the most sinister creations of humanity. According to their 'final solution', the Nazis in this camp exterminated Jews in gas chambers and in death blocks. It is now estimated that 1.5 million people died in Auschwitz–Birkenau, 1.1 million of them Jews. Others were gypsies, and Poles, Czechs, Austrians, Danes, French, Dutch and Germans who

The camp motto, "Work Makes You Free".

known that Jews themselves were not always loyal to their fellow men. War and fear of death evoked all sorts of emotions and behaviour.

One of the most tragic moments in the history of the Jewish nation is connected with the Polish capital Warsaw. During the occupation of the city by Germans, they locked part of the city and brought into it Jews from all over Poland. Cramped and oppressed, hungered and persecuted, in desperation the Jews took to using guns in April 1943. For about one month a desperate fight took place. To combat the uprising, the Germans used tanks and soldiers. The Jewish fighters either died of bullet wounds or took their own lives. A very few of them escaped through the sewer canals

opposed the Nazi regime. It remains a place of great sorrow for people from all over the world, regardless of their faith (see page 62).

Auschwitz was also a place of great sacrifices and the noblest of human behaviour, as people risked their lives to help others. One such prisoner, Gertruda Stein, a nun of Jewish origin who helped and tended other prisoners, was recently beatified.

Great hopes for Israel

In the first half of 1946, some 137,000 Jews who had either fled or been deported returned from the Soviet Union to Poland. The new government was anything but charitable towards the survivors of the Holocaust and often actively prevented the Jews from reconstructing their communities. There were even isolated cases of anti-Semitic riots, culminating in the Kielce pogrom of 1946, when Poles killed 46 Jews. Because of this climate, many Jews finally decided to emigrate to Palestine to make a new life for themselves.

Immediately after the war the Communist leadership of Poland was still hoping that the new state of Israel that was just coming into being would be socialist-orientated, or would at least sympathise with the countries within Moscow's sphere of influence. For this reason, a military camp was set up to offer training to

Stained glass in Kraków's Old Synagogue.

volunteers who belonged to the Zionist Haganah movement.

However, these friendly feelings soon evaporated when it became evident that Israel was developing along the lines of a western democratic society. The Jewish exodus reached record levels during the political crises of 1956–57 and 1968–69, which were often accompanied by anti-Semitic propaganda. Soviets now needed good relations with the Arabs and enticed this attitude, which was not always in tune with the general feeling of the people. This all took place against the background of the Arab–Israeli war, when the whole of the Eastern Bloc was vociferous in its condemnation of the Israelis.

Many artists, scientists and students were of Jewish origin, and the Polish rulers found that the simplest thing to do was to make the Jews the scapegoat, since they were likely to offer the least resistance. To the country, however, it was a tremendous loss of much of its intellectual capital as hundreds of artists, journalists and academics, including world-famous sociologist Zygmunt Bauman, chose to leave the country.

In order to stir up the population against them, the Polish rulers drew attention to the inglorious part some of the Jews had played during Stalin's reign of terror. The campaign forced at least 20,000 Poles of Jewish origin to turn their backs on the country of their birth and which they considered to be their homeland to seek a new life in Israel or the US.

Jewish renaissance

The reduction of the Jewish population from 3.5 million to 5,000 was an irreplaceable loss to Polish society. As a result of a shortage of pupils, the three Jewish high schools had to be closed and rabbis brought over from the US. It is even more startling that, at election time, old demagogic formulas have been revived and the 'Polishness' of Jewish candidates is often questioned. In recent years, however, attitudes are changing again. The post-war Jewish minority has had its own cultural, religious and scientific institutions, folklore, magazines, a theatre, as well as a Jewish Historical Institute with a library and a museum in Warsaw. Poland also now has a Chief Rabbi and Kosher restaurants are in great demand.

Recent years saw a strong revival of interest in Jewish tradition and folklore among the young generation of Poles who want to grow up without the label of prejudice their parents had. Annual Jewish culture festivals organised in Kraków (Jewish Culture Festival) and Warsaw (Singer Festival of Jewish Culture) have become very popular, and successfully promote modern artists and musicians of Jewish origin from around the world. Opened in 2013, the spectacular Museum of the History of Polish Jews or *Polin* (see page 159) offers much more than just an interactive and insightful presentation of the 1,000-year history of the Polish Jews, but it is also a vibrant cultural and educational centre hosting exhibitions, film screenings, concerts, workshops, performances and lectures.

Consequently, Poland has become a destination favoured by Jews from all over the world, in search of their roots and traditions.

Stained glass in Kraków's Franciscan Church.

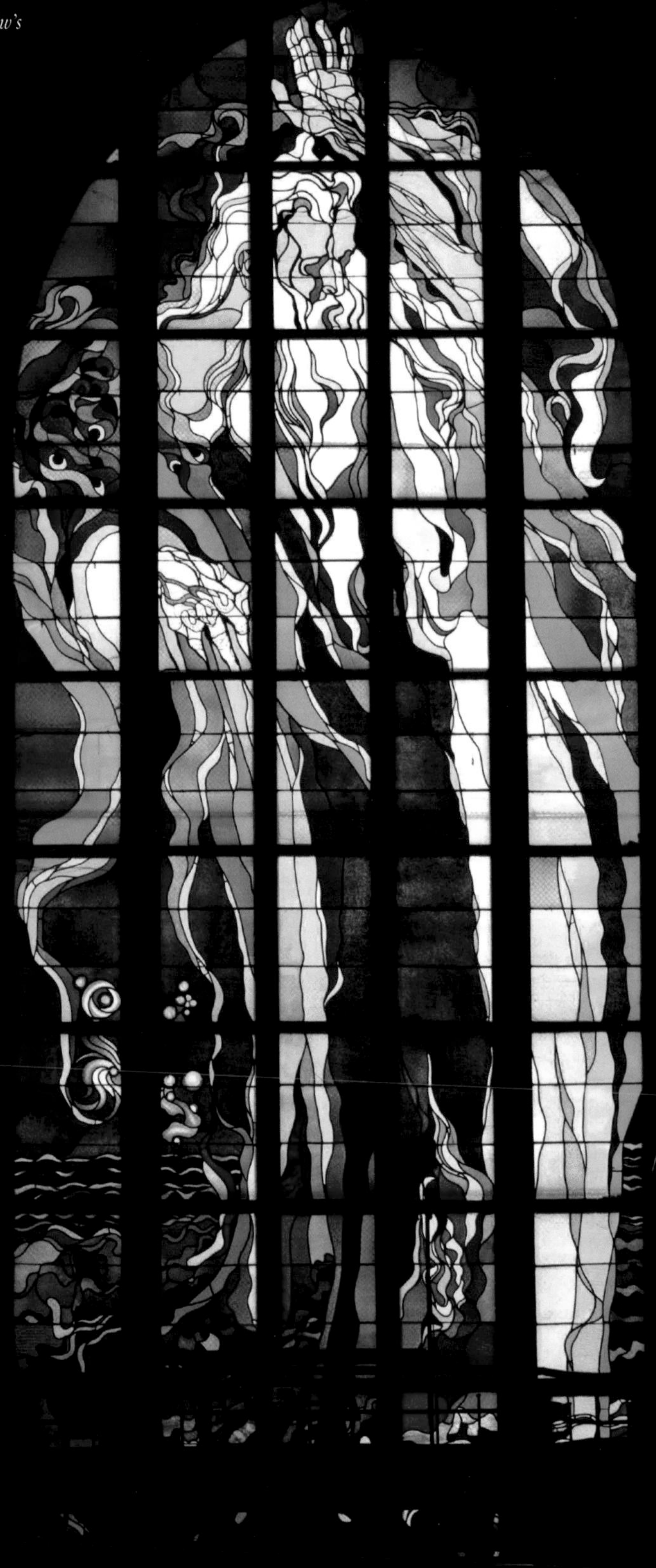

THE CATHOLICS

Until recently the Catholic Church played a hugely significant role in the country's politics. Today its cultural and social role is dominant.

I f on a Sunday you are anywhere near a church it is as well not to be in a hurry. The roads and squares are full of families dressed in their Sunday best making their way to mass. And on special religious holidays the procession of brightly coloured flags extends for miles as the miraculous picture of the Madonna of Częstochowa is carried for several hours from house to house. In the home of every family a picture of the Virgin Mary or a portrait of Pope John Paul II occupies pride of place.

Religious origins

Christianity was introduced to Poland in the 10th century. It was primarily for political reasons that the first ruler of the land Mieszko I, the Polish Duke, had himself baptised and took the country from the Pope as a fiefdom. He did not consult all of his subjects and followers, who were members of the Slavic tribes and adhered to a very different religion based on ancestor and nature worship, and resistance to Christianity continued for two centuries.

In spite of this, at around the turn of the first millennium the archdiocese of Gniezno proceeded to expand its influence. In AD 1000 it became the Archdiocese of Poland, with subordinate dioceses of Kraków, Wrocław, Kołobrzeg and Poznań. Missionary-style groups left from here with the purpose of converting neighbouring tribes. The first Christian missionaries did not have an easy time, and many, like Bishop Wojciech of Prague, who sought to convert the Prussians, met a martyr's death: he became the first Polish saint, St Adalbert. His brother Gaudenty became first Archbishop of Poland.

Confession time.

Gradually the rulers imposed their will. Polygamy and working on religious holidays was prohibited, times of fasting and contributions to the church were made compulsory. The Cistercians established the new religion in the towns as well as a new economic system in the country. Religion brought with it a rich cultural tradition and skilled craftsmen from all over Europe worked on the construction of places of worship. By the middle of the 12th century all babies were christened and the old faith merged with the new without conflict.

In Poland, as in most of Europe, the Church made concessions to tradition by allowing memorials to be built to ancestors, tolerating ancient customs and introducing festivals involving intercessions for good weather and rich harvests. With the breakdown of central secular power in the 13th century, it was able to escape secular domination and to perpetuate the doctrine of St Thomas of Aquinas, according to which it was the duty of the Church to admonish tyrants and protect the rights of the faithful.

As early as the 11th century, the Kraków bishop Stanisław had publicly opposed a king. The conflict resulted in the fall of the ruler, which strengthened the authority of

Shrine in a Gdańsk park.

the clergy as defenders of justice, and the Polish Church has taken this role seriously ever since. At the beginning of the Reformation the Catholics lived in the western half of the enormous Polish-Lithuanian state and the adherents to the Orthodox Church were in the eastern half. In order to establish a counterweight to an increasingly powerful Moscow and to the patriarch of Constantinople, some Orthodox bishops joined the Roman Catholic Church at the Synod of Brest (Brześć) in 1596, creating an act of union between the two traditions (Unia Brzeska). The 'Uniates', or Unici, kept their Slavonic rites but recognised the supremacy of the Pope.

In later years, with misfortunes falling

upon the country from Protestant Germany and Orthodox Russia, the maxim 'to be a Pole is to be a Catholic' overruled all else.

The church and the people

The church in Poland was always tuned to the worship of saints. In the 17th century the Mother of God, the mother and queen of Poland, was the chief object of veneration, especially after the attack by the Swedish army on Jasna Góra monastery in Częstochowa. Success in the uneven defence was accredited to her divine protection.

While the state fell apart, religion flourished. Superstitious beliefs were also popular. There were over 400 local cults based on miraculous manifestations and pictures that were supposed to save people from having impure thoughts. It was at this time that the idea of 'Catholicism under siege' became part of the ideology – the idea of the one true faith in a heretical world.

Historic events such as the wars against Swedish and Turkish infidels, whom the Poles resisted at Częstochowa and Vienna respectively, reinforced their belief that they and their nation were a bulwark of true Christianity. Some members of the high-ranking clergy – who were, after all, principally aristocrats from the ruling Polish families then fighting for power and influence – were not entirely blameless when Poland was partitioned in 1772, and frequently made deals with the various occupying powers. But the bond between the church and the people was never destroyed.

LAND OF RELIGIOUS TOLERANCE

Although Poland is a Roman Catholic country, religious tolerance has always gone hand in hand with national belief. There has never been widespread religious persecution in Poland. Protestant Scots, fleeing the Counter-Reformation in Scotland, Huguenots and followers of Jan Hus, and Jews fleeing the Inquisition all found in Poland a safe haven.

Calvinism and Lutheranism had their followers, especially in Pomerania and Gdańsk, and a radical group – the Aryans, or Polish Brothers – separated from the Calvinists. Despite activity by the Jesuits, the Counter-Reformation in Poland did not fully develop.

Aided by the uprising against Russia and the Vatican's defence of Polish independence, the church was able to win back the trust of the nation. It became a stronghold of what the nation stood for; it educated, often in conspiracy conditions; it taught patriotism and, above all, it gave hope to the majority of people.

Numerous monastic orders settled in Poland and established the image of the church through their ministering work. At the dawn of Polish Christianity monks taught the art of writing and copied books. The Cistercian Order, established in the 12th century was noted for its role in the development of education, culture and economy. The Dominican Friars opened schools. The Franciscans taught how to construct brick buildings. The Bernardine Order built monasteries and churches. The monks of the Pauline Order built the most famous of Polish sanctuaries, Jasna Góra, with its icon of the Black Madonna. The Piarists and Jesuits established colleges. Ursuline Nuns opened orphanages and worked as nurses in hospitals.

A momentum developed, and became something for the people to hold on to: the idea that the cultural identity of Poland, including its freedom and religious tolerance, was guaranteed as long as the Catholic Church continued to exist, even if state sovereignty was a long way off. The church went along with this, at first tentatively then more actively. Throughout the occupation by Nazi Germany and the terrors of the Stalinist regime, as well as the persistent endeavours of the Communist leaders, the church held firm.

Two men stand out among the countless heroes who confronted these troubled times. The Franciscan friar Maksymilian (Rajmund) Kolbe went voluntarily in 1941 to the hunger block to be killed with a phenol injection through the heart to save the life of an unknown man. He was later canonised. In October 1984, Father Jerzy Popiełuszko, a young Warsaw priest, was abducted by the secret police and brutally murdered for his defence of his community and the political goals of Solidarity which he supported.

Spokesman of the nation

When in 1976 the Polish conference of bishops published a pastoral in which the Catholic Church was portrayed as the legitimate representative of the people and the nation, it received the people's unanimous approval. The election of Cardinal Karol Wojtyła as Pope in 1978 further strengthened this claim. In 1979, on his first journey home, he encouraged millions of his countrymen with the words 'Do not be afraid!' John Paul II visited his homeland on seven occasions: in 1979; in 1983 after martial law was lifted; in 1987 to help Poles cope with the communist stronghold and in 1991 (twice) to celebrate a free Poland. He returned again for short visits in 1997 and

Catholic nuns.

again in 1999. In 2005, Pope John Paul II died and was buried in the Vatican.

Today Poland is still synonymous with Catholicism, but westernisation and secularisation of the Polish society have taken its toll, and less than 40 percent of believers regularly attend the Sunday mass. Moreover, a few highly publicised cases of paedophilia among Polish priests, as well as the church's intransigent position on several social issues, including contraception, divorce and homosexuality, have further tarnished its image and reduced its popularity, particularly among young people in large cities. That said, the Catholic Radio Maryja still has more than its fair share of listeners.

THE ARTS

Poland has always had a high profile in the international arts scene because of the deep cultural awareness of its population and its artistic traditions.

Although Poland's historical presence in Christian Europe dates from the 10th century, Polish literature was late in emerging. Medieval Poland was frequently attacked by foreign invaders and weakened by division into small principalities. Additionally, as in other European countries, Latin was the only literary language. Early medieval writings are confined to the lives of the saints and historical annals and chronicles.

Poetry and drama

Even though the Renaissance reached Poland late and lasted for a comparatively short period, the country flourished during that time and the name 'golden age' was attributed to it. The leading personality of the period is Jan Kochanowski (1530–84) whose influence on future generations of poets gained him the title 'Father of Polish poetry'. His masterpiece, *Treny* (*Laments*, 1580), speaks of the death of his infant daughter and of his subsequent recovery of spiritual harmony. The poems put him among the great European poets of that era.

In contrast with the Renaissance, the Baroque period appeared in Poland very early, almost at the same time as in Italy. The 17th century was dominated by constant military conflict with Russia, Sweden and Turkey and by internal unrest and disputes over constitutional reforms. The masterpiece of Baroque lyrics is the poetry of Jan Andrzej Morsztyn (1613–93) who supplied the royal theatre with superb translations of Corneille's tragedies.

After the decadent period of the Saxon reign in Poland, the Enlightenment literature was genuinely preoccupied with building political awareness and recreating Polish national culture in order to save the weakened country from its

Igor Mitoraj's Eros Bendato, in Kraków's market square.

inevitable collapse. The notable event was the inauguration in 1765, on the king's initiative, of the first public theatre. The comedies by Franciszek Zabłocki (1754–1821) and Aleksander Fredro (1793–1876) successfully combine the foreign plots borrowed from Molière and Goldoni with typical Polish archetypes and their anxieties. The period was mainly didactic in character, yet it saw the emergence of the first professional periodicals, the first *Dictionary of the Polish Language* (1807–14), the introduction of the sentimental novel and, in poetry, of western genres, all of which were practiced with high artistic standards.

Romanticism coincided with the most tragic moments in Polish history. The juxtaposition of the loss of national independence with the uplifted Romantic ideology led to the emergence of some extraordinary poetic output, which makes Polish Romanticism one of the most distinctive literary periods in Europe. On the one hand there was the poet's duty to keep the spirit of the Polish identity alive, on the other there was the fascination with Byron and Shelley's Promethean myth. According to the formula, the evil Gods were either the oppressors or the Christian God who let them reduce the nation's position to mere martyrdom. The human being was the poet who 'suffers for millions'. The rebellion was, of course, the fight

Wisława Szymborska won the Nobel Prize for Literature in 1996.

against the tyrants – often in a truly Promethean situation – as the genius trio of Polish Romantic poets went into exile. Had they stayed they would have been deported to Siberia with the most luminous people of their generation.

The star trio are Adam Mickiewicz (1798– 1855), Juliusz Słowacki (1809–49) and Zygmunt Krasiński (1812–59). Mickiewicz is the most popular and accessible of them all. His works have been translated into many languages, and among the highlights are *Dziady* (*The Forefathers' Eve*, 1823), a Messianic drama presenting Poland suppressed by foreign powers as the Christ among the peoples destined to rise in glory. His poetic tour de force is *Pan*

> The oldest Polish literary text is a song in honour of the Virgin Mary, the *Bogurodzica*. The first copy dates from the 14th century but it was probably written earlier.

Tadeusz (1834) presenting the Polish landed gentry in the context of Napoleon's expedition to Moscow in 1812.

Practicality and realism

The Romantic vein continued until 1863 when another unsuccessful uprising began. After the nation was severely punished for rebelling against the Russian oppressors, all hopes were abandoned and the period that followed is now called Positivism. It was a mood of practical thinking that expressed a rationalist reaction against Romanticism and the domination of literature over life. 'Work from the foundations' was the new realistic slogan, implying the renunciation of armed resistance and the concentration on the preservation of the ideological and cultural assets of the nation. The period produced two extraordinary novelists Bolesław Prus (1847– 1912) and Henryk Sienkiewicz (1846–1916). The latter was the first Polish winner of the literary Nobel Prize in 1905. Recently published in England, Prus's *Lalka* (*The Doll*, 1890) is an accomplished and vivid picture of contemporary Warsaw with an intricate plot and a collection of unforgettable characters. *Trilogy* (1884–88) by Sienkiewicz is a picture of Poland's struggles against its 17th-century enemies, and the Nobel Prize winning *Quo Vadis* (1896) is a historical novel of Rome under Nero. Historians argue over their factual value but their literary qualities are undeniable.

While Positivism flourished in Warsaw, Kraków saw an emergence of the Young Poland movement, which proclaimed a return to the expression of feelings and to imaginative writing. The most outstanding figure of the movement was Stanisław Wyspiański (1869–1907). In his play *Wesele* (*The Wedding*, 1901), based on the foundations of primitive folk theatre, he created a visionary drama as a vehicle to criticise the problems of his age.

The newfound freedom of 1918 turned the artists' attention to matters other than independence, which had dominated Polish literature for over 120 years. Between the two world wars Polish writers produced a wide range of distinguished literary works. One of the most interesting writers of that time was Witold Gombrowicz (1905–1969), whose satiric prose influenced the birth of the Theatre of the Absurd on an international scale. Other playwrights who exercised the genre were Stanisław Ignacy Witkiewicz (1885–1939), known as Witkacy (see page 238) and later Sławomir Mrożek (born 1930). Both have been translated into many languages and given numerous international performances.

The reconstruction of an independent Polish state was harshly interrupted by the invasion of the Germans and the Soviet Russians in 1939.

by Socialist Realism. The factory worker or collective farmer was now to become a literary hero. After 1956 Polish literature concentrated on the nuances and contradictions of life in a communist country. The most important authors of this epoch are Tadeusz Konwicki, Sławomir Mrożek, Zbigniew Herbert, Stanisław Barańczak, Tadeusz Różewicz, Andrzej Szczypiorski and the two Nobel Prize winners Czesław Miłosz and Wisława Szymborska. Ryszard Kapuściński gained international acclaim with his books on dictatorships in Africa and Asia, exposing parallels with communist rule in Poland.

The movie Kanal, about the Warsaw Uprising, was directed by Andrej Wajda, a leading light of the Polish Film School.

The epic Chłopi (The Peasants, 1909) by Władysław Reymont (1868–1925) was translated into every European language and was awarded the Nobel Prize in 1924.

The rich literary harvest of these years was only fully revealed after the end of the war. One of the most devastating works of this period is Tadeusz Borowski's *Proszę Państwa do Gazu* (*Would You Please Proceed to the Gas Chamber*, 1949) based on the author's personal experiences in the concentration camp at Auschwitz–Birkenau.

From 1945 until the political 'thaw' after Stalin's death, literary life in Poland was dominated

Since the collapse of Communism, the Polish literary scene is enjoying all the privileges of democracy. Along with the discovery of the writers whose works were banned under the Communist regime, the young generation of writers is preoccupied with such phenomena as feminism, sexual revolution and the discovery of the national identity under the new political system. There remains a literary bequest; a moral issue of a dichotomised nation, split over the last 50 years into oppressors and oppressed. The contemporary literary climate that facilitated the extraordinary success of Paweł Huelle's novel Weiser *Dawidek*, looks set to resolve this.

Post-modernist fiction by Dorota Masłowska, including her widely acclaimed debut novel

White and Red, has been widely praised for 'creative use of the common language and original take on Polish reality' and translated into several European languages. Marek Krajewski's crime novels (see page 264), set in pre-war Wrocław (then Breslau), have also enjoyed unfaltering popularity among both Polish and foreign readers. Another representative of this genre is an award-winning Zygmunt Miłoszewski, whose novels such as *Entanglement* and *A Grain of Truth* delve deep into the national psyche offering a nuanced – albeit often unflattering – portrait of the modern Poland. Following in the footsteps

Frederick Chopin.

of his mentor and friend Ryszard Kapuściński, Wojciech Jagielski's internationally acclaimed books provide an invaluable insight into the grim realities of living in the most troubled and dangerous parts of the world.

A national rhythm

Frederick Chopin (see page 186) is not the only Polish contribution to world music, although he is undoubtedly the most important composer to represent Polish music abroad. The first international success was probably the polonaise, a lofty court dance in simple triple time. It became fashionable from the 18th century onwards and features in the works of Bach, Mozart, Beethoven, Schubert and Liszt, and of course the famous piano polonaises by Chopin. The most famous Polish polonaise is Michał Oginski's *Pożegnanie ojczyzny* (*Farewell to the Homeland*) written soon after the country disappeared from the map of Europe in 1795. For the following 120 years Polish music, like literature and fine arts, was an expression of national spirit full of allusiveness and political message. Chopin (1810–1849) and his contemporaries were putting elements of folk music into their works – elements that achieved the status of a national Polish musical style in the words and music of the 'father of Polish national opera', Stanisław Moniuszko (1819–72). They allude to the heroic era of Polish nobility in works such as *Straszny Dwór* (*The Haunted House*, 1864) and introduce common people as victims (*Halka*, 1858). The patriotic plots, along with a great use of Polish dance rhythms such as the mazurek and polonaise, were to foster deep patriotic feelings.

Henryk Wieniawski (1835–80) was both a patriotic composer and one of the most important violinists of the generation after Paganini. He combined the technical advances of the great Italian virtuoso with Romantic imagination and Slavonic spirit.

After the country regained its independence in 1918 folk tradition was still present in music. The most distinguished composer of the entre-guerre period was Karol Szymanowski (1882–1937) who took the challenge of translating folk music into the symphonic spirit of Modernism. He spent half his life in the Tatra Mountains resort of Zakopane, where he studied the songs and dances of the mountaineers, which led to the composition of an exotic ballet *Harnasie* (1935). His other

MUSIC AND POLITICS

The combination of music and patriotism found its best expression in the life of Ignacy Paderewski (1860–1941), who was not only an outstanding composer and a world-class pianist, but also an important politician. His works are deeply rooted in the Romantic Polish national school among which the opera Manru and the Fantasie polonaise are most noteworthy. During World War I Paderewski represented the Polish nation abroad, making speeches and assisting victims of oppression, and eventually became Prime Minister in 1919. He lived much of his life in exile, but in 1992 his remains were returned for burial in Warsaw.

Many musical festivals are held in Poland: the annual Warsaw Autumn Festival of modern music, the International Chopin Piano Competition in Warsaw (every four years) and the Wieniawski Violin Competition in Poznań (every five years).

major works are the opera *King Roger* (1924) and the choral orchestral *Stabat Mater* (1926), both outstanding examples of modern Romanticism. Szymanowski's villa in Zakopane is now a museum and a popular tourist attraction.

Post-war music is represented by Witold Lutosławski (1913–1994), Tadeusz Baird (1928–1981) and Krzysztof Penderecki (born 1933). Their works are closely linked with history. On the one hand they were influenced by the horrors of World War II and on the other were dependent on the political situation in Communist Poland. Lutosławski's early works were composed under official restraints insisting on a style based on folk-song. When the political repression lifted, he became internationally active as a teacher and conductor of his own music. Baird also started out toeing the party line, but the cultural thaw of 1956 enabled him to pursue his own artistic vision. Penderecki gained international acclaim with *Threnody for the Victims of Hiroshima* (1961), *St Luke Passion* (1965) and his dynamic operas.

A younger generation of artists includes one of the best classical pianists in the world, Krystian Zimerman, mostly known for his interpretation of Chopin piano concertos, as well as Rafał Blechacz, winner of the International Frederick Chopin Piano Competition in 2005 and recipient of the prestigious Gilmore Artist Award in 2014).

Fine Arts

As with literature and music, it is impossible to appreciate Polish art without an understanding of its references to the historical situation. Polish artists worked either in exile or in the partitioned country trying to convey some implicit political message.

One of the most outstanding figures of the first half of the 19th century was Piotr Michałowski (1800–55), who settled in Paris and produced works on a level with those of Géricault and Delacroix. His patriotic scenes of horsemen from the Kościuszko Uprising

and the Napoleonic wars (now in the Kraków Museum) demonstrate a more lively and explosive temperament than the Paris artists trained in the tame classical tradition.

Michalowski's successors in allegorical and historical art were Juliusz Kossak (1824–99), Artur Grottger (1837–67) and Jan Matejko (1838–93). Their works portray the nation's grand historic events with patriotic emotiveness. The depiction of the nation's fate and the fight for independence fulfilled the criteria of the patriotic mission being enthusiastically received by large sections of the population.

Pianist Rafał Blechacz performing.

Matejko's pupil, Stanisław Wyspiański (1869–1907) was a versatile painter, poet, playwright, architect and man of letters who translated historic Romanticism into eerie visions of Symbolism. His paintings revealed a genius for dramatic construction, but the loss of the use of his hand forced him to turn to designing and writing.

Most of Wyspiański's architectural designs still exist on paper. Notably, he turned the attention of his generation to the wooden homesteads and churches built by the Polish peasants, wishing to apply the rural forms to monumental buildings in order to create a national style. Wyspiański was one of the first artists to choose Zakopane as his home, which was to later become an artistic centre.

Another outstanding artist of early 20th-century Polish Symbolism was Jacek Malczewski (1854–1929), who combined the dreamlike visions of the past with a psychoanalytical perception of humanity.

Following independence, the major creators of Polish Impressionism were Leon Wyczółłkowski (1852–1936) and Julian Fałat (1853–1929). In Poland the younger generation was no longer prepared to convey patriotic duty, and new artistic groups emerged. The Futurists and late Expressionists made a break from all that had gone before.

Katarzyna Kozyra in front of her Pyramid of Animals artwork.

For more than a decade after World War II artists had to conform to painting in the style of Socialist Realism in order to gain any recognition. One of the most interesting alternative movements was the Blok Group, which introduced its own interpretation of constructivism. Its reference points were architecture, sociology and the new technical civilisation. Władysław Strzemiński (1893–1952) and Henryk Stażewski (1894–1988) gave their particular approach to arts the name 'unism'. The movement had a charismatic influence on the constructivist avant-garde. Recently Stażewski has become the central figure of the younger generation of art analysts and representatives of concrete art.

Contemporary aesthetics embrace instalment art: instead of pictures there are now 'environments'. The showing of slides and films is being used to supplement the traditional media. The opening up of the Eastern Bloc and the consequent free-flow of ideas across Europe means that Polish art now participates within a universal framework as opposed to the isolated national movements of before.

Known for her use of fibres as a sculptural medium, Magdalena Abakanowicz (b.1930), won international acclaim in the 1960s for her Abakans, giant three-dimensional sculptures made with woven materials. Igor Mitoraj (1944–2014), who was inspired by Greek and Roman mythology, has some of his bigger sculptures displayed in Paris, London, Rome, Warsaw and Kraków. Younger Polish sculptors such as Katarzyna Kozyra (b.1963), Mirosław Bałka (b.1958) and Paweł Althamer (b.1967) have also won acclaim both at home and throughout the world.

POLISH JAZZ

As a musical genre born in the 'rotten West', jazz was officially forbidden soon after World War II. However, it went underground and was played at private parties. After Stalin's death in 1953, soon followed by the 'political thaw' of 1956, Polish jazz reached new heights as several groups of musicians including Krzysztof Komeda, Michał Urbaniak, Tomasz Stańko, Jan Ptaszyn Wróblewski and Zbigniew Namysłowski, to name just a few, blended cool and hard bob with technical mastery and Polish traditional melodies. Indeed, Komeda's *Astygmatic* (1966) is still considered the best Polish jazz album ever.

The reputation of the genre was later cemented with the appearance of popular jazz festivals such as Jazz Jamboree, which every year attracts the best musicians from Poland and the rest of the world. At the end of the 1980s a totally new jazz genre was created in Gdańsk by the band Miłość (Love), which included leader Ryszard Tymon Tymański, pianist Leszek Możdżer and saxophonists Maciej Sikała and Mikołaj Trzaska. Their creative music called 'yass' was a mix of new wave, free jazz, modern rock and poetry. Though the group has broken up, it has continued to inspire young generations of Polish jazz musicians.

Film School of Łódź

After World War II, Łódź became the centre of cinematography in Poland, launching the careers of a string of world-famous film-makers.

In his autobiography, Roman Polański writes: 'It was through a mere whim of history that Łódź became the film capital of Poland... after the war the capital, Warsaw, lay in ruins and... the government chose the nearest suitable town when looking for a place to establish a centre of cinematography'. Two years after World War II the Kraków film course was also transferred to Łódź and from then on it was here that film-makers received their training. The Communist authorities appropriated a small palace belonging to an industrialist, and by 1948 they had already promoted the school to the status of a college. From the outset, the school was orientated towards the production of an élite, and, despite the war devastation, it was well equipped and had excellent teachers – no expense spared. The reason is summed up in the quote by Lenin carved in marble in the hall: 'Of all the forms of art we have, film is the most important'.

In the 1950s Polish film was bound by the Socialist style, with no room for originality. Only after Stalin's death did it become possible to make films that did not reflect the propaganda clichés of the Communists. There emerged what came to be known as the Polish Film School and its founders portrayed the war and the heroism of that period in a new light. For the first time they were able to focus on the problem of human loneliness. *Kanał* (Silver Palm winner in Cannes, 1957) and *Ashes and Diamonds* (FIREPRESCI in Venice, 1959) by Andrzej Wajda and *Eroica* by Andrzej Munk – the best-known postwar productions – all date from this period. A few years later Jerzy Kawalerowicz made *Mother Joanne of the Angels* (Silver Palm in Cannes, 1961) and Roman Polański made the Academy-Award nominated *Knife in the Water* (FIREPRESCI in Venice, 1962).

Almost all contemporary Polish directors are graduates of the Łódź film school, including world-famous Andrzej Wajda and Roman Polański. Wajda (b. 1926) has been heaped with prizes: for *The Promised Land* (Moscow 1975; Valladolid 1976; Cartagena 1978; Academy Award nomination), *Man of Iron* (Grand Prix Cannes 1981), *Danton* (Prix Delluc 1983; César 1983) and an honorary Oscar in 2000, to name but a few. Today Wajda is the undisputed authority among

young directors. In 1989, he also became a member of the Senate. Polański, in contrast, left Poland at an earlier stage in his career and made films abroad that enjoyed huge international success, including *Rosemary's Baby, Repulsion, Cul-de-Sac, Chinatown, The Tenant* and *Dance of the Vampires*.

Towards the end of the 1980s the films being produced by young directors dwelt with painful precision on the social realities of the decade while attempting to establish a new manifestation of solidarity. A good example is Krzysztof Kieślowski's 10-part television series *Dekalog*, about the Ten Commandments. While his works, such as *Film about Love* and *The*

Roman Polański, a leading Polish film maker.

Double Life of Véronique, received more acclaim abroad than at home, his trilogy *Three Colours: Blue, White, Red* did bring greater recognition among his compatriots. Another Łódź graduate, Janusz Kamiński, has won two Oscars for Best Photography (*Schindler's List* and *Saving Private Ryan*) while cameramen Sławomir Idziak and Paweł Edelman were nominated for Oscars for Best Photography for *Black Hawk Down* and *The Pianist* respectively.

Today, the school continues to spawn talented directors and cameramen. Wojciech Smarzowski is one of the most popular new directors. His adaptation of the classic Stanisław Wyspiański play *The Wedding* draws a caricature of the Polish society, its complexes and sins, while *Dark House* and *Rose* debunk many myths about post-war Poland.

MAINTAINING TRADITIONAL CULTURE

Numerous ethnographic museums showcase regional folk arts, crafts and architectural styles.

Skansens (open-air museums) comprise different types of buildings, brought together within a park to recreate a village community. The range of buildings shows how peasants as well as owners of small-holdings lived and worked, with houses decorated in period style and windmills or blacksmith's forges showing how these rural crafts were operated.

Top *skansens*

Visitors interested in Kashubian culture should go to the vast Ethnographic Park at Wdzydze Kiszewskie (www.muzeum-wdzydze.gda.pl). One of the earliest *skansens* (1906), it has 58 cottages, manors, a schoolhouse, a smithy, windmills, churches and craftsmen's workshops from the 18th and 19th centuries, as well as a centre of folk arts and crafts. There is also the Museum of Agriculture (www.muzeumrolnictwa.pl), which displays 300 historic agricultural machines in a 19th-century palace and gardens at Ciechanowiec.

The Museum of the Mazovian Village (www.mwm skansen.pl) in Sierpc features a reconstructed Mazovian row village from the turn of the 20th century. Cottages with small flower and vegetable gardens give the illusion that the village is still full of life.

The Open-Air Village Museum in Maurzyce (www. muzeumlowicz.pl), part of the museum in Łowicz just 7km (4.3 miles) away, displays farms, storage and livestock buildings and farming equipment dating from the late 19th and early 20th centuries.

Zielona Góra's Ethnographic Museum (www.muz eumochla.pl) has the oldest well-preserved wooden house in Poland (1675) and a vintage wine press.

Foodies should not miss the museum inside the Upper Silesian Ethnographic Park (http://muzeumgpe-chorzow.pl), located between Chorzów and Katowice. It is well known for its popular Potato Day festival.

The Open-Air Museum of Rural Architecture (www. muzeumwsiopolskiej.pl) in Opole, Silesia, showcases historic wooden architecture and hosts well-known festivals, such as the Eastern Fair.

This skansen in Lublin has an idyllic lakeside setting.

Skansens contain a wide range of wooden Russian orthodox churches, mosques and Roman Catholic churches.

Bee keeping is an ancient rural occupation, with honey also made into alcoholic mead. Skansens such as Biskupin display historic bee hives.

Windmills were essential to every rural community. This one is from the Olsztynek skansen near the town of Olsztyn in the Mazurian lake district.

GÓRAL CULTURAL STYLE

One thriving ethnic community culture is the Górals, who live in the Podhale and Pieniny regions of southern Poland. Traditionally shepherds and farmers, they have their own dialect and maintain traditional customs and regional costumes. Góral style can be seen in the local architecture with ornately carved wooden houses and churches still remaining in Tatra villages, as well as in Zakopane. There is also an important collection of Góral folk art in Zakopane's Tatra Museum. In addition to architecture, music and folk dancing are essential elements of the culture. Among a varied programme of cultural events, Zakopane hosts the annual international Festival of Highland Folklore in September.

Ladies in local costume at the Lublin skansen. Old churches, manor houses and windmills can be seen at the Open-Air Village Museum in Lublin (www.skansen.lublin.pl). It also plans to open a typical 'provincial Eastern European town'.

...his skansen includes 18th- and 19th-century houses with ...eir characteristic small front gardens collected from the ...tra mountains.

...ansen buildings are maintained using traditional skills.

Sausage stand in Kraków's market square.

FOOD AND DRINK

Polish food is a delicious blend of contemporary
and traditional dishes with influences drawn
from Russia, Ukraine, Italy and France.

For a long time Poland has been better known for its politics than its cuisine, and when the cuisine is mentioned it is usually in terms of clichés, such as herrings, stuffed cabbage leaves and various other rich, stodgy dishes. This type of food does exist, as it does in virtually every national cuisine, but Polish fare also offers a wealth of modern, light and elegant dishes. Specialities include Baltic salmon, ceps and other wild mushrooms, and a wide range of game, led by venison and wild boar, typically flavoured with juniper berries. Various dishes are garnished with dill (the national herb).

Polish cuisine has constantly evolved as new ingredients and techniques became known to cooks. In the 12th century Poland was already on the spice route from the East to Western Europe and Scandinavia, and the salt mines at Wieliczka, just outside Kraków, were in production from that time.

In the 16th century the Italian Princess Bona Sforza married King Zygmunt Stary and introduced Italian favourites such as tomatoes, chicory, asparagus, artichokes and, of course, pasta. King Jan III Sobieski, who reigned in the 17th century, had a French wife who brought the omelette and various French specialities with her, and Jan Sobieski's defeat of the Turks at Vienna in 1683 resulted in him bringing back coffee. The Austrian emperor also gave the king some potato plants, which were initially planted at Wilanów, the royal summer residence outside Warsaw, and were considered an 'exotic', novelty. In the 17th century, the Polish and Lithuanian commonwealth was Europe's largest country except for Russia, reaching from the Baltic to the Black Sea, with Lithuanian dishes like boiled meat dumplings being

Drinks flowing in Kraków.

integrated. A large Jewish community also contributed various dishes.

Soup and dumplings

Polish hospitality is warm and generous, summed up by a popular saying: 'a guest in the house, God in the house'. Breakfast is typically a selection of sliced charcuterie, tomatoes and cheese, fried or boiled eggs, rye bread and plenty of strong tea or coffee. A late lunch is usually the day's main three-course meal, with a light buffet-style supper typically comprising cold cuts, vegetables such as tomatoes and pickled cucumbers, with rye bread.

Soup is a popular starter. Poland's more than 30 types of mushrooms are put to good use in numerous versions of mushroom soup, while *kapuśniak* is a hearty winter warmer of boiled cabbage. The most popular soup is *barszcz* (beetroot soup), served either 'clear' or with chopped beetroot and boiled potatoes added. Ukranian barszcz means extra chopped vegetables including cabbage. *Chłodnik* is the summer version, served cold garnished with a freshly boiled egg, chopped dill and soured cream, which turns the soup a shade of lilac. Another favourite is *pomidorowa* (tomato soup), preferably made with fresh tomatoes and served with noodles or rice, a generous scoop of sour cream and a spoon of fresh dill.

A plate of pierogi.

Pierogi are variously translated as dumplings or ravioli, but this makes them sound like a derivative rather than a speciality in their own right. Where they originated is unclear – they may have arrived during the 12th century from Russia or they may already have been an original Slavic folk dish. Pierogi are prepared by placing a small amount of stuffing in a circle of dough, which is then folded over the stuffing and sealed with a scalloped edge, making them look rather like large ears. The most popular filling, *z serem* (with cheese), also known as *ruskie* (Russian), means a combination of curd cheese, mashed potato and chopped fried onion.

Another preferred style *z kapustą* (with cabbage) means either cabbage or sauerkraut (or a combination of both) mixed with chopped sautéed mushrooms; while *z mięsem* (with meat) is minced beef mixed with breadcrumbs and onion. Buckwheat, a staple of the Slav diet, is the most historic style. Once boiled, the typical garnish is finely chopped onion fried in butter. Alternatively, the *pierogi* can be lightly sautéed to give a crispy texture, and served with soured cream. Sweet *pierogi* are also served, stuffed with curd cheese mixed with candied zest and raisins, or various fruits such as blueberries, diced apples or thick preserves, which are served with caster sugar and soured cream. Less orthodox fillings include spinach and lentils.

Meat and vegetables

Bigos ('hunter's stew') is a classic example of a one-pot dish, originally prepared with whatever game a hunter (or poacher) could get. The line-up of extras is also variable, though the usual basis of *bigos* is chopped white cabbage, sauerkraut and dried mushrooms, cooked with pork, bacon and Polish sausage. Adding a little lard is traditional and gives a wonderful depth of flavour, whereas the question of whether or not to add a few tablespoons of tomato purée is a great talking point among serious cooks.

Meat essentially means pork in Poland, whether a fried breaded cutlet, roasted with prunes or served with stewed cabbage. Chicken is typically served as de *volaille* (stuffed with butter and garlic) or roasted with sour apples and prunes. Beef is less common, unless it is served as the ultra-popular *zrazy*, established in the 14th century by King Władysław himself. Pieces of beaten, seasoned sirloin of beef are fried, rolled around a filling of chopped fried bacon, breadcrumbs, dill cucumber and mushrooms, and then simmered. Roast duck or goose is yet another Polish speciality, usually reserved for special occasions such as Christmas or Easter.

The traditional accompaniment of *zrazy* – and indeed other meat dishes (but never fish) – is buckwheat or potatoes. Other favourites are *gołąbki*, literally 'little pigeons', which are stuffed cabbage leaves and roast suckling pig. Another popular side dish with various roast meats is a cucumber salad named *mizeria* ('misery'). The name is no indication of the wonderfully refreshing flavours, with wafer-thin slices of cucumber dressed in a combination of soured cream, lemon juice, a dash of caster sugar and salt, garnished with minced dill or spring onion, and chilled before serving. The origins of *mizeria* are attributed to Queen Bona Sforza, but the reasons vary. The name may have stemmed from her weeping nostalgically for Italy whenever she ate it (before settling in and living happily in Poland). Alternatively, she may have eaten *mizeria* in such quantities that the consequent pain of indigestion made her ask for a misericord (a dagger for committing suicide).

Modern Polish cuisine

Under Communism Polish cuisine virtually disappeared, with rationing and frequent shortages a daily reality. Not surprisingly, restaurants offered a very erratic menu, and chefs also had to endure various other restrictions. The end of Communism in 1989 meant regular supplies, and chefs had the freedom to use their creativity. Not only was real Polish food back on the menu, but Polish chefs who had been working abroad began to return, bringing with them a modern European perspective. As chefs began to re-interpret their

Buying pretzels.

Meat dishes are also frequently accompanied by various beetroot dishes. *Ćwikła* is one of the most historic, made with baked or cooked beetroots, sliced and layered with a dressing of vinegar, caraway seeds, horseradish and lemon juice. Beetroot is also popular puréed, sliced and fried in batter, or grated and combined with a little soured cream or minced onion.

Despite the plentiful lakes and long coastline, fish is not high on the list of Poles' favourite dishes. This is slowly changing as fresh fish becomes more widely available in large cities, not just on the coast. Pickled herring fillets and fried carp are traditionally eaten on Christmas Eve while smoked eel is considered a delicacy.

POLISH SWEETS AND CAKES

Many Polish cakes and pastries originally arrived from France, such as *napoleonki* (millefeuille) and *eklerka* (eclair). Among the classic Polish cakes are *sernik* (cheesecake), prepared with curd and/or cream cheese and either baked or unbaked topped with a layer of jelly. Variations include adding cream to the cheese, raisins (Viennese-style), and with a top layer of either icing sugar or dark chocolate and crushed nuts. *Makowiec* is a sponge cake rolled around a filling of poppy seeds or a 'poppy seed cream'. During carnival and particularly on Fat Thursday, doughnuts filled with rose petal jam and *chrusty*, or *faworki* (little flavours), are eaten.

national dishes, so Modern Polish cuisine began to emerge in a few key Warsaw restaurants during the mid-1990s. Well-known restaurateur families, including Gessler and Kręgliccy, were among the key pioneers.

Modern Polish cuisine is, fortunately, retaining the authentic character of classic dishes, but producing lighter, more subtle and interesting versions. A new style *barszcz*, for instance, comprises delicate jellied consommé with soured cream and a beetroot julienne; herring appears as a tartare, *pierogi* may feature brains or Baltic seaweed, while *bigos* benefits

Waiting for customers at Szara na Kazimierz.

As early as the end of the 16th century vodka was established as the Polish national drink.

from a wider repertoire of choice cuts such as smoked duck and venison.

It took a perfect blend of fresh Polish seasonal products, imagination and perfectly mastered modern cooking techniques for chef Wojciech Modest Amaro's Atelier Amaro to win Poland's first Michelin star in 2013. This success gave yet another boost to the culinary revolution in Poland. As Poles fell in love with cooking, TV programmes dedicated to modern Polish and

international cuisine gained immense popularity, with contestants and judges alike becoming instant celebrities.

Warsaw and other large cities are at the centre of this culinary movement, with new restaurants springing up almost everywhere. They offer not only innovative Polish dishes but also vegetarian, vegan, oriental and exotic delicacies likely to satisfy even the most demanding tastes. Devotees of simple fare will find plenty of choice too: fresh-made burgers, sandwiches (often sold from food tracks), falafels and the ubiquitous kebabs have become another feature of the Polish culinary landscape. Moreover, eating out is still substantially cheaper than in Western Europe. With the slow food movement firmly established in Poland, many Poles have come to consider food and cooking as yet another expression of their individuality.

Vodka

There has been a long-standing dispute between the Poles and Russians about the origins of vodka. After all, who wouldn't want to take the credit for inventing such a drink. While there is no definitive proof, circumstantial evidence points to Poland. Knowledge of distillation spread from France across Europe around the 14th century, and is likely to have reached Poland before going on to Russia via Lithuania and the Ukraine. Moreover, the earliest recorded use of the word 'vodka' in Eastern Europe is on a Polish document, dated 1405. The Russians, however, claim vodka was first distilled in a monastery outside Moscow in the 14th century.

At least the Poles and Russians agreed on the name for this drink, with vodka being the diminutive of *woda*, meaning water (so vodka literally means 'little water.') When this term was coined using the diminutive it indicated that it was an improved version of the original. The earliest centres of commercial distillation, during the 16th century, were Kraków, Poznań and Gdańsk. By then vodka had developed from being purely medicinal into a social drink.

Commercial distillation was originally limited to the aristocracy (providing plenty of tax revenue), though early distillation methods were inevitably rudimentary, as it was impossible to rectify (purify) the spirit. This meant

Numerous 'vodka sayings' have evolved in Poland, such as 'wodka grzeje, wodka chlodzi, wodka nigdy nie zaskodzi', meaning 'vodka cools and vodka warms, but vodka never harms.'

that the vodka was marred by unpleasant flavours and aromas. The answer was to disguise these imperfections by adding aromatic oils, fruit, herbs and spices, and to sweeten it with honey. When rectification was developed dur-

bison grass to create this complex, aromatic vodka with herbaceous, fresh grass/hay aromas, and beautifully balanced flavours of thyme and lavender, together with lemon, tobacco and hints of chocolate.

High strength vodkas extend the range of choice, with Polish Pure Spirit at either 57 percent or 79 percent ABV, while Rectified Spirit (*Spirytus Rektyfikowany*) at 95 percent ABV, the world's strongest spirit, is distillation strength vodka. These styles are usually a base for home-flavouring, a favourite combination being Rectified Spirit and cherry cordial: *wiśniówka*;

Café life in Zamość.

ing the 19th century, flavourings were added for their own sake, as there was nothing left to hide.

During the 19th century around 100 flavoured styles were available, and Poland continues to produce the world's largest range of flavoured vodka.

A classic style dating from the 16th century and still going strong is Żubrowka, which includes the simpler reference of 'Bison Vodka' on the label. The flavour is derived not from any part of a bison but entirely from bison grass, a wild herb growing only in the Białowieża Forest, a national park in eastern Poland. A blade of grass features in each bottle of Żubrowka, but that is merely decorative, as it takes far more

VODKA PARTIES

A great benefit of having a vodka session in true Polish style is that it's an instant party, because Poles always serve food with vodka. There is actually a specific range of specialities called *zakąski* (literally 'a nibble'), all of which have a genuine rapport with vodka: salted herring fillets and blinis with soured cream, pickled cucumbers, pickled mushrooms, sausage, ham, rye bread and curd cheese. These flavours are substantial enough to stand up to the vodka, while the vodka tames the saltiness of herring fillets and melting soured cream. Moreover, rich, salty, spicy flavours naturally encourage another glass of vodka, so it's a perfect match.

karmelówka has a sugar syrup added to Rectified Spirit for an instant caramel vodka.

The Polish toast *'na zdrowie'* (meaning 'to your health') is not simply a polite line. Vodka is renowned for purity, and actually contains a lower level of congeners (impurities responsible for hangovers) than other spirits. While devotees claim that drinking vodka is a guarantee against hangovers, this also depends on the quantity of vodka consumed, particularly as an enthusiastic refrain in Poland is *'do dna',* meaning 'to the bottom' (of the glass). A recent phenomenon is bars serving shots of vodka

A drop of Krupnik – honey vodka.

with snacks called *zakąski*. There are even vodka tours, during which a knowledgeable guide unveils all of vodka's secrets.

Beer and wine

Beer and mead (honey wine) were the earliest alcoholic drinks prepared by the Slavs, and major cities like Warsaw and Wrocław still feature mead bars. Mead is kept hot by serving it in ceramic beakers that stand on a tray heated by a small candle.

Polish beer is generally lager, though porter, stout and other dark beers are also brewed in a growing number of breweries across the country. Some of the most famous brands come from the south, including Żywiec and Okocim,

> *If, after all this vodka and alcohol, you have a hangover, you can try a classic Polish remedy – drinking the juice drained from a glass of sauerkraut. Failing that it's back to the drink that caused the problem.*

both produced at the brewery and town of the same name. Unfortunately, these and many more Polish beer brands have been sold to big international companies, thus losing their distinctive character. On the other hand, independent breweries serving unfiltered, naturally brewed beers are thriving as the popularity of 'beer-only' bars in large cities rises.

Even though the climate is not ideal, wine production in Poland began as early as the 10th century, mostly in the south and southwestern part of the country. By the 14th century wine became nearly as popular as beer and mead. However, the following centuries saw most vineyards fall into disuse mainly due to the popularity of wines imported from Hungary. In recent years, wine making has seen a sudden revival, with several vineyards being established in the southwest of Poland, notably at Zielona Góra and Wrocław. Though not cheap, Polish wines are getting positive reviews from wine lovers looking for distinctive flavours and new experiences.

Soft drinks

Poland's huge number of spas also means there's a comprehensive selection of mineral waters, with varying taste profiles, and spas across the country are increasingly commercialising their finest liquid assets. Mineral water mixed with bottled fruit juice is refreshing, and a wide range of fresh juice is produced from indigenous fruits. The clear leader in popularity must be *sok z czarnej porzeczki* (blackcurrant juice), deliciously ripe and rich, but with a dry finish; strawberry and apple are also among the favourite flavours.

Coffee (*kawa*) is typically served cappuccino style, strong and full-bodied with a dash of milk, while tea (*herbata*) is served without milk but with a slice of lemon. In a café or restaurant this usually means a glass of boiling water and a tea bag on the saucer will arrive at the table for you to brew the tea according to your own preference.

Festive Food

The food served during religious celebrations is as important as the events themselves.

Christmas

The religious and gastronomic focus of Christmas is Christmas Eve rather than Christmas Day. However, until the Christmas Eve dinner (traditionally comprising 12 dishes, one for each apostle) a semi-fast is observed, involving a small helping of rye bread and salted herring fillets.

There is no set time to assemble for Christmas Eve dinner, known as Wigilia – it depends on when the first star appears, symbolising the star that guided the Three Kings to Bethlehem. The table is laid with a white tablecloth, under which a small amount of hay is placed, recalling the hay of the crib. Traditionally an extra place is set so that no unexpected visitor will be turned away, to experience the same treatment that inns in Bethlehem extended to the Holy family. Christmas greetings are then exchanged and food is served.

Everyone has a small wafer, blessed by a priest, and small pieces of wafer are exchanged. As this is a Holy day, the entire meal excludes meat products of any kind, even animal fat. Consequently, the Christmas Eve barszcz (soup) is based on vegetable stock. The soup can be garnished with uszka (literally 'little ears'), which are scaled-down pierogi filled with sliced mushrooms. Several types of fish, prepared in various ways, provide the subsequent dishes. Salted herring fillets, for example, are served with a garnish of chopped onion and soured cream or apple. Baltic salmon and pike are popular, though the archetypal choice is carp, either fried or served with szary sos (grey sauce) prepared from ground honeycake, raisins and almonds. Some say that saving a scale from the carp and keeping it in your wallet ensures prosperity in the coming year. Fish is followed by a selection of pierogi. Fruit compote is the classic dessert, prepared by stewing dried fruits flavoured with a vanilla pod, followed by makowiec and other cakes with tea. Then it's off to church for Midnight Mass.

Roast goose is the main event on Christmas Day, with the festive period known as Carnival lasting until Shrove Tuesday. This is the season when people go from house to house celebrating. Hot honey vodka is the usual tipple, accompanied by jam doughnuts and chrusty (literally 'brushwood'), also known as faworki

(little favours). These light deep-fried pastry twists are served with a sprinkling of icing sugar.

Easter

Easter celebrations begin with a semi-fast on Good Friday, usually herrings and rye bread, prior to the Easter Sunday breakfast served after an early morning mass. A basket of hardboiled eggs decorated with rustic motifs forms the centrepiece of the table, with the host and hostess exchanging an Easter greeting by passing everyone a small piece of egg. The breakfast fare represents daily staples, which are taken to church to be blessed on Easter Saturday in baskets

Traditional bryndza (smoked cheeses) are a speciality of the southern highlands.

decorated with colourful napkins and greenery. These foodstuffs, known as święcone (blessed) include various types of Polish sausage, hardboiled eggs, rye bread, salt and horseradish. There are also cakes, including Easter Babka, a yeast cake flavoured with chocolate and vanilla, baked in a tall fluted tin. Eggshells and sausage skins are burned, as anything that has been blessed must be eaten or burned.

Easter Monday sees a ritual known as śmigus dyngus. Until noon everyone has the 'right' to splash people with water. The victim is not supposed to retaliate. Traditionally young boys sought out unsuspecting girls. A sprinkling of cologne water is more gentlemanly, though jugs of cold water are not uncommon.

POLAND'S NATIONAL PARKS

The country's national parks have excellent hiking, cycling and horse riding trails as well as exceptional opportunities for anglers, climbers and skiers.

Nature lovers will find few other countries in Europe that can offer such a diverse range of natural landscapes and rare fauna and flora as Poland. The woods, marshland and valleys feature plants and animals that are now extremely rare elsewhere in Europe.

The most valuable areas are now designated as national parks and are generally open to the public. There are currently 23 national parks in Poland, covering a total area of approximately 314,570 hectares (786,425 acres). Nine of them, the Babiogórski, Białowieski, Bieszczady, Bory Tucholskie, Kampinoski, Karkonosze, Poleski, Słowiński and ,Tatrzański national parks have been registered on the Unesco list of World Biosphere Reserves; additionally, the Białowieski National Park has been included in Unesco's list of Humanity's World Heritage, and five – Biebrzański, Narew River, Poleski, Wigry and Słowiński – have been made a part of the International Ramsar Convention of protection of waterways.

All aspects of the Polish natural world are preserved here: from the rocky, almost alpine Tatra Mountains to the wooded Pieniński and Bieszczady mountains, from the shifting dunes in the mini-desert beside the Baltic to the lakes and rivers hidden among the forests of the Suwalskie region and the Roztocze Heights.

Accommodation and restaurants can be found in or near to all the national parks. Tourist trails and educational paths leading through the parks also make getting acquainted with nature much easier. Way-marked footpaths and nature trails help visitors explore deep into the parks, and the nearby natural history museums invariably have interesting collections. Services offered

The Dunajec Gorge in the Pieniński National Park.

by professional guides and specialist travel agencies are available to those who wish to explore different forms of nature tourism.

The most enticing region for nature-loving tourists is the Nizina Polnocnopodlaska lowland plain (Bialystok and Lomza provinces) with the Puszcza Białowieska primeval forest and the marshes of the Biebrza and Narew River valleys. This area, together with a section of the Suwalki-Augustów Lakes and the Mazurian Lake District, is often described as Poland's 'Green Lung'.

Białowieski National Park

The preservation of this area as a park goes back to 1921, when the forestry 'Reservation' was created. In 1932 it was transformed into the National Park in Białowieski and restored in 1947 as Białowieski National Park; the area was enlarged again in 1996. It is the oldest national park in Poland and one of the most precious natural legacies to be found in this part of Europe. The park is in the central part of Białowieski Forest, in the eastern part of the Podlasie-Byelorus Uplands, on Mazurian-Podlasie Land, in the natural forest region of the Białowieski Primeval Forest. According to biogeographical division, it lies in the bore-onemoral province.

leafy deciduous trees, with a distinctive Central European flavour; and another part which is full of spruce trees and much more reminiscent of Eastern Europe. Altogether the park is host to 600 types of flora – including many 300-year-old trees – and some 11,000 types of fauna, including 62 species of mammals and 120 bird species. Here one can come across, elk, fawn deer, wild lynx and wolves. But the park is probably most famous for its wild bison, now restored to their natural habitat.

There are many outstanding attractions in the park, but particularly recommended are

Bison in Białowieski National Park.

At first sight it seems an untidy place, with trees growing in strange ways and places. But this is the key to Białowieski – this is how nature intended and is much the way forest would have looked in prehistoric times. The untidiness of the forest also allows an amazing range of flora and fauna to flourish freely. The most protected part of the forest is its central-northern region, where all types of human activity are strictly banned – even gathering berries or collecting dead leaves. Nature alone is king here.

The most common trees are oak, hornbeam, lime, maple and spruce. Much of the forest is covered with a mixture of trees and vegetation and there are two very distinct areas: one with

SAVING THE BISON

One of the species that may be encountered in Białowieski is the bison, Europe's largest animal. Once these were plentiful, numbering almost 2,000 in the mid-19th century, but by 1914 their number was reduced to around 700, and during the war the Germans killed them for food. The national park was set up to protect what was left and in 1929 wild bison were reintroduced into a closed perimeter. Although there are currently more than 500 bison living in the park, they remain a threatened species. The bison population in Europe amounts to a little over 3,000, of which almost 2,000 live in the wild in special reserves like Białowieski.

the grounds surrounding the palace built by the Czar of Russia in the latter half of the 19th century.

From water to desert

The Biebrzański National Park, which covers an area of 59,223 hectares (146,280 acres) is an eldorado for ornithologists. This, the largest and probably the most popular of Poland's national parks, extends along the River Biebrza and contains some marshland and peat bogs unique to Europe. The wide range of bird wildlife includes golden eagles, whitetail eagles, owls and ruff. The main attraction of Słowiński National Park (see page 325), stretching for 33 kilometres (21 miles) along the Baltic coast, are probably the shifting dunes, some of which can reach 42 metres (140 ft) high. The most spectacular of these are found on the sandbar between the sea and the River Łeba. They can move at a speed of 10 metres (35 ft) per year, burying everything in their way. Nearby are attractive lakes, rich in birdlife, beaches and a mini-desert.

Tourism is rapidly gaining ground in the Pieniński National Park in the Pieniński Mountains in the southeast of Poland. The Dunajec Gorge is a spectacular stretch of river, which snakes for about 8 kilometres (5 miles) between steep cliffs, often over 300 metres (1,000 ft) high. Although raft rides have been an attraction since the 19th century, the modern versions, consisting of coffin-like canoes tied together with rope and navigated by local guides, attract 200,000 passengers every year.

Mountain country

A narrow belt running along the Czech frontier, the Karkonosze National Park includes the peaks of the Karkonosze Mountains in the western Sudetens with Mount Sniežka (1,602 metres/5,254 ft) the highest point. Characteristic of the Karkonosze are the *kotły* (cirques) – huge hollows carved by glaciers during the Ice Age. Kocioł Małego Stawu and Kościół Wielkiego Stawu near Mount Sniežka are the most spectacular. The climate in this region is notoriously unpredictable and yet it is popular with hikers. Warm, waterproof clothes are essential whatever the time of year.

The natural beauty of the West Carpathians is preserved by Bieszczady National Park, created in 1973 (see page 231). It is in the southeast of the country, at the frontier with Ukraine and Slovakia, and covers 27.834 hectares (68,780 acres).

In the highest part of Polish upper West Bieszczady are *połoniny* (mountain pastures) – peaks which are free from forests and above the tree line, such as Carynska and Wetlinska. These mountain meadows host a great number of rare, East Carpathian plant species. The forests, mostly beech with some fir and sycamore stands, cover 87 percent of the park. About 50 species of mammals are native to the area, including typical forest species: European

Waterfalls in the Karkonosze Mountains.

bison, brown bears, wolves, red deer, the lynx and the wild cat. About 150 species of birds have found a haven here. If visitors wish to spot the wild inhabitants of the park, they should walk quietly along the trails in small groups. The best time for wildlife watchers is the early morning – grazing red deer may be seen even from the roads in the valleys. At Ustrzyki Dolne is the park's natural science museum and educational centre.

Tatrzański National Park encompasses 21,164-hectares (52,297-acres) and surrounds and protects the whole Polish portion of the Tatra mountain range, the youngest and highest mountains in the country. It is the only region of alpine character in Poland, with the highest peak being Mount Rysy, 2,499 metres (8,198 ft) above sea level. There are post-glacial pot-holes (Czarny Staw), the Śnieżna cave which is 780 metres (2,560 ft) deep, and an abundance of lakes, including Morskie Oko, with an area of 34 hectares (84 acres) and Wielki Staw Polski, 79 metres (260 ft) deep. Spruce forests mixed with fir, larch, beech and sycamore dominate the foothills, and the highland zone is covered with spruce with a few stone pine stands; the dwarf pine layer gives way to alpine meadows and pastures, while crags and peaks soar above the 2.300 metres (7,546 ft) mark.

One of the pleasures of Poland's mountain areas is its accessibility. Hiking trails are aimed more at leisurely walks than strenuous hard climbing.

mountain pine predominate in the upper zones. Next comes the alpine zone with its rare mountain plant species. Gullies filled with rubble can be found in the top rocky zone. The forests shelter a multitude of animals including bear, red deer, wolf and lynx; they are also a habitat for the rare wood grouse.

The Gorczański National Park comprises the central part of the Gorce Range, with the exception of its highest peak, Turbacz. This is a typical mountain forest park with storied layers of tree stands. The Carpathian beech and fir woods make up the lower layer, while the upper layer is dominated by spruce forest. Both alpine and endemic plants cover the numerous mountain glades. The park's fauna includes such typical forest animals and red deer, roe deer, wild boar, lynx, wildcat and wolf. Worthy of special note is the population of wood grouse and the spotted salamander.

The Góry Stołowe National Park envelops the Góry Stołowe (Table Mountain) massif. The main attraction is the original landscape of rocky plateaux with sheer ledges, which has developed due to the specific tabular geological structure of these mountains. Nature has formed labyrinthine passages among the rocks.

A day out on the mountain trail.

The flora and fauna of the Tatra range abounds in indigenous and alpine plant species as well as and marmot, chamois and a small population of bears. The Tatra range is also one of Poland's last refuges of the golden eagle. The park has a natural history museum with many interesting objects and a scientific laboratory. The main tourist base is Zakopane, the winter capital of Poland.

The Babiogórski National Park encompasses Mount Babia Góra, at 1,725 metres (5,660 ft) the highest peak of the Western Beskid Range. The woods here are very much like a primeval forest. The lower plant zone is dominated by fir and beech forest mixed with spruce and sycamore. Spruce, mountain ash and dwarf

The most interesting clusters of rock formations may be seen in the Błędne Skały reserve and on Mount Szczeliniec Wielki (919 metres/3,015 ft). The slopes and foothills of the plateaux are covered with spruce and beech forests, while the high moors with marsh plants developed in places on the flat table-like tops.

The territory of Świętokrzyski National Park includes the Łysogóry Mountains, with Mount Łysica reaching 612 metres (2,007 ft) above sea level, the highest range of the Świętokrzyski Mountains and fragments of the adjoining valleys. The Świętokrzyski Mountains, the oldest in Poland, were formed of paleozoic rocks. Worth particular attention are the small, deforested areas (*gołoborza*), covered with quartzite boulders and stripped of green vegetation. The Łysogóry Range is covered with fir forests mixed with pine, beech and larch. The park's rich plant population includes many rare species of mountain and lowland plants. The king of the wildlife here is the red deer.

Forested landscapes

The Bory Tucholskie National Park protects the most valuable area of the Bory Tucholskie Forest. The sandy flat land is overgrown with pinewoods, cut across with river valleys and dotted with lakes, nestling in deep ravines. In depressions and at the edges of some lakes are bogs, home to rare species of post-glacial plants. The wildlife includes trout found in the crystal-clear rivers, as well as waterfowl, birds of prey, beaver and elk.

The Drawieński National Park, in the Drawska Forest, contains parts of the Drawa river valley (one of the most beautiful rivers in Polish Pomerania), the Płociczna river, its tributary and 13 lakes.

Pine forests cover 78 percent of the park's total area, but there are also forests where pine is mixed with oak, beech and alder. Of particular interest are the high moorlands in the Płociczna river basin, which abound in rare species of marsh plants and post-glacial remains. Various species of fish inhabit the crystal-clear waters of the park. The park is also home to a colony of beavers, otter and osprey, a rare bird of prey.

The Kampinoski National Park, in the vicinity of Warsaw, encompasses the Kampinoski Forest, spreading over the Vistula river proglacial valley. Belts of inland dunes, overgrown with pinewoods, add to the beauty of the park's landscape. In the depressions between the dunes there are peat bogs, meadows and marshes covered with a growth of alder. The park's flora abounds in rare protected species and wildlife includes elk, beaver and lynx.

The Magurski National Park occupies the central part of the Lower Beskid Range, dominated by Mount Magura Watkowska (846 metres/2,775 ft). It covers areas typical for the Beskid Range landscape, with forested dome-like hills separated by rivers and brooks.

The river Wisłoka is born in the park and runs across its territory, forming numerous scenic gorges and meanders. The hills are overgrown with beech, fir and spruce forests. The flora of the park boasts many rare mountain

species and protected plants and fauna is represented by bear, wolf, lynx, wildcat, golden eagle and eagle owl.

Valleys and plateaux

The greatest natural asset of the Narew River National Park is its well-preserved and unspoilt swampy River Narew valley which features a unique system of flood waters, meanders, old river beds, bulrushes and low-bogs, all of which are called "Polish Amazonia". It has particularly rich birdlife with over 200 species, out of which 154 species have their

Ojcow National Park rock formation.

nesting grounds in the park. Some species of the local water birds are difficult to spot elsewhere in Europe.

The Ojcowski National Park (19 sq km/7 sq miles), near Kraków, occupies the southern part of the Kraków Częstochowa Upland and the valleys of the Prądnik and Saspówka rivers. Numerous caves, scenic ravines, rocky passes and spectacular rock formations, including the famous "Hercules Club", have been created by nature. Forest covers the majority of the park area.

The most characteristic species of the park's flora are those of stenothermal lichens. The insect population is extremely diversified (over 3,000 species) including 1,142 species

The Ojcowski National Park is popular with history buffs as well as nature lovers for its location near the Eagles' Nest Trail of ancient castles and fortresses.

of beetles and 520 species of butterflies. The caves are a shelter for a multitude of species of bats.

The Poleski National Park is in the Łęczyńsko-Włodawskie Lake District (Lublin Poleski) and includes a unique flatland

Wooden houses by the lake, Wolin National Park.

of extensive peat bogs and swamps, which in places is reminiscent of the tundra or the transitional zone between tundra and taiga. The peat bogs shelter many species of rare plants. The park is also a refuge to elk, wolves and the rare marsh turtle.

The Roztoczański National Park encompasses the central part of the Roztocze region, where eminences are divided by deep ravines; the Wieprz and Tanew rivers gently wind their way across the park. Forests, mainly beech and fir, cover 93 percent of the park's territory. The rich flora includes lowland and highland species, as well as stenothermal species originating from southeastern Europe. There are also some 190 species of birds.

Lakes and islands

The Wielkopolski National Park near Poznań, in the Wielkopolskie Lake District, has all the characteristic elements of a post-glacial landscape. Thus, there are hills 130 metres (426 ft) above sea level, subglacial channels and plenty of lakes. Pine and mixed forests cover the majority part of the park. The park's flora includes many rare and protected species and the forests are home to such animals as red deer, roe deer, wild boar, marten, badger, hare and numerous bird species.

Lake Wigry, one of the largest lakes in northeastern Poland, is an important element of Wigry National Park. In addition, there are 25 lakes in the park, interconnected by a network of rivers, the biggest being the Czarna Hańcza river. Small, marshy mid-forest lakes, surrounded by peat bogs are one of the special features of this park, and although the dominant vegetation is pine and spruce forests, there are also large colonies of moor, aquatic and meadow plants. Mammals living in the forest include elk, red deer, roe deer, wolf and beaver. There is a profusion of water birds, and the park waterways teem with such rare fish as lavaret, European whitefish, bulltrout and European smelt.

The Wolin National Park occupies the western part of Wolin Island. It includes the morainic heights, which end with a picturesque, steep 95-metre (312-ft) high cliff at the shore of the Baltic Sea and the Bay of Szczecin. Here the shore continuously retreats because of the destructive action of the waves. Almost the entire park is densely forested, the most valuable areas being the beech stands.

A group of lakes and sandy beaches is found in the southern part of the park. The diversified plant cover is made up of many rare species of undergrowth, stenothermal and sand plants. Among the wildlife are such rare species as the white-tailed eagle, Aquila pomarina and numerous species of water birds. In the heart of the park there is a bison exhibition reserve (see page 389).

For visitors to Poland who wish to take full advantage of the many national parks, as well as learn about much of its unique flora and fauna, the addresses of the national park headquarters and the Polish tour operators specialising in tourism for naturalists can be found in the *Travel Tips* section (see page 388).

Outdoor Paradise

Nature and outdoor sports enthusiasts will find plenty of reasons to pursue their favourite pastimes in Poland.

Rugged mountains, pristine rivers and lakes, long Baltic seashore, charming countryside, ancient woods and marshes – Poland has a lot to offer. Be it kite-surfing, windsurfing, swimming, rock climbing, paragliding, diving, skiing or simply walking, all these

Climbers will love the Polish Jura region (between Kraków and Częstochowa) with limestone formations in the most bizarre shapes, picturesque cliffs and steep-walled valleys featuring some 220 caves. Ever popular 'skałki', as the area is known, offer rather short (up to 30 metres/98 ft on average) climbing routes of varying difficulty. Another perfect spot to hone mountaineering skills are the Tatra Mountains, which make for a good alternative, particularly in winter, for seasoned climbers.

Way-marked footpaths and trails for hikers and bikers criss-cross the Tatra, Sudety and Bieszczady mountains, as well as many lowland areas of out-

Trekking in the Tatra Mountains.

sports can be practised amid beautiful, unspoilt scenery. Every day more Poles, particularly in big cities, ditch their sedentary habits and turn to outdoor activities, with running and cycling coming to the fore.

In summer water sports fans head for Hel, known for its good winds and nearby kite- and wind-surfing schools. The shallow Puck Bay is ideal for beginners, while the Baltic Sea, though often rough, offers a thrilling experience for seasoned wave riders and sailors. The real mecca for Polish sailors, though, is the Mazurian Lakes, in the northeast. Yachts can be hired and cruises organised at all major ports, such as Węgorzewo, Sztynort, Giżycko, Wilkasy, Rydzewo, Mikołajki or Ruciane-Nida. Dubbed a 'land of a thousand lakes', the Mazurian Lakes District is equally popular among fishermen, kayakers and cyclists.

standing beauty. Scarcely populated Bieszczady is popular with backpackers, who may stroll for miles without seeing another human being. Horseriding is another good way to explore the Polish countryside; there are numerous riding schools in the popular tourist areas and within, or very close to, large cities.

With so many Polish pilots regularly winning the most coveted international trophies, gliding, paragliding and other aerial sports remain popular outdoor activities. Numerous aero clubs across the country organise flying courses and hire out equipment. An increasing number of Poles have taken up golf, and practise it on more than 60 courses across the country as well as on outdoor and indoor driving ranges. The number of tournaments for amateurs and professionals is also on the rise (see page 388).

A windfarm in rural Gdańsk.

THE ENVIRONMENT

During the Communist era, Poland
suffered years of environmental damage
from heavy industry. Now regulations are
in place and the clean-up is under way.

Poland is a land of contrasts and that applies just as much to the country's politics and its society as it does to the culture and the different landscapes. When it comes to the demands of the environment and the conservation of the natural world, there are also some huge disparities.

Large parts of Poland have a reputation as refuges for rare fauna and flora, but many visitors are still shocked to discover how carelessly the Communist authorities treated the environment, particularly in the industrial regions. For years the damage that the natural surroundings were suffering was ignored by the people and covered up by the party; now, however, everyone is aware of the problems – and they are posing a major headache for the government.

Nature protection

Nearly one third of Poland's surface area (29 percent) represents natural attractions and is protected by law. This includes national parks, nature reserves, landscape parks and protected natural landscapes.

National parks are the highest form of nature protection in Poland (see page 119). They generally encompass a protected area distinguished by its singular scientific, natural, cultural and educational values. All nature and the characteristic features of a particular landscape are protected within the boundaries of 23 national parks throughout the country. These parks can be visited for a small fee – nearly 1,700 km (1,050 miles) of tourist trails have been marked out within the parks' territories.

Apart from offering very popular hiking routes, the park areas are also available to skiers, mountain climbers and canoeists. Some trails for cycling have also been marked out

Many species of birds thrive in protected nature reserves.

within some of these national parks. Nature reserves are the second most important form of nature protection and they embrace natural or only slightly changed ecosystems, selected species of plants and animals, and elements of still nature; all these of particular value from either scientific, natural or cultural viewpoints.

In 2014 there were nearly 1,500 nature reserves in Poland, with areas ranging from 0.5 to 5,000 hectares (1.25 to 12,355 acres).

Landscape parks and special protection zones occupy about 10 percent of the country's area. Landscape parks are created in areas that have not only natural but historical value as well. Unlike the national parks, they may be economically exploited under certain conditions, but no activities undertaken in the parks must ruin their landscape values: the beauty of the landscape should be preserved.

Certain zones are marked out and used for short-term holiday recreation, holiday stays and special interest tourism. Therefore, landscape parks often contain organised campsites with good facilities, bivouac fields, and even recreation and holiday centres.

Other areas of protected landscape include individual forms of nature surviving in clusters, which have either scientific, cultural, historical or landscape value, such as large, old trees, springs, waterfalls, rock formations, ravines, boulders and caves. The most fascinating caves are found in the Pieniński, Ojcowski and Karkonoski national parks.

Communist legacy

For decades Polish industry used far too much water, and contaminated the air, the forests and the soil with toxins and discarded raw materials. As early as the 1950s, the government introduced laws and regulations that would, in theory, have protected the

Visible signs of industrial pollution are just the tip of the iceberg.

ENVIRONMENTAL DISASTER AREAS

Despite an apparent concern for the landscape shown in its many national parks and nature reserves, there are many regions in Poland that have suffered badly at the hands of an economic system that paid only lip service to environmental concerns.

Areas such as the Upper Silesia-Kraków agglomeration, Turoszów and Konin brown coal-basins, Bełchatów Industrial District, Legnica-Głogów Copper-Basin and Tarnobrzeg Sulphur-Basin, have highly degraded natural resources as a result of long-term destructive factors. Katowice and Kraków, however, are the regions with the worst problems. As well as coal, zinc ore and lead ore mining, energy and steel production are the main sources of employment in those regions. Consequently, both cities suffer from serious, health-damaging air pollution.

To this day, politicians tread warily in this part of the country, any major restructuring would inevitably have devastating consequences in social costs. Kraków's air quality is amongst the worst in Europe, especially in winter when residents fire up more than 40,000 coal or equally polluting heating furnaces. They will all need to be replaced by 2018 and city authorities are offering subsidies to those switching to more environmentally friendly heating systems. The pollution is likely to gradually diminish over the next few years.

The EU has accepted Polish requests for transitional periods to conform to EU standards on the environment covering such areas as air quality and water, waste management, industrial pollution and radioactivity.

environment, but in the years that followed the pollutant emissions from manufacturing industries increased.

An Environment Ministry was established in 1972 and plans were drawn up for the clo-

the State Inspectorate for Protecting the Environment, due to the decreased use of energy, water and other resources by the government. A major part was also played by the reduction in output of heavy industry and the bankruptcy of many polluting enterprises, as well as the implementation of EU regulations after Poland's accession in 2004, when large subsidies for environmental projects started pouring in from Brussels.

Polish taxes have also been changed to provide greater tax relief for pro-ecological activities, while new areas went under protection

Environmental awareness is increasing.

sure of the worst industrial plants by 1990, but these measures were purely for the sake of propaganda and were never taken seriously by the government. And if the truly committed environmental campaigners were able to point to some small successes in their battles with the government at first, such as the abandoned plan for a nuclear power station, it seems as though it was all in vain. According to the current government plan, the first Polish nuclear plant should become operational by 2024.

Ecological optimism

The state of the natural environment has greatly improved in recent years, according to

as Poland implemented the EU's Nature 2000 programme.

In recent years, many non-governmental organisations have done a great deal to change social attitudes towards nature protection and sustainable development. However, their goals often clash with big business interests, making conflicts unavoidable. Polish environmentalists have already won several important battles, including making the government reroute the Augustów bypass expressway, which was to cut through the protected wilderness area of the river Rospuda valley. It was also thanks to their efforts that the Wisła, the largest Polish river, has seen its water quality substantially improved in recent years.

Cross-country skiing in Jakuszyce,
near the Czech border.

Sunrise over the spring floodwaters of the Biebrza river, Biebrzański National Park.

The Leba Dunes in Slowiński National Park are a Unesco World Biosphere Reserve.

Spring blooms at Wawel Castle.
Kraków.

INTRODUCTION

A detailed guide to the entire country,
with principal sites clearly cross-
referenced by number to the maps.

Feeding the pigeons in Zamość.

Despite the world becoming a smaller place, Poland typically remains an unknown quantity, even among seasoned travellers. Moreover, not having visited Poland
doesn't prevent people from having definite views of 'how it
really is.' The Communist era gave rise to an image of cities of
bleak concrete blocks, inhabited by amorphous people who
spent their lives either working, or queuing outside almost
empty shops. As for the countryside, the only landscapes were imagined
to be industrial, dwarfed by towering chimneys belching out toxic fumes.

The reality is that the Polish landscape offers a great variety of immense
natural beauty, protected by a large number of national parks throughout
the country. In the east, the Białowieski National Park is a primeval forest, sheltering various rare species, including herds of European bison. In
the northeast the Mazurian Lake District comprises more than 1,000 lakes,
many of which are linked by rivers and canals, and bordered
by vast areas of natural wetlands including bogs and marshes.
Meanwhile, the Carpathian Mountains extend across the southern border of Poland, offering skiers as well as hikers some magnificent terrain. In the north, the Baltic coast is characterised by
secluded beaches fringed by pine trees and small cliffs.

Kraków lamppost.

Every architectural genre can be seen in Poland, with some
stunning examples of Romanesque, Gothic, Renaissance,
Baroque, neoclassical and Secessionist buildings. Most cities have
retained their medieval layouts, which means an 'old town' district with a central market square, town hall and burghers' houses. Having
been a Roman Catholic country since the 10th century there are also many
historic churches to see. Thanks to EU funding, most Polish cities have
undergone extensive restoration and are now considerably more tourist ori-
ented. It's no longer just Kraków that foreign tourists consider worth visiting but also other cities, including Warsaw, Gdańsk, Poznań and Wrocław.

Joseph Conrad, the Polish-born novelist, referred to Poland as 'that
advanced outpost of western civilisation.' Having endured various oppressors, most recently 45 years of Communism, Poles have tremendous resilience and spirit. These characteristics were at the heart of the Solidarity
movement, which defeated the Communist regime and, in turn, led to the
liberation of the entire Eastern bloc. Poland has rapidly acclimatised to a
'Western' lifestyle, but Polish culture and national identity remain stronger
than ever.

Poland

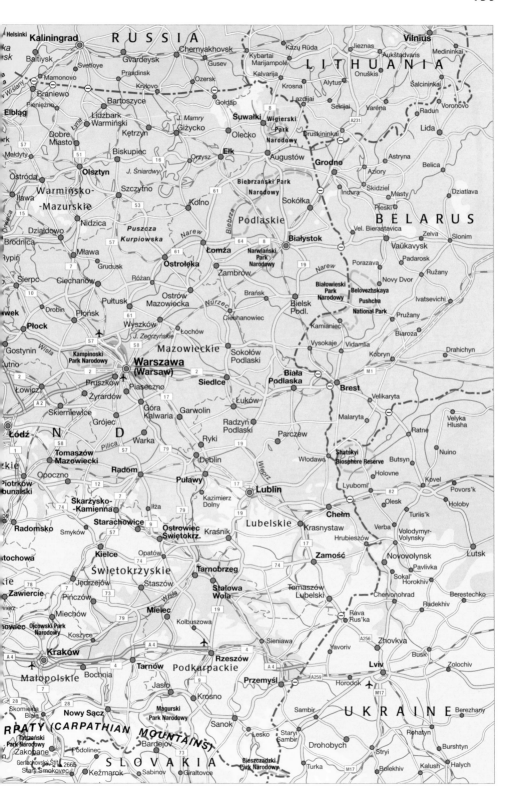

The distinctive oval roof of Plac Wilsona metro station.

WARSAW AND MAZOVIA

Warsaw's successful transformation into Central
Europe's financial hub will draw more visitors to
the city and to the surrounding region of Mazovia.

Royal Castle tower.

Warsaw encapsulates Poland's extraordinary history, with the city subjected to a continual cycle of invasion, destruction, rebuilding and resurrection. While much of the historic centre was reconstructed after the city was devastated by the Nazis, the ensuing regime also established monuments to Communism and modernism. This helps to account for the city's diversity of architecture and atmosphere, which can take you from aesthetic highs to bleak depths.

As Poland's most progressive city, Warsaw is a touchstone of modernity, yet also provides a direct link to the past. The city's rapidly developing infrastructure – with skyscrapers springing up in the centre, a second metro line and meticulously renovated main streets – means that visitors can now enjoy a classic Polish experience, whether it's shopping for specialities such as amber, crystal, pottery and leather goods, or dining on modern or classic Polish cuisine, while also having the pick of international restaurants, brand names and services.

Manufaktura shopping centre, Łódź.

The following chapter includes a comprehensive tour of Warsaw, spanning the city's historic, architectural and cultural extremes, which could be completed in a day, although several museums deserve leisurely visits.

Warsaw is also an ideal base for visiting the surrounding Mazovian region. The chapter entitled Through Mazovia (see page 167) includes suggestions for day trips, as well as more extended tours of the region's historic towns and villages. This includes Żelazowa Wola, the manor house in which Frederick Chopin was born, the enchanting Nieborów Palace and the deeply romantic landscaped park of Arkadia. Mazovia's low-lying, pastoral landscapes also lead on to the Białowieski National Park, a vast primeval forest extending to the border with Belarus, where European bison and other rare species still roam.

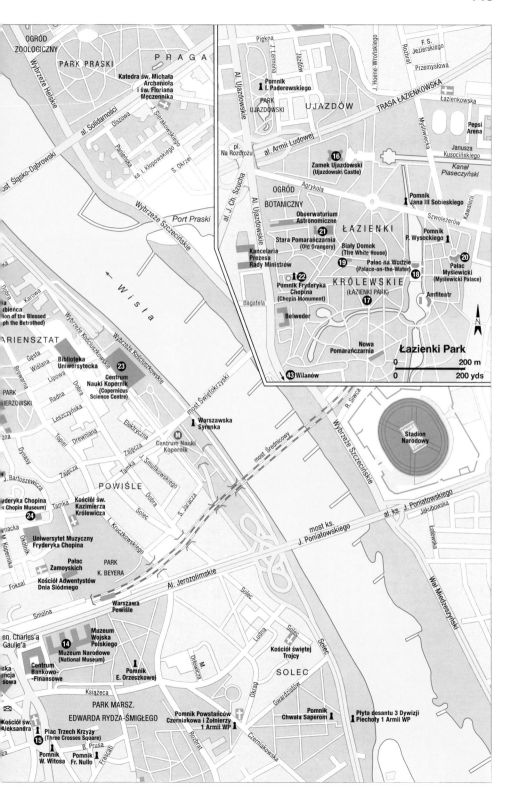

OGRÓD
ZOOLOGICZNY

PARK PRASKI

P R A G A

Katedra św. Michała
Archanioła
i św. Floriana
Męczennika

Wybrzeże Helskie

al. Solidarności

Olszowa

J. Sierakowskiego

Panieńska

ks. J. Kłopowskiego

S. Okrzei

Jmost Śląsko-Dąbrowski

Wybrzeże Szczecińskie

Port Praski

Piękna

J. Lennona

Jazdów

Jazdów

Al. Ujazdowskie

Pomnik
I. Paderewskiego

PARK
UJAZDOWSKI

U J A Z D Ó W

al. Armii Ludowej

J. Hoene-Wrońskiego

F.S.
Jezierskiego

Rozbrat

Przemysłowa

TRASA ŁAZIENKOWSKA

Łazienkowska

Myśliwiecka

Pepsi
Arena

pl.
Na Rozdrożu

al. J. Ch. Szucha

Al. Ujazdowskie

OGRÓD

BOTANICZNY

Zamek Ujazdowski
(Ujazdowski Castle)

Agrykola

Ł A Z I E N K I

Szwoleżerów

Kawalerii

Janusza
Kusocińskiego

Kanał
Piaseczyński

Pomnik
Jana III Sobieskiego

Obserwatorium
Astronomiczne

Stara Pomarańczarnia
(Old Orangery)

Kancelaria
Prezesa
Rady Ministrów

Biały Domek
(The White House)

Pałac na Wodzie
(Palace-on-the-Water)

Pomnik
P. Wysockiego

Pałac
Myślewicki
(Myślewicki Palace)

Bagatela

Pomnik Fryderyka
Chopina
(Chopin Monument)

K R Ó L E W S K I E

(ŁAZIENKI PARK)

Amfiteatr

Belweder

Nowa
Pomarańczarnia

Łazienki Park

N

0   200 m

0   200 yds

Wilanów

Wisła

Karowa

Dobra

labieńca
ion of the Blessed
oph the Betrothed)

ARIENSZTAT

Wybrzeże Kościuszkowskie

Wybrzeże Kościuszkowskie

Gęsta

Wiślana

Browarna

Ligowa

Dobra

Biblioteka
Uniwersytecka

Centrum
Nauki Kopernik
(Copernicus
Science Centre)

most Świętokrzyski

PARK
IIERZOWSKI

Radna

Leszczyńska

Elektryczna

Warszawska
Syrenka

R. Siwca

Wybrzeże Szczecińskie

Stadion
Narodowy

zna

Dynasy

Topiel

Drewniana

Zajęcza

Centrum Nauki
Kopernik

Zajęcza

Tamka

J. Smulikowskiego

most Średnicowy

J. Bartoszewicza

P O W I Ś L E

Dobra

ryderyka Chopina
(Chopin Museum)

Tamka

Kościół św.
Kazimierza
Królewicza

Solec

L. Kruczkowskiego

S. Jaracza

most ks.
J. Poniatowskiego

al. ks. J. Poniatowskiego

Jakubowska

Łotewska

nacka

Uniwersytet Muzyczny
Fryderyka Chopina

Okólnik

Pałac
Zamoyskich

PARK
K. BEYERA

Kościół Adwentystów
Dnia Siódmego

Al. Jerozolimskie

Solec

Wał Miedzeszyński

Foksal

Warszawa
Powiśle

Smolna

Muzeum
Wojska
Polskiego

en. Charles'a
Gaulle'a

Muzeum Narodowe
(National Museum)

Pomnik
E. Orzeszkowej

Ludna

Solec

M.
Orłowicza

Kościół świętej
Trójcy

Okrąg

Solec

S O L E C

Gwardzistów

ska
ncja
sowa

Centrum
Bankowo-
-Finansowe

Książęca

PARK MARSZ.

EDWARDA RYDZA-ŚMIGŁEGO

Kościół św.
Aleksandra

Plac Trzech Krzyży
(Three Crosses Square)

Pomnik
W. Witosa

Pomnik
Fr. Nullo

B. Prusa

Rozbrat

Frascati

Pomnik Powstańców
Czerniakowa i Żołnierzy
1 Armii WP

Czerniakowska

Pomnik
Chwała Saperom

Płyta desantu 3 Dywizji
Piechoty 1 Armii WP

The Palace of Culture and Science.

WARSAW

Warsaw's post-war reconstruction produced an eclectic mix of contrasting architectural styles, from the monolithic Palace of Culture and Science to the quaint streets of the Old Town.

arsaw (Warszawa) is a bustling city which has reinvented itself as a tourist attraction and Central Europe's financial hub. High-rise glass and steel buildings contrast with the luscious green of its numerous parks and squares, and a long and often bitter history has left a lasting imprint on its architecture.

Enormous changes since the 1989 democratic elections have turned Warsaw into a thoroughly European, metropolitan capital. Cafés are full of people enjoying a leisurely break of coffee and cakes, bars and restaurants are full of business people in power-suits brandishing mobile phones, and a growing number of shops stock everything from Cartier, Versace and exotic foodstuffs, to local specialities such as folk crafts. The city has a thriving nightlife scene with numerous bars and nightclubs, particularly in the centre and, in summer, along the riverside.

Warsaw lies in the heart of the Mazovia (Mazowsze) region in central Poland, on the banks of the River Vistula (Wisła). As the capital and commercial centre of Poland, with a population of around 1.8 million, Warsaw is also a major cultural hub. Various institutions such as the Academy of Science, the National Library, National Museum and National Philharmonic are based here, while the city also hosts international events such as

the International Chopin Competition and the International Book Fair. Nevertheless, anyone from Kraków will tell you that their city is, and always has been, Poland's cultural centre. Throughout Poland, Varsovians (people from Warsaw) are caricatured as being fast-talking, fast-driving, corporate climbers who consider themselves superior to the rest of the country. The fact is, however, that only 53 percent of the city's inhabitants were born in Warsaw. Each year thousands of Poles from all regions come in search of job

Main Attractions
Old Town & Royal Castle
Łazienki Park
Palace of Culture
Museum of the History of Polish Jews
The Fryderyk Chopin Museum
Warsaw Rising Museum
Copernicus Science Centre
Wilanów Park & Palace

Hanging in there.

Using one of the 25 tram routes in Warsaw is a great way to get about the city. Tram stops and routes are marked in red on city maps.

opportunities and a better life. The locals fondly call them *słoiki* (jars) because every weekend they return to their home towns and bring back plenty of food in jars.

Warsaw's history

While the exact origins of Warsaw have eluded historians, one legend states that an amalgamation of the names of two historic lovers, Wars and Sawa, who lived by the Vistula river, provided a name for the city. Another legend states that a mermaid swimming in the Vistula told Mazovian fishermen of an indestructible city that would be founded there. Warsaw has certainly fulfilled the mermaid's prophecy, with the city's history being a continual cycle of invasion, destruction, rebuilding and resurrection.

The Old Town evolved around the residence of the Mazovian dukes, established on the site of the present Royal Castle in 1281. The city's evolution continued on the basis of its key position on trade routes through Poland. Moreover, Mazovia was also growing in importance as the central

Old and new Warsaw.

point between the two capitals of the Polish-Lithuanian Commonwealth, Kraków and Vilnius.

Parliament first met in Warsaw in 1529, and from 1573 royal elections were held here (the king being elected rather than hereditary). However, the king continued to reside in Kraków, the capital of Poland since 1040, until King Zygmunt III Waza proclaimed Warsaw the capital city in 1596.

Between 1655 and 1660 the Swedish invasion, known as '*Potop*' ('The Deluge') devastated Poland, and seriously depleted Warsaw's buildings and population. Under King Jan III Sobieski, elected in 1674, the city enjoyed great prosperity, with numerous buildings, palaces and principal thoroughfares dating from this time, including the king's summer residence, Wilanów, on the outskirts of the city.

During the period of the Enlightenment, during the second half of the 18th century, commerce and culture evolved rapidly, which included the founding of the National Theatre and several periodicals, while the first constitution in Europe was ratified in Warsaw on 3 May 1791.

However, three successive partitions of Poland, beginning in 1772, saw the country progressively divided between Prussia, Austro-Hungary and Russia. Initially under Prussian rule, Napoleon established the city as the capital of the Grand Duchy of Warsaw. Following the Congress of Vienna in 1815, Warsaw was capital of the Congress Kingdom of Poland, ruled by the Tsar of Russia. Warsaw was also the centre of numerous insurrections during this time, with the uprisings of 1830 and 1863 the most significant.

One of the most tragic periods in the city's turbulent history was World War II, with more than 700,000 citizens killed during the German Occupation. After the Warsaw Uprising (see page 59), Hitler ordered that the Poles be punished, by razing Warsaw to the ground. The city was systematically destroyed and left virtually

uninhabited, with the total wartime damage resulting in almost 85 percent of the city being reduced to rubble. The **Warsaw Rising Museum** explains more about this terrible time. A massive post-war rebuilding programme recreated the Old Town and New Town districts, as well as numerous palaces, churches and important civic buildings. Ironically, the Communists demolished 19th-century mansion blocks and tenement buildings in the centre of Warsaw, which had survived the Nazi regime, and converted this area into a 'showpiece' of Socialist Realism architecture. The wartime legacy means that various poignant sites are marked throughout the city. There are numerous plaques set on walls and pavements, stating when and how many Poles were executed on each site by the Nazis, with candles and flowers still placed by many of these memorials. The Old Town and adjacent New Town took around 30 years to reconstruct – this was carried out so authentically that both were awarded Unesco World Heritage status. If you didn't know the history you'd never guess they were reproductions. Fortunately they are not a case of 'splendid isolation' either, as the surrounding areas are also historic and aesthetic.

Old Town Market Square

The centre of the Old Town is **Old Town Market Square ❶** (Rynek Starego Miasta). It's always bustling with people visiting the square's numerous cafés, bars and restaurants, while street-traders and artists ply their wares outside the galleries and shops. During the summer the square is covered with café tables, while horse-drawn carriages clip-clop from here to the Old Town (which is closed to traffic). Beautifully recreated burghers' houses, dating from the 15th and 16th centuries, line the square, each with individual architectural features. This includes a late Gothic portal at Number 21, while the house *Pod Bazyliszkiem* (Under the Basilisk) at Number 5 features the mythical Old Town monster, whose stare apparently brought instant death. *Pod Murzynkiem* (Under the Negro), featuring a Renaissance

Dining out in the Old Town.

portal, is one of three burghers' houses which were linked behind their façades to accommodate the **Warsaw Museum**  (Muzeum Warszawy; Rynek Starego Miasta 28–42; tel: 022-596 67 00; http://muzeumwarszawy.pl), which also has other branches in the city. It is currently closed for renovation and is due to reopen in mid-2017.

Also within a burgher's house is the **A. Mickiewicz Literature Museum** ❸ (Muzeum Literatury im A. Mickiewicza; Rynek Starego Miasta 20; tel: 022-831 40 61; muzeumliteratury.pl; Mon–Tue, Fri 10am–4pm, Wed–Thu 11am–6pm, Sun 11am–5pm; closed last Sun of the month). Dedicated to Adam Mickiewicz (1798–1855), Poland's greatest Romantic poet (see page 301), the museum also provides insights into the life and work of other Polish writers and temporary exhibitions of authors of other nationalities. Beyond this museum, in the square's northeast corner, are the **Stone Steps** (Kamienne Schodki), a picturesque thoroughfare leading from the Old Town to the Vistula.

Leaving the Old Town Square along Swiętojańska leads to **St John's**

Cathedral ❹ (Katedra Św Jana Chrzciciela; Swiętojańska 8; daily). Warsaw's oldest church, and the largest church in the Old Town, the cathedral was rebuilt after World War II in the original 14th-century style known as Vistulan Gothic, defined by an austere but spiritual simplicity. The crypt contains various Mazovian dukes and some of Poland's most renowned leaders and artists, including Nobel Prize-winning novelist Henryk Sienkiewicz (1846–1916), author of *Quo Vadis*, and the first president of independent Poland, Gabriel Narutowicz. A side altar contains the sarcophagus of Poland's former primate, Cardinal Stefan Wyszyński.

Warsaw's Royal Castle

Swiętojańska culminates at Castle Square (Plac Zamkowy), dominated by the **Royal Castle** ❺ (Zamek Królewski; Plac Zamkowy 4; www.zamek-krolewski.pl; May–Sept Mon–Sat 10am–6pm, Thu until 8pm, Sun 11am–6pm, Oct–Apr Tue–Sat 10am–4pm, Sun 11am–4pm; tel: 022-35 55 170; ticket office at Plac Zamkowy 4; free on Sun). A castle was first established here in the 13th century as the residence of the Mazovian dukes. From the end of the 16th century it became the royal residence, as well as the seat of the Sejm (Parliament). In 1791 the 3rd of May Constitution was drawn up here, the first of its kind in Europe. Between the two World Wars, the castle was the president's official residence. The Nazis' total destruction of the castle extended to drilling thousands of holes in the foundations for sticks of dynamite (a few holes can still be seen in parts of the crypt). The decision to reconstruct the castle was taken in 1971, funded by private subscriptions raised in Poland and from émigré Poles around the world. The Communists did not contribute, considering this to be too overt a symbol of Polish sovereignty. Opened to the public in 1984, the surviving architectural fragments, including Baroque, Gothic and

Waiting for a fare in the Old Town.

rococo styles, were incorporated into a recreation of the 17th-century façade.

The interiors are largely 18th-century, with most of the works of art and furniture either original to the castle (some items were sent to Canada prior to the outbreak of war) or donated by museums and collectors. All the rooms have individual characteristics. The pillared and gilded ballroom is in contrast to the mausoleum-like character of the Marble Room, or the Picture Gallery devoted to views of Warsaw painted by Bernardo Bellotto (known as the 'Polish Canaletto', he was the nephew of the renowned Venetian painter). In the former chapel is an urn containing the heart of the Polish hero Tadeusz Kościuszko (1746–1817). He led Polish troops against the Russians in a bid for freedom during the partitions, and was also a hero of the American War of Independence.

Adjoining the royal castle, but also offering a different experience is **Lubomirski Palace** (Pałac Pod Blacha; Plac Zamkowy 2; tel: 022-657 21 70; www.zamek-krolewski.pl; May–Sept Mon–Sat 10am–6pm, Sun 11am–6pm, Oct–Apr Tue–Sat 10am–4pm, Sun 11am–4pm; free on Sun). This Baroque palace has a collection of rugs and carpets, with rare examples from Persia and Turkey, and the world's largest collection of Caucasian rugs. The castle's gardens, by the old riverbed, contain the beautifully restored **Kubicki Arcades** (Arkady Kubickiego; May–Sept Mon–Sat 10am–6pm, Sun 11am–6pm, Oct–Apr Mon–Sat 10am–5pm, Sun 11am–5pm; free on Sun), built from 1818 to 1821. The arcades are used as an exhibition and cultural centre, but eventually will be the main entrance to the castle.

The Royal Route

Plac Zamkowy features Warsaw's oldest monument, **Zygmunt's Column** (Kolumna Zygmunta). Erected in 1644, it depicts the king bearing a sword and a large cross (reflecting his counter-reformatory stance). This square also marks the beginning of the so-called Royal Route (Trakt Królewski), a favourite stroll for Varsovians and a good way to see numerous

The Royal Castle and Zygmunt's Column.

historic sights with almost no visual interference from modern buildings. Extending along Krakowskie Przedmieście, the Royal Route continues along Nowy Świat and Aleje Ujazdowskie, past Łazienki Park and ends at Wilanów Palace. Walking all the way to Wilanów is unrealistic, but a leisurely stroll with café breaks en route should get you to Łazienki Park (see page 164).

The name Krakowskie Przedmieście (Kraków Suburb) originated shortly after Warsaw replaced Kraków as the capital, as this street eventually leads south to that city. It was on this thoroughfare, and adjacent streets, that magnificent churches were established, while numerous aristocrats constructed palatial residences. At Krakowskie Przedmieście 68 is **St Anna's Church** ❻ (Kościół Św Anny). The earliest sections are late 15th-century Gothic, though the church was refashioned several times. Its current neoclassical incarnation includes a façade modelled on Venice's Il Redentore, designed by the renowned 16th-century Italian architect Andrea Palladio.

The Adam Mickiewicz Monument.

Ornate interiors, predominantly cream and gilt, create a sense of restrained flamboyance. Continuing along Krakowskie Przedmieście, decorative railings delineate a small square with lawns and flowerbeds featuring the **Adam Mickiewicz Monument** ❼ (Pomnik Adama Mickiewicza). This monument dates from 1898, the centenary of the poet's birth. At Numbers 52–54 is the mid-17th-century **Church of the Assumption of the Blessed Virgin Mary and St Joseph Betrothed** ❽ (Kościół Wniebowzięcia NMP i Św Józefa Oblubieńca; open daily). A neoclassical façade belies the dazzling Baroque interiors, culminating in a beautiful altar. Another grand neoclassical building is **Presidential Palace** ❾ (Pałac Prezydencki; not open to the public), established as the residence of the Polish president in 1994. Formerly owned by various aristocratic families, it served as the residence of the Viceroy of the Kingdom of Poland, the Russian Tsar's official representative, during the partition of Poland. In 1955 the Warsaw Pact was signed at the palace (see page 66),

and in 1989 the historic round-table talks between the Communist government and the Solidarity trade union movement were held here.

The neighbouring **Hotel Bristol** at numbers 42–44, which reopened as the city's premier deluxe hotel in 1992, is classified as a national monument, being a superb example of Secessionist architecture and interiors. A coffee in the hotel's Viennese-style café is the least expensive way of enjoying its immense style. Opposite, at Krakowskie Przedmieście 13, is Warsaw's oldest hotel, formerly known as the Europejski Hotel. Dating from 1855, it features an impressive neo-Renaissance façade. The interior is currently being renovated and the hotel is scheduled to reopen in July 2015.

One of the few churches to survive the Nazis, the **Church of the Visitation Order** ❿ (Kościół Wizytek; open daily) has an elaborate façade. This artistry continues within, providing some of Warsaw's finest Baroque and rococo interiors. Adjacent to the church is the Nuns of the Visitation convent. At Krakowskie Przedmieście 26–28 is the entrance to **Warsaw University** ⓫ (Uniwersytet Warszawski). This aesthetic enclave provides a delightful diversion, animated by the bustle of students arriving for lectures and meeting friends. Several imposing buildings that serve as the university's lecture halls, set amid courtyards and greenery, have a distinguished provenance. The most commanding building is the Kazimierzowski Palace (Pałac Kazimierzowski), originally the summer residence of King Władysław IV Vaza and the royal family during the 17th century. The neoclassical Tyszkiewicz Palace, the Baroque Uruski Palace and other buildings were the residences of aristocratic families.

Opposite the university is the **Holy Cross Church** ⓬ (Kościół Św Krzyża). This imposing twin-towered Baroque church, completed in 1760, also managed to survive the Nazis. By the entrance is an impressive double stairway, with a poignant figure of Christ carrying the cross. In a side pillar of the main nave are urns containing the hearts of Frederick Chopin and the writer Władysław Reymont, who was awarded the Nobel Prize for literature in 1924.

Nowy Świat to Ujazdowskie Avenue

A monument to the astronomer Nicholas Copernicus (Mikołaj Kopernik), the work of Danish sculptor Bertel Thorvaldsen, stands in front of the early 19th-century neoclassical Staszic Palace, at the point where Krakowskie Przedmieście meets **Nowy Świat** ⓭ (New World Street). This has a totally different character, being much narrower and more uniform in style than Krakowskie Przedmieście. Rebuilt in its early 19th-century neoclassical style, both sides of the street feature attractive façades. As one of the city's smartest shopping venues, just as it was in the 1920s and 1930s, the street has designer boutiques, jewellers, art galleries, smart delicatessens, bakers and bookshops. All the street's cafés are eclipsed by

Warsaw University gate.

FACT

Ironically, Sunday can be a good day for 'church tourism'. The city is much quieter as many Varsovians head off for the weekend to their *działka* – small, usually wooden houses set in a small plot, within about an hour's drive from Warsaw.

Food fare on Nowy Świat.

Blikle Café at Number 33. This traditional rendezvous, with excellent patisseries, has an elegant pavement section screened by greenery, and *fin-de-siècle* Bohemian interiors. At Number 45 is an apartment in which novelist Joseph Conrad (born Józef Korzeniówski) spent his childhood, before leaving Warsaw for Marseille at the age of 17.

Nowy Świat leads to Charles de Gaulle Roundabout, with a surrealistic giant palm at its centre. Varsovians fell in love with Joanna Rajkowska's artistic provocation and opposed any plans to get rid of the artificial tree. A less famous monument, of the French president making a giant stride, stands at the corner of Nowy Świat and Aleje Jerozolimskie. The imposing building behind it is a former headquarters of the Polish Communist Party (so called **Party's House**, Dom Partii), now housing the trendy bar Cuda na Kiju, which offers great beers and excellent pizza. Not far from the roundabout, heading west on Aleje Jerozolimskie, is the poshest department store in Warsaw – **VITKAC** (www.vumag.pl), with nearly 40 luxury boutiques.

Also on Aleje Jerozolimskie, but east from the roundabout, is the **National Museum** ⓮ (Muzeum Narodowe; Aleje Jerozolimskie 3; tel: 022-621 10 31; www.mnw.art.pl; Tue–Sun 10am–6pm, Thu until 9pm). In a Modernist building dating from 1927 to 1938, it houses an amazing collection. The visitor-friendly layout makes it easy either to do a grand tour or to select your own highlights. The choice includes 12th- to 20th-century Polish paintings, with works by Jan Matejko (1838–93), Poland's greatest historical painter, as well as Jacek Malczewski, Józef Pankiewicz, Aleksander Gierymski, Wilhelm Sasnal and many others. The foreign art gallery, with paintings by French, Flemish and Dutch masters, is also worth seeing. Another highlight is the wonderful Faras Gallery, the only permanent exhibition in Europe of medieval Nubian art, including amazing early Christian frescos. The café on the museum's patio offers a welcome respite for tired visitors.

Back on Nowy Świat, you reach **Three Crosses Square** ⓯ (Plac Trzech Krzyży). On an island at the centre of

the square is the neoclassical St Alexander's Church (Kościół Św Aleksandra), dating from 1818. From here, turn into Mokotowska Street to get to the circular Saviour Square (Plac Zbawiciela), Warsaw's hipster hub, with plenty of cafés, bars and restaurants. A colourful rainbow at its centre has been burnt down several times by right-wing demonstrators offended by what they saw as a 'gay symbol'. Each time it has been reinstated.

Alternatively, take Ujazdowskie Avenue (Aleje Ujazdowskie), which marks another change of character. This avenue is considerably wider and busier than Nowy Świat, and showcases a different architectural genre, being lined with elegant *fin-de-siècle* Secessionist villas and mansion blocks. Many of these are embassies, diplomatic buildings or headquarters for foreign legations. Nearby at Numbers 2–6 Wiejska is the seat of the **Sejm** (Polish Parliament) and the Senate of the Republic.

The Centre for Contemporary Art Ujazdowski Castle (Centrum Sztuki Współczesnej Zamek Ujazdowski) is housed within **Ujazdowski Castle** ⑯ (Zamek Ujazdowski; Aleje Ujazdowskie 6; tel: 022-628 12 71; www.csw.art.pl; Tue–Sun noon–7pm, Fri until 9pm; free Thu). The site of the castle was the first residence of the 13th-century Mazovian dukes, and subsequently became the summer residence of the Vaza royal family during the 17th century. Burned down during World War II, the remains of the castle were demolished in 1954. After careful reconstruction it is totally credible in its 17th-century Baroque incarnation, with this 'modern-ancient' castle holding temporary modern art exhibitions. A terrace at the rear of the castle has extensive views over the Ujazdowski Park below and the castle has a post-modern style restaurant, Qchnia Artystyczna.

The **Botanic Garden** (Ogród Botaniczny; Aleje Ujazdowskie 4; tel: 022-553 05 11; www.garden.uw.edu.pl; Apr–Aug Mon–Fri 9am–8pm, Sat–Sun 10am–8pm, Sept daily 10am–6pm, Oct daily 10am–5pm; greenhouses open only on Sun 10am–5pm) was established in 1819 and has a comprehensive, layout including flower beds,

Holy Cross Church overlooks Nowy Świat.

medicinal herbs and water plants, set around a fountain and pool. The beautiful grounds are also the site of the neoclassical **Astronomical Observatory** (Obserwatorium Astronomiczne), dating from 1824, which is part of Warsaw University.

Łazienki Park and Palace

One of Europe's most beautiful palace-park complexes, **Łazienki Park** ⑰ (Łazienki Królewskie; entrances along Ujazdowskie, or Agrykola; tel: 022-506 00 28; www.lazienki-krolewskie.com; open daily until dusk; guided tours to the Palace-on-the-Water) extends to 200 acres (81 hectares). Originally used as royal hunting grounds, the park's numerous avenues, woodlands and formal gardens were laid out by Johann Christian Schuch, who created both French- and English-style gardens during the late 18th century. He was commissioned by Stanisław August Poniatowski, Poland's last king, who was a great patron of the arts during the Polish Enlightenment. The park opened to the public in 1818, and continues to be a favourite

A boat trip on the lake in Łazienki Park.

promenade for Varsovians, particularly on a Sunday afternoon, with cafés in the park doing a roaring trade. While obviously peaking in the summer, the park is popular throughout the year for the escapism it offers – here you can totally forget you are in the centre of a major city. Autumn is spectacular, with the densely wooded park assuming various hues.

Several palaces, pavilions and other buildings in the park were designed by the Italian architect Domenico Merlini, in conjunction with the king. This resulted in a combination of neoclassical and Baroque elements referred to as the 'Stanislaus style', which is exemplified by the **Palace-on-the-Water** ⑱ (Pałac na Wodzie). Romantically located in the centre of a lake, and approached by bridges, the palace was built in stages from 1784 to 1793, on the site of earlier bathing pavilions. The Bacchus room, decorated with Delft tiles, was part of the original bathhouse. The palace also features a ballroom, a portrait gallery with works by the court painter Marcello Bacciarelli, and the principal reception

room, Solomon's Hall. While these rooms were always intended to be showpieces, other rooms nevertheless provide a more personal insight into life at the palace. The king's bedroom, for instance, has a discreet little gallery from where he could keep an eye on proceedings in the ballroom below; in the dining room, the king held his celebrated 'Thursday dinners', a salon for writers, artists and intellectuals. The bedroom of the king's valet also gives another perspective.

The neighbouring **Theatre on the Isle** (Teatr na Wyspie), dating from 1790, was modelled on an ancient amphitheatre. The stage is a 'ruined temple', while a canal separates the auditorium, which can also be used as part of the stage. The park includes several other romantic neoclassical buildings within walking distance of each other: the Temple of Sibyl (Świątynia Sybilli), Water Tower (Wodozbiór) and Egyptian Temple (Świątynia Egipska). The compact Hermitage (Ermitaż) accommodated the king's fortune-teller, Madam Lhullier, who is said to have predicted his election to the throne.

The White House ⑲ (Biały Domek) does indeed have a white façade, and this small square villa was completed in 1774 as a residence for the king's sisters. Between 1801 and 1805 the exiled Louis XVIII of France lived here. The dining room bears exquisite murals in the 'grotesque' style (floral motifs in conjunction with human, animal and fantasy figures), while the drawing room and bedrooms are decorated with superior chinoiserie. **Myślewicki Palace ⑳** (Pałac Myślewicki; Mon 11am–6pm, Tue–Sun 9am–6pm) is early neoclassical with two semicircular wings and took its name from a former Myślewice village nearby. This was the residence of the king's nephew, Prince Józef Poniatowski. In addition to paintings and furniture, the palace includes elements of chinoiserie, while murals in the dining room depict views of Rome and Venice. The compact but fascinating museum creates a lasting impression; it has been so skilfully assembled that the aristocratic residence still feels as if it is occupied as it was in its heyday.

A sculpture gallery occupies one wing of the **Old Orangery ㉑** (Stara

Students painting by the lake in Łazienki Park.

FACT

If you are visiting Warsaw in summer, try to visit the Chopin Monument on a Sunday afternoon, when concerts are held. Despite a hint of kitsch, the combination of the statue, lake and surrounding park create an ideal setting for the romanticism of Chopin's music.

Pomarańczarnia), while another wing houses one of Europe's few remaining 18th-century court theatres. It is worth seeing for the extravagant Baroque interiors in what is otherwise an intimate setting. The New Orangery (Nowa Oranżeria) provides an atmospheric setting for the Belweder restaurant, one of Warsaw's finest. There are two dining rooms, one decorated in a neoclassical style, and one in the original glazed section of the orangery amid lush greenery. Nearby is the **Chopin Monument ㉒** (Pomnik Chopina), a reconstruction of the original 1926 work by Secessionist sculptor Wacław Szymanowski.

Around Powiśle

Powiśle, an area close to the riverbank, is currently one of the most sought-after addresses in Warsaw. The construction of the University of Warsaw Library (www.buw.uw.edu.pl), with its popular roof garden, and the Copernicus Science Centre has turned it into a thriving neighbourhood, full of young people chatting in the countless cafés and bars. The district also abounds with elegant housing developments, which offer breathtaking views over the river, and luxury car dealerships. The renovated riverbank, where several bars open in summer, adds to Powiśle's charm. The **Copernicus Science Centre ㉓** (Centrum Nauki Kopernik; Wybrzeże Kościuszkowskie 20; tel: 022-596 41 10; www.kopernik.org.pl; Tue–Fri 9am–6pm, Sat–Sun 10am–7pm) is probably the most popular of all Warsaw's museums at the moment. With a superb location on the riverbank, it offers six permanent exhibitions with amazing hands-on displays, multimedia presentations, logical puzzles and simulators. Visitors can even experience an earthquake! There are also labs, workshops and a top-notch planetarium with 3D films and laser shows. A roof garden offers splendid views over the river and towards the National Stadium.

Opened in 2010, the **Fryderyk Chopin Museum ㉔** (Muzeum Fryderyka Chopina; Okólnik 1; tel: 022-44 16 251/252; www.chopin.museum; Tue–Sun 11am–8pm) has interactive multimedia displays covering the history and works of the great Polish composer. The collection includes manuscripts, personal letters, photographs and even Chopin's calligraphy exercise book, which he used at school in Warsaw. The museum also runs educational workshops for children and organises trips to its branch in Żelazowa Wola (tel: 046-863 33 00; Tue–Sun Apr–Sept 9am–7pm, Oct–Mar 9am–5pm; Mon park only), where Chopin was born in 1810.

Around the Palace of Culture and Science

Returning to the central district known as Mid-town (Śródmieście), the predominant character is Socialist Realism and Modernism, exemplified by the **Palace of Culture and Science ㉕** (Pałac Kultury i Nauki; Plac Defilad 1; tel: 022-656 76 00; www.pkin.pl). Built on Warsaw's largest square, Plac Defilad, between

ON YOUR BIKE

Like many other European capitals, Warsaw has its own bicycle sharing system called Veturilo (the name comes from Esperanto). Bicycles can be hired at over 100 locations, most of them located in the city centre and in the vicinity of metro stations. A list of all hire points can be found online: http://en.veturilo.waw.pl/locations. The system operates from March to November. To hire a bicycle you will need to either register online (http://en.veturilo.waw.pl) or with a credit card at terminals located at every bicycle station. The first 20 minutes are free of charge.

Warsaw's cycling community is extremely active and puts a lot of effort into making cycling in the city safer and a more pleasant experience for all road users. Every last Friday of the month it organises a ride through the city. Called Masa Krytyczna (Critical Mass), it starts at 6pm on Zamkowy Square (in front of the Royal Castle), regardless of weather conditions. The number of cycling paths in Warsaw is also growing, with the longest and most popular one linking Młociny in the north with Powsin forest in the south. At the end of 2013 there were more than 350km (217 miles) of cycling paths and lanes in the capital. As the traffic jams get worse, the bicycle is rapidly becoming a favourite means of transport in Warsaw. It is also a perfect way of discovering the city.

952 and 1955, it was officially a gift' to the Poles from the Soviet Union. Needless to say, at that time the Palace of Culture was universally loathed – as both a symbol of Communist oppression and for its uncompromising architecture. Today this is no longer the case, as most people see it as one of the city's hallmarks. Moreover, the construction of several skyscrapers nearby – including one designed by world-famous architect Daniel Libeskind and dubbed 'The Sail' – has softened its impact.

Meanwhile, the statistics make interesting reading: 3,288 rooms on 30 floors and a total height of 235 metres (770ft). The palace plays an important scientific and cultural role, comprising scientific institutes, cinemas, theatres and a multi-purpose Congressional Hall (Sala Kongresowa) seating 3,200. The observation terrace on the 30th floor (daily 9am–6pm) offers a magnificent panorama of Warsaw and its suburbs. Maintaining such a colossus, however, has become such a financial burden that office space within the palace has been let to businesses.

Opposite the east side of the Palace of Culture is Marszałkowska, a principal thoroughfare on which numerous office buildings, fast-food outlets and department stores are located. Some of the surrounding streets only provide more of the same, with the **Central Railway Station** (Warszawa Centralna) an example of 1970s Modernist architecture. Nearby is **Złote Tarasy**, an elaborately designed shopping mall (ul Złota; www.zlotetarasy.pl; Mon–Sat 10am–10pm, Sun 10am–8pm) and the new **Museum of Modern Art** ❷❻ (Muzeum Sztuki Nowoczesnej w Warszawie; Pańska 3; tel: 022-596 40 10; www.artmuseum.pl; Tue–Sun noon–6pm; free), located temporarily in the former furniture shop Emilia. Across the street from the Central Railway Station at Aleje Jerozolimskie 51 is Warsaw's **Fotoplastikon** (Kaiserpanorama; tel: 022-629 60 78; www.foto plastikonwarszawski.pl; Tue–Sun 10am–6pm; free on Sun), showing 3D photographs of the city. The Fotoplastikon is more than 100 years old and one of the few of its kind still in operation in Europe.

Złote Tarasy, Warsaw's futuristic shopping mall.

Guard at the remembrance stone monument on Miła Street in the Warsaw Ghetto.

Warsaw's business centre.

In a former tram power station west of the Central Railway Station, the **Warsaw Rising Museum** ㉗ (Muzeum Powstania Warszawskiego; Grzybowska 79; tel: 022-539 79 05/06; www.1944.pl; Mon and Wed–Fri 8am–6pm, Thu until 8pm, Sat–Sun 10am–6pm) was the late president and former Warsaw mayor Lech Kaczyński's flagship project. The museum opened in 2004 on the eve of the 60th anniversary of the Warsaw Rising as a tribute 'to those who fought and died for independent Poland and its capital.' It depicts not only the 63-day military struggle but also the everyday life of civilians at the time. Among more than 30,000 exhibits is a full-size replica of a Liberator B-24J bomber, weapons and documents. Particularly moving are audio recordings of former Polish fighters talking about the Warsaw Rising. The 'sewer experience' (sewers were used for communication and escape during the uprising) is not for the faint-hearted.

The Warsaw Ghetto

Northwest of the Palace of Culture is the area of the former Warsaw Ghetto, which has obviously los some of its pre-war Jewish charac ter, though various monuments and important buildings between Stawk and Świętokrzyska convey the tragic plight of Warsaw's Jews. The suffer ings of the Jews in the ghetto and their courageous uprising are com memorated by the Memorial To The Struggle and Martyrdom of the Jew (**Trakt Pamięci Męczeństwa i Walk Żydów**) on Zamenhofa Street, in one of the most poignant areas of the city Nearby, at the intersection of Miła and Dubois streets, is the grass Anielewicz Mound (Bunkier Anielewicza). It was one of the last stands of the Jewish Combat Organisation (ŻOB) fighters Many of them, including ŻOB com mander Mordechaj Anielewicz, pre ferred suicide to surrender.

The emotive **Monument to the Heroes of the Ghetto** ㉘ (Pomnik Bohaterów Getta; Anielewicza 6) symbolises the Jews' bravery and even tual helplessness in the face of Nazi anti-Semitism; in 1970 the German Chancellor Willy Brandt knelt here as a gesture of reconciliation. Opposite

the monument is the **Museum of the History of Polish Jews** ㉙ (Muzeum Historii Żydów Polskich Polin; Anielewicza 6; tel: 022-471 03 00; www.polin.pl; daily 10am–6pm, Wed, Sat and Sun until 8pm; free on Thu), designed by Finnish architect Rainer Mahlamäki. The core exposition, developed by more than 120 international scholars and displayed in eight galleries, is a fascinating journey through 1,000 years of history. The heritage and culture of Polish Jews is presented through paintings, interactive installations, artefacts, hands-on exhibits, video projections, reconstructions and models. It is a story of coexistence and cooperation, but also of rivalry and conflicts. The museum aims to celebrate life not death, so the section dedicated to the Holocaust is comparatively small. The museum is also a vibrant cultural centre hosting concerts, workshops and film screenings, among other activities. It is worth having a look inside the museum shop, which has many interesting books on Jewish culture and history.

It's worth making a detour from here to the former **Pawiak Prison** ㉚ (Więzienie Pawiak; ul Dzielna 24–26; tel: 022-831 92 89; www.muzeum-niepodleglosci.pl; Wed–Fri 9.30am–5pm, Sat–Sun 10am–4pm), a place of detention, torture and execution from 1830, when it was built as a Tsarist Prison, until 1944, when the retreating Nazis blew it up. More than 100,000 people were processed here during the Nazi occupation. The recreations of the hellish conditions in which prisoners were forced to live are chilling.

Memorial stones mark the route to **Umschlagplatz Monument** ㉛ (Pomnik Umschlagplatz) in Stawki Street. It was here that Jews were assembled before being transported in cattle trucks to concentration camps.

Krasiński Gardens to the New Town

Continuing to another historic area, Krasiński Gardens (Ogród Krasińskich) provides a nice stretch of greenery leading to **Krasiński Square** ㉜ (Plac Krasińskich), where Krasiński

Menora sculpture on Willy Brandt Square.

SKINNY HOUSE

Squeezed in between a pre-war house and an apartment building, between Chłodna 22 and Żelazna 74, the two-storey Keret House (www.kerethouse.com) was designed by Polish architect Jakub Szczęsny for the Israeli writer and film-maker Etgar Keret, whose mother was born in Poland. Measuring a mere 152cm (5ft) at the widest point (and only 92cm/3ft at the narrowest), it is believed to be the narrowest house in the world.

The tiny house features one bedroom, a bathroom, a kitchen and a living area. Light filters through two small windows and translucent glass panels that make up the walls. As it doesn't meet Polish construction regulations, the house is officially called an art installation.

Palace (Pałac Krasińskich) houses the **National Library** (Biblioteka Narodowa). The elegant façade was designed by Dutch architect Tylman van Gameren in 1677. Opposite the palace are the contrastingly modern Law Courts (completed in 1999) and a **Monument to the Heroes of the Warsaw Rising**. Unveiled in 1989, this moving monument includes figures emerging from the sewers, which were a vital means of communication and escape during the uprising. Długa Street takes you towards the bustling, expansive metropolitan **Bank Square** ❸ (Plac Bankowy), with its multi-laned roaring traffic and multiple tram lines.

Plac Bankowy leads to **Saxon Gardens** ❸ (Ogród Saski), Warsaw's first public gardens, opened in 1727, where you immediately leave behind the roar of the traffic. Originally Baroque in design, the gardens were laid out in the style of an English garden in 1827, and include a neoclassical water tower, decorative statuary and a fountain. At the edge of the gardens, on Plac Piłsudkiego, is

Changing of the Guard at the Tomb of the Unknown Soldier.

the **Tomb of the Unknown Soldier** ❸ (Grób Nieznanego Żołnierza). Consecrated in 1925, it includes urns from battlefields in which Polish troops fought, as well as from the graves of Polish officers murdered by the Red Army in Katyń (see page 63). The tomb is under a small section of a colonnade, which is all that remains of the former Saxon Palace (Pałac Saski) destroyed by the Nazis. Every Sunday at noon a ceremonial changing of the guard takes place by the tomb.

A nearby sleek office building with a nice piazza at the centre is called Metropolitan. It was designed by Sir Norman Foster and boasts cutting-edge technologies. Across **Piłsudski Square** (Plac Piłsudskiego) stands the Hotel Sofitel Warsaw Victoria, built in 1974–1976 and renovated a few times since then. It used to be the most expensive and elegant hotel in Warsaw.

Ul Wierzbowa leads to **Theatre Square** ❸ (Plac Teatralny), which is dominated by the Grand Theatre (Teatr Wielki), also known as the

National Theatre (Teatr Narodowy). Dating from 1833, the monumental neoclassical façade was designed by the Italian architect Antonio Corazzi. With an auditorium of almost 2,000 seats, this is Poland's largest opera house. Opposite is the former Town Hall building, recreated in 1997–8 to its original splendour. The area around the theatre abounds with restaurants and cafés, perfect for a quick bite to eat or a more elegant dinner before a night at the opera.

Senatorska leads to the tranquil street **Miodowa** ❸, which features several palaces (mainly used as government buildings and so inaccessible to the public) and historic churches. From here Długa and Podwale streets lead to the **Barbican** ❸ (Barbakan) fortress, which dates from the 16th century as part of the Old Town's defensive wall, and is now a popular haunt of street artists and entertainers. Continuing along the elegant street **Freta** takes in the Baroque St Jacek's Church (Kościół Św Jacka), opposite which stands the Church of the Holy Spirit (Kościół Św Ducha), founded in 1688 to commemorate King Jan III Sobieski's victory over the Turks at Vienna.

The **Marie Skłodowska-Curie Museum** ❸ (Muzeum Marii Skłodowskiej-Curie) is set within her former home (Freta 16; tel: 022-831 80 92; muzeum. if.pw.edu.pl; June–Aug Tue–Sun 10am–7pm, Sept–May Tue–Sun 9am–4.30pm). Twice winning the Nobel Prize, Curie is best known for her experiments with radium, conducted with her husband Pierre Curie in Paris. The museum documents her life and work. Freta leads on to **New Town Market Square** ❹ (Rynek Nowego Miasta). Less formal than the Old Town Market Square (and not a perfect square shape either), it is also far less busy. Nevertheless, there are several cafés and restaurants from which to admire this beautifully re-created area, dominated by the domed **St Casimir's Church** ❹ (Kościół Św Kazimierza;

open daily), designed by Tylman van Gameren, one of the most prominent Baroque architects in Poland. Go down Rynek Starego Miasta Street and turn right into Kościelna to get to the **Multimedia Fountain Park** ❹ (Multimedialny Park Fontann; intersection of Boleść and Sanguszki streets; www. parkfontann.pl), which stages laser and music shows from May to September (Fri and Sat 9 or 9.30pm).

Greater Warsaw

Just to the south of Warsaw is King Jan III Sobieski's summer residence, **Wilanów** ❸ (Muzeum Pałac w Wilanowie; ul S. K. Potockiego 10/16; tel: 022-544 27 00; wilanow-palac.pl; palace: mid-Jan–late Apr and late Sept–mid-Dec Mon, Wed, Fri–Sun 9.30am–4pm, Thu 9.50am–4pm, late Apr–late Sept Mon 9.30am–8pm, Tue, Fri 9.30am–4pm, Wed, Sat–Sun 9.30am–6pm, Thu 9.50am–4pm. Park: open until dusk in spring/summer, till 4pm in autumn/winter). Wilanów is a popular day out for many Varsovians, even if it's only for a stroll through the park rather than a full museum visit.

DESTRUCTION OF A RACE

Before World War II the Jewish community accounted for around one-third of Warsaw's population – the largest Jewish community in the world. In November 1940 the Nazis began rounding up and confining Jews to the ghetto, a district of about 4 sq km (1.5 sq miles) – the largest of its kind in Nazi-occupied Europe. Ultimately around 500,000 Jews were enclosed within the ghetto, where they endured inhumane conditions, suffering inevitably from overcrowding, disease and starvation.

Even the Nazis realised that the situation was untenable. In 1942 they began transporting Jews to the death camps of Auschwitz and Treblinka (see page 62) until only 60,000 Jews remained.

An underground resistance movement led by the Jewish Combat Organisation (ŻOB) culminated in the desperate month-long uprising of April 1943, but the ŻOB did not have the manpower or arms to defeat the Nazis (see page 93). A few ŻOB commanders escaped through the network of sewer canals, but 7,000 fighters were shot and the rest were deported to the camps, leading Himmler to declare 'the Jewish quarter in Warsaw no longer exists.'

Today many Jews from around the world come to Warsaw in search of their roots.

Dating from 1679, the palace was built on the site of a country manor house, with the new royal residence named 'Villa Nova' (New Villa), which was 'translated' into Wilanów. The architect was Augustino Locci, who subsequently designed some of Poland's most renowned Baroque buildings. After the king's death (1696) the property changed hands, and in the following decades various extensions and annexes were added to accommodate galleries and towers, while pavilions were added in the grounds. Renovation work, following the Nazis' ruination of the palace, also uncovered 17th- and 18th-century paintings which had been concealed by plasterwork applied in the 19th century. The Nazis also plundered the most valuable works of art.

Nevertheless, the palace has one of the largest collections of portraits by Polish artists, spanning the 16th to 19th centuries. This includes a portrait by Jacques-Louis David of Stanisław Kostka Potocki, who acquired Wilanów in 1799. As a connoisseur of fine art, Potocki established one of the first public museums in Poland at Wilanów in 1805, exhibiting *objets d'art* from the time of King Jan III Sobieski, together with furniture, Chinese and Japanese art and ancient ceramics. A tour of the palace includes royal apartments from the 17th to the 19th centuries, decorated with period furniture and works of art.

Two sculpted horses stand at the entrance to the mid-19th-century Riding School, which now houses the **Poster Museum** (Muzeum Plakatu; www.postermuseum.pl; Tue–Sun 10am–4pm; free on Mon noon–4pm). Established in 1968, this was the first of its kind in the world, housing a collection that acts as a vivid record of Poland's post-war history. The Orangery (Oranżeria) exhibits Polish arts and crafts. On the east side of the palace is an Italian Baroque garden, comprising several parterres, while the English-style garden was laid out between 1799 and 1821 and includes a Chinese pavilion with a pagoda roof, dating from 1806. Also within the grounds are the Potocki family mausoleum, built in the early 19th century

The Barbican.

in a neo-Gothic style, and the late 19th-century neo-Baroque St Anne's Church (Kościół Św Anny).

In **Żoliborz**, one of Warsaw's more exclusive residential areas and political hotbeds, is the Modernist church dedicated to St Stanisław Kostka, on ul Hozjusza 2. By the church is the grave of Father Jerzy Popiełuszko, a priest who was a prominent supporter of Solidarity, murdered by members of the Communist security intelligence service (SB) in 1984. His grave has now become a national memorial. A Stations of the Cross route in the church grounds pinpoints landmarks in modern Polish history. Adjacent to the church there is a modern pilgrim's house with comfortable rooms and a restaurant. It is worth taking a stroll around Żoliborz Oficerski (Officers' Żoliborz), for instance on Śmiała Street, with its well-preserved Modernist pre-war villas inspired by 18th-century manor houses of the Polish aristocracy.

The right bank of the Wisła (Vistula) River includes the district of **Praga**, which became part of the city of Warsaw in 1916 and was relatively undamaged during the war. Although this district is also where most of the city's industrial and manufacturing plants are located, there is also plenty of *fin-de-siècle* architecture with characteristic alleys and small courtyards to see, as well as the Russian Orthodox Church of St Mary Magdalene (Cerkiew Św Marii Magdaleny), in al Solidarności, with its splendid interiors. A particularly local character thrives at Różycki Market (Bazar Różyckiego), where the **Museum of Praga** (Muzeum Pragi; ul Targowa 50/52; www.muzeumpragi.pl; Tue–Sun noon–8pm) opened in 2014. Although the exhibition itself is not yet ready, the historic buildings and restored Jewish murals are worth visiting. Praga has become a favourite place for Polish designers and artists, who take advantage of low rents and amazing post-industrial spaces.

A good example is the thriving Soho Factory (Mińska 25; tel: 022-323 19 00; www.sohofactory.pl), with its workshops, design shops and trendy restaurants (see page 372). The **Neon Museum** (Mińska 25, Building 55; tel: (0) 516 608 881; www.neonmuzeum. org; Wed–Sat noon–5pm, Sun noon–4pm) has more than 50 original neon signs from the Communist era, many of which were created by the best Polish architects and graphic designers.

The versatile **National Stadium**, constructed for the Euro 2012 football championships, is also one of Praga's attractions. As well as football matches, it also hosts conferences, exhibitions and, to the dismay of people living nearby, rock concerts. The 'Basket', as some Varsovians call the stadium, has even hosted a windsurfing competition! In winter there is an ice rink open to the public.

Also on the right bank of the river, across from the Old Town, is the Warsaw Zoo (tel: 022-619 40 41; www.zoo. waw.pl; daily 9am–3.30pm). Established in 1928, it has animals from around the world.

WARSAW CEMETERIES

Warsaw cemeteries are very special places, where the tragic history of the city is reflected in almost every gravestone and monument. The best day to visit any Polish cemetery is November 1st, when families come to lay flowers on the graves of their relatives. At night cemeteries are enshrouded in the smoke of burning candles. **Powązki Cemetery** (Stare Powązki; Powązkowska 1), founded in 1790, is the city's oldest. Many of its gravestones are works of art in their own right, and a number of celebrated writers, artists and scientists are buried here.

Within walking distance of Powązki, the **Military Cemetery** (Cmentarz Wojskowy; Powązkowska 43/45), is the final resting place for soldiers who lost their lives in the two world wars, as well as prime ministers, politicians and artists. This cemetery also contains the graves of elite soldiers from the Home Army (Armia Krajowa – AK) who lost their lives during the Nazi occupation and the 1944 Warsaw Rising, and a symbolic tomb containing earth from the graves of Polish officers murdered at Katyń in spring 1940. Nearby, at 49/51 Okopowa Street, is the **Okopowa Street Jewish Cemetery** (Cmentarz Żydowski), the second-largest Jewish cemetery in Poland, founded in 1806.

Dating from the late 1800s, **Bródno Cemetery** (Cmentarz Bródnowski; św Wincentego 83), on the right bank of the Vistula River, is one of the largest in Europe with over 1.2 million people buried here.

THE BEAUTY OF ŁAZIENKI PARK

The extensive woodland of Łazienki Park features several palaces, pavilions, orangeries and even an amphitheatre in the very heart of Warsaw.

Łazienki Park is a delightful haven, with avenues lined by chestnut trees and beautiful formal gardens leading to several palaces, pavilions, orangeries and other historic buildings. Visitors can enter the park free of charge until sunset every day.

Apart from the big attractions of the palaces and the Theatre on the Isle, contemporary art exhibitions are held in the Old Guardhouse, on the edge of the lake to the north. Another highlight is the Ignacy Jan Paderewski and Polish Expatriates in America Museum, housed in the Great Outbuilding next to the Old Guardhouse. It was opened in 1992 to celebrate the life of the great Polish pianist and composer and the return of his body to Warsaw from America. It contains personal memorabilia of the exiled composer, along with exhibits relating to Polish emigration to America.

The park also features a circular neoclassical water tower which was used to supply water to the palace, an Egyptian temple, another small pavilion called the Hermitage and the early 19th-century Astronomical Observatory. The Belweder Palace, an official residence made available to visiting foreign dignitaries, is also within the grounds. The 18th-century building was redesigned for the governor of Warsaw in the 1820s and has not been used to house the Polish head of state since 1995, when the official residence was moved to the Namiestnikowski Palace by Lech Wałęsa. (For more information on Łazienki Park see page 154.)

The southern elevation of the palace was a bathing pavilion before being turned into a summer residence for the last Polish king.

Peacock strutting his feathers near the lake.

Water features in the park include lakes, fountains set amid formal gardens, canals and water's-edge paths.

The northern elevation of the Palace-on-the-Water, as seen from the bridge featuring a monument of King Jan III Sobieski.

RELAXING IN THE PARK

Łazienki Park is a favourite place to relax and unwind for the people of Warsaw, and while visitor numbers obviously peak in the summer months, the park is popular all year round for its sheer beauty and the escapism it offers. In August through September park alleys are decorated with Chinese lanterns to celebrate the festival of the light. Clusters of artists sell views of the park or offer their services as portrait painters, while buskers provide a musical background as you leave the city far behind. Many visitors choose to sit at one of the two cafés in the park and watch the world go by. One café occupies a neoclassical pavilion neighbouring the Palace-on-the-Water, while another is within the Theatre on the Isle. If you're looking for a more formal atmosphere, the botanical garden of the New Orangery provides a highly atmospheric setting for the Belvedere Restaurant. Specialities of the house include roast fillet of beef with fois gras and truffles and hazelnut grouse.

The park's lake provides the perfect setting for summer Chopin concerts, held on Sunday at noon and 4pm by the Chopin statue.

he Belweder Palace is an elegant example of early th-century neoclassical architecture.

rt Nouveau sculpture of Chopin contemplating the beauty nature.

THROUGH MAZOVIA

Day trips from Warsaw to the region of
Mazovia can be made by public transport.
Places to visit include dense forests,
historical towns and Chopin's birthplace.

The region that surrounds **Warsaw** ❶ is known as **Mazovia** (Mazowsze). From the early Middle Ages to 1526 it was ruled by an independent branch of the Piast Dynasty, yet because of its geographical situation between the two capitals of the Polish-Lithuanian crown, Kraków and Vilnius, the region's bridging function made it inevitable that eventually the town in the middle, Warsaw, would be elevated to the capital of Poland. After the Third Partition, Mazovia was shared between Prussia and Austria, but in 1815 the Congress of Vienna set up the Congress Kingdom of Poland; effective power over the region passed to the Russian tsar. Mazovia became part of independent Poland in 1918. The landscape of Mazovia was formed by Ice-Age moraines. Its broad river valleys, sandy plains and rolling hills are particularly beautiful. Visitors will discover fascinating national parks, national costumes and folk art in the Łowicz and Kurpie regions, two mosques and a stud farm for Arab horses. Mazovia is one of Poland's poorer regions.

On the outskirts of Warsaw

Immediately adjacent to Warsaw is **Kampinoski National Park** ❷ (Kampinoski Park Narodowy; see page 123) which, with an area of 38,544 hectares (95,244 acres), is the second-largest

national park in Poland. Moors, dunes – some 20 metres (65ft) high – and large areas of broadleaf and conifer woodland between the Vistula and Bzura rivers are accessible via signposted footpaths. Rare black birches grow in the wetlands, while elks, boars, beavers and lynx have been reintroduced.

During World War II many Poles, including politicians, artists and scientists, were secretly brought to this wooded region and executed by Nazi firing squads. The most notorious location of such executions is

Main Attractions
Płock Museum of Mazovia
Puszcza Białowieska
Biebrza National Park
Nieborów and Arkadia
Łódź

Bison in the Białowieża National Park.

Palmiry in the Puszcza Kampinowska (Muzeum Miejsce Pamięci Palmiry; tel: 022-720 81 14; www.palmiry. muzeumwarszawy.pl; May–Oct Tue–Sun 10am–6pm, Nov–Apr till 4pm; free) at the northern edge of the park. After the war a proper cemetery was constructed, which contains the graves of 2,500 victims.

Not far from Palmiry, where the Bug and Narew rivers flow into the Vistula, stands the gigantic **Modlin Fortress** (Twierdza Modlin; tel: 0 696-081 633/0 604-607 092; www.twierdza modlin.pl; daily 24hrs; free), made of earth bricks and constructed in 1806 under the orders of Napoleon. Later it was reinforced and extended by Russian troops; the barracks alone have a perimeter of 2,800 metres

(8,650ft) and it is the longest building in Europe. It accommodated the entire garrison of the fortress, with 26,000 men, and it remains in the hands of the military. East of Modlin is the Zegrzyński Reservoir (Jezioro Zegrzyńskie), created in 1964 by high water and the water pressure of the Narew. It's a popular place of relaxation for Varsovians, especially for those who enjoy water sports.

North of Warsaw

Further down the Narew is **Pułtusk** ❸, an old town situated on an island. This town has twice achieved world fame: in 1806 a battle was fought here between the Napoleonic and Russian armies, and in 1868 the enormous Pułtusk meteorite landed nearby. The

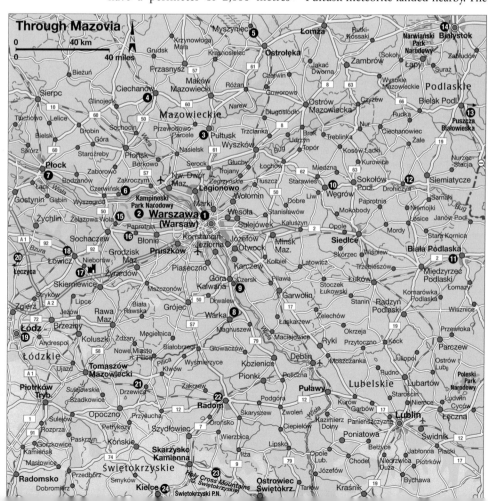

marketplace is the longest in Poland – a cobbled square dominated by a Gothic town hall, now home to a regional museum (Muzeum Regionalne w Pułtusku; Rynek 1; tel: 023-692 51 32; Tue–Sun 10am–4pm). The tower affords a fine view of the surrounding area that extends as far as the Collegiate Church. This dates from 1443, with a splendid Renaissance nave added in 1554. Pułtusk has a number of other attractive old churches that are worth visiting, as well as parts of its original town wall. Pułtusk is also an academic centre, seat of the higher school of humanities (Wyższa Szkoła Humanistyczna).

The road that leads northwest out of Pułtusk passes next through **Gołymin-Ośrodek**, which is also famous for its Gothic church. A further 40km (25 miles) from Pułtusk is **Ciechanów** ❹. Old Gothic buildings testify to the town's long history; the impressively large castle and two churches are striking examples of Mazovian brick Gothic architecture. The **Museum of the Mazovian Nobility** (Muzeum Szlachty Mazowieckiej; ul Warszawska 61a; tel: 023-672 53 46; http://muzeum-ciechanow.pl; Tue–Sun May–Sept 10am–6pm, Oct–Nov 10am–4pm) includes military exhibits as well as decorative arts. The renovated castle of the Mazovian Dukes (Zamek Książąt Mazowieckich; http://zamek-wciechanowie.pl; Tue–Sun May–Sept 10am–6pm, Oct–Nov 10am–4pm) is also worth a visit. The countryside north of Ciechanów was the scene of a massive battle in September 1939, when the Germans attempted to march straight through to Warsaw. The many military cemeteries in this area serve as a reminder of the conflict. Close to Ciechanów is the little village of **Opinogóra**. In the crypt of the church is the tomb of one of the greatest Polish romantic poets, Zygmunt Krasiński. The town's neo-Gothic castle houses the **Museum of Romanticism** (Muzeum Romantyzmu; ul Krasińskiego 9; tel: 023-671

70 25; www.muzeumromantyzmu.pl; daily May–Sept 10.15am–5.45pm, Oct–Apr 8.15am–3.45pm), and in the splendid park there is a monument to the poet.

Further to the east is an expanse of wooded countryside known as **Kurpie**. The wooden houses here are some of the most beautiful in all Poland. The best place to stay and admire them is Nowogród, where the River Pisa flows into the Narew. The town has an attractive open-air museum.

Between Nowogród and Myszyniec lies the village of Łyse, where people congregate each Palm Sunday to see a prize presented for the most beautiful Easter Palm. The palms are kept for a long time in the wooden church, the work of carpenters from Kurpie, with an impressive interior decorated by local artists. From Łyse the road continues to the "capital" of Kurpie, **Myszyniec** ❺. Every year on the Thursday after Trinity Sunday the Corpus Christi procession sets out from the square in front of the neo-Gothic church. A similarly colourful procession can also be seen in nearby **Kadzidło**. This is the place to watch

The Narew haff (lagoon).

Płock Cathedral has copies of the Płock bronze doors made for the town in the 12th century in Magdeburg.

Vernacular architecture in Podlasie.

women skilfully cutting traditional silhouettes from coloured paper. In the town's church there is an exhibition devoted solely to this form of folk art.

Continuing eastwards, **Łomża** on the River Narew, has an interesting permanent exhibition of amber, which was once mined in Kurpie. Also in Łomża, surrounded by one of the oldest cemeteries in Mazovia (18th century), is an attractive Gothic cathedral with a beautiful interior. The local Jewish cemetery is from the 19th century.

On the banks of the Vistula

The lower reaches of the Vistula northwest of Warsaw are lined by many interesting towns with long histories. In **Czerwińsk** ❻ a church displaying both Romanesque and Gothic features towers above the river valley. Romanesque frescos in the east chapel are among the art treasures within. In the adjoining monastery an ethnographical museum houses many exhibits which were brought back by monks returning from missionary work abroad (www.czerwinsk. salezjanie.pl/muzea; open daily). The late

Gothic bell-tower contains some of the oldest bells in the country. During the summer it is possible to climb the bell-tower for a magnificent view of the town, with its dilapidated wooden houses and its surroundings.

Further down in a pretty setting by the Vistula lies **Płock** ❼, the 'capital' of northern Mazovia. The ruins of a castle, churches from all periods and styles and the oldest grammar school in Poland (founded in 1180) are the dominant features of this historic town. In the crypt of the impressive Romanesque cathedral are the tombs of two dukes of Poland, Władysław Herman (1040–1102) and Bolesław Krzywousty (1086–1138). The **Museum of Mazovia** (Muzeum Mazowieckie; ul Tumska 2; tel: 024-364 70 71; www.muzeumplock.art.pl; Tue–Sun 10am–5pm, mid-Oct–Apr until 4pm) is well worth a visit. It houses one of the best Secession collections in Poland, including paintings and ceramics from the Młoda Polska movement. In the adjacent town house is a new interactive permanent exhibition presenting 1,000

years of Płock's history. Another branch, in a former synagogue at Kwiatowa, is dedicated to the history and culture of the local Jewish community (www.muzeumplock.art.pl; Tue–Sun 10am–5pm, mid-Oct–Apr until 4pm). North of Płock, near Sierpc, is an open-air museum (Skansen Wsi Mazowieckiej w Sierpcu; tel: 024-275 28 83; http://mwmskansen.pl; July–Aug daily 10am–6pm, Apr, June, Sept Tue–Fri 9am–5pm, Sat–Sun 10am–6pm, Oct Tue–Fri 8am–4pm, Sat–Sun 9am–5pm, Nov–Mar Tue–Sun 9am–3pm), with examples of the traditional architecture of northern Mazovia.

South of Warsaw, on the right bank of the Vistula, lies Maciejowice where in 1794 Kościuszko led his troops into battle against Russia: their defeat was to seal the fate of the Polish state.

Warka ❽, on the opposite bank, is best known as the birthplace of General Kazimierz Pułaski, the freedom hero of Poland and the USA, and the town contains both a museum (tel: 048-667 22 67; www.muzeumpulaski.pl; Tue–Fri 10am–5pm, Sat–Sun until 6pm) and two monuments named after him. Continuing in the direction of Warsaw, you will come to **Góra Kalwaria**, which was modelled on the city of Jerusalem and is the destination of many Catholic pilgrims. Later in its history it also became a centre for Orthodox Jews. The area has 400km (250 miles) of wonderful cycle paths (www.krainajeziorki.pl). The most popular is Chojnowski Cycling Path (Warsaw Kabaty-Piaseczno-Góra Kalwaria) and Vistula River Cycling Path (Warszawa–Konstancin–Czersk).

Czersk ❾, with a medieval castle commanding a fine view over the banks of the Vistula, lies about 3km (2 miles) from Góra Kalwaria. During the 14th and 15th centuries the town was home to the dukes of Mazovia. It lost much of its prominence due to the rise of Warsaw's importance and the reflowing of the Vistula, cutting it off from commercial trade. The Gothic castle (tel: 022-727 35 22; www.zamekczersk.pl; daily 8am–3pm, May–Aug until 8pm, Sept until 7pm, Apr until 6pm, Mar, Oct until 5pm) is still worth a visit, including its exhibition of regional art. There are nice views

Czersk Castle.

from its three towers and sometimes there are knights' tournaments. If you have a sleeping bag you can sleep over in one of the towers.

The Podlasie lowlands

The open countryside of the region known as **Podlasie** begins east of Warsaw and extends right to the eastern border of Poland. In the early Middle Ages this area was first settled by Ruthenians, then Lithuanians and Poles; even today there are places that contain both a Russian Orthodox and a Catholic church. Until 1939 every town in this region also had a synagogue, and in addition there were many Protestant churches and even two mosques in the area. Podlasie was always a melting pot for many different cultures and peoples, a region where the Latin traditions of Western Europe met the Byzantine culture of Eastern Europe.

The town of **Węgrów** ❿ is now within Mazowieckie voivodeship (it was formerly in Siedleckie) and is typical of the Podlasie region. Next to the market square is a Gothic parish church, which was rebuilt in Baroque style and decorated with frescos by Michelangelo Palloni in the early 18th century. In the sacristy hangs the famous 'Magic Mirror' dating from the 17th century. The Church of the Reformation was built by the Polish architect of Dutch origin, Tylman van Gameren. It also has frescos by Palloni and the splendid tomb of Jan Krasiński, which dates from 1703. Among those buried in the Protestant cemetery are Scottish weavers who settled in this area. The Jewish settlement has long since vanished. The village of **Liw**, west of Węgrów and within the borders of Mazovia proper, is dominated by a massive castle (tel: 025-792 57 17; www.liw-zamek.pl; Tue–Sat 10am–4pm, Sun 11am–4pm, May–Sept Sat and Sun until 6pm). It was built in the 15th century and after being destroyed twice by the Swedes was only partially reconstructed. A later building dating from the Baroque era houses a museum of weaponry. Every year the museum organises the Knight Contest of the Ring of Princess Anna and an Archaeological Feast, with shows and workshops in archery and crafts such as pottery and weaving.

Siedlce, the administrative centre of the *powiat* (district), is predominantly an 18th-century town. The figure of Atlas crowns the Ratusz (Town Hall). The former prison (1841–44) is now a regional museum (ul Piłsudskiego 1; tel: 025-632 74 70; www.muzeumsiedlce. art.pl; Sun–Fri 10am–4pm, until 6pm Tue and Fri Apr–Sept), and the town has many monuments to the persecution of the community's Jews during World War II and the advance of the Soviet army in 1944. The highlight of a visit is the Diocesan Museum (Muzeum Diecezjalne; ul Biskupa I. Świrskiego 56; tel: 025-644 98 65/0 602-514 789; http://elgreco.siedlce.pl) because it has on display the painting Ecstasy of St Francisco by El Greco.

Biała Podlaska ⓫, now within Lubelskie voivodeship, is a town which, like Siedlce, is on the railway

Poland's stud farms are world famous.

line between Warsaw and Moscow. It was founded in the 15th century and for a long time belonged to the Radziwiłłs, one of the richest families in Poland. Radziwiłł Castle only partially survived the upheavals of Polish history. A pavilion with towers and a chapel, surrounded by a parapet, are all that remains. The castle's newly refurbished museum, the Museum of South Podlasie (Muzeum Południowego Podlasia; tel: 083-341 67 57; http://muzeumbiala.pl; closed Mon), however, illustrates just how impressive the original structure once was and has a large collection of icons.

The churches of Biała Podlaska date from the 16th and 17th centuries, although the Greek Orthodox church was consecrated only in 1989. The monument to Józef Ignacy Kraszewski (1812–87) recalls that this was where the famous Polish writer went to school. The museum (tel: 083-379 30 14; www.muzeumkraszewskiego.pl; Tue–Sun 10am–4pm, park till dusk) dedicated to his memory is located in **Romanów**, the picturesque village, in which Kraszewski spent his childhood, approximately 50km (30 miles) southeast of Biała Podlaska.

In the east

A few kilometres east of Romanów run the tranquil waters of the River Bug, which forms the border between Poland, Byelarus and the Ukraine. An EU-sponsored project to revitalise the riverbanks and the nearest towns, called 'Bug is a paradise', is on-going, with the aim of making them more attractive to tourists (www.bugrajem.eu). **Jabłeczna** is the centre of the Greek Orthodox faith in Poland. The most important buildings in the town are the Church of St Onufry (built in 1840) and the only Greek Orthodox monastery and seminary for priests in Poland (www.klasztor-jableczna.pl). Each June a country fair is held here. Still further upriver is Kodeń, destination of many pilgrimages because of the miraculous picture, the *Virgin of Kodeń*, in the town's church. Kodeń has a special significance for the Catholics of Podlasie and Byelarus, similar to that of Częstochowa for the rest of Poland (see page 252). On the site of the former castle is a Gothic

TIP

Janów Podlaski, 20km (12 miles) from Biała Podlaska, is famous as an equestrian centre and home to a stud farm that produces world-class Arab horses.

The calm waters of the River Bug.

FACT

Białystok is also notable as the birthplace of Ludwik Zamenhof (1859–1917), the creator of Esperanto, the 'international language' made up of common words from several European tongues. Although it never truly caught on, there are an estimated 100,000 speakers in the world today.

Białystok's Market Square.

church that was once Greek Orthodox; it contains a wooden sculpture depicting the martyrdom of the Polish people and the Stations of the Cross. The most interesting town on the Bug, however, is **Drohiczyn** ⓬. It was the scene of a coronation when Prince Daniel Halicki (1201–64) crowned himself King of the Ukraine. The barrows in the area surrounding the town date from the 7th to the 9th centuries and the settlement itself, with a history that goes back to the 7th century, was once the customs post between the Congress Kingdom of Poland and the Ukraine.

Archaeological excavations uncovered thousands of lead seals from all over Europe, some of which are now on display in the town's museum (which also contains a museum of kayaking). A dominant feature of the town is the castle hill, which towers over the river. Also of interest are the Orthodox church and the three Baroque churches, which were badly damaged in World War I.

Northwest of Drohiczyn is the little town of Ciechanowiec, with a fascinating Museum of Agriculture (Muzeum Rolnictwa im Ks Krzytofa Kluka; tel: 086-277 13 28; www.muzeumrolnictwa. pl; Mon–Fri 8am–6pm, Sat–Sun 9am–7pm, Oct–Apr till 4pm). The museum has an open-air section (*skansen*) with a range of wooden buildings from Podlasie. On the other side of the Bug, near Małkinia Górna, is **Treblinka** (tel: 025-781 16 58; www.treblinka-muzeum.eu; daily 8am–7.30pm). In the work camp Treblinka I (1941–44) and the extermination camp Treblinka II (1942–43) nearly 800,000 people were murdered by the Nazis (see page 63).

The **Puszcza Białowieska** ⓭, a vast forest that has been left untouched since the Middle Ages and the largest of its kind in Europe, runs along the eastern border of Poland. Once the hunting ground of Lithuanian princes, Polish kings and Russian tsars, this national park is now a world reserve under the special protection of UNESCO. Around 1,000 bison roam free, and other species of animals and plants threatened with extinction are also protected. Wild horses (tarpans), bears, wolves, beavers, lynx and rare species of bird, such as the black-headed eagle, live in the wild.

In the village of **Białowieża** the former palace (www.palaccarski.com) has been converted into a hotel, next to which is an informative natural history museum with exhibits relating to species found in the forest (tel: 085-681 22 75; www.muzeum.bpn.com.pl; mid-Apr–mid-Oct Mon–Fri 9am–4.30pm, Sat–Sun 9am–5pm, mid-Oct–mid-Apr Tue–Sun 9am–4pm). There is also a small open-air museum dedicated to the local wooden architecture (tel: 085-683 36 28; open only in summer and public holidays). On the way to **Hajnówka** there is a reserve for bison and wild horses. In the town itself, on the western edge of the park, stands an imposing Greek Orthodox church, the combined work of artists from Poland, Greece and Bulgaria. The largest town in northeast Poland is **Białystok** ⓮, the administrative capital of the Podlaskie voivodeship (Województwo)

of the same name. In the 18th century the town was dominated by the Branicki aristocratic family, and their massive Baroque palace is a particularly interesting piece of architecture, also called the Versailles of Podlasie. Today it houses the Medical Academy. The adjacent arsenal, built in 1755, is used for exhibitions. Extensive gardens in French and English style surround the palace. In the Town Hall is the Podlaskie and **Białystok** Museum (Muzeum Podlaskie w Biełymstoku; Rynek Kościuszki 10; tel: 085-742 14 73; www.muzeum.bialystok.pl; May–Aug Tue–Sun 10am–5pm, Fri till 8pm, Sept–Apr Tue–Sun 10am–5pm), with an exhibition of 18th- to 20th-century Polish art. The Orthodox cathedral of St Nicolas dates from the 19th century when Białystok was under Russian rule: the 1920s modernistic Church of St Roch provides an interesting contrast. The former summer palace of the Branickis in Choroszcz (Muzeum Wnętrz Pałacowych w Choroszczy; Pl Brodowicza 1; tel: 085-719 12 33; www. muzeum.bialystok.pl; May–Aug Tue–Sun 10am–5pm, Fri till 8pm, Sept–Apr

Tue–Sun 10am–5pm), 12km (7 miles) away, is worth a detour for anyone with a keen interest in interior design. There are other branches of the Podlaskie Museum worth seeing: the Museum of Icons in Supraśl (ul Klasztorna 1; May–Aug Tue–Sun 10am–5pm, Fri until 8pm, Sept–Apr Tue–Sun 10am–5pm), the Museum in Tykocin (ul Kozia 2; Tue–Sun 10am–6pm, Oct–Apr until 5pm), presenting the interiors of a synagogue and Jewish houses, and an open-air museum (Białostockie Muzeum Wsi; www.bialostockiemuzeum wsi.pl; daily until dusk; free on Mon, but you can't enter the houses).

Some 42km (26 miles) northeast of Białystok is Sokółka. It was in this region that Jan III Sobieski allowed Tatar prisoners-of-war to settle, and a whole section of the local museum is given over to the arrival of this ethnic Muslim group. The villages of **Bohoniki** and **Kruszyniany** each have a mosque (the 18th-century mosque in Kruszyniany is the oldest in Poland) and there is an active Tatar community here. Many of the characteristics of Polish woodcarving can be seen in the

Deer in Biebrza National Park.

Early spring in Biebrza National Park.

architecture of these wooden Islamic buildings, which date from the 18th and 19th centuries. The *mizars*, as the Islamic cemeteries are known, are also of interest, with gravestones inscribed in both Polish and Arabic.

Nearby, on the banks of the Biebrza River, the **Biebrza National Park** (Biebrzański Park Narodowy, see page 121) is the largest marshy area in Poland, and almost certainly one of the largest unspoilt river landscapes in Europe to be preserved in its original state. Beavers, wolves and thousands of waterfowl, including sea eagles, sandpipers and herons, enjoy this protected environment of some 592 sq km (228 sq miles). The Biebrza is ideal for water sports, and safaris are organised on the river and in the surrounding area with guides who are expert in Biebrzanski's natural history.

Between Warsaw and Łódź

There are two possible routes that can be taken west from Warsaw. The northern route runs along the edge of the Puszcza Kampinowska and passes through the village of **Kampinos**.

Here the little wooden church dating from the 18th century is a good example of how the craftsmen in the villages made use of the simple building materials available to them to imitate the Baroque stone churches in the towns. If you wish to explore the Kampinoski National Park, horse-drawn carts and sleighs can be hired in the village.

Further along this route is Żelazowa Wola ⓱, the birthplace of Frédéric Chopin in 1810 (see page 186). In his childhood home is a museum documenting his life and work (tel: 046-863 33 00; http://chopin.museum/pl; Tue–Sun Apr–Sept 9am–7pm, Oct–Mar 9am–5pm; Mon park only). The house has been restored and the music room has manuscripts of early works and a cast of Chopin's left hand on display. In the summer piano recitals by internationally renowned performers are held almost every day in the park. In **Brochów**, where Chopin's parents were married, Chopin's baptismal certificate is kept in the late medieval fortified church.

The second route along the E30 from Warsaw to the west runs south

Corpus Christi procession in Łowicz.

through **Paprotnia** , which has a classic inn and a smithy, both at least 200 years old. Napoleon is said to have once feasted in the restaurant, hence the name Kuźnia Napoleońska. The Franciscan Niepokalanów Monastery (www.niepokalanow.pl) was built in 1927 by St Maximilian Kolbe. Abbot of the monastery, Kolbe died to save the life of a fellow prisoner in Auschwitz in 1941 and was canonised in 1982. The church of Niepokalanów was built between 1948 and 1954; it also houses a Maximilian Kolbe memorial. In the vault is an exhibition, One Thousand Years of Polish History.

The two routes leading west out of Warsaw meet in **Sochaczew**, which contains the ruins of the palace of the princes of Mazovia and a museum devoted to the Battle of the Bzura (Muzeum Ziemi Sochaczewskiej i Pola Bitwy nad Bzurą; Pl Kosciuszki 2; www.e-sochaczew.pl; Tue–Sun 10am–4pm, Wed, Fri until 3pm). This was the biggest defensive battle fought by the Poles in 1939. The Narrow Gauge Railway Museum (Muzeum Kolei Wąskotorowej; tel: 046-862 59 75; http://mkw.e-sochaczew.pl; Tue–Sun 10am–3pm; free on Wed) sets a happier tone. From Sochaczew there is a road branching off to the south to **Bolimów**. This community has no buildings of architectural interest, but is well known as the place where, on 31 December 1915, the Germans first used chlorine gas as a weapon on the eastern front.

Not far from Bolimów is **Nieborów** , one of Poland's most magnificent palaces and parks (Muzeum w Nieborowie i Arkadii; www.nieborow.art.pl; Mar–Apr, Oct Tue–Sun 10am–4pm, May–June daily 10am–6pm, July–Sept Mon–Fri 10am–4pm, Sat–Sun 10am–6pm). The palace, designed by Tylman van Gameren and built from 1690 to 1696, today houses a museum with valuable exhibits, among them a Roman sculpture of Niobe, portraits of European monarchs and a huge Italian globe dating from the 17th century. These works of art were collected by the Radziwiłł family, which owned Nieborów until 1945. A second romantic park known as **Arkadia** (daily 10am–dusk, closed Mon out of the summer season) is 5km (3 miles) from Nieborów. It contains almost everything you would expect to find in a park laid out at the end of the 18th century: a Gothic house, Greek temple, aqueduct, lakes and a ruined castle.

The 12th-century trading city of **Łowicz**  was for several centuries the seat of the archbishops of Gniezno. Here, folk arts and crafts have not yet degenerated to the level of mass-production for the tourists. The woodcarvings, paper silhouettes and colourful hand-woven materials of Łowicz are famous throughout Poland, and can be bought from shops around the main square. Anyone who is especially interested in traditions of this kind should pay a visit to the museum in a Baroque palace right on the market square (Muzeum w Łowiczu i Skansen w Maurzycach; tel: 046-837 39 28; www.muzeumlowicz.pl; Tue–Sun 10am–4pm, open-air museum in Maurzyce May–Sept

Nieborów Palace.

10am–6pm, Apr and Oct till 4pm, Nov–Mar park only). The processions that take place at Corpus Christi in late May are particularly lively affairs.

The nearby Collegiate Church contains the tombs of the Polish primates, the princes of the church who took over leadership of the state between rulers, until the new king was crowned. South of Łowicz, close to the railway line, is the village of **Lipce**. The famous Polish writer and Nobel prize winner Władysław Reymont lived here from 1889 to 1891, and set the story of his best-known novel *Chłopi* (*The Peasants*) in this village (see pages 151 and 163). There is a small museum dedicated to his work and to popular country crafts, especially weaving (Muzeum Regionalne im Wł St Reymonta w Lipcach Reymontowskich; ul Wiatraczna 10; tel: 046-831 61 12; May–Sept Tue–Fri 10am–4pm, Sat from 10am, Sun 11am–5pm, Oct–Apr Tue–Fri 9am–2pm, Sat from 10am, Sun noon–3pm).

Łódź

With its 708,500 inhabitants, **Łódź** ⓲ is today the third-largest city in Poland, with light industry and 50 percent of the Polish textile industry located within its boundaries. Above all, however, it is a dynamic and quickly developing place with a rich cultural life to rival nearby Warsaw. Every year dozens of festivals are organised in Łódź, including the Łódź of Four Cultures Festival celebrating the Jewish, German, Russian and Polish roots of the city, as well as its tradition of tolerance and openness. Design, fashion and film festivals are so numerous that no matter when Łódź is visited, at least some of them will be under way.

Łódź was granted a town charter as long ago as 1423, but in 1820 still only had 800 inhabitants – a place of no significance whatsoever. Things began to change in 1823 with the building of Nowe Miasto, the first textile workers' estate. The removal of the customs barriers between Poland and Russia led to an enormous increase in the export of textiles to Russia, and in the second half of the 19th century Łódź became one of the most important textile centres in the world.

The vast Manufaktura complex.

During World War II the Germans opened two large transit camps in Łódź for Polish prisoners-of-war, as well as a camp for Russian airmen, a camp for 5,000 gypsies from Germany, Austria and the Balkans, and also a camp for 4,000 Polish children. Approximately 260,000 Jews were murdered in nearby Chełmno nad Nerem, and the people of Łódź itself were also affected; of its 600,000 inhabitants only around half survived the war.

After the war new estates grew up around the original districts of the town. In addition to the traditional textile industry, electrical engineering and chemical industries also came to Łódź. The first institutions of further education were founded, the most famous being the State College of Cinematic Art, Drama and Television (see page 107). Typical of Łódź are a group of buildings that date from the 19th century: an industrialist's villa, a factory and the modest little houses of the textile workers. They were built in imitation of previous architectural styles, Gothic and Baroque in particular, as were the interesting town residences in Piotrkowska and Moniuszko streets. At least 30 houses in the Art Nouveau mode, *Secesja* in Polish, have also been preserved. A stroll on Piotrkowska Street is a must, not only because of its elegant architecture, but also because the changes taking place in Łódź are nowhere more visible than in this neighbourhood. In 2014 the street was covered with granite and equipped with 178 new lampposts. Not all of the beautiful town houses have been renovated yet, but some sections have been refurbished with a lot of creativity. Probably the most interesting project is **Off Piotrowska** (Piotrkowska 138/140, entrance also from Roosvelt and Sienkiewicz streets; www.offpiotrkowska.pl). In the former cotton mill of Franciszek Ramish several workshops, galleries, shops and restaurants have opened, creating a bustling place with a unique atmosphere.

The **Museum of the City of Łódź** (Muzeum Miasta Łodzi; Ogrodowa 15; tel: 042-254 90 00; www.muzeum-lodz.pl; Mon 10am–2pm, Wed 10am–6pm, Tue, Thu 10am–4pm, Sat–Sun 11am–6pm; free on Sun) is in the Poznański family's palace, which has a flamboyant interior. The museum documents the town's past, showing how it looked prior to World War II's devastation. The museum is today just one part of the enormous **Manufaktura** complex. Inside this series of former textile mills is Poland's largest shopping centre, hundreds of cafés and restaurants, a cinema, art galleries and a huge public square which regularly hosts concerts. The massive red-brick building at the front of the complex once housed the mill's offices and is now an impressive five-star hotel (www.vi-hotels.com/pl/andels-lodz). The Manufaktura also houses The Art Museum (Muzeum Sztuki MS; ul Ogrodowa 19; tel: 042-634 39 48; http://msl.org.pl; Tue 10am–6pm, Wed–Sun 11am–5pm) – the red-brick, three-storey building with enormous windows is home to an extraordinary collection of

Piotrkowska Street is lined with elegant townhouses.

Polish 20th- and 21st-century art. The permanent exhibition is constantly changing and the works are ordered thematically and not chronologically. The museum has two other branches. The MS1 (Więkowskiego 36; Tue 10am–6pm, Wed–Sun 11am–5pm) is in another historic palace once owned by the Poznański family, which has been transformed into a contemporary exhibition space, with the Neo-plastic Room designed by Władysław Strzemiński. The Herbst Palace (Pałac Herbsta; ul. Przędzalniana 72; Tue–Sun 11am–7pm), surrounded by tranquil gardens, houses a collection of 19th-century and early modern art. The **Central Textile Museum** (Centralne Muzeum Włokiennictwa; Piotrkowska 282; tel: 042-683 26 84; www.muzeumwlokiennictwa.pl; Tue–Wed, Fri 9am–5pm, Thu 11am–7pm, Sat–Sun 11am–4pm) is in the White Factory, in 1838 the first spinning mill in Łódź to be fitted with a steam-driven engine. There is a portrayal of the development of technology in the textile industry and its social consequences in Poland, and the museum is

The Poznański Mausoleum in the Jewish Cemetery, Łódź.

rounded off with a collection of 16th- to 19th-century textiles from all over the world, along with impressive displays of modern textile work. Not far from the Textile Museum is the **Film Museum** (Muzeum Kinematografii; Pl Zwycięstwa 1; tel: 042-674 09 57; www.kinomuzeum.pl; Tue 10am–5pm, Wed, Fri 9am–4pm, Thu, Sat–Sun 11am–6pm), almost in front of the Film School of Łódź (see page 107) in a former palace of Karol Scheibler, the German-Polish textile magnate and philanthropist. The collection may not be for everyone (posters, cameras and film-makers' equipment), but it offers a glimpse into the opulent yet also a little gloomy interior of this 19th-century palace. In this part of the city there are a lot of examples of red-brick industrial architecture. It's worth taking a stroll around, especially in **Księży Młyn**, a red-brick neighbourhood of small houses founded by Karol Scheibler for his textile workers; the philanthropist didn't forget about building a school and a hospital.

Before the war over 30 percent of the inhabitants of Łódź were Jewish. The

Jewish community, both synagogues and the old Jewish cemetery were destroyed during the war. Only the new **Jewish Cemetery** survived, with around 120,000 gravestones and the Izrael Poznański Mausoleum erected between 1893 and 1939. Today it is the largest Jewish cemetery in Europe and one of the largest in the world.

North of the cemetery (on Al Pamięci Ofiar Litzmannstadt Getto 12, around 20 minutes' walk away; there is no public transport) is the moving **Radegast Station**, from where the Jews of the Łódź Ghetto were deported to the extermination camps at Chełmno and Auschwitz. Three original Deutsche Bahn cattle trucks stand at the eerily empty platform (tel: 042-291 36 27; www.muzeumtradycji.pl; Mon–Tue 9am–5pm, Wed–Thu until 6pm, Sat–Sun until 4pm).

Villages around Łódź

North of Łódź is **Łęczyca** ⑳ which, in the Middle Ages, was one of the most powerful towns in Poland. It still has a number of monuments: a Gothic castle with an ethnographical museum (www.zamek.leczyca.info.pl; May–Sept Tue–Fri 10am–5pm, Sat–Sun from 11am, Oct–Apr Tue–Fri 10am–4pm, Sat–Sun 10am–3pm; free on Thu), well-preserved town walls and a classical Town Hall. In the nearby village of Tum is a Romanesque church dating from 1141–45, and, adjacent to it, the ruins of an old castle. The town also has an open-air museum of local country culture (Muzeum Łęczycka Zagroda Chłopska;tel: 088-822 4867; www.maie.lodz.pl/tum; Apr–Sept daily 10am–6pm, Oct–Mar Tue–Sun 9am–4pm; free on Tue). Not far from Kutno is **Oporów**, which has an attractive Gothic castle (tel: 024-28 59 122; www.zamekoporow.pl), situated on a man-made island.

To the southwest is the industrial town of **Piotrków Trybunalski**, which has a well-known glassworks. The former Royal Palace, which was built between 1511 and 1519, now

houses a museum (www.muzeum piotrkow.pl). Other historic sights in Piotrków include the remains of the town walls, some fascinating churches and the synagogue. The municipal station dates from 1850, when the railway line was built from Warsaw to Vienna. Brick-built stations like this are typical of this particular area. A favourite place for weekend excursions is the River **Pilica**, with its romantic villages and medieval castles surrounded by water. In **Inowłódz** is a Romanesque church founded by the duke of Poland, Władysław Hermann, with a high stone tower that dominates the surrounding countryside. Also in Inowłódz is a castle built by King Kazimierz Wielki in the 14th century and since reconstructed several times. It is now a centre of local culture, with classes for children and a library (tel: 044-710 18 54; www.gckinowlodz.naszgok.pl). In the suburb of Tomaszów Mazowiecki there is the **Niebieskie Źródła**. Literally meaning 'blue springs', its name is a reference to the blue sheen of the water, which is caused by the minerals it contains. There is also an open-air

---

CHAIM RUMKOWSKI

One of the most controversial figures in the whole tragic history of Polish Jewry during World War II was Chaim Rumkowski.

A former textiles manager, Rumkowski was chosen by the Nazis to lead the Łódź ghetto that they set up in the north of the city, a position that involved negotiating – some say collaborating – between the Germans and the ghetto inhabitants as their spokesman and leader.

The Łódź ghetto soon became one of the most productive in Poland, but stories abound of Rumkowski's dictatorial manner and power-hungry motives, including offering children up to the camps in place of healthy adults – he believed that he would emerge as the head of a Jewish protectorate after the war. Nevertheless, it cannot be denied that under his leadership the number of deportations to the concentration camps was reduced and that the ghetto became a place of culture and education, not simply slave labour.

In 1944, at the height of the Final Solution frenzy, Himmler ordered that the Łódź ghetto be shut down despite its profitability, and Rumkowski volunteered to go to Auschwitz, where he died soon after – possibly murdered by vengeful fellow ghetto residents, although this has never been proved.

museum (Skansen Rzeki Pilicy; ul A. Frycza Modrzewskiego 9/11; tel: 044-723 00 03; www.skansenpilicy.pl). Further upriver, in **Sulejów**, is an old Cistercian monastery, one of Poland's most important architectural monuments. It was founded and financed by Duke Kazimierz the Just in 1177. The well-fortified complex includes a church, the ruins of a monastery, defensive walls with bastions and farm buildings. Today it houses a hotel (www.hotel podklasztorze.pl).

Southwest of Łódź is **Zduńska Wola**, where, in 1894, the abbot, later to become St Maximilian Kolbe, was born (see page 99). As long ago as the 6th century a settlement stood by the River Warta, not far from Sieradz. Churches dating from the 14th century and castle ruins are worth a detour. In **Wieluń** the fortified walls and the Kraków Gate have also been preserved; the classical Town Hall was built in 1842. The Pauline Church, which was originally Gothic, also has a splendid Baroque interior. There are 37 old wooden churches in the vicinity of Wieluń. One of them, the **Church of the Holy Spirit** which stands in Sieradz cemetery, was built after the victory over the Teutonic Knights near Grunwald in 1410. The church in **Grębień**, near Wieluń, has interiors decorated with well-preserved Gothic-Renaissance wall paintings which date from 1500 to 1531. Also well worth seeing is the 18th-century manor of the Walewski family in nearby **Trubadzin**. Now it houses an interesting museum of aristocratic interiors, the Walewski and Trubadzin Museum(Muzeum Walewskich w Tubądzinie; http://muzeum-sieradz.com.pl; Tue–Fri 9am–3pm, Sun 10am–3pm).

Between the Vistula and the Pilica

In the past this area was part of Little Poland (see page 213). In the north it is mainly flat, but towards the south it becomes hilly. Between Radom and Puławy is **Czarnolas**, where Jan Kochanowski (1530–84) lived. This poet was one of the first to write in Polish rather than Latin, the usual written language in those days (see

The State Archives building in Radom.

page 101). He is buried in the church of nearby Zwoleń. The Museum of Jan Kochanowski (Muzeum Jana Kochanowskiego w Czarnolesie; tel: 048-677 20 05; http://cyfrowyczarnolas.pl; May–Aug Tue–Fri 8am–4pm, Sat–Sun 10am–6pm, Sept–Apr until 4pm), is in the 19th-century manor house of the Jabłonowski family and surrounded by a beautiful park with a neo-Gothic chapel. (The poet's house burned down in the late 18th century.)

Further to the west a monumental Gothic-Renaissance palace, now in ruins, towers above the town of **Drzewica** ㉑. This region was the scene of the fiercest partisan battles in Poland, and in the whole of Europe, during World War II. The commander of the Polish freedom fighters, Henryk Dobrzański, generally known as 'Hubal', did not capitulate in 1939 but fought on with his uniformed division for another eight months. He fell not far from the village of Studzianna, which is well known for its Baroque church. In revenge for Hubal's resistance, many of the surrounding villages were burned down by the Germans and all men over 15 years of age were murdered. The village that suffered the most was Skłoby, the 'Village of Widows', where 265 people lost their lives and 400 buildings were set on fire.

The area surrounding Drzewica and Studzianna is referred to by ethnologists as the **Opoczyński region**. Here traditional costume is rather like those of Mazovia, with different striped patterns. Timber is still frequently used as a building material in this region and there are many folk artists dedicated to continuing the silhouette tradition.

The largest town in this region is **Radom** ㉒, an important centre with a metal industry and leather and tobacco factories. The oldest monument is the Church of St Wacław. The medieval town centre has also been preserved, and there is a *skansen* (open-air museum) with examples of the various building styles of this area (Muzeum Wsi Radomskiej; tel:

048-332 92 81; www.muzeum-radom.pl; Tue–Fri 9am–5pm, Sat–Sun 10am–6pm, in winter until 3pm). There is also a display of old beehives in many shapes and sizes. In a monumental building on the main square is a museum dedicated to one of the most popular Polish painters of the symbolism movement, the Museum of Jacek Malczewski, (Muzeum im Jacka Malczewskiego; www.muzeum.edu.pl; Sun–Thu 10am–3pm, Fri 10am–5pm). On display, besides paintings, are archaeological artefacts and decorative arts. There is another branch in two colourful town houses on the square, with an extraordinary collection of modern Polish art. The latest addition to Radom's cultural scene is the impressive Centre of Contemporary Art (Mazowieckie Centrum Sztuki Współczesnej; www.elektrownia.art.pl), in a former power station. A little further along road E77, in the local palace of Szydłowiec, is the **Folk Musical Instrument Museum** (Muzeum Ludowych Instrumentów Muzycznych; http://muzeuminstrumentow.pl), the only one of its

Farmland and chapel in the mountains.

kind in Poland. Other features of Szydłowiec are a Renaissance Town Hall, a large Jewish cemetery and a well-known sandstone quarry.

An alternative route, the B9, leads from Radom to Sandomierz. Immediately after Radom you come to **Skaryszew**. The horse market held here on the first Monday of Lent attracts large numbers of gypsies, farmers and horselovers from all over Poland. It's an event well worth catching if you can.

Further along this road is Iłża, the scene of a major battle in 1939. The tower of the palace of the bishops of Kraków, a building that is now a ruin, was used as an observation point by the Polish army in the battle. A few kilometres from Ostrowiec Swiętokrzyski in **Krzemionki Opatowskie** there is a quartz mine, which is known to have been in existence in the Neolithic period, when it was one of the largest in Europe. One section of it can be visited, the **Quartz Mine Museum** (Muzeum Archeologiczne i Rezerwat 'Krzemionki'; Sudół 135a; tel: 041-330 45 50; http://krzemionki.pl; May–Sept Mon–Fri 9am–7pm, Sat–Sun

11am–7pm, Apr, Oct daily 9am–5pm, Nov–Mar Tue–Sun 8am–4pm; guided visits only). It's a branch of the Museum of History and Archaeology of Ostrowiec Świętokrzyski (Muzeum Historyczno-Archeologiczne Krzemionki; www.muzeumostrowiec.pl).

Between the industrial town of Skarżysko-Kamienna and Starachowice is **Wąchock**, which has a Romanesque-Gothic church and a **Cistercian monastery**(Opactwo Cysterskie w Wąchocku; tel: 041-275 02 00; www.wachock.cystersi.pl) dating from the beginning of the 13th century. The monastery contains the most beautiful examples of Romanesque art in the whole of Poland. Another famous partisan leader from World War II, Jan Piwnik 'Ponury', is buried here.

The Holy Cross Mountains

Further to the south runs a line of rocky mountains known as the **Holy Cross Mountains** ㉓ (Góry Świętokrzyskie). This is the oldest Polish mountain range, an area of pine forests, exposed mountain peaks, quartz rock, a type of larch peculiar to the region, the remains of coral in the pre-Cambrian rock and a multitude of rare but protected fauna and flora. Amid the wild and romantic scenery there are many places worth taking the time to visit.

In **Samsonów** are the ruins of a metalworks dating from the beginning of the 19th century and now a technological monument. Nearby is 'Bartek', one of the largest and oldest oak trees in Poland. The trunk has a circumference of over 9 metres (29ft). Nearby **Oblęgorek** is where Nobel laureate Henryk Sienkiewicz, author of the novel *Quo Vadis*, lived until 1914. There is a museum dedicated to the writer (Tue–Sun 8am–3pm).

The capital of this region is **Kielce** ㉔. Its bishop's palace was built in the 17th century, and now houses the National Museum (Muzeum Narodowe w Kielcach; Plac Zamkowy 1; http://mnki.pl/pl; Tue–Sun 10am–6pm): this includes a gallery of Polish art and

Świętokrzyski National Park.

a section dealing with interior design. It is possible to spend a night in the palace, in a guest room in the southern wing. Just opposite the palace is a Baroque cathedral (Bazylika Katedralna Wniebowzięcia NMP) with an interior preserved in its original style and a beautiful sculpture of the Virgin Mary made of galena, a lead ore. The castle at nearby Chęciny (15km/9 miles from Kielce on the road to Kraków), built at the turn of the 14th century, was once the strongest fortress in Poland. The castle was recently renovated. Another must-see in the area is the fabulous **Paradise Cave** (Jaskinia Raj; http://jaskiniaraj.pl; daily Jan–Apr, Sept–Nov 10am–5pm, May–June 9am–7pm, July–Aug 9am–6pm; guided tours only). Discovered in 1964, it is one of the most beautiful karst grottos in the world. The corridors of the cave, formed around 360 million years ago at the bottom of the sea, feature stalactites and stalagmites in the most bizarre shapes.

To the east of Kielce rises the Bare Mountain (Łysa Góra), with its forbidding scree slopes. On this mountain is the **Holy Cross Monastery** (Święty Krzyż) belonging to the Benedictine order, where a relic of the Holy Cross is kept. Before the monastery came into existence there was a pre-Christian sanctuary on this spot. Legend has it that the mountain was a meeting place for the country's witches. Today the countryside is sadly marred by a television broadcasting tower.

The whole area surrounding Łysa Góra is the **Świętokrzyski National Park** (Świętokrzyski Park Narodowy), which extends over a total of 6,000 hectares (15,000 acres). The heath has splendid pine and larch woods and there are numerous clearings and deforested areas, dotted with large boulder fields. At the foot of this range of mountains is the attractive village of **Nowa Słupia**. Some experts claim there was already an iron industry here 2,000 years ago and it is perfectly possible that iron was exported from this area to the Roman Empire. Remains of the old furnaces are on display in the local history museum (Muzeum Hutnictwa Starożytnego im Radwana), which is a branch of Warsaw's Museum of Technology.

All these mountains are composed of sandstone, and it is only north of Kielce that limestone begins to predominate. Here magnificent marble is also to be found, and even semiprecious stones such as malachite and azurite are relatively common.

On the road towards Kraków is **Jędrzejów**, whose 13th-century Cistercian monastery was rebuilt in Baroque style. However, the town is best known for its Przypkowski Museum (Muzeum im Przypkowskich w Jędrzejowie; Tue–Sun 8am–4pm, mid-Apr–Oct until 5pm), which is named after the local Przypkowski family and includes their fascinating collection of sundials. In the region east of Jędrzejów lies **Szyłdów**, a sleepy little village that once had a town charter. It's a pleasant place to stop for a wander; its town walls and church have survived the upheavals of the ages undamaged.

Holy Cross Monastery.

THE SPIRIT OF POLISH ROMANTICISM

Frederick Chopin's lyricism and unparalleled melodic genius has produced some of the most beautiful and spiritual music ever written.

Chopin was born in 1810 in a country manor house in the village of Żelazowa Wola, outside Warsaw. His baptismal certificate is kept in the medieval church of the nearby village of Brochów, where his parents were married and his father, an immigrant from France, was engaged as a tutor at the nearby estate of Count Skarbek. He made his professional debut as a child prodigy, appearing at charity concerts organised by Warsaw's aristocratic circles. While Chopin was studying at the Warsaw School of Music he was captivated by Polish folk music and become familiar with various songs and dances in the villages surrounding Warsaw. In the autumn of 1830 Chopin left Warsaw and never returned to his beloved Poland. After performing in Dresden, Vienna, Salzburg and Munich, he finally arrived in Paris, where he initially gave numerous recitals before concentrating on composition. Chopin's social circle included many prominent musicians, including Franz Liszt, and the love of his life, George Sand, the pseudonym of the French writer Aurore Dudevant. Their intense relationship resulted in her nursing Chopin for several years after he contracted tuberculosis. She finally left him in 1847, when he was seriously ill and virtually penniless. A desperate but highly successful visit to London briefly revived his fortunes, where he gave his final public concert in 1848. Returning to Paris, Chopin died in 1849 in his home in the Place Vendôme.

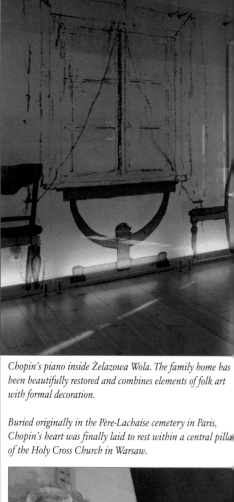

Chopin's piano inside Żelazowa Wola. The family home has been beautifully restored and combines elements of folk art with formal decoration.

Buried originally in the Père-Lachaise cemetery in Paris, Chopin's heart was finally laid to rest within a central pilla of the Holy Cross Church in Warsaw.

The state-of-the-art museum is not only full of modern technology but is also child-friendly.

Chopin's music on a glass panel at Żelazowa Wola.

CHOPIN'S MUSICAL LEGACY

Chopin's earliest compositions date from his childhood. He began composing seriously when he settled in Paris in the 1830s, and it was while convalescing in Mallorca in 1838 that he composed the renowned Preludes, the Polonaise in A major, and the Sonata which includes the Funeral March. His music was as controversial as it was passionate, and his most vehement critics condemned its overt emotionalism as the ravings of a lunatic. Nearing the end of his life he wrote: "Where have my abilities gone, what has happened to my heart? I can hardly remember how they sing at home. The world is sinking round me in a strange fashion." At Chopin's funeral service, Mozart's Requiem was played according to his wishes and he was buried in the Père-Lachaise Cemetery in Paris.

Chopin's restored 19th-century family home is now a branch of Warsaw's Fryderyk Chopin Museum, with a collection of family possessions and early piano manuscripts.

…mmer concerts are held on the terrace at Żelazowa Wola, which …rrounded by delightful parkland containing a small lake.

…engraving of Żelazowa Wola.

Traditional wooden houses of the Tatra region.

*Waiting for a train at
Kraków station.*

MAŁOPOLSKA – LITTLE POLAND

Małopolska (Little Poland) is not small in either size or significance. From the historic city of Kraków to trekking in the Tatras, this region is packed with things to see and do.

Façade detail, Zamość.

A region of immense natural beauty, which also includes some of Poland's most attractive and historic towns, Małopolska embraces the southern and south-eastern corner of Poland, between the Ukraine and Slovakia. To the south the Carpathian Mountains and foothills extend along the border with Slovakia, while the centre of the region features the low-lying Koltina Sandomierska basin. To the north rises the Małopolska Upland (Wyżyna Małopolska), comprising a number of separate, low-lying ranges of hills, bordered by the Krakowsko-Częstochowska Upland (Wyżyna Krakowsko Częstochowska). To the east the Lublin Uplands (Wyżyna Lubelska) jut out above the surrounding plains. The region is also traversed by important rivers, such as the Vistula, Dunajec and San, as well as numerous picturesque streams and lakes, which continually add variety and heighten the appeal of the surrounding countryside.

The region's most important city is Kraków, the capital of Poland between the 11th and the 16th century. Although the city's political power subsequently diminished, it continues to be regarded as Poland's cultural and intellectual capital. Kraków is also one of Poland's most beautiful cities, with a wealth of museums including the Royal Castle and Wawel Cathedral, and a comprehensive range of architecture that includes definitive examples of Renaissance style.

Rural landscape, Pieniński mountains.

The chapter entitled *Through Little Poland* (see page 213) highlights the vast number of attractions within easy reach of Kraków, including the salt mines at Wieliczka, dating from the 12th century, a network of ruined castles along the so-called Trail of the Eagle's Lair on the border with Slovakia; Łańcut, one of Poland's most impressive palaces (now a museum) and the town of Zamość, a remarkable example of Renaissance architecture and town planning.

KRAKÓW

There's so much to do in Kraków that the city requires a week's stay to do it justice. It contains both low-brow and high-brow culture mixed with vitality and a sense of history.

ormerly the capital of Poland, Krakovians have always continued to think of their city as Poland's cultural and intellectual capital – despite the counter-claims of Varsovians. But no one can dispute the city's immense beauty, which is readily accessible within the pedestrianised Old Town. Hailed as European City of Culture in 1992 and 2000, Kraków (Cracow) is frequently termed an 'al fresco museum', with Unesco's World Heritage Listing classifying 55 of the city's buildings and monuments as of the highest class. Meanwhile, its numerous museums, containing more than two million works of art, span an amazing range of themes, including rarities such as the pharmacy museum and the insurance museum.

Alongside the sense of history, Kraków is also a vibrant, progressive city, with a full cultural programme of music (classical, jazz, alternative, whatever), film and theatre, including the country's foremost theatre, the Helena Modrzejewska Theatre, as well as avant garde troupes. More than 100 annual festivals include the Music in Old Kraków International Festival in August, with concerts held in atmospheric burghers' houses, churches and palaces throughout the Old Town. The Kraków Film Festival in September continues the city's heritage as the site of the first Polish film screening in 1896, while the Jewish Culture Festival that starts at the end of June is one of the most important events of its type in the world.

The Jagiellonian University (the 'Oxbridge' of Poland) ensures a high youth quota, with the inevitable accompaniment of Bohemian and various alternative sub-cultures. Even during the summer vacations there is an 'academic' influx, as the university holds summer schools with courses on Polish language, culture and history

Main Attractions

Main Market Square
Rynek Underground
Cloth Hall
St Mary's Church
Royal Castle and Wawel Hill
Kazimierz Jewish Quarter
Museum of Contemporary
  Art (MOCAK)
Oskar Schindler's Factory
Wieliczka Salt Mines

Inside the Cloth Hall.

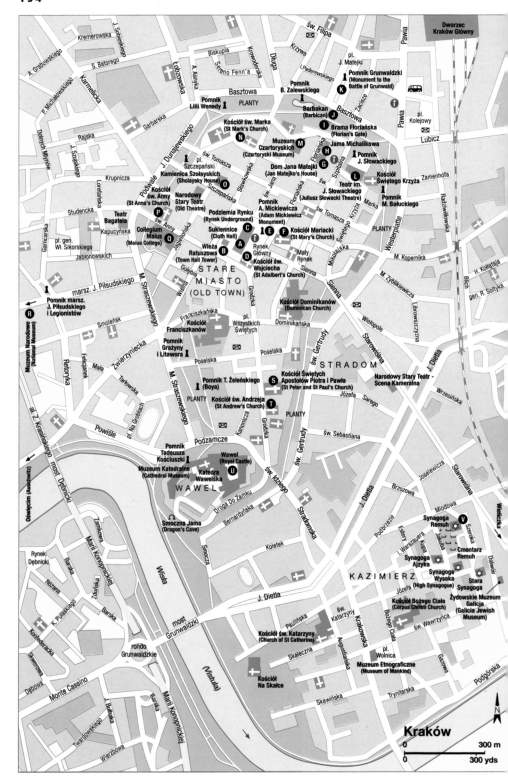

Kraków

0   300 m

0   300 yds

for overseas students, particularly Polish émigrés.

The history of Kraków

According to legend, Krakus, the leader of a Slavic tribe called the Wiślanie (Vistulans) erected a fortified settlement on a hill known as Wawel. Being on key trade routes meant the settlement developed into a town, with the earliest recorded reference dated ad 965, when a Jewish merchant from Cordoba, Ibrahim ibn Jakub, wrote that Kraków was already a major town known throughout Europe.

The diocese of Kraków was founded in 1000, following the country's conversion to Christianity in 966. In 1040 King Casimir 'The Restorer' made Kraków Poland's capital. In 1241 the town was destroyed by a Tartar invasion, although it was rapidly rebuilt, and blossomed again under the Jagiellonian dynasty (1386–1572), with commerce developing alongside art and culture. The Jagiellonian University was founded in 1364. The country's first university has retained its reputation as one of the country's premier educational institutes. During the 15th century Kraków became a town of some 30,000 inhabitants, surrounded by fortified walls and turrets. Situated at the junction of trade routes from western Europe to Byzantium, and from southern Europe to the Baltic, the city joined the Hanseatic League in 1430, which attracted many German craftsmen and merchants. The first half of the 16th century saw trade and handicrafts flourish, with as many as 60 different guilds. However, the union of Poland and Lithuania in 1569 decreased Kraków's status, as Mazovia and Warsaw emerged as the new 'centre' of Poland, with King Zygmunt III making Warsaw the capital in 1596. Yet, as Polish kings continued to be crowned and buried in Kraków's Wawel Cathedral, the city retained some of its importance.

The eagle of Kraków is also Poland's coat of arms.

Foreign rule

Under the Third Partition of Poland in 1795, Małopolska became part of the Austrian Habsburg Empire. After the Congress of Vienna, Kraków was a free city and capital of the so-called

The arches of the Renaissance-style Cloth Hall in the Main Market Square.

Kraków Republic from 1815 until, in 1846, the city was incorporated into the province of Galicia. The relatively liberal attitude of the Austrian authorities enabled Polish culture and science to progress; even the activities of the independence movement were tolerated. It was during this period that the painters Jan Matejko, Jacek Malczewski and Leon Wyczółkowski emerged as maestros. Subsequently, the forerunners of Secessionism (Polish Art Nouveau), Stanisław Wyspiański and Józef Mehoffer, developed a movement called *Młoda Polska* (Young Poland) centred in the city. Austrian rule also transformed Kraków into a resilient 'fortress' which even managed to withstand the Russian offensive of 1914.

In November 1939 the Nazis established the headquarters of the General Government in the city, with the Governor General Hans Frank taking up residence in the Royal Palace. Having wiped out the Jewish population, as well as the Polish intelligentsia, the Nazis mined the city for systematic destruction (which was the fate of Warsaw) in 1945. However, nothing was detonated as they retreated from a sudden advance by the Red Army, which liberated the city on 18 January 1945. In fact, this is one of the few Polish cities to have survived the war more or less intact (see page 53).

Kraków, the second-largest city in Poland, now has a population of 759,800, with the post-war suburbs being purpose-built industrial centres, including engineering, metal processing, electronics, pharmaceuticals and foodstuffs. However, it was for political rather than economic reasons that the Lenin steelworks employed a vast proletarian labour-force. A horrific consequence was pollution from the factories, which attacked not only the inhabitants, but also the historic buildings. Fortunately, a tough policy of dealing with industrial waste has brought this under control. Despite these efforts, air pollution levels in Kraków remain among the highest in Europe. The ubiquitous coal furnaces, which spew smoke and contribute to smog, especially in winter, are the main cause. The city authorities have already started a campaign to replace

Feeding the pigeons in the Main Market Square.

them with more ecological alternatives but it will take some years.

The Main Market Square

The heart of the city, the **Main Market Square** (Rynek Główny) is always busy with locals and tourists, and during the summer this continues until late into the night. Measuring 200 metres (650ft) on each side, it is one of Europe's largest medieval squares (only St Mark's Square in Venice is larger), with plenty of space for numerous restaurants and cafés, as well as flower stalls, pavement artists and street performers. Being such a cultured town, there are plenty of duos and trios playing exquisite classical refrains, with some buskers having a cheerful placard stating: 'I'm healthy and happy, I'm just collecting money for beer.'

The market square is surrounded by grand burghers' houses and palaces, with façades reflecting various architectural genres, while many of the rear courtyards serve as al fresco cafés and restaurants. It's essential to dine at **Wierzynek** (Rynek Główny 15; www. wierzynek.com.pl), which serves some of the city's finest dishes. This restaurant occupies three Renaissance houses, one of which belonged to the patrician Wierzynek family. In 1364 King Kazimierz invited a number of European monarchs to a royal wedding in Kraków – a case of strategic political union rather than true love – with the wedding feast hosted by the Wierzynek family in one of these houses. One of the restaurant's dining rooms has a copy of a 14th-century painting depicting this wedding feast. Other options include the Clock Room (featuring a wall full of antique clocks) and the Sala Rycerska (Knight's Hall); 14th-century sandstone Gothic arches are also a feature of the restaurant. The cellar is a wine bar specialising in Hungarian Tokay wines, continuing a vogue established by Hungarian-born Queen Jadwiga.

At the centre of the market square stands the **Cloth Hall Ⓐ** (Sukiennice;

daily 9am-5pm, May–Oct until 7pm), originally a covered market with stalls, shops and warehouses. The current Renaissance façade was designed by Giovannia Maria of Padua (known as Padovano) between 1556 and 1560. The Italian sculptor Santi Gucci of Florence decorated the façade with mascarons (faces), for which (apparently) Kraków's most distinguished burghers posed.

The ground floor of the Sukiennice continues its commercial role, with stalls selling folk arts and crafts, amber jewellery, leather goods and souvenirs, which are definitely a cut above the usual, while the arcades on either side house cafés.

On the first floor of the Sukiennice is the superbly renovated **Gallery of Polish 19th-century Painting and Sculpture** (Galeria Sztuki Polskiej XIX Wieku; Rynek Główny 1; tel: 012-433 54 00; Tue–Sun 10am–8pm; free on Sun in winter). The name says it all, with this small but concentrated museum enabling you to see a lot in a short time. The collection includes Polish landscapes, portraits and historic

St Adalbert's Church cupola.

scenes by Jan Matejko and Adam Chmielowski, together with some works by late 18th-century artists such as Marcello Bacciarelli, the court artist of Stanisław August Poniatowski, Poland's last king. The **Town Hall Tower** Ⓑ (Wieża Ratuszowa; 20 Apr–Oct daily 10.30am–6pm) provides fine views of the immediate area. The tower also includes a museum (Wed–Sun) detailing the city's evolution.

Rynek Underground Ⓒ exhibition (Podziemia Rynku; Rynek Główny 1; www.podziemiarynku.com; Apr–Oct Mon 10am–8pm, Tue 10am–4pm, Wed–Sun 10am–10pm, Nov–Mar Wed–Mon 10am–8pm, Tue 10am–4pm; closed 1st Tue of the month) is the result of five years of archaeological excavations under Kraków's main square, which had originally been planned to last only six months. It tells the history of the city through archaeological finds. On display are architectural relics, ornaments, coins and numerous everyday objects from the time when Kraków was the second most important and magnificent city in this part of Europe, after Prague.

The tiny Romanesque **St Adalbert's Church** Ⓓ (Kościół Św Wojciecha) dates from the 11th and 12th centuries, and features ornate interiors. The vaults include Romanesque and pre-Romanesque architectural fragments.

In front of the Cloth Hall is the **Adam Mickiewicz Monument** Ⓔ (Pomnik Adama Mickiewicza), commemorating Poland's greatest romantic poet; meeting 'by the monument' is a favourite rendezvous for locals. The Main Market Square also hosts cultural events such as the colourful Lajkonik pageant, which takes place shortly after Corpus Christi. This procession of Tartars marching through the streets is led by the Lajkonik, a legendary Polish hero disguised as a Tartar, 'riding' a hobbyhorse which dances to the sound of drums. Being touched by the Lajkonik's wooden mace is considered good luck.

The imposing, twin-towered **St Mary's Church** Ⓕ (Kościół Mariacki; Mon–Sat 11.30am–6pm, Sun 2–6pm) was built during the 14th to 16th centuries. The triple-naved design features ornate interiors including an

The Adam Mickiewicz Monument.

incredible late-Gothic altarpiece entitled 'The lives of Our Lady and Her Son Jesus Christ'. Completed between 1477 and 1489 by the master carver of Nuremberg, Veit Stoss (known in Poland as Wit Stwosz), it entailed carving around 2,000 realistic figures and decorative elements in linden, which were given the features of contemporary Krakovians. The central panel, 13 metres (43ft) high and 11 metres (36ft) wide, depicts the death of the Virgin Mary, while side panels depict scenes from the life of the Virgin Mary and Jesus. Stoss remained in the city for 20 years, fulfilling commissions for the king and other Polish aristocrats. The interiors, including 19th-century murals by Jan Matejko, are so rich and concentrated that it requires a leisurely visit to appreciate the various details. There are two entrances to the church, one for tourists and another for those who wish to pray or attend a service. Tourists are not admitted during mass.

Every hour on the hour a trumpeter plays the '*hejnał*' (bugle call) from the taller of the two church towers, which originally served as a warning against attack by the Tartars. One watchman who began the *hejnał* during an attack in the 12th century was struck by an arrow mid-note and it took a few moments before a replacement continued: now there is always a pause after the first few notes, in the watchman's honour. The *hejnał* now acts as a greeting for visitors.

Around the old town

Taking Floriańska street from the market square leads to **Jan Matejko's House** ❻ (Dom Jana Matejki; Floriańska 41; tel: 012-433 59 60; www. muzeum.krakow.pl; Tue–Sat 10am–6pm, Sun 10am–4pm). The grandeur of the neoclassical façade and first floor wrought-iron balcony immediately distinguish this house, where Poland's greatest historical painter, Jan Matejko (1838–93), was born and subsequently worked. Retaining the sense of a private house, the original interiors

include a salon with neo-Renaissance furniture commissioned by Jan Matejko in Venice. The top floor studio, where his linen jacket and walking stick hang on coat hooks, contains easels and various accessories such as palettes and preparatory sketches.

Nearby, at Number 45, is **Jama Michalikowa** ❿ (tel: 012-422 15 61; www.jamamichalika.pl), a famous café and restaurant which was traditionally the haunt of the city's Bohemian set, including the *fin-de-siècle* '*Młoda Polska*' (Young Poland) group which pioneered Secessionism (Art Nouveau). The café was also the home of the Zielony Balonik (literally 'Green Balloon') cabaret troupe. The interiors are a potpourri of Secessionist decor, including a stained-glass dome, eccentric chandeliers, elaborate mirrors, drawings and one of the Christ Child's cribs for which the city is renowned. The restaurant's speciality is traditional Polish cuisine, while the café serves delicious cakes and desserts.

The street culminates at **Florian's Gate** (Brama Floriańska) ❶. This is the Old Town's only remaining

Statue outside the Juliusz Słowacki Theatre.

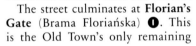

LIFE UNDERGROUND

The original medieval buildings of Kraków were not built with cellars because of their shallow foundations. Instead, they had three levels, the top level being used as the attic room.

As the city became wealthier and expanded, new houses were built on top of the old and the street level was raised when new roads were added. The old houses consequently 'developed' basements, as the original ground floors were now located below street level. The majority of basements were largely ignored by their owners for hundreds of years and the situation was exacerbated by stringent Communist property laws which controlled the use of all buildings. As a result, for a long time, only two buildings around the Main Market Square (Rynek Główny) had cellars that were accessible to the public.

It has only been since the late 1980s and 1990s, after a change in the property law, that these cellars, so distinctive of the city's architecture, have been put to use and celebrated as a unique feature. Today, many of the cellars have been converted into atmospheric bars and restaurants – even art galleries. The cosy ambience, combined in many instances with unique medieval ceiling decoration, makes them an experience not to be missed by any visitor to the city.

The arcaded courtyard of Maius College, restored almost to its original form.

Da Vinci's exquisite Lady with an Ermine.

gateway, and features a section of the city wall together with four fortified turrets dating from the 14th century. The city wall is hung with pictures by local artists (spanning the usual range from kitsch to artistic). Beyond Florian's Gate is the **Barbican** (Barbakan) ❶ (www.mhk.pl; Apr–Oct daily 10.30am–6pm; closed 2nd Mon of the month), a circular Gothic bastion built in 1499, and the largest example of its kind in Europe. The rest of the city walls were pulled down in the 19th century, and this area was laid out as the **Planty**, a wooded park with fountains and numerous benches that extends for almost 3.5km (2 miles), encircling the historic centre.

Various monuments erected in the Planty include a statue of astronomer Nicholas Copernicus, who studied in the city. **Pomnik Grunwaldzki** ❶ on Plac J. Matejki is the monument to the Battle of Grunwald in 1410, when Poland defeated the Teutonic knights (see page 362). The monument was commissioned by the pianist and statesman Ignacy Paderewski in 1910, on the 500th anniversary of the battle.

Modelled on the Paris Opera House, the flamboyant neo-Renaissance late 19th-century **Juliusz Słowacki Theatre** ❶ (Teatr im J. Słowackiego; Plac Świętego Ducha; tel: 012-424 45 00; www.slowacki.krakow.pl) is one of the city's leading theatrical venues, while one of the city's most important museums is the **Czartoryski Museum** ❶ (Muzeum Czartoryskich; Św Jana 19; tel: 012-370 54 60; www.muzeum-czartory skich.krakow.pl; Tue–Sun 10am–4pm). This palace, former monastery and armoury provides a suitably historic setting for an art collection which includes German, Italian and Dutch masters, including *Landscape with the Good Samaritan* by Rembrandt. At the time of printing the museum was partially closed for renovations, and the renowned *Lady with an Ermine*, painted by Leonardo da Vinci around 1490, was on temporary display at the Royal Castle.

A prime example of Gothic architecture, **St Mark's Church** ❶ (Kościół Św Marka) on Św Marka 10 has impressive interiors including a Passion scene in the apse. The nearby **Sholaysky House** ❶ (Kamienica Szołayskich; pl Szczepański 9; tel: 012-433 54 50; Tue–Sat 10am–6pm, Sun 10am–4pm) is home to a branch of Kraków's National Museum, with paintings by Poland's leading 20th-century painter, Stanisław Wyspiański. The collection is currently under renovation, but the museum still has permanent exhibitions devoted to art collector and critic Feliks 'Manggha' Jasieński, temporary exhibitions, lectures, concerts, theatre plays, a museum shop, information centre and café.

The Baroque **St Anna's Church** ❶ (Kościół Św Anny) on Św Anny 13 was designed by Tylman van Gameren between 1689 and 1703 as the university church. The stucco works and polychromy of the magnificent ceiling, let alone the side chapels, make this a worthwhile visit. Opposite the church is **Maius College** ❶ (Collegium Maius; Jagiellońska 15; tel: 012-663 15 21/13 07

(reservations); www.maius.uj.edu.pl; Apr–Oct Mon–Sat 10am–2.20pm, Tue and Thu till 5.20pm, Nov–Mar Mon–Sat 10am–2.20pm, Tue, till 3.20pm; book in advance). This is the oldest college of Kraków University, established by the Jagiellonian dynasty in 1364. It was also Poland's first university college, and the second in Central and Eastern Europe after Prague. The Gothic arcaded court-yard is magnificent, and you can stroll through it whenever the college is open (daily, until dusk). Admission to the museum is only as part of a guided tour (leaving every 20 minutes). This takes in the original library with its blue sky-scape ceiling, senate room, professors' dining room and chambers, including numerous *objets d'art*, and scientific instruments used by Nicholas Coper-nicus (Mikołaj Kopernik), who studied here from 1491 to 1495. The Golden Globe of 1510 is one of the first to show the New World (America), with the inscription '*America, terra noviter reperta*' ('America, a newly discovered land').

A detour to the main building of the **National Museum** (Muzeum Narodowe; 3 Maja 1; tel: 012-433 56 00; www.muzeum.krakow.pl; Tue–Sat 10am–6pm, Sun 10am–4pm) gives you the chance to see one of the city's most important and extensive galler-ies. It covers 20th-century art, from Secessionism to contemporary art, and details Kraków's history as Poland's most important centre of fine art. Other galleries in the museum include a collection of military uniforms and weapons, and a collection of decora-tive arts, including furniture. Despite the vast number of exhibits, you can get around the entire building in a morning or afternoon session without experiencing gallery fatigue.

Grodzka leads to the Royal Castle and Cathedral, but before this it is worth exploring the numerous gal-leries and restaurants on this street, such as the traditionally Polish 'Pod Aniołami' ('Under the Angels'; www.podaniolami.pl) at Number 35. It is famous for its marinated meats, grilled over a beech hardwood fire, and many other traditional dishes. Among the historic buildings is the city's earli-est Baroque church, **St Peter and St Paul's Church** (Kościół Św Piotra

The passageway within Florian's Gate.

i Pawła). In front of the church is an impressive walled courtyard with 12 late-Baroque sculptures of the apostles. The architect modelled his designs on Il Gesù, Rome's renowned Jesuit church. A 46.5-metre (153ft) Foucault's pendulum inside the church is the longest in Poland. Every Thursday there are demonstrations which illustrate, albeit indirectly, Earth's rotation. The austere and strikingly simple Romanesque **St Andrew's Church** ❶ (Kościół Św Andrzeja) is one of the city's oldest, with elegant stucco work by Balthasar Fontana and a pulpit in the shape of a horse-drawn carriage.

Parallel to Grodzka is one of the city's most beautiful streets, Kanonicza (as it once housed clergymen), with ornate Renaissance and Gothic houses. At number 19 is the former **home of Pope John Paul II** (Muzeum Kardynała Wojtyły; tel: 012-422 75 23; www.muzeumkra.diecezja.pl; Tue–Fri 10am–4pm, Sat–Sun 10am–3pm), who lived here while serving as Bishop of Kraków. Besides the exhibition of his personal effects there is also a fine collection of sacred art.

Wawel Castle and Cathedral

At the end of Grodzka, which is an easy stroll from the main market square, you have an inspiring view of the **Wawel Castle** ⓤ (also known as Royal Castle; Zamek Królewski na Wawelu; tel: 012-422 51 55; www.wawel.krakow.pl; each exhibition has a separate entrance and ticket), built on a limestone hill rising above the River Vistula (Wisła). Serving as the royal residence between 1038 and 1596, this complex of buildings includes medieval defensive walls and towers, the royal castle, royal cathedral, treasury and armoury. The earliest surviving architectural fragments date from the 10th century, and each architectural genre, from Romanesque and Gothic to Renaissance and Baroque, can be seen here. The immense importance of the castle to Poland's heritage is summed up by the eminent artist Stanisław Wyspiański, who wrote: 'Here everything is Poland, every stone and fragment, and the person who enters here becomes a part of Poland.'

The perfectly proportioned, three-storey arcaded courtyard, from which the castle extends along four wings,

Maius College Assembly Hall.

is one of Europe's finest examples of Renaissance architecture. Built from 1502 to 1536, it was designed by the Italian architects Francisco the Florentine and Bartolomeo Berrecci. The royal apartments (Apr–Oct Tue–Fri 9.30am–5pm, Sat–Sun 10am–5pm, Nov–Mar Tue–Sat 9.30am–4pm) include a magnificent collection of arrases (woven wall hangings) depicting Biblical scenes, commissioned in the mid-16th century by King Zygmunt August. While many treasures were saved from the Nazis, having been shipped to Canada prior to the outbreak of World War II, only 142 of the original 360 arrases survived the war. The tour passes through Renaissance and Baroque apartments, and there are usually a couple of musicians in period costume performing medieval songs. The **Treasury and Armoury Museum** (Apr–Oct Mon 9.30am–1pm, Tue–Fri 9.30am–5pm, Sat–Sun 10am–5pm, Nov–Mar Tue–Sat 9.30am–4pm) includes coronation regalia and royal jewels, including the 13th-century szczerbiec ('jagged sword') used at Polish coronations from 1320.

At the entrance to the Gothic **Wawel Cathedral** (Mon–Sat, 9am–4pm, Sun 12.30–4pm, until 5pm Apr–Oct; free) is a prehistoric tusk, which has hung here for centuries; superstition states that so long as the tusk hangs by the entrance the cathedral will be safe. Built on the site of an earlier Romanesque church, the triple-naved design includes side chapels that were added later. The most spectacular are the Renaissance Kaplica Zygmunta (Sigismund's Chapel), built from 1519 to 1533, crowned with a magnificent gilded dome, and **Holy Cross Chapel** (Kaplica Świętego Krzyża), with frescos incorporating Ruthenian and Byzantian elements. From the 14th century the cathedral was used for royal coronations and funerals. Royal tombs (charge) vary in design from the highly ornate, such as the marble sarcophagus of the Jagiellonian King Kazimierz IV, completed by Veit Stoss, to the entirely modest, such as the tomb of St Stanisław Szczepanowski in the central nave.

The labyrinthine **crypt** is usually much quieter than the cathedral,

Inside the National Museum.

which can be full of tour groups, and is the final resting place for members of the royal family and national figures such as Adam Mickiewicz, Tadeusz Kościuszko (who led uprisings during the partition of Poland) and the 20th-century statesman Marshal Józef Piłsudski. There is also the tomb of late president Lech Kaczyński and his wife Maria, who both died in the Smoleńsk air crash in 2010 (see page 79).

One of the cathedral's three towers contains Zygmunt's Bell (Dzwon Zygmunta; charge), which was cast in 1520 and weighs 8 tons. Climbing the steep and cramped staircase is a bit of a struggle, but it's worth it, particularly as a Polish superstition states that anyone touching the bell will enjoy good fortune. Moreover, an observation terrace provides great views of the Old Town.

Opposite the main entrance to the cathedral is a separate building housing the **Cathedral Museum** (Apr–Oct Mon–Sat 9am–5pm, Nov–Mar 9am–4pm), established on the initiative of Pope John Paul II when he was

Wawel Castle.

Cardinal Karol Wojtyła, Archbishop of Kraków.

Beneath the Wawel is the **Dragon's Cave** (Smocza Jama; daily Apr–June 10am–6pm, July–Aug 10am–7pm, Sept–Oct 10am–5pm), home of the mythical Wawel dragon. The entrance to the cave is marked by an incongruously modern metalwork sculpture of a slimline, 1960s-style dragon periodically breathing gas flames. Apparently the dragon was woken from a deep thousand years' sleep by the constant noise as the castle was constructed, and ventured out in search of something to eat. As the dragon preferred virgins, he soon depleted Kraków of this valuable commodity. King Krak, by then too elderly to take up the challenge of slaying the dragon himself, said that whoever defeated the dragon would receive half the kingdom and his daughter's hand in marriage. An apprentice shoemaker used ingenuity rather than brawn. Filling a sheepskin with sulphur and salt, he sewed it up, equipped it with four wooden legs to make it appear life-like and left it outside the cave. The dragon had it

for breakfast. At this point there are two versions of what happened next. Either the contents made the dragon so thirsty that he went to the river and drank so much that he burst, or the sheep blew up inside him, ignited by the fire that the dragon breathed. The shoemaker consequently married the princess and, true to fairy-tale tradition, they lived happily ever after. By the Wawel, on Bulwar Czerwińskiego, you can join boat trips (tel: 012-427 20 03; www.zeglugawkrakowie.pl; Apr–Oct) along the River Vistula.

Across the river is the popular **Manggha Museum of Japanese Art and Technology** (Muzeum Sztuki i Techniki Japońskiej Manggha; Marii Konopnickiej 26; tel: 012-267 27 03; www.manggha.pl; Tue–Sun 10am–6pm), which opened in 1994. Founded by the famous Polish film director Andrzej Wajda, the museum collection comprises contemporary Japanese, Korean and Polish art, including works by Toshihiro Amano. Manggha is also a vibrant cultural centre that offers classes in Japanese, tea brewing, Ikebana (flower arranging) and more in order to promote Japanese culture in Poland. The ultra-modern museum building was designed by renowned Japanese architect Arata Isozaki and inspired by the traditional architecture of Japan.

Kazimierz, Kraków's Jewish Quarter

Kraków's Jewish quarter, Kazimierz, was originally a separate walled town established in the 14th century by King Casimir the Great (Kazimierz Wielki), with its own gateways, town hall and market place, centred around what is now **Szeroka**  (literally 'Wide Street'). Kazimierz became part of Kraków in the 18th century. In 1941 the Nazis confined Jews to the Kazimierz ghetto before sending them to the death camps. Of the 68,000 Jews who lived in Kazimierz in 1938, only a few hundred survived the war. Kazimierz itself escaped destruction by the

Nazis – but only because they planned to establish a macabre museum here of what they termed 'vanished races'. However, after the war it fell into ruin as Communist authorities neglected the quarter. Things changed when the first annual Jewish Culture Festival was organised in 1988, soon becoming one of the biggest such events in the world. A seven-hour concert, 'Szalom na Szerokiej', on Szeroka street, which presents Jewish music from all over the world, remains one of its highlights. The festival succeeded in awakening interest in the nearly forgotten culture of Kraków's Jews. Steven Spielberg's film *Schindler's List*, mostly shot in Kazimierz, also contributed to the quarter's revival. As a result, renovation work started, with once-dilapidated streets and houses being slowly restored to their former glory.

Szeroka has retained its Jewish character, though parts of this and some surrounding streets are still so run-down you would think the war had only just ended. Restoration work is ongoing, and in the meantime the area receives plenty of tourists,

Star of David on a wall in Kazimierz, now a thriving Jewish quarter.

The fire-breathing dragon of sculptor Bronisław Chromy.

particularly American Jews tracing their roots, or other visitors taking 'Oskar Schindler tours'. Making the most of this, wandering musicians play nostalgic tunes in Szeroka's Jewish cafés and restaurants. Szeroka also has three synagogues. The **Jewish Museum** (www.mhk.pl; Apr–Oct Mon 10am–2pm, Tue–Sun 9am–5pm, Nov–Mar Mon 10am–2pm, Tue–Thu and Sat–Sun 9am–4pm, Fri 10am–5pm; free on Mon) is housed in the **Old Synagogue** (Stara Synagoga; Szeroka 24; tel: 012-422 09 62). Dating from the 15th and 16th centuries, the façade has Gothic and Renaissance elements, while period interiors house an exhibition of Jewish history and culture. A monument in front of the synagogue marks the site where 30 Jews were shot by the Nazis in 1943.

The **Remuh Synagogue** (May–Sept Sun–Fri 9am–4 pm, May–Sept until 6pm, currently under renovation), the smallest in the city, is not only a historic monument but still has a small congregation. A courtyard opens onto one of Europe's only Renaissance Jewish cemeteries, laid out in 1533 (the other is in Prague). The renowned writer and philosopher Rabbi Moses Isserle, known as Remuh, was laid to rest here. This cemetery has a very poignant atmosphere, with some highly ornate tombstones.

One of the restored buildings is the **Isaac Synagogue** (Synagoga Izaaka; Kupa 18; Sun–Thu 9am–7pm, Fri 9am–3pm). Dating from the 17th century, this was the city's largest and originally the most lavishly furnished synagogue. Retaining a Renaissance façade, the Baroque hall has fragments of recently uncovered 17th-century wall murals, while the women's gallery is separated from the main hall by an arcade of Tuscan columns. Having been left unfurnished as a 'shell', the slightly austere appearance makes visiting this synagogue all the more moving. On the premises there are also kosher and Judaica shops, a Hebrew/English library, study hall and kosher restaurant.

The Judaica Foundation Centre for Jewish Culture, which includes a picture gallery, antiquarian bookshop and café, is nearby at Meiselsa 17, while

Inside the Tempel Synagogue in Kazimierz.

the former Town Hall (Ratusz) now houses the Ethnographic Museum (Muzeum Etnograficzne; PlacWolnica 1; tel: 012-430 55 75; www.etnomuzeum. eu; Tue–Sat 11am–7pm, Thu until 9pm, Sun 11am–3pm; free on Sun). Its extensive collection of folk art and culture from villages in the Kraków, Podhale and Silesian regions includes paintings, sculpture and folk costumes, as well as exhibits relating to traditional folk-rites such as Christ Child's cribs and Easter eggs. Recreated rooms comprising authentic furniture and decor mean you can walk around in what still feels like someone's home.

Across the river from Kazimierz there are two museums not to be missed. The first is the **Museum of Contemporary Art,** also known as **MOCAK** (Lipowa 4; tel: 012-263 40 00; www.mocak.pl; Tue–Sun 11am–7pm; free on Tue). Opened in 2011 in the former Schindler's enamel factory warehouse, it presents international contemporary art, mainly of the last two decades, organises educational workshops and holds temporary exhibitions. The permanent collection includes works by Marina Abramowic, Mirosław Bałka, Krzysztof Wodiczko, Wilhelm Sasnal and many others. It also houses a library (building B) and a bookstore.

Across the street (a single ticket can be bought for both museums), the former **Oskar Schindler's Factory** houses a branch of Kraków's Historical Museum (www.mhk.pl/branches/ oskar-schindlers-factory; Apr–Oct Mon 10am–4pm, Tue–Sun 10am–8pm, Nov–Mar Mon 10am–2pm, Tue–Sun 10am–6pm; last admission 90 mins before closing) dedicated to Oskar Schindler, who saved more than a thousand Jews from extermination in concentration camps (see page 62). Its permanent exhibition 'Kraków under Nazi Occupation 1939–1945' documents the lives of Kraków's residents, as well as their oppressors, during World War II. Multimedia presentations, reconstructions – for instance, of basements where Jews were hidden – and other exhibits keep their stories alive. Schindler's former office in the administrative building

FACT

The International Biennial of Regional Dolls and the Annual Folk Art Fair in September are held in Kraków, as part of the Ethnographic Museum.

Kazimierz teems with bars and cafés.

hasn't been changed much since he left it and features a symbolic 'survivors' ark' made from thousands of enamelled products made by Schindler's employees during the war.

Modern Kraków

The most recent part of the city is **Nowa Huta**, a large post-war housing and industrial area featuring the uncompromising style of 'concrete blocks' typical of the Communist era. This long-neglected area has recently become very popular with foreign tourists interested in its unspoilt Communist legacy. A statue of Lenin stood in the central square until the beginning of 1990, when it was pulled down.

Nowa Huta, once a model socialist town, was a popular destination among Polish and foreign apparatchiks. At the heart of the district is a vast steelworks (now owned by ArcelorMittal Poland) which at its height employed nearly 40,000 workers (now only 3,500). The neighbourhood was designed to provide its inhabitants with all they needed

for living. However, with the demise of the steelworks, Nowa Huta begin to slide into oblivion. It gained the unenviable reputation of being the most dangerous district in the city (even though statistics didn't confirm this), which has begun to change only recently. Today Nowa Huta has turned its bleak socialist legacy into an advantage as several tourist companies organise tailor-made 'Communism tours' (www.crazyguides.com) that offer a ride in a vintage Trabant or Polonez, lunch in a traditional milk bar and many other attractions. To learn more about history of the district, head for the **History of Nowa Huta Museum** (16 Słoneczny Estate; Apr–Oct Tue–Sun 9.30am–5pm, Nov–Mar Tue–Sat 9am–4pm, Wed until 5pm; free on Wed). But Nowa Huta is not all gloomy industrialisation: it also has some historic buildings, including the 11th-century Cistercian Abbey in Mogiła, which is opposite the wooden elaborate 15th-century Church of St Bartholomew. The neighbourhood of Bieńczyce features the vast Church of the Holy Mother Queen of Poland, built in the shape of a ship, which was used as a rendezvous and shelter for opposition groups during the period of martial law declared by President Jaruzelski in December 1981.

The pleasant **Zakrzówek** lake in VIII Dębniki district is one of Krakovians' favourite leisure spots. The former quarry was flooded in 1990 and soon became a popular weekend destination. It is also a divers' paradise as the water is clear and visibility reaches 15 metres (49ft). The maximum depth of the artificial lake is 32 metres (105ft). To dive here, contact Kraken Diving Centre (Centrum Nurkowe Kraken; www.kraken.pl).

Greater Kraków

Various national parks, historic towns, palaces and attractions are within easy reach of Kraków. The region has also preserved its *Folklor Krakowski*, the

OSKAR SCHINDLER AND PŁASZÓW

Oskar Schindler was a German industrialist living and working in Kraków during World War II, who is credited with saving hundreds of Jews by employing them in his factory. Although his motives remain controversial and were not altogether altruistic – he was a businessman at heart and the Jews were effectively slave labour – the number of lives saved cannot be disputed. Schindler has now reached hero status to many, immortalised first in the award-winning book *Schindler's Ark* by Thomas Keneally and later in the Academy Award-winning film *Schindler's List*, directed by Steven Spielberg, much of which was filmed in and around Kraków. Schindler's Emalia factory is still standing on Lipowa street and now houses a branch of Krakow's History Museum.

Also immortalised in Spielberg's film is the Płaszów concentration camp, located just south of Kazimierz, which was overseen by the cold-blooded Nazi commander Amon Goeth. Many of Kraków's Jews were imprisoned and murdered here. Although the Nazis blew up much of the camp as they retreated in 1945, leaving behind little more than a deserted wilderness, parts of the gate remain and on the hill there is a monument to the victims of the camp, which was erected in the 1960s. Goeth's villa is now a private residence.

traditional folklore, which includes a dance known as the Krakowiak (similar to the polka). Many surrounding villages have also retained the architectural style typical of this region. A visit to the Benedictine Abbey in **Tyniec** (www.tyniec.benedyktyni.pl), 10km (6 miles) from Kraków, is highly recommended. Formerly a Romanesque abbey fortress, it is romantically situated on the summit of a limestone cliff overlooking the River Vistula. While the church and cloisters are a prime example of Baroque, much of the abbey lay in ruins until the beginning of the 21st century, when the last stage of a long renovation project was completed. In summer, the abbey hosts the Benedictine Music Summer Festival. A stroll along the banks of the River Vistula beneath the abbey is also very picturesque.

Around 13km (8 miles) outside Kraków is the **Wieliczka Salt Mines** (Kopalnia Soli Wieliczka; Daniłowicza 10; tel: 012-278 73 02; www.kopalnia.pl; daily Apr–Oct 7.30am–7.30pm, Nov–Mar 8am–5pm; guided tour only). Listed by UNESCO on the World Cultural Heritage List, this is Poland's (and possibly the world's) oldest working salt mine, dating from the 12th or even the 10th century. There are nine levels, down to a depth of 327 metres (1,072 ft), with galleries, chambers and tunnels totalling over 300km (93 miles). More than a million visitors a year now come to see the amazing features of this salt mine, including a vast underground cathedral carved from salt, including an altar, gallery and chandeliers, three further chapels also carved from salt, a gallery of salt gnomes carved by miners in the 1960s, and caverns with lakes, while the extraordinary effect of refracted light creates a magical 'underworld'. The mining museum exhibits local geology, tools, clothing and documents dating back 600 years. There is also a subterranean sanatorium treating patients suffering from asthma and various allergies.

To the east of Kraków, at the confluence of the Wisła and Raba rivers, lies **Puszcza Niepołomicka**, a primeval forest which was formerly hunting grounds for the royal court,

The Benedictine Abbey in Tyniec.

and which now includes a reserve for aurochs. At the edge of the forest in the town of Niepołomice is a castle with a delightful arcaded courtyard, modelled on Kraków's Royal Castle (see page 202) and now serving as a regional museum (tel: 012-261 98 51; www.muzeum.niepolomice.pl). Trails from the town lead into the forest. On the other side of the Wisła, about an hour's drive from Kraków, is the village of **Wiślica**. This was the main fortress for the Wiślanie tribe between the 9th and 10th centuries. The crypt of the town's Gothic church has Romanesque foundations and a handsome floor relief, as well as fragments of an earlier church, complete with a font – evidence that Christianity was already established in this region long before Poland's official conversion to Christianity in ad 966. The village of **Igołomia** is the home town of Brother Albert (Adam Chmielowski). This painter and monk founded the order of St Adalbertus, devoted to caring for the poor. Numerous archaeological digs have also taken place in the Igołomia region.

The beauty of the surrounding countryside is spectacularly displayed throughout the **Jura Krakowsko-Częstochowska**. This mountain range to the northwest of Kraków includes limestone hills and cliff-faces, caves, deep valleys and extraordinary rocks in the shape of clubs and needles. The region is also home to wild boar and roe deer, not to mention 12 different species of bat. Part of the Jura now comes under the auspices of the Ojców National Park (Ojcowski Park Narodowy), which covers an area of 1,890 hectares (4,650 acres). The most interesting part of this park is the 14km (9-mile) long valley of the River Prądnik near Ojców, surrounded by thick forests which provide a dramatic backdrop to limestone cliff-faces. The valley's unique flora includes the so-called *brzoza ojcowska* (shrubby birch). Two caves, Ciemna (literally 'dark'; tel: 012-380 10 11; end Apr–mid-Oct 10am–5pm) and the larger Łokietek (tel: 012-419 08 01; www.grotalokietka.pl) are open to the public. It is said that King Władysław Łokietek hid here

St Kinga's Chapel in the Salt Mines, Wieliczka.

after an attack by King Wenceslas of Bohemia. Some traces of human settlement found in the Ciemna Caves are thought to be about 120,000 years old, and are on display in the Władysław Szafer Museum in Ojców (tel: 012-389 20 40; Tue–Fri 9am–3pm, Sat–Sun 10am–4pm). The town also has ruins of a 14th-century castle.

A few kilometres from Ojców on a dramatic elevation overlooking the Prądnik Valley is the Renaissance castle of **Pieskowa Skała** ('Dog's Rock'). Once the residence of aristocratic families, it is now a branch of the Wawel's National Art Collection (the museum is closed for renovation until 2016), with an exhibition of household and castle furnishings dating from the Middle Ages to the 19th century. On the ground floor of the palace is the historic Zamkowa restaurant, while a short walk from the castle leads to an unusual 25-metre (82ft) rock called the Club of Hercules. Pieskowa Skała was one of several hilltop castles built on the so-called 'Trail of the Eagle's Lair', in order to secure the route from Kraków to Silesia during the Middle

Ages. Most of those castles are now in ruins, with one of the most impressive being Ogrodzieniec, which lies further west.

At the plateau's western edge is **Olkusz**, once known as 'silver city'. This is Poland's oldest mining region. Lead and zinc ore, both with a high silver content, were found in this area. The Błędow Desert (Pustynia Błędowska) covers 30 sq km (11 sq miles) and is the only large expanse of sand in Poland. It was once much larger, but it is progressively giving way to vegetation.

En route to Bielsko-Biała (see page 254) is **Wadowice**, 50km (35 miles) from Kraków. Set in the valley of the River Skawa at the foot of the Little Beskid Mountains, this is the town where Pope John Paul II was born and spent his youth. His childhood home is now a museum (Kościelna 7; www.domjp2.pl; daily May–Sept 8.30am–5.30pm, Nov–Mar 8.30am–2.30pm, Apr and Oct 8.30am–4.30) documenting his life and work, while on the Market Place is the 15th-century church where the Pope was baptised.

Climbing in the Jura.

A window-view in Lublin.

THROUGH LITTLE POLAND

On this route through Małopolska, places of outstanding natural beauty alternate with the Renaissance and Gothic architecture of cities such as Zamość and Łańcut.

Main Attractions
Tarnów
Łańcut
Ujazd
Krasiczyn
Zamość
Lublin
Kazimierz Dolny

In the south and east of Little Poland (Małopolska) large tracts of land have retained the character of primeval forest – the Puszcza Niepołomicka, Puszcza Sandomierska and Puszcza Solska. Amid broadleaf and coniferous woodland live indigenous wolves, lynx, bison and brown bears. National parks, about a dozen protected areas and several hundred nature reserves have been established in the area.

East of Kraków

If you travel from **Kraków ❶** (see page 193) eastwards along the E40, which leads through Tarnów, Rzeszów and Przemyśl all the way to Medyka on the Ukraine border, you will come to yet another region of Małopolska. In Bochnia, not far from Wieliczka, is a second salt mine, almost as old as that in Wieliczka (see page 193). It is also open to visitors.

To the south of Bochnia, in the village of **Nowy Wiśnicz ❷**, stands a palace (tel: 014-612 85 89; www.zamek wisnicz.pl; May–Oct Mon–Fri 8am–6pm, Sat–Sun 10am–6pm, Nov–Apr Mon–Fri 8am–4pm, Sat–Sun 9am–5pm) owned by the Lubomirski family. After the war, the property was confiscated by the state as part of the land reform policy, but the land registry documents were never altered, so when democracy was restored to Poland and changes were made to the constitution,

the property was legally returned to its former owners. It is an impressive structure with five towers, massive walls and a pentagonal courtyard. Formerly a Gothic fortification, the palace was renovated in the 17th century by Mattia Trapole and the walls and interior are decorated with wall paintings and stucco work. A small municipal museum in the former poorhouse, funded by Duke Stanisław Lubomirski, features a few Nikifor sketches (see page 235) and a 17th-century brass canon. The next town along the

Rural life in the Lublin countryside.

FACT

Located on a so-called 'thermal island', Tarnów is the warmest place in Poland, with a long-term average temperature of 8.8°C. It is also the sunniest, with the fewest number of cloudy days (55) in a year.

route is **Brzesko**, justly famous for its excellent beer, Okocim, brewed in the nearby village of the same name. The brewery (currently owned by Carlsberg) was founded in 1845 by the Bohemian industrialist Baron Goetz. Not far from Brzesko, in the town of **Dębno**, is a small but interesting Gothic castle where a museum keeps an interesting collection of weapons, paintings and furniture.

The next important settlement along the route through Małopolska is **Tarnów ❸**, the administrative centre for the *powiat* (county), with a charter dating back to 1330. It was once the seat of the powerful noble Tarnowski family, ancestors of the Polish military commander hetman Jan Tarnowski. Some 350 buildings in Tarnów are listed under the Polish national monument protection scheme and the town, which was a provincial capital during the era of the Austro-Hungarian empire, is sometimes called a "Pearl of the Renaissance".

Medieval Tarnów is built on two levels, with the upper and lower towns connected by steps. The former

defensive walls were removed and replaced in the late 19th century by a road around the old town centre. Sights of particular interest in the Old Town include the Town Hall, its arcades, patrician houses and a vast 15th-century cathedral containing the tombs of the Tarnowski and Ostrogski families.

The Town Hall houses a branch of Tarnów Regional Museum (Rynek 1; Muzeum Okręgowe w Tarnowie; www.muzeum.tarnow.pl; Tue 9am–5pm, Wed–Fri 9am–3pm, Sun 10am–2pm), with a collection including portraits, military equipment, china and silverware. Other museums worth seeing include: the Diocesan Museum (Plac Katedralny 6; Tue–Sat 10am–3pm, Sun 9am–2pm) and the Ethnographic Museum (ul Krakowska 10; Muzeum Etnograficzne; Tue 9am–5pm, Wed–Fri 9am–3pm, Sun 10am–2pm), with a rich collection on Roma culture.

Before World War II, some 45 percent of Tarnów's inhabitants were Jews. Following the German invasion they were enclosed in the ghetto and subsequently killed or sent to concentration camps. In the winter of 1944 the

Germans declared the city *Judenrein* (Jew-free). Today a Jewish tourist trail in Tarnów includes characteristic tenement houses from the 17th and 18th centuries on Żydowska and Wekslarska streets, as well as one of the oldest and best-preserved Jewish cemeteries in southern Poland, and the bimah (the central part of a synagogue).

Not far from the Old Town is the **Square of the Ghetto Heroes** (Plac Bohaterów Getta) and, beside the square, the baths where the Jewish community performed their ritual washing ceremonies. It was from here on 14 June 1940 that the first transport left for the concentration camp at Auschwitz with 738 people on board (see page 62). Dating from 1517, the **Church of St Stanislaus**, with two chapels, a tower and adjacent cloisters, is the largest wooden church in Małopolska. Among the most interesting relics are Gothic sculptures on the altar and the sculpture of St Barbara from 1500.

The nearby village of Wierzchosławice is the birthplace of Wincenty Witos (1874–1945), leader of the radical peasant movement which gained momentum between the two world wars. His home and the adjacent buildings house a museum (Wed–Fri 8am–3.30pm, Sun 10am–2pm) with tools that belonged to the peasant leader.

The village of Ciężkowice, dating back to the 10th century, lies in the Biała valley. Wooden houses with open galleries looking out onto the town make a picturesque sight. The **Petrified City** (Skamieniałe Miasto) nature reserve is nearby. An amazing rock formation here has given rise to numerous myths and legends.

The Sandomierz Basin

The central region of Małopolska is dominated by a wide depression known as the Sandomierz Basin (Kotlina Sandomierska). Fields interspersed with large wooded areas are typical of this flat, rural landscape. Most of the farms are small, about 2 hectares (5 acres) in area, and the narrow strips of cultivated land form a regular pattern.

The most important town in this region is **Rzeszów ❹**. Founded in

Folk art on a Zalipie dwelling.

COLOURFUL VILLAGE

Lovers of folk art should take a detour to the village of **Zalipie**, about 32km (20 miles) to the northwest of Tarnów, where local folk artists have covered the interiors and exteriors of their houses, their tables, barns, fences, furniture and even their dog kennels with colourful and original paintings of plant motifs. The custom originated at the end of the 19th century when old furnaces were replaced. Women tried to cover the blackened walls with brightly coloured spots made of lime. These later evolved into flower bouquets. Zalipie is also renowned for its embroidery, hand-cut silhouettes and straw dolls. In the house where the painter Felicja Curyłowa (1904–74) lived, a museum (Tue–Fri and Sun 10am–4pm) keeps alive these unusual rural crafts.

FACT

Every other July since 1969, Rzeszów has been the venue for the World Festival of Polish Folklore Groups Living Abroad.

the 14th century, the capital of the Podkarpackie voivodeship has seen a dynamic growth in recent years. A modern international airport, Rzeszów–Jesionka, links the city with several European capitals including London, Oslo, Paris and Rome, as well as with Warsaw and Gdańsk. It boasts the country's second-largest runway. The landmark of the "new" Rzeszów is a futuristic **round footbridge** over the intersection of Piłsudski and Grunwald streets – the first such construction in Europe. Modern shopping centres and a technological university catering for the growing number of foreign IT and innovation companies that have set up their offices here complete the picture of a vibrant town which, fortunately, hasn't forgotten its past. A splendidly renovated main square features a spectacular underground cellars tour, which explores the basements of nearby town houses. The route is nearly 400 metres (435 yards) long and goes as deep as 10 metres (33ft). The cellars were used mainly for storing goods, but also as shelters during the war. Remains of the medieval walls,

elements of iron bars and hinges can be seen during the excursion, while numerous secret passages just wait to be explored. A magnificent **Town Hall** originally built at the end of the 16th century dominates the main square. Elements of the old walls and cellar vaults are its main attraction. Two synagogues, rebuilt from the rubble of the war, and a Jewish cemetery serve as memorials to the town's former Jewish community which made up half the population before World War II.

The townscape today is dominated by the magnificent Lubomirski Palace, which dates from the late 16th century, although it was reconstructed at the turn of the 20th century. Surrounded by bastions and moats; it now houses a court and prosecutor's office. The Baroque church and the Bernardine Monastery (dating from the beginning of the 17th century) have also been preserved. The adjacent Italian-style **Bernardine Gardens** (Ogrody Bernardyńskie; daily 7am–9pm), with thousands of plants, a fountain and neat alleys, form a popular recreational area open to the public. A

Łańcut in the autumn.

Regional Museum (ul 3 Maja 19; tel: 017-853 52 78; www.muzeum.rzeszow.pl; Tue–Thu 9am–3.30pm, Fri 10am–5.30pm, Sun 10am–4pm) is housed in the former Piarist cloister. It contains a collection of Polish and European paintings and documents the history of the region and its people.

Every day a bustling market takes place in Rzeszów on Dołowa street. A great variety of produce, but above all low prices, attract not only locals but also shoppers and vendors from the whole region. It's not only food that's on sale – there have even been items such as a set of second-hand golf clubs brought from Germany in a car boot.

Situated on the E40 motorway, 17km (10 miles) east of Rzeszów, is the medieval town of **Łańcut** ❺, with its magnificent castle. This former residence of the aristocratic Lubomirski and Potocki families was built on old foundations between 1629 and 1641 by Stanisław Lubomirski. At the beginning of the 19th century the structure was expanded into a modern residential castle with the encouragement of Princess Elżbieta Lubomirska (1736–1826). This renovation was carried out according to plans drawn up by the famous architect Piotr Aigner. Later, at the turn of the 20th century, a façade in the French neo-Baroque style was added.

Today the castle is a museum (www.zamek-lancut.pl/en; castle: Mon noon–4pm, Tue–Sat 9am–4pm, Sun 9am–5pm; stables and coach house: Mon 1–5pm, Tue–Sat 10am–5pm, Sun 10am–6pm; opening times may vary according to season). The centrepiece of the castle is an almost square structure with corner towers and a central inner courtyard. A bulwark in the form of a five-pointed star surrounds the complex. The castle is famous for its interiors, dating from the 18th, 19th and 20th centuries and considered the most beautiful in Poland. The unusual library contains over 22,000 precious tomes. The upstairs living quarters, the ballroom, large dining hall and

theatre, as well as the Turkish room on the ground floor, are all remarkable. Visitors to the former stables will find a priceless collection of about 55 old carriages that belonged to the Potocki family. There is also another collection of about 80 carriages from after World War II at the nearby Castle Carriage House. Several outbuildings were added at a later date: the library, a greenhouse, orchid house and a court building which is now a restaurant and hotel (www.zamkowa-lancut.pl). The castle is encompassed by a park, laid out on a grand scale. A smaller palace and a riding school are located within the grounds. An international music festival (www.festiwallancut.pl) has been held in the castle every May since 1961.

Traditional country fairs are still held in the small towns around Rzeszów, such as Sokołów, Kolbuszowa and Strzyżów. Visitors to these fairs will find authentic arts and crafts on sale made by local craftspeople. A few of the villages in this region, in particular Medynia Głogowska, Pogwizdów, Medynia Łańcucka and Zalesie, are also centres for the traditional craft

Łańcut Castle.

The sundial on the Town Hall.

The rooftops of Sandomierz.

of pottery. Here almost 120 potters produce decorative ceramic dishes and sculptures, as well as traditional crockery for everyday use.

A range of hills known as the **Pogórze** lies to the south of Rzeszów. The River Wisłoka meanders peacefully through this picturesque landscape. In the many little towns and hamlets, wind-battered farmhouses recall a bygone age, but following the expulsion of the native, mainly Jewish, population, these primitive settlements have lost much of their charm.

The village buildings of Małopolska were originally built almost entirely out of wood. Although many examples of this type of construction still exist, an exceptionally good one is the small church in **Blizne**, which is situated between Rzeszów and Sanok. Built in Gothic style at the end of the 15th century from thick larchwood beams, it has remained, remarkably, unchanged (albeit renovated) to this day. It is now a Unesco Heritage site, just like its counterpart in **Sękowa** village near Gorlice. This splendid example of wooden architecture dates from the beginning

of the 16th century and is known for its wonderful setting. It proved very popular among 19th- and 20th-century Polish painters, including Stanisław Wyspiański and Józef Mehoffer.

North of Rzeszów

The section of the Kotlina Sandomierska to the north of Rzeszów is covered with the rich forests of the vast **Puszcza Sandomierska**. Mushrooms, berries and wild game all flourish in this environment. The region is inhabited by the Lesowiaki, a people who pride themselves on their self-sufficiency. Old farmhouses remain unspoilt, quaint traditions and intriguing rituals survive. Some aspects of the local folk customs have been preserved in the open-air museum at **Kolbuszowa** ❻ (www.muzeumkolbuszowa. pl; 16 April–15 Oct; Mon–Fri 9am–5pm, Sat–Sun 10am–7pm, 16 Oct–15 Apr daily 9am–3pm). This museum also hosts cultural events.

During World War II, the German army established two large military training grounds in Puszcza Sandomierska. Several prison and work camps also formed part of this complex. The most notorious work camp was in **Pustków**. Some 15,000 people lost their lives here.

Experiments with V-1 and V-2 rockets were carried out on a strictly guarded site close to the village of **Blizna** ❼. The underground intelligence wing of the Polish Home Army (*Armia Krajowa*) recorded a major success in its struggle against the occupying forces when locals managed to retrieve a rocket which had been fired by the Germans and, after dismantling it, smuggled it to London.

The ancient town of **Leżajsk** ❽ lies about 50km (31 miles) to the northeast of Rzeszów, not far from the River San. Numerous historic buildings and other reminders of a distant past can be found here. Produce markets take place weekly. In the northern part of the town is a 17th-century Bernardine monastery, which was later converted

into a fortress. The beautiful and richly decorated interior of the monastery is dominated by the organ, one of the largest in Poland. Built at the end of the 17th century, this instrument, with its 74 organ stops and 5,894 pipes, spans all three naves of the church. The International Organ and Chamber Music Festival has been held here for 20 years, from June to August. In other months the in-house organist will perform by special request. *The Miraculous Image of the Virgin Mary with Child* has been famous since 1634 as a painting that performs miracles. On Assumption Day in August, believers and nonbelievers alike are drawn here by the festivities.

Economically, the northern portion of this region, at the confluence of the Vistula and San rivers, is the most interesting. The centre of this area is the village of **Tarnobrzeg**. Once poverty-stricken and neglected, its sulphur deposits have brought employment and prosperity. The former open-cast mine at Machów was closed down in the late 1990s, and later flooded to form an artificial lake. The lake opened to the public in 2010

and its popularity has been growing ever since, particularly among sailors and windsurfers, who praise the lake's excellent wind conditions.

Baranów Sandomierski ⑨, located on the right-hand bank of the Vistula, is especially renowned for its palace, known as "little Wawel", a building regarded by many as one of the brightest jewels of Polish Renaissance architecture. All that remains from the original 16th-century fortress, however, is a rectangular structure with corner towers and a gate. The courtyard with arcaded passageways, an unusual stairway and rooftop attics, which are certainly the most distinctive features of the palace, were added between 1591 and 1606. Inside, the superbly renovated palace is richly decorated with murals and stucco works and is the site of a museum (Zamek w Baranowie Sandomierskim; www.baranow.com.pl; Tue–Sun Apr, Oct 9am–5pm, May–Sept 9am–6pm, Nov–Mar 9am–4pm), as well as a luxury hotel.

A short distance to the east of Tarnobrzeg is **Stalowa Wola**, one of Poland's newer towns and an important centre

Baranów Sandomierski's unusual staircase.

for the metal industry. Stalowa Wola was built in 1937, in conjunction with a weapons manufacturing plant. Today, the works manufacture steel and construction machinery. Nearby, on the opposite side of the San, lies the old village of **Radomyśl nad Sanem ⑩**. This is the venue for an unusual patriotic and religious play, performed every year at Easter. A group of residents, dressed in the colourful robes of Turkish soldiers (Turki), head a military parade through the village. Afterwards they go from house to house wishing the inhabitants luck and asking for a donation to pay for their costumes. They are accompanied by a marching band and countless spectators, many of whom travel great distances to watch the spectacle. The parade commemorates events of 1683, when a local detachment of the Polish infantry joined King Jan III Sobieski's troops heading for Vienna, which was besieged by the Turks. After the great victory they returned to their village wearing trophy Turkish uniforms.

This area is also very well known for its crafts. A little further to the east of Stalowa Wola, along the road leading from Nisko to Janów Lubelski, lie the villages of Łążek Ordynacki and Łążek Garncarski. These two woodland settlements, with craftsmen working in traditional family potteries, are renowned for the production of imaginative and beautiful ceramic designs. The small town of **Rudnik** lies half-an-hour's drive away from Stalowa Wola in the direction of Jarosław. Rudnik is famous for its basket-making. Manufacturing workshops and several thousand helpers working in their homes produce baskets, which are then exported to many different countries all over the world.

Sandomierz ⑪, one of Poland's finest towns, is situated to the north of the basin on a terrace above the banks of the Vistula. Once the capital of an independent duchy, the town was an important trading port. Founded on the site of an ancient settlement, it is one of the oldest and most picturesque towns in Poland. Thanks to its strategically important fortress, as early as the 12th century it was one of Poland's three largest commercial centres and enjoyed great prosperity during the

The clock tower of the Town Hall, Sandomierz.

Renaissance. The Old Town is perched on an oval-shaped hill 30 metres (100ft) above the river valley and has managed to preserve much of its medieval character, including several narrow streets with nooks and crannies. Like so many Polish towns, these old quarters successfully convey the impression of working communities where ordinary people still lead normal lives.

The remains of a royal palace can be seen at the southern edge of the town. Adjacent to these is a triple-naved Gothic cathedral dating from the 14th century. The Russo-Byzantine frescos in the chancel merit special attention. Adjacent to the cathedral is the Gothic house of **Długosz**, a medieval historian and chronicler of Poland (1415–80). Today, the Diocesan Museum (Tue–Sat 9am–3.30pm, Sun 1.30–3.30 pm, May–Sept until 4.30pm), with its collection of art and objets d'art, is housed here.

Nearby is the **Church of St James**, which formerly belonged to the Dominicans. This is Poland's best remaining example of a Romanesque brick church and serves as a memorial to the bloody Tartar invasion of 1259. The plain Romanesque north portal is particularly impressive, while the interior is tastefully finished with glazed bricks. Glass cases contain the bones of the monks who were murdered during the 13th-century Tartar attack.

The marketplace in the centre of the town is surrounded by a number of stylish houses. One, belonging to the Oleśnicki family, stands out, mainly because of its ornate gallery. The Town Hall dominates the middle of the marketplace and the remains of the old fortifications, with the tall Brama Opatowska (Abbot Gate), mark the northern boundary of the Old Town.

Visitors to Sandomierz should spend some time exploring the surrounding area as there are a number of places of interest. The arable land here is well suited to the production of fruits and vegetables. An old Cistercian abbey and a late-Romanesque church dating from the early 13th century are found in **Koprzywnica**, 17km (10 miles) to the southwest of Sandomierz. In the small village of **Ujazd ⓬**, the impressive Krzyżtopór Palace (www.krzyz topor.org.pl; daily Apr–Aug 8am–8pm, Sept–Oct 8am–6pm, Nov–Mar 8am–4pm) can be seen. This enormous edifice was built in the 17th century by the Ossoliński family, but was partially destroyed soon afterwards by the Swedes. Before the construction of the Palais de Versailles near Paris, this was the largest official residence in Europe. It has some very unusual design features: four towers for the four seasons, 12 large halls for each month, 52 rooms for each week of the year and 365 windows. There was even an additional window for leap years, which was covered up for the rest of the time.

Some 16km (10 miles) to the northeast of Ujazd lies **Opatów**, with its Romanesque theological college. A far-reaching system of passageways, cellars and vaulted chambers winds its way under the streets and houses. Five centuries ago, this served as a refuge from the marauding Tartars; today part of it is open to the public.

Wooden Orthodox church, Przemyśl.

Eastern Małopolska

The economy of the eastern section of Małopolska, which nestles in the valley of the River San, is dominated by agriculture. Those journeying eastwards from Rzeszów should make plans to stop off in **Jarosław** , close to the Ukrainian border. Sited on the banks of the river, Jarosław is one of the oldest towns in this area. During the Middle Ages its markets and fairs attracted merchants from all over Europe. The Old Town, with its abundance of interesting architecture, is still a veritable paradise for photographers.

The old houses around the marketplace, with their distinctive passageways, covered courtyards, decorated stairways and galleries, are particularly picturesque. The house that formerly belonged to the patrician Italian Orsetti family, built in Renaissance style with an open gallery and attic, is definitely worth seeking out. It now houses the Regional Museum (www.jaroslaw.pl; Wed–Sun 10am–2pm, 9am–5pm in July–Aug; free on Sun). Other interesting sights in Jarosław are the attractive Town Hall, a number of older churches, one of which is Russian-Orthodox, and several synagogues. Entering the town from Rzeszów, you will be able to see the late-Baroque **Dominican Monastery** hidden behind its surrounding walls. Outside these walls is a small well, which is enclosed in a chapel. The water in the well not only tastes good, but is also reputed to work magical powers on those who drink it. According to legend, a sculpture of the Madonna was found here in ancient times. Soon afterwards, the sculpture was found to have miracle-working powers. An exceptionally valuable work of art is the Gothic wooden sculpture of Mater Dolorosa from Zbawiec which is now located on the main altar.

Near Jarosław is **Sieniawa**, further downstream, where the restored palace of the Czartoryski family is well worth a visit. Equally interesting are Zarzecze, with the Dzieduszycki Castle, and **Węgierka**, with its ruins of a medieval manor house. In the small town of **Pruchnik** , a few miles south of Jarosław, time seems to have stood still for several centuries. The wooden houses by the marketplace and nearby streets have open galleries and precise, extremely complex decorative woodwork. Many are very old and, as they represent rare examples of Polish architecture, are now officially listed as ancient national monuments. Long-standing traditions have also been preserved: for many years now it has been the custom to hang an effigy of Judas publicly on the Saturday before Easter.

East meets west

The border between the Catholic world and the Orthodox runs to the east of the River San. For centuries this stretch of land has been the scene of confrontations between the east and west, and the various nationalities in the regions have lived and fought both together and against each other. At the end of World War II, for example, the Ukrainian nationalists here fought a bitter and cruel two-year battle for

Western Capercaillie, Roztocze National Park.

their right to independence. In the end, having suffered enormous destruction and the loss of many lives, they gave up their fight. In April 1947, regardless of whether they had supported the resistance movement, the Ukrainians living in southeastern Poland were forcibly resettled in the former German regions of Poland that were incorporated into Poland after World War II. Only evacuated and burnt-out villages remained. Even today many regions are only thinly populated and settlements can be found that are almost totally overgrown by woodland and shrubs.

Characteristic of this part of Poland is the wooden architecture of the Orthodox churches, which frequently occurs in the old villages. These are real gems of folk architecture. Some of the more beautiful Orthodox churches are found in Rudka near Sieniawa and in Chołyniec (both 17th-century), in Pożdziacz and Piątkowa near Przemyśl (18th-century) and in Radruż near Lubaczów (16th-century). Some of the old churches in the Ukrainian villages, also excellent examples of folk art, are now used as Roman Catholic churches.

The iconostases have been preserved in many of the churches. These traditional altar screens often show icons dating from the 17th to 19th centuries and many are of great artistic value. In 2013 eight wooden *tserkvas* (Eastern Orthodox churches) in Radruż, Chotyniec, Smolnik, Turzańsk, Powroźnik, Owczary, Kwiatoń and Brunary Wyżne were inscribed on Unesco's World Heritage List.

In the town of **Przemyśl** ⓯ the National and Archidiocesan Museum (Muzeum Archidiecezjalne w Przemyślu; Pl Katedralny 2–3; Tue–Sat 10am–4pm) houses an interesting collection of painted icons and other examples of sacred art. The countryside surrounding the border town of Przemyśl, a melting pot of various cultures and traditions since the 7th century, is enchanting. The densely wooded and hilly Przemyśl foothills (Pogórze Przemyskie) stretch out to the south of a town that receives few tourists. In recent years, the Ukrainian minority here has started celebrating its national holiday, the **Feast of St Jordan**, again. On a winter morning, the faithful, bearing flags

FACT

The eastern area abounds with sacred myths. Near Jarosław is the Sanctuary of the Holy Virgin in Jodłówka, with a chapel and well. Legend has it that here, too, the Virgin Mary appeared and performed miracles.

The Renaissance palace in Krasiczyn.

and crosses, congregate on the banks of the San and the deeply religious, almost mystical festival then begins. After the ceremony, the people wash their faces and eyes with river water. Freshly cleansed, they then consider themselves able to face up to their daily lives with renewed vigour.

A charming Renaissance palace belonging to the Krasicki family is located in **Krasiczyn** (Zamek w Krasiczynie; www.krasiczyn.com.pl; daily Apr–Oct 9am–4pm, tours every hour; Nov–Mar reserve at least a day ahead), 10km (6 miles) west of Przemyśl. Once the seat of one of Poland's most powerful families, it is a large building with fortifications comprising four bastions and a tower over the entrance. Stylish stucco work and paintings decorate the meticulously restored palace. There is a hotel and a restaurant in the revitalised Coach House, which is a good base for exploring the scenic area, ideally on a bike. Sword-fighting shows and lessons are other attractions.

Not far from Krasiczyn, 16km (10 miles) south of Przemyśl, is **Kalwaria Pacławska ⑯**, where a Franciscan monastery with a painting of the Virgin Mary has been revered for centuries because of its miracle-working powers. In the area around the monastery, the Stations of the Cross are illustrated in 42 picturesquely situated chapels. The wooden houses in the village that grew up around the monastery are also worth taking the time to see. This is an extremely quiet and almost deserted area. Only in August, when the annual fair takes place, does it show any real signs of life.

A little further to the south, in the woods around the former village of **Arłamów**, is a holiday hostel that used to belong to the Communist Party and where Lech Wałęsa was kept prisoner for a time (see page 72). Today it is open to the public and, among other activities, hunts are organised in which visiting foreigners can participate. Anyone who enjoys horses and riding will want to visit **Stubno** to the northeast of Przemyśl, where the Polish state maintains a stud farm with English thoroughbreds and a riding club.

The Roztocze, which begins a bit further to the north, is also an extremely picturesque region. A unique mixture of flora and fauna can be found in the rolling forest-covered hills. In the most beautiful part of the Roztocze around the towns of Zwierzyniec and Krasnobrod, the **Roztocze National Park ⑰** (Roztoczański Park Narodowy, see page 124) has been established. About 10 percent of this 7,900-hectare (19,500-acre) park is under very strict protection. Geologically, the landscape is mixed and the climate changes dramatically with altitude. Consequently the vegetation is very varied: tough steppe plants, an abundance of mountain flora and other species that require warmth. The wooded regions are also very varied: pine, oak and beech forests proliferate. Running through the centre of the park is the spectacular River Wieprz. Varieties of game, wolf, tarpan, beaver, eagle, osprey and capercaillie are all native species to this park and thrive in great numbers.

Town house façades, Zamość.

On the southern faces of the Roztocze hills the remains of the Molotov Line fortifications from World War II can still be identified. Maps of hiking routes are available but small areas of the park are restricted and require the accompaniment of a guide.

Zamość

At the northeastern end of the national park in the Zamość Basin (Kotlina Zamojska) lies the attractive settlement of **Zamość** ⑱. This fascinating town, founded in the heart of the wilderness during the Renaissance (1579–1616) by the chancellor and Grand Hetman of the Crown, Jan Zamoyski, was designed by the Venetian Bernardo Morando.

The Old Town of **Zamość** consists of a palace and residential area surrounded by fortified walls with bastions and gates. This mighty fortress was built so solidly that it was able to resist the attacks of both the Cossacks and the Swedes. The palace, renovated between 1821 and 1831, now houses the prosecutor's office and court. Zamość Old Town is so greatly prized as an example of Renaissance architecture that it has been awarded Unesco World Cultural Heritage status.

The **Market Square** (Rynek Główny) lies at the heart of the Old Town. Its famous Town Hall (designed by Morando between 1591 and 1600) includes later additions of a grand double staircase (1768) and the octagonal 50-metre (165ft) high tower (1770) with a Baroque roof. Today it houses city council offices. The square is surrounded by town houses in Renaissance style, linked together with arcades. The German revolutionary and socialist-feminist theorist Rosa Luxembourg was born at Number 37 in 1871. The colourful houses on the northern frontage of the square shelter Zamojskie Museum (Muzeum Zamojoskie; Tue–Sun 9am–4pm, till 5pm in summer), with archaeological, ethnographic and historic collections. The Collegiate Church (1587–98), another of Morando's works, is located to the southwest of the market square. The high altar paintings here are usually ascribed to Domenico Tintoretto. The cathedral's bell-tower has an observation terrace (tel: 084-639 26

Town Hall on Market Square, Zamość.

Candy-floss stand in Market Square.

Market day in Kazimierz Dolny.

14; May–Oct Mon–Fri 10am–9pm, Sat–Sun 1–10pm, Nov–Apr reserve ahead). Adjoining this central marketplace are two other squares: the Salt Marketplace (Rynek Solny) and the Water Marketplace (Rynek Wodny). The western part of the Old Town is dominated by the palace formerly owned by the Zamoyski family (1585). An impressive statue of Jan Zamojski on a horse stands in front of it.

Zamość was once a town with a multicultural population, including Poles, Russians, Jews and Armenians. During the Nazi occupation, it was renamed Himmlerstadt. The Polish population was expelled and Germans were brought in to create what Hitler hoped would become the eastern bulwark of the Third Reich. Consequently, the historic buildings, including the old Orthodox church, the synagogue and an Armenian meeting house, survived the war. The Germans were unable to complete their inhumane resettlement plan, but thousands of Poles still lost their lives in the prisoner-of-war camps and mass shootings in the Rotunda, now a Museum of Martyrology (Apr–Oct daily 7am–8pm; free), a ring-shaped fort 10 minutes from the Old Town. Many of the town's inhabitants were transported to the extermination camp at Bełżec, 42km (26 miles) away, and the Jewish population was completely wiped out.

Lublin

The region of Lublin in the northeastern part of Małopolska is an agricultural area, but with industry concentrated in the larger towns. The largest town in eastern Poland, **Lublin** ⓳, is an important centre for industry, culture and science. It has been a busy trading centre since medieval times and during several periods in its history has been a target for invaders. Its finest moment occurred in 1569 when the Polish and Lithuanian rulers met here to agree the Lublin Union. A period of prosperity followed, but this ended with the First Partition (see page 38). When Poland regained its full independence in 1918, Lublin's Catholic University, the only Catholic university in the whole of eastern Europe, became the centre for Poland's

Catholic intelligentsia. It is now called the **John Paul II Catholic University of Lublin**, known as KUL (Katolicki Uniwersytet Lubelski Jana Pawła II; www.kul.pl). In July 1944, after liberation, Lublin was also the provisional capital of Poland and the seat of the transitional government that Stalin installed.

The small **Old Town** (Stare Miasto) is full of interesting sights: the marketplace with its old town houses (16th–18th century); the cathedral (16th–17th century) and the Dominican monastery (14th–17th century) are noteworthy. The Gothic church has 11 chapels and two are worth seeking out: the Firlej family chapel has a two-tier grave, and the dome above the Tyszkiewicz family chapel has a large fresco depicting *The Last Judgement*. The first building on the hill to the east of the town was erected during the 9th century, but the tower that stands there now is 13th century. The Holy Trinity Chapel, with its Russo-Byzantine paintings, has survived the ravages of time. Recently restored, this 15th-century art treasure can now be admired

in all its splendour. Western European Gothic architecture and Orthodox frescos make strange bedfellows. The neo-Gothic castle complex houses Lubelskie Museum (Muzeum Lubelskie; June–Aug Tue–Sun 10am–5pm, until 6pm on Wed and Sun, Sept–May Tue–Sun 9am–4pm, until 5pm on Wed and Sun), a museum of Polish painting, folk art and archaeology. Head for the Holy Trinity Chapel (Kaplica Trójcy Świętej), dating from the second half of the 14th century, to see the amazing medieval frescos. The Donjon has a terrace on top with a commanding view of the surrounding area.

During the years of the German occupation, thousands of Poles were tortured and killed in the neo-Gothic prison (1823) and, following the war, Polish freedom fighters and anti-Communists were imprisoned here. Lublin used to have a large Jewish population and they mainly occupied the part of the Old Town around Grodzka, where a few memorial plaques can be seen. During the 19th century, Lublin was also one of the centres of Hassidic Jewry and its Talmud school, the Jeschiwa,

Lublin's busy main thoroughfare.

was among the most distinguished of its kind anywhere in the world. The Germans closed the school and its fine library was plundered, but the building remains, now housing Lublin's medical faculty. The Nazis also destroyed all the synagogues and Jewish quarters in 1943, but some graves from both the old and new Jewish cemeteries escaped destruction. In 1941 German forces established a ghetto in the north of the Old Town by the Lubartowska. In the same year they built one of their most terrible extermination camps in **Majdanek**, a suburb of Lublin. During the following year most of the 40,000 inhabitants of the ghetto were systematically murdered, if not in Majdanek, then in Treblinka or Bełżec. The State Museum at Majdanek (Państwowe Muzeum na Majdanku; Droga Męczenników Majdanka 67; www.majdanek. eu; Tue–Sun Apr–Oct 9am–6pm, Nov–Mar 9am–4pm) is a sombre reminder of those atrocities. Between Lublin and the Vistula lies the region known as Płaskowyż Nałęczowski. The town of **Nałęczów**, which gives this high plateau its name, owes its existence to the mineral springs discovered here in the 18th century. It is still a popular health resort for patients suffering from circulatory disorders and heart disease. Many famous Polish writers and artists, including Bolesław Prus and Stefan Żeromski, often came to this spa during its heyday to relax and take the waters. Biographical museums have been erected in their honour.

Kazimierz Dolny to Chełm

On the right bank of the Vistula lies the delightful town of **Kazimierz Dolny** ⑳. Founded by King Kazimierz III Wielki (The Great), who died in 1370, Kazimierz Dolny originally earned its living from the grain trade and the town enjoyed great prosperity for many centuries. During the 16th century, the grain merchants built themselves some fine town houses – their naïve interpretation of Renaissance motifs seems quite touching nowadays. Stucco work covers the whole of the façades. Also worth looking out for are Kazimierz Dolny's three regional-style 16th-century churches and the unusual grain stores.

Strolling along the Vistula river in Kazimierz Dolny.

A network of footpaths and cycling trails crisscross the landscape in the immediate vicinity of the town. Many visitors enjoy a relaxed walk up to the ruined castle and the watchtower. It is also possible to arrange kayaking trips on the Vistula river. Kazimierz Dolny has also become a popular haunt with actors, writers and painters, particularly during the summer holiday period and at weekends. Poland's first monument to the dog (called Werniks), on the main square, is very popular with tourists, particularly children. In the spring, orchards explode into flower all around this town on the Vistula. In June each year a fair, which includes a folk music competition, is held in the town, while at the beginning of August the popular Two Riversides Film and Art Festival (http://dwabrzegi.pl) takes place.

A short way downstream from Kazimierz Dolny is **Puławy**. This town can also look back on a rich cultural tradition. Towards the end of the 18th century, a centre for Polish culture and a focal point for political activity grew up here on the Czartoryski family estate. It was because of these seditious activities that the family's property around Puławy was confiscated by the Tsarist authorities, the members of the family were forced into exile, and the name was changed to New Alexandria.

During the time of Izabella Czartoryska (1789–1810), a fabulous palace with English gardens (open daily till dusk) was built alongside the Gothic, Chinese and Alexander pavilions, the recently renovated Temple of Sibylle (Świątynia Sybilii) – which sheltered the first Polish national museum – and the small Palace of Marynka (Pałac Marynki). Due to on-going renovation, most of the park's buildings can be seen only from the outside. A museum dedicated to the aristocratic family can be visited at the Czartoryski Palace (Pałac Czartoryskich; daily 9am–5pm), also in the park.

The medieval town of **Chełm** ㉑, which was famous for many centuries for its chalk industry, lies at the eastern edge of the Lubelszczyzna. The town itself is perched on a 221-metre (722ft) high chalk hill known as the Chełmska Góra, an easily defensible spot in the Middle Ages. At the highest point stands an impressive group of buildings including a cathedral, bishop's palace, monastery and gate. In order to mine the chalk on a commercial basis during the Middle Ages, a network of lengthy passageways and deep shafts was carved out of the soft stone. This multilevel labyrinth of chalk cellars (Chełmskie Podziemia Kredowe; tel: 082-565 25 30; daily, guided tours at 11am, 1 and 4pm; guided tours available in English or German with advance booking), some 40km (25 miles) long and 27 metres (89ft) deep, is open to the public; warm clothing is advised.

To the south of the line connecting Lublin and Chełm is the **Poleski Lubelskie** region. This beautiful, tranquil area is covered with woods, meadows and marshland. The variety of flora and fauna is protected by nature reserves and parks, with the most interesting being Jezioro Białe, Krowie Bagno and the Poleski National Park.

The Vistula and Kazimierz Dolny.

Hiking in the Tatra mountains.

KARPATY

The mountainous Karpaty region is characterised by beautiful scenery, quaint timber houses and rustic churches. Culturally it is one of the best preserved regions in Poland.

The outstanding natural beauty of the **Carpathian Mountains** (Karpaty), Europe's largest chain of mountains after the Alps, extends through the whole of southern Poland. The highest range in the Carpathians are the **High Tatras**, reminiscent of the Alps, which adjoin the **Bieszczady** and the **Beskidy**, characterised by woodlands, lakes and forests. Hiking trails and established tourist facilities make many areas within these mountain chains readily accessible. Meanwhile, fascinating historic towns, including some of Poland's most renowned spas, provide an ideal base from which to explore the surrounding area, and enable you to combine the urban with the rural.

This unique mountain terrain became a series of national parks in the 1920s and 1930s, to preserve the countryside from any prospect of industrial development. This foresight means that the natural landscape remains virtually unaffected, with rare animal and plant species thriving among its dense woodlands. The clean air, microclimates and mineral-rich spring waters also provide a natural habitat for health spas (which date from the 18th and 19th centuries).

The western region of the Carpathian Mountains is readily accessible to tourists, with convenient road and rail connections, and an established

Exploring Bieszczady National Park.

tourist infrastructure, including a wide range of hotels, resorts and guesthouses. The eastern region is far less populated, and consequently less developed. This appeals more to hikers who prefer heading off with a rucksack, tent and their own supplies, and who enjoy exploring rugged and beautiful countryside independently.

Bieszczady National Park

The **Bieszczady**, a region of primeval forest at the southeastern tip of Poland, is one of those rare places in

Main Attractions

Open-air museum in Sanok
Krynica Zdrój
Pieniński National Park
River Dunajec
Osada Czorsztyn
Zakopane
Morskie Oko
Babia Góra

Mountain shelters in the High Tatras.

Europe that has scarcely been touched by tourism. The long, gentle slopes, covering a large part of the *powiat* (county) of Krosno, run along the border with Slovakia and the Ukraine. The highest peak here is the **Tarnica** (1,350 metres/4,500ft). The steppe-like pastures (*połoniny*) are definitely worth exploring, using the extensive network of hiking trails, which do not present any great difficulties, but are quite long and often require considerable stamina.

More than half of this region is thickly wooded. Right in the middle of the mountain area is the **Bieszczadzki Park Narodowy** (www.bdpn.pl; see page 388), a national park that is a haven for brown bears, herds of bison, lynx, wildcat, sparrow hawk, black stork and kingfisher. Even covering the area by car provides panoramic views from the roadside, with the Bieszczady Loop (Pętla Bieszczadzka) winding through the most interesting sections of the foothills, which is one of the most unusual landscapes in Europe.

Another major attraction in Bieszczady is the **Solina reservoir** (Jezioro Solińskie). Also known as the Sea of Bieszczady, this lake covers an area of 21 sq km (8 sq miles) and was created in 1968 when a dam was built. Pleasure boats cruise the lake, which also has numerous tourist and holiday centres providing accommodation and leisure activities.

Some of the original inhabitants of these mountains belong to two small ethnic groups, the Lemkos (*Łemkowie*) and the Boykos (*Bojkowie*), Greek-Catholic and Russian-Orthodox respectively. These groups are now a minority, as the government resettled much of the region's current population from other parts of Poland after World War II. Many of the originally Orthodox wooden churches, which are typical of the area, have now been converted into Catholic churches. The most beautiful are in **Komańcza**, **Hoszów**, **Równia**, **Turzańsk**, **Rzepedz** and **Szczawne**. It's also worth visiting the open-air **Museum of Folk Architecture** (Muzeum Budownictwa Ludowego w Sanoku; ul Rybickiego 3; tel: 013-493 01 77; www.skansen.mblsanok.pl; daily

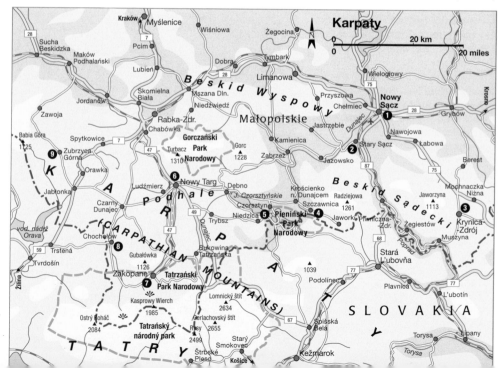

Apr 9am–4pm, May–Sept 8am–6pm, Oct 8am–4pm, Nov–Mar 9am–2pm) in **Sanok** to see examples of architecture typical of the different ethnic groups of southeast Poland. Also interesting is the **Museum of Millingi** (Młyn Muzeum Młynarstwa i Wsi w Ustrzykach; ul Fabryczna 12; tel: 607-477 110; daily 10am–5pm) **in Ustrzyk**, which has a nice café and restaurant serving local food (see page 376).

Beskid Sądecki

Two main rivers, the Poprad and Dunajec, cross the next mountain region, which is known as the **Beskid Sądecki**. Numerous hiking trails – all of them classified as 'easy' and therefore suitable for less experienced hikers – cross the beautiful wooded slopes of the two main mountain ridges: the Radziejowa, which reaches a height of 1,261 metres (4,186ft) and the Jaworzyna, rising to 1,113 metres (3,677ft).

Beskid Sądecki is best known for its numerous mineral-rich springs. The water from these streams, considered highly effective in treating stomach, kidney and rheumatic complaints, flows down the hillsides into the River Poprad, which rises on the southern Slovakian slopes of the Tatra Mountains, and then flows through rocks and woods into Poland.

The Beskid Sądecki region is also known for its lively folk traditions. However, the number of mountain villages in which the **Łemkowie** maintain their folk customs in their original form is rapidly diminishing. The foothills of this region are also home to the tiny ethnic group known as the *Lachowie Sądeccy*.

The administrative centre for this region is **Nowy Sącz ❶**. Founded in 1292 by the Czech king, Wenceslas II, it developed into a regional centre during the reign of King Kazimierz Wielki (1333–70). The original layout of the town is intact, with some buildings dating from the 15th and 16th centuries. The **Museum** (Okręgowe w Nowym Sączu; Lwowska 3; tel: 018-443 77 08; www.muzeum.sacz.pl; Tue–Thu 10am–3pm, Fri 10am–5.30pm, Sat–Sun 9am–2.30pm) contains a collection of folk arts and crafts, as well as Orthodox sacred art. It has an open-air

Farmland in Bieszczady.

FACT

Known as 'Polish Davos', the annual Economic Forum in Krynica is a meeting place for business and political elites. Experts and current and former heads of states from Poland and abroad come to the popular resort every September to take part in lectures, panel discussions and report presentations.

Raft-riding on the River Dunajec.

museum and several branches in Nowy Sącz and other towns, including the **Museum of Lachowie Sądeccy** in Podegrodzie (Mon–Fri 8am–3pm). Nowy Sącz has a comfortable hotel, the Beskid (Limanowskiego 1; tel: 018-440 40 00; www.hotelbeskid.pl), and a few guesthouses to choose from.

To the south of Nowy Sącz (New Sącz) is the small town of **Stary Sącz** ❷ (Old Sącz), which dates from the 13th century. The town is linked historically with Kinga, a duchess beatified by the Church, who founded a nunnery for the order of St Clare. The fortified convent complex and the town's historic fortifications, as well as several interesting churches, and medieval arcaded town houses, have survived. With its peaceful setting, mild climate and wealth of cultural events, such as classical concerts in historic churches, and the Annual Festival of Ancient Music (www.festiwal.stary.sacz.pl), Stary Sącz is thoroughly recommended for a longer stay in the region. Another great attraction is the excursions on the Radziejowa railway into the Poprad valley.

The most historic spa in the Beskidy is the small town of **Krynica Zdrój** ❸, 45km (28 miles) to the southeast of Nowy Sącz. This is also one of the most beautiful spas, being surrounded by wooded hills, with various sanatorium facilities located on the mountain slopes. A cable car (daily in summer) provides access to the peak of the Góra Parkowa at a height of 741 metres (2,400ft), from which there are magnificent panoramas and marked trails leading in various directions. It was during the 18th century that the springs, and the medicinal benefits of the waters, were discovered here. The waters continue to be used for drinking and bathing, as well as to treat stomach, intestinal, heart, kidney and respiratory disorders. The main Dom Zdrojowy, where you can 'take the waters', has recently been refurbished and a new musical fountain added in front of the building. From the end of the 19th century, Krynica became increasingly popular as a retreat for famous Polish artists, writers and musicians. One such patient was the

world-famous Polish opera singer Jan Kiepura, whose regular visits during the 1920s and 1930s helped to boost Krynica's international reputation. The renowned naïve artist Nikifor (1895–1968) was born here and continued to work here after World War II. His old house is now the Nikifor Museum (**Muzeum Nikifora**; ul Bulkwary Dietla 19; tel: 018-471 53 03; www.muzeum.sacz.pl; Tue–Sat 10am–1pm, 2–5pm, Sun 10am–3pm).

Touring by car, the region is best explored via the Poprad Loop (Pętla Popradzka), which extends through wonderful scenery from Krynica via the spas of Muszyna, Żegiestów and Piwniczna, all the way back to Stary Sącz. Also worth visiting is the Obrożyska linden tree reserve near Muszyna – it's also the biggest habitat of the fire salamander in Poland.

The town of **Szczawnica** ❹, situated on the River Dunajec, between the Pieniński and the Beskid Sądecki mountains, also has a sanatorium (www.uzdrowiskoszczawnica.pl). This dates from the second half of the 19th century, and specialises in treating respiratory complaints, which includes inhalation therapy. The town was regularly visited by the novelist Henryk Sienkiewicz. Fascinating wooden buildings and long-standing folk traditions are among the town's other attractions. It is also recommended as a base for excursions into the Pieniński, an individual mountain range with a complex geological structure and varied climatic conditions.

Almost the entire mountain range is within the **Pieniński National Park** (Pieniński Park Narodowy, see page 389). The highest peak, **Wysoka**, at 1,000 metres (3,350ft), is in the southern part of the range, and can easily be reached from Szczawnica. The route to the peak passes the spectacular gorge known as **Wąwóz Homole**, which is cut deep into the rock. The mountain peak in the area that attracts most hikers, however, is **Trzy Korony** or the 'Three Crowns', which rises to 980 metres (3,200ft). If you want to reach the summit of Trzy Korony, the best starting point is undoubtedly Krościenko, a picturesque village by the River Dunajec.

FACT

It is a mystery why the Niedzicka museum includes the will of the last Inca ruler, Túpac Amaru. Amaru's daughter Umina married the last owner of the castle, and his will is said to have been discovered within the castle by a descendant, who vanished in mysterious circumstances.

Pieniński National Park in its winter coat.

Sailing the River Dunajec

A raft ride on the River Dunajec, which winds through the dramatically beautiful Pieniny gorges, is one of the most popular tourist attractions in Poland. As the river flows rapidly between steep gorges up to 300 metres (980ft) high, has many sharp turns and a couple of loops, rafting is not for the faint-hearted. It is more dangerous when water levels are higher, but the trips are led by experienced Góral guides. The two-hour excursion, which covers about 15km (9 miles), beginning in **Sromowce Wyżne** and ending in Szczawnica, is an unforgettable experience.

The Pieniny region is divided between Poland and Slovakia, with the border running across the top of the mountains and along the Dunajec. Despite the ruggedness of this terrain, it has been a vital route for traders and armies for centuries. That's why castles and fortresses were built on various hilltops to protect the route, and to observe any enemy movements. Many ruined castles and strongholds now provide a poignant reminder of this era.

The remains of an ancient fortress known as **Zamek Pieniński**, near the summit of Trzy Korony, are open to the public. Further west are two 14th-century castles, **Czorsztyn** (daily summer 9am–6pm, winter 10am–3pm) and **Niedzica** ❺ (daily summer 9am–6.30pm, winter 10am–3.30pm) (first mentioned in records in 1325 as Dunajec Castle), which face one another on opposite sides of Lake Czorsztyn (a man-made reservoir of the Dunajec). Both were built on the ruins of pre-Christian fortresses, and were important territorial markers, frequently occupied by opposing warlords. Czorsztyn is now a ruin, while part of Niedzica castle serves as a folk art museum. Near Czorsztyn Castle is the open-air museum (free access) of regional architecture, **Osada Czorsztyn** (www.osada.czorsztyn.pl). The beautiful wooden villas from the turn of the 19th and 20th centuries were moved here when the artificial Lake Czorsztyn was created. One of the villas was converted into a hotel and fancy restaurant (tel: 018-265 03 02).

Cow bells for sale in Zakopane.

The **Gorce** and **Beskid Wyspowy** mountain ranges form the region's northern boundary. Most visitors to this region are experienced mountain-hikers, who are undeterred by its remoteness, basic accommodation or the limited road and rail links.

Podhale

Between Gorce and the Tatra mountains lie the **Podhale** – an area which is of great ethnographic and historic interest. The largest town in Podhale is **Nowy Targ** ❻, a settlement dating from the 13th century. It was traditionally the centre of the entire region, serving as the seat of the royal administration and judiciary. The town also became famous for its annual country fairs, a tradition that continues today. Additionally, the town market, selling livestock, local produce and domestic utensils every Thursday and Saturday, is a principal attraction for locals and visitors. Among the historic buildings, of what is otherwise an unremarkable industrial town, are the Church of St Katharina in the town centre, and the small **Church of St Anna** by the town's cemetery, which dates from the 14th century and is thought to have been founded by brigands from the Podhale region (presumably trying to salve their conscience).

The sculpture of the Madonna and Child in the sanctuary in nearby **Ludźmierz** (www.mbludzm.pl) is revered throughout Podhale. Every year countless devout Catholics from the Polish and Slovakian foothills come to Ludźmierz for the festival on 15 August, celebrating the Feast of the Assumption of the Blessed Virgin Mary.

The village of **Dębno**, also near Nowy Targ, is renowned for its beautifully preserved larchwood church, dedicated to the Archangel Michael. Constructed during the 15th century using dowels in place of metal nails, the church was decorated with splendid paintings in the early Renaissance style by unknown artists. Similar paintings can be seen in the churches of **Harklowa** and **Grywald**, but these are not as well preserved.

EAT

Every visitor to Zakopane should try a traditional spindle-shaped *oscypek*. Made of salted sheep's milk, this smoked cheese reveals its distinctive flavour best when grilled and accompanied by a tablespoon of home-made cranberry jelly. Since 2007 *oscypek* has been a brand name protected under EU regulations.

Sheep grazing in the Podhale region.

SKIING IN POLAND

Fed up with queues and archaic lifts, Poles used to look down on their ski resorts and head for the Czech Republic, Slovakia, Austria, France or Italy. Not anymore. Things have improved considerably as new, modern ski stations are springing up in the Polish mountains. Among the best are Kluszkowce, Jaworzyna Krynicka and Muszyna-Wierchomla. Traditional ski stations such as Zakopane, Bukowina Tatrzańska, Białka Tatrzańska, Korbielów, Szczyrk, Zieleniec or Szklarska Poręba have also been modernised. That said, the most popular remains Kasprowy Wierch in the Tatra mountains near Zakopane, which offers excellent high alpine skiing and the longest runs. Downsides include obsolete lifts and strong winds. Nordic ski fans should head for Jakuszyce, with its first-class cross-country ski trails.

Witkacy

One personality who is closely linked with Zakopane is Stanisław Ignacy Witkiewicz (1885–1939).

Generally known as Witkacy, he was one of the most original exponents of Polish culture, combining the roles of painter, art theoretician, philosopher, writer and dramatist. Although born in Warsaw, Zakopane became the centre of Witkacy's life: his father, Stanisław Witkiewicz, a painter, art critic and creator of the 'Zakopane Style', which he applied to architecture and the design of everyday objects, had established himself here.

The Zakopane influence

In 1890, at the age of five, Witkacy made his debut as an artist in the magazine *Przegląd Zakopianski*, and only a few years later his pictures were exhibited in Zakopane for the first time. Brought up to be an artist by his father, he enjoyed the companionship of many of the cultural elite who came to spend their holidays in

The Fight, (1921–22) by Stanisław Witkiewicz.

Zakopane. After the suicide of his fiancée Witkacy fled Zakopane, travelling first to Australia, then to Sri Lanka and on to Russia, where he served as a soldier, surviving World War I. From 1918 he lived permanently in Zakopane, usually staying in one of the guesthouses run by his mother. In 1933, he moved to Witkiewiczówka on Antałówka Hill, and lived in a house built in the Zakopane Style; there are now plans to found a Witkacy Museum here.

Distorted style

Witkacy was a prolific artist. He produced several hundred portraits in his studio, often under the influence of alcohol or hallucinogenic drugs. Even as a young man his paintings were surreal, with visionary and Utopian elements. His early self-portraits reveal carefully chosen colour and psychological depth, but the sharp lines already show signs of the caricature of his later portraits, in which faces were distorted and grotesque.

His *Composition with Three Female Forms* (oil on canvas, 1917–20) is indicative of this development. It is also an example of the way in which he incorporated his impressions of the exotic Tropics and the horrors of the war. Most of his works are exhibited in the museums of Słupsk, Stolp and Warsaw, and in the Tatra Museum in Zakopane.

Theatre work

He wrote the majority of his plays in the dramatic surroundings of the Tatra Mountains. His major works, including *Mother* (*Matka*), *Cobblers* (*Szewcy*) and *New Deliverance* (*Nowe Wyzwolenie*), became popular in the 1960s. In 1925 he founded the Formistic Theatre and put on several productions in Morskie Oko's Eye of the Sea Room, such as *The Madman and the Nuns* (*Wariat i Zakonnice*) and *New Deliverance* (*Nowe Wyzwolenie*). Witkacy was also involved in philosophy and art theory: before World War II he was one of the organisers of the General Vacation University in Zakopane. In conjunction with his belief in 'catastrophism', the disintegration of civilisation, the Soviet army's invasion of Poland shocked him into committing suicide.

Witkacy is commemorated in Zakopane cemetery with a symbolic gravestone. The S. I. Witkiewicz Theatre on Chramcówki was founded with the aim of producing his plays, so that people can continue to profit from the life and work of this brilliant outsider.

Zakopane

The small town of **Zakopane** ❼ at the foot of the Tatra mountains was originally a Góral village until it was 'discovered' by a Warsaw doctor, Tytus Chałubiński. It became increasingly important in Poland from the 1870s. A growing number of Polish intellectuals and artists soon began to settle in what was then a village, drawn by the area's natural and rustic beauty. Moreover, the Górals' love of freedom and indomitable sense of independence became a source of inspiration for the entire country, and a symbol for the national struggle against Prussia, Russia and Austria. Consequently, Zakopane was elevated into a cultural and political centre.

After World War I this small town in the Tatra Mountains continued to be a meeting point for prominent politicians and artists, many of whom made Zakopane their permanent home. Elements of Góral culture and folk music also inspired various artists, such as the composers Karol Szymanowski, Mieczysław Karłowicz and Artur Masławski; the writers Jan Kasprowicz, Kornel Makuszyński and Kazimierz Przerwa-Tetmajer, the Dutch pianist Egon Petri and the painter, architect and theoretician Stanisław Witkiewicz (see page 238).

Individual museums dedicated to the lives and work of Karol Szymanowski (see page 101), Jan Kasprowicz and Kornel Makuszyński have been established in the town. A memorial also stands in the Old Cemetery, honouring many renowned figures who have contributed to public life in Zakopane.

Several artists, such as Stanisław Witkiewicz, built houses in the Zakopane style at the end of the 19th century. This is a synthesis of various types of folk art and was an attempt to integrate elements of local art and architecture with their Polish counterparts. The most beautiful example is the Dom pod Jedłami (tel: 012-345 67 89; www.dompodjedlami.pl), built in **Koziniec** in 1897 for the Pawlikowski

family and recently renovated. Equally worth seeing is the chapel in **Jaszczurówka** (tel: 012-206 10 19; open in summer) built in 1908. The traditional Góral houses that have survived on Kościeliska give the impression of being part of an open-air museum of regional architecture.

Zakopane's **Tatra Museum** (Muzeum Tatrzańskie im Dr Tytusa Chałubińskiego; Krupówki 10; tel: 018-201 52 05; www.muzeumtatrzanskie.com.pl; Wed–Sat 9am–5pm, Sun 9am–3pm) has an important collection of local folk art and several branches. One of the most interesting is the **Gallery of 20th-Century Art** (ul Zamoyskiego 25; tel: (0) 692-029 817; Wed–Sat 10am–6pm, Sun 11am–4pm) at **Oksza Villa**. Decorative arts made by members of the artistic community that lived in Zakopane before World War II, such as Zofia Stryjeńska, are displayed in this impressive masterpiece of Witkiewicz's architecture. It's the best place to understand what a true *styl zakopiański* (Zakopane style), heavily influenced by the culture of Podhale, really is about. The

Folk art at the Tatra Museum.

GÓRALS

The Górals (*górale*) are a small ethnic group of highlanders, living in the Podhale and Pieniny regions. Traditionally farmers and shepherds, they speak their own dialect, and maintain their traditional customs and regional costumes – regardless of living among Poles, or, for that matter, the dominant influence of tourism. In fact, as the Górals are a major attraction of the region, tourism is actually helping to ensure the continuation of their culture.

A distinctive feature of Góral folk culture is the local architecture: ornately carved wooden houses and churches, many of which can be admired in the Tatra villages. These traditional houses are often well maintained – one of the greatest ironies of recent Góral culture is that poverty forced generations of them to migrate to the United States, but the money they sent back to their relatives was used to preserve the traditional farmhouses they left behind.

In addition to architecture, music and folk dancing are other easily accessible elements of Góral culture, and there are plenty of opportunities for visitors to enjoy performances by Góral choirs, string bands and dance troupes. Some restaurants in Zakopane have regular performances in the evenings.

Museum of the Zakopane Style (at Droga do Rojów 6) and Villa Koliba (at Kościeliska 18) are other branches of the Tatra Museum (same opening hours) and are also worth visiting.

Zakopane's reputation as a Bohemian town continues to attract artists, writers and composers, while various cultural events – such as the concerts held in the villa housing the Atma museum – underline the continued importance of art and culture to the locals, as well as visitors. Galleries, such as the Władysław Hasior Gallery, dedicated to the famous Polish artist and now a branch of Tatra Museum (ul Jagiellońska 18b; tel: 018-206 68 71; Wed–Sat 9am–5pm, Sun 9am–3pm), organise regular exhibitions of work by professional and amateur artists. The **Witkacy Theatre** (Teatr im S. Witkiewicza w Zakopanem; Chramcówki 15; tel: 018-200 06 61; www.witkacy.pl) has received critical acclaim and is very popular with visitors. Zakopane also hosts the annual international **Festival of Highland Folklore** (Międzynarodowy Festiwal Folkloru Ziem Górskich; http://festiwal.

ezakopane.pl) in mid-August, which attracts large crowds.

The Tatra Mountains

Zakopane is the gateway to one of Poland's greatest natural treasures, the beautiful Tatry (Tatras) mountain chain, which has established the town as Poland's premier skiing resort. The highest mountains between the Alps and the Caucasus, the Tatras extend to almost 800 sq km (300 sq miles), part of which is in Poland, while two-thirds are in Slovakia. The highest peak within Poland is the Rysy at 2,499 metres (8,200ft). The Tatra area is totally enchanting, with alpine scenery and an abundance of attractive water features: streams, waterfalls and lakes, of which the **Morskie Oko** ('Eye of the Sea') is the largest. It can easily be reached by bus from Zakopane, followed by a short walk.

About three million visitors each year, many from Western Europe and Russia, use the peaks for mountaineering and skiing. The most beautiful spots are connected by an extensive network of hiking trails, which range in difficulty from simple walks to skilful rock climbs. It must not be forgotten that this entire mountain area is part of the Tatra National Park, with its own strict regulations protecting the fauna and flora. If you want to trek in the mountains, it is strongly recommended that you seek the assistance of professional local mountain guides; there is also a volunteer rescue service looking after hikers in case of accidents. Make sure you have suitable insurance when planning more serious climbing. You can go hiking in the Tatras in both the summer and the winter, but always take all the necessary precautions and equipment before venturing out, whatever the season, and inform rangers of where you are going.

While you can ski at Zakopane, it should be noted that the visitor who comes primarily with winter sports in mind might be a bit disappointed. Lift queues, especially for the cable car and

Typical wooden houses in the Podhale region.

funicular up to the main ski areas at **Kasprowy Wierch** and **Gubałówka**, tend to be long, especially in high season, while the resort's other slopes are spread out around the town. Far more satisfactory are the facilities for ski jumping: five jumps of varying height are regularly used in international competitions, and crowds at these events can be huge. Cross-country skiing is another good option.

Besides skiing, ski jumping and hiking, Zakopane is an increasingly popular base for other mountain pursuits, such as mountain biking and paragliding. There are now a number of designated biking trails in the resort.

Orawa and Babia Góra

To the north of Zakopane lies the extraordinary village of **Chochołów** ❽ which can be reached by car or by a four-hour walk. The traditional wooden houses and church lining the main street provide some of the finest examples of the Podhale region's typical architectural style. A characteristic feature of these houses is the absence of any nails, with pieces of timber skilfully slotted together through joints.

From here the road leads on to **Orawa**, the least known of all areas in the foothills. From the gentle hills of this delightful countryside there are wonderful views of the nearby Tatra and Beskid Wysoki mountains. As the public transport system is limited, it is advisable to travel here by car, either from Kraków, Katowice or Zakopane. Although this area has only a few places of interest, these are certainly special enough (and refreshingly uncrowded) to make the effort worthwhile. Foremost among these is the small holiday village of **Orawka**, which dates from the 16th century. The exceptional wooden church of St John the Baptist, decorated with interesting paintings (including a *biblia pauperum*, an illustration of the Ten Commandments, on the chancel wall), was built in the 17th century. A little farther on from Orawka is the larger village of **Zubrzyca Górna**

❾, where many wooden buildings typical of this region have been preserved.

Definitely not to be missed is the Orawa Ethnographic Park (**Orawski Park Etnograficzny**; May–Sep Tue–Sun 8.30am–5pm, Oct–Apr Tue–Sun 8.30am–2.30pm). This is a *skansen* (open-air museum) with rural buildings from the region, some of which date from the 17th century. This includes an entire farmstead that once belonged to a local mayor, as well as other farm buildings and stalls, each containing original traditional tools and household objects.

To the northwest of Orawa, the mountain of **Babia Góra** rises to a height of 1,725 metres (5,690ft). A number of hiking trails offering varying degrees of difficulty lead to the summit, and in clear weather it is well worth the climb for the unforgettable and all-embracing panorama it offers: of the Tatras, the Beskids, large areas of the foothills and, in the distance, Silesia. If you're tired after the climb, you can recover by checking into the mid-market Hotel Markowe Szczawiny, which is conveniently close to the summit.

Chairlift from Zakopane to Gubalowka.

Silesian landscape.

SILESIA

Silesia offers the beauty of the Sudety Mountains, health resorts, sightseeing and the cosmopolitan city of Wrocław.

Ostrów Tumski Cathedral, Wrocław.

Long established as the industrial heartland of Poland, Silesia's turbulent history has been dominated by Germany and the Austro-Hungarian Habsburg Empire – a legacy that can be traced throughout the region. Silesia is thought to have been named after an early Slavic tribe of settlers, the Silings, and was ruled by the Polish Piast dynasty from the 11th century. In the 12th century the region was divided into two duchies: Lower Silesia was governed by Duke Bolesław, while Duke Mieszko controlled Upper Silesia. This historic division has remained, with Lower Silesia surrounding the city of Wrocław in the northwest, and Upper Silesia, which includes Katowice, in the southeast.

As Silesia prospered during the 13th century, the population also began to diversify, with many new towns and villages principally settled by Germans. Moreover, the death of Bolesław III in 1348 brought the Piast's rule to an end, and Silesia became part of Bohemia. From 1526 Silesia was ruled by Ferdinand I, and remained part of the Habsburg Empire for 200 years. The Silesian wars of 1740–63 resulted in Frederick the Great annexing Lower Silesia and much of Upper Silesia, leaving only part of Upper Silesia under Habsburg rule.

The lookout on Mount Sniezka.

Following World War I, the Treaty of Versailles incorporated a small area of Silesia within Czechoslovakia, and the rest was divided between Poland and Germany in 1921. After World War II Silesia was returned to Poland, after an absence of 600 years. The German population was replaced by those Poles who had been forced to leave the eastern areas of Poland, which had become part of the Ukraine.

Silesia's industrial prowess is, inevitably, an aspect of the region's heritage and character, with various museums depicting the evolution of key industries such as mining and steelworks. However, the region also has numerous attractions which can be visited without going anywhere near an industrial unit.

Wrocław is a fascinating and dynamic city, the Jasna Góra monastery in Częstochowa is Poland's holiest shrine, while the Beskid mountains, part of the Carpathian mountain range, provide endless vistas of outstanding natural beauty.

The New Silesian Museum reflects the area's industrial heritage.

UPPER SILESIA AND KATOWICE

In the country's industrial centre, coal
and steel production have shaped the
landscape and its people for centuries.

Upper Silesia is the industrial heartland of Poland, offering attractions such as museums of mining or weaving – even industrial towns yield architectural and cultural gems. The surrounding countryside offers enormous natural beauty, as well as historic towns and villages. During the Middle Ages, Silesia was a gold-mining centre. However, the economic policies of Frederick the Great encouraged the mining of coal and iron ore, which led to the construction of iron and steel works. Industrialisation in Silesia made rapid strides. By the turn of the 19th century, it was a major competitor to the great industrial areas beside the Rhine and the Ruhr.

Upper Silesia's main natural resource is hard coal, extracted in nearly 30 mines. The Katowice steel works are the largest in Poland, while the iron, chemical and automobile industries are also major factors. In fact, it's a way of life. Of the region's 2.5 million inhabitants, almost one million are employed in industrial concerns. With such a large population concentrated into a relatively small area, many cities have merged to form conurbations. The heavy industry located between Gliwice and Dąbrowa Górnicza created a serious pollution problem which culminated in it being declared a disaster area in the 1980s. The main reason for this was the Communist

regime's planning policies, or rather lack of planning. Heavy industry was seen as the key to economic prosperity, which entailed misusing natural resources and ignoring environmental consequences. Once the Communist government was out of office, a major clean-up began, with environmentally harmful and unprofitable factories closed down, while modern technology was also introduced to prevent damaging emissions. An added impetus was the Polish government's determination to meet the environmental

Main Attractions

New Silesian Museum,
  Katowice
Historic Silver Mine,
  Tarnowskie Góry
Jasna Góra Monastery,
  Częstochowa
Memorial and Museum
  Auschwitz–Birkenau
Skiing in Szczyrk
Śląsk Opolski Museum,
  Opole

Katowice steelworks.

criteria established as a pre-condition for joining the EU.

Katowice

The capital of Upper Silesia (Górny Śląsk) and centre of the Upper Silesian industrial belt, **Katowice ❶**, the administrative seat of Śląskie voivodeship, is also a scientific and cultural centre. With a population of over 300,000, Katowice was once a typical 19th-century industrial town, but now embraces some 70 small towns scattered across the southern highlands. The oldest of them, Bogucice and Dąb, were founded in the 13th and 14th centuries.

Urbanisation began in the 1860s and for this reason there are numerous examples of Revivalism, Art Nouveau and Modernism in the town's architecture, the theatre and the old railway station in particular. Most of the churches date from around the turn of the 20th century and were designed in the neo-Romanesque or neo-Gothic styles that were popular at the time.

One particularly striking example of the ecclesiastical style that prevailed between the two world wars is Christ The King's Cathedral (Archikatedra Chrystusa Króla), designed by Zygmunt Gawlik and Franciszka Mączyńskiego. The sandstone structure is the largest 20th-century church in Poland. The Council Offices, representative of the secular architecture of this period, were a showpiece for Upper Silesia in the inter-war years.

Close by is a Monument to the Silesian Insurgents, commemorating the inhabitants who fought against the Germans in the uprisings of 1919–21 for Silesia to join the newly independent Poland. After World War I it required three uprisings and a plebiscite before Katowice finally joined Poland. Nearby is a giant sports and entertainment complex, the Wojewódzka Hala Widowiskowo-Sportowa, known locally as Spodek ('the saucer') because of its shape. In 2014 thousands of fans inside and outside the arena roared with joy as the Polish national volleyball team won the world championship.

The futuristic **New Silesian Museum** (Nowe Muzeum Śląskie; al Korfantego 3; tel: 032-779 93 00; www.

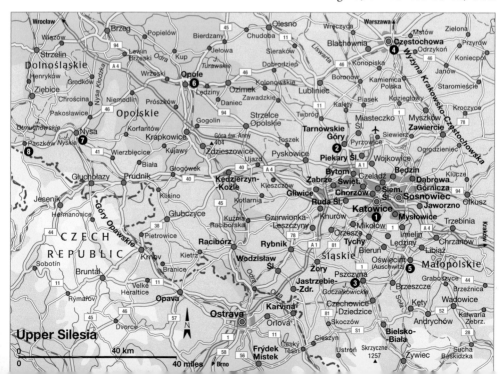

muzeumslaskie.pl; Tue–Fri 10am–5pm, Sat–Sun 11am–5pm) is in the old coal mine 'Katowice', which has been superbly converted. The major part of the two-storey museum is hidden underground, with glass boxes on the surface providing daylight. The museum houses a valuable collection of Polish art, including paintings by Jan Matejko, Aleksander and Maksymilian Gierymski, Józef Chełmoński, Leon Wyczółkowski, Jerzy Nowosielski and other 19th- and 20th-century artists.

Other museums worth a visit include the **Archdiocesan Museum** (Muzeum Archidiecezjalne; Wita Stwosza 16; tel: 519 546 023; www.muzeum.archidiecezja.katowice.pl; Tue–Thu 2–6pm, Sat 11am–3pm), with an impressive collection of carved Madonnas, and the **Katowice History Museum** (Muzeum Historii Katowic; ul Ks. J. Szafranka 9; tel: 032-256 18 10; www.mhk.katowice.pl; Tue, Thu 10am–3pm, Wed, Fri 10am–5.30pm, Sat–Sun 11am–2pm), which documents the city's history.

On the edge of the city centre is **Kościuszko Park** (Park im Tadeusza Kościuszki), with a Parachute Tower and the nearby monument commemorating the Silesians who attempted to fight off the German invasion in 1939. Other large parks in Katowice include Chorzów's **Park Śląski** (www.parkslaski.pl), featuring the legendary football stadium where the Polish national football team defeated England in 1973, as well as a planetarium and observatory, and the Upper Silesian Ethnographic Park (Muzeum Górnośląski Park Etnograficzny; May–Sept Mon 9am–5pm, Tue–Sun 9am–7pm, Oct daily 9am–5pm, Nov–Apr daily 9am–4pm), showing examples of local wooden buildings.

Around Katowice

In **Bytom**, 12km (7 miles) north of Katowice, the Museum of Upper Silesia (Muzeum Górnośląskie; ul Wojciecha Korfantego 34; tel: 032-281 82 94; Tue, Thu, Fri 9am–3pm, Wed 10am–6pm, Sat 11am–4pm, Sun 11am–3pm) has an interesting collection of Polish and European painting, as well as folk arts and crafts, and discoveries from archaeological digs in the region. The town is also home to the Silesian Opera (Opera Śląska; http://opera-slaska.pl). A little further north is the mining town of **Tarnowskie Góry ❷**, which developed after rich deposits of silver and lead were discovered in the area during the 13th century. While this form of mining ended in the 1920s, the ancient silver mine (Zabytkowa Kopalnia Srebra; www.kopalniasrebra.pl; daily 9am–3pm, till 5pm on Sat–Sun in summer) is a great tourist attraction, where you can follow a 1,500-metre (5,000ft) long trail through chambers and galleries, at a depth of 40 metres (130ft). Trolleys and tools have been deliberately left in place to help conjure up the working atmosphere, with guides explaining the history of mining during escorted tours. The huge silver chamber is of particular interest. Another extraordinary attraction in the area is the so-called **Black Trout**

Katowice old town.

TIP

A more colourful aspect of the mining tradition in Tarnowskie Góry is the annual Miner's Day Festival in September.

Pilgrims to Jasna Góra Monastery.

Adit (Sztolnia Czarnego Pstrąga), a canal around 30 metres (100ft) below ground level, bored out of dolomite rock. A boat takes you across the 600-metre (1,960ft) wide canal, which separates two mine shafts. It is advertised as the longest underground boat trip in Poland.

The regional museum in Tarnowskie Góry (Rynek 1; www.muzeumtg.pl; Tue–Fri 10am–4pm, Sat–Sun 10am–3pm) also details the history of mining in the area. The first steam-driven engine in Continental Europe went into operation in the town in 1788, which also explains why there is a *skansen* (open-air museum) of steam engines (ul Szczęść Boże 81; daily; free).

Gliwice, one of Upper Silesia's oldest towns, has a significant place in the outbreak of World War II. In 1939 Hitler accused the Poles of attacking a German radio station in the town and used this as a pretext for invading Poland. The attack had, in fact, been carried out by SS troops. The main points of interest in the well-preserved medieval town are the Gothic All Saints Parish Church, the neoclassical Town Hall surrounded by restored town houses, and the Piast Palace Museum (Zamek Piastowski; Tue 9am–3pm, Wed 9am–4pm, Thu–Fr 10am–4pm, Sat–Sun 11am–4pm).

Będzin is on the border between Silesia and Little Poland (Małopolska). In the 14th century it occupied a key position in the new Polish state's defensive system. The Zagłębie Museum (Muzeum Zagłębia; http://muzeum.bedzin.pl) comprises a 14th-century castle (July–Aug Tue–Sun 10am–6pm, Thu until 5pm, Sept–June Tue–Fri 8am–4pm, Sat–Sun 9am–5pm), which hosted several Polish kings and now shelters an armament collection, and Mieroszewski's Palace (Pałac Mieroszewskich; Tue, Thu, Fri 8am–4pm, Wed, Sat–Sun 9am–5pm, until 6pm in summer; free on Thu), featuring 18th- and 19th-century interiors. There is also an underground route (reserve ahead; tel: 032-267 77 07/47 31) exploring the World War II shelter.

The industrial town of **Dąbrowa Górnicza**, east of Będzin, has the largest iron and steel works in Poland, known as the 'Katowice', which began

operating in 1976. This replaced the traditional local industry, the mining of precious metal ores, which ceased at the beginning of the 19th century.

Since the 15th century **Piekary Śląskie** has been a shrine for Catholic pilgrims, and since the 17th century their focus has been a painting of the Virgin Mary of Piekary. The painting's miraculous powers were said to heal people from the Black Death. The last Sunday in May sees the largest influx of pilgrims, worshipping in the 19th-century basilica on Cerekwica Hill.

Jastrzębie-Zdrój and Pszczyna

North of the Silesian highlands is the region of Rybnicki Okręg Węglowy, where **Jastrzębie-Zdrój** has been a spa town since 1861. However, it is also the site of a large modern coal mining centre, and the mass strikes held here in 1980 – together with strikes in Gdańsk and Szczecin – led to the founding of the Solidarity trade union movement (see page 71). Between Katowice and Bielsko-Biała, adjacent to a woodland region, lies the medieval town

of **Pszczyna ❸**. Until 1945 Pszczyna Palace was the seat of the Hochberg-Fürstenstein family, although it was originally constructed for the Piast dynasty, who made the town the capital of their Duchy. During the late 19th century it was refashioned from the original Gothic into an exquisite, highly decorative neoclassical style, by the renowned French architect Hippolyte Destailleur. It is now a museum (Muzeum Zamkowe w Pszczynie; tel: 032-210 30 37; www.zamek-pszczyna.pl; for opening hours check website) with a superb collection of decorative arts and furniture from the Renaissance to the 20th century. Concerts of chamber music composed by the former court bandmaster Philipp Telemann, a resident of the town from 1704–8, are held in the Hall of Mirrors. The palace is surrounded by one of Silesia's most attractive and largest parks, totalling 44 hectares (109 acres). Laid out in an English style, the park is traversed by the River Pszczynka. Interiors at the other end of the scale, though nonetheless beautiful, can be seen at the Pszczyna Village and Farm Skansen

Lutheran church in Pszczyna.

(Skansen Zagroda Wsi Pszczyńskiej; ul Parkowa; tel: 032-210 57 77; www. skansen.pszczyna.pl; daily Apr–Aug 9am–7pm, Feb, Oct 9am–5pm, Mar, Sept 9am–6pm, Nov–Jan 9am–4pm).

Częstochowa

Częstochowa ❹, in the Wyżyna (Jura) Krakowsko-Częstochowska region, part of the Małopolska upland, is a major industrial centre concentrating on metallurgy, textiles and chemicals, although the city is much better known for the **Jasna Góra Monastery** (tel: 034-377 74 08; www.jci.jasnagora.pl; daily 9am–5pm, Nov–Feb until 4pm). This is the most important Catholic shrine in Poland for the cult of the Virgin Mary. Pilgrims arrive here throughout the year from around the world, including those who walk from Warsaw, particularly on 15 August, the Feast of the Assumption of the Virgin Mary, and 26 August, the feast day of the Blessed Virgin Mary of Częstochowa. The object of veneration is a painting of the so-called Black Madonna, a miraculous icon of the Blessed Virgin Mary holding the infant Jesus.

Winter in the Jura Krakowsko-Częstochowska.

This medieval Byzantine icon is believed to be a copy of a painting by St Luke, made on a piece of wood which came from the table on which the Holy family ate. Originating in the Ukraine, the icon was brought to Silesia by Pauline monks led by Prince Władysław of Opole in 1382, in whose care the icon remained. The prince ordered that the icon be kept in a church and monastery constructed on a limestone hill above the town.

This resulted in a fortified 14th-century monastic complex, extended in the 16th and 17th centuries, which is now one of Poland's most important sacred buildings. The monastery even withstood a heavy siege during the Swedish invasions in the 17th century. When the Swedes inexplicably retreated from the monastery and were subsequently driven from the country, the cult of the Virgin Mary was intensified even further. King Jan Kazimierz laid his crown before the icon and officially declared the Virgin Mary as Queen of Poland. The icon is hung above an early Baroque altar made of ebony and silver in the beautiful Chapel of the Virgin Mary of Częstochowa, which is high Baroque. It is uncovered every day before the first mass and covered again at midday. A poignant showcase in the chapel features walking sticks, crutches and other medical items left behind by people who have been miraculously cured here.

The basilica is equally magnificent, with priceless votive offerings from several Polish kings exhibited in the treasury. The armoury includes rare weapons and suits of armour including Middle Eastern examples, which Jan III Sobieski brought back with him after his victory over the Turks at Vienna. The library contains numerous rare tomes, illuminated manuscripts and liturgical works. Other rooms which can be visited include the refectory, with its extraordinarily beautiful vaulted ceiling painted with religious scenes.

The **Częstochowskie Museum** (**Muzeum Częstochowskie**; al NMP

47; www.muzeumczestochowa.pl; June–Sept Tue–Fri 11am–5pm, Wed and Fri until 5.30pm, Sat–Sun 11am–6pm, Oct–May Tue, Thu, Fri 9–3.30pm, Wed 11am–5.30, Sat–Sun 11am–5pm) is in the Town Hall, although it has branches spread across the city. Detailing the history of the Częstochowa region, the collection also includes local folk arts and crafts.

The **Jura Krakowsko-Częstochowska**, a rocky area running from Częstochowa to Kraków close to the border between Upper Silesia and Little Poland (Małopolska), is now a popular holiday region. The natural beauty, characterised by caves, wild gorges, gentle valleys and variegated woodland, is the attraction. The highest point is the Podzamcze Ogrodzienieckie at 500 metres (1,650ft). In the Middle Ages this border area was defended by a series of imposing castles and fortresses, known as eagle's lairs because of their inaccessibility. Ruins of these old castles can still be seen today along the **Trail of the Eagle's Lair Route**, which starts with the Wawel in Kraków (see page 202) and finishes with Jasnógorski Castle in Częstochowa. Near Olsztyn beside the Eagle's Lair Route are the ruins of a castle built by Kazimierz the Great, which was badly damaged by the Swedes in 1655. Not far away, in Potok Złoty, is a palace formerly owned by the Raczyński family, and a manor house where the romantic poet Zygmunt Krasiński (1812–59) worked. In Mirów and Bobolice further castle ruins testify to the eventful history of this region.

Certainly worth a short detour are the ruins of Ogrodzieniec Palace (www.zamek-ogrodzieniec.pl), just to the south of **Zawiercie**. The palace was so sumptuously furnished by its owner, a wealthy merchant by the name of Boner, that it even rivalled the opulence of Kraków's Wawel. The oldest building in the Jura Krakowsko-Częstochowska is the small Romanesque Church of St John the Baptist, near Siewierz.

Auschwitz (Oświęcim)

Located on the border between Silesia and Małopolska, where the River Sola flows into the Vistula, **Oświęcim** ❺ was the site of a 12th-century castle. In 1317 it became the capital of an independent

SILESIAN PEOPLE

In the 2011 national census, nearly 850,000 people declared themselves of Silesian nationality, with nearly half choosing it as their only nationality, thus maintaining their position as the largest minority group in Poland.

Recent years have seen the emergence of several organisations, including the Movement for Silesia Autonomy (RAŚ) and the Association of People of Silesian Nationality, that are trying to revive Silesian culture and make, so far without much success, Polish authorities recognise Silesians as a separate people with their own language.

For many centuries Silesia was part of the Austrian Empire or Prussia. Ties with Poland, broken in the 14th century, were not restored until 1918 when, following three uprisings and a plebiscite, almost all of Silesia was divided between Poland and Germany.

During World War II many Silesians, considered Germans by the Nazis, were conscripted, often against their will, into the Wehrmacht. As a result, a large number of Poles regarded them with suspicion. In 1945, when Silesia returned to Poland after some 600 years of separation, the Communist government issued its inhabitants with documents confirming their Polish nationality but with a warning that it 'may be revoked at any time'. The Silesian language was often mocked as a 'crippled' version of Polish, while the Silesians' knowledge of German was a cause of major concern. Consequently, nearly 600,000 Silesians emigrated to Germany between 1945 and 1989.

Things have changed with the restoration of democracy and the Silesian culture revival, which has taken place in the last decade. Torn between Poles and Germans for so long, Silesians are finally finding their own voice. Nowhere is this more evident than in film, art and literature. Director Kazimierz Kutz and writer Szczepan Twardoch, to name just a few, have embarked on a mission to explain the Silesian conundrum to the Poles.

Being Silesian always meant being different, but today it is more than ever before a source of pride rather than shame.

Block 5 in Auschwitz displays belongings stripped from prisoners as they arrived. Most poignant are the children's shoes and toys, while the piles of glasses and artificial limbs are equally harrowing.

Chilling sign, Auschwitz.

principality, incorporated into Poland in 1457. In 1772, under the First Polish Partition, the town was ceded to the Habsburg Empire. It is now an industrial centre, but will always be synonymous with the Holocaust.

Begun in 1940, Auschwitz-Birkenau was the largest Nazi camp complex, with two camps covering an area of 40 sq km (15 sq miles). Auschwitz was a slave-labour camp, largely reserved for political prisoners, members of the resistance and other 'opponents' to the Nazi regime, while a second camp, Birkenau, was an extermination camp. A total of 1.5 million prisoners of 28 nationalities lost their lives here, brought by train from all over Europe. At the end of the unloading ramp new arrivals were divided into those capable of work, and those to be taken straight to the gas chambers. The great majority of the victims were European Jews, together with Poles, Russians and gypsies, who were forced to endure inhuman conditions. Many died as a result of slave labour, hunger, illness and torture, while the genocide reached a peak in 1942 with up to 24,000 people

being murdered every day in the gas chambers. The corpses were burned in crematoria and then buried in mass graves. In 1944 the Nazis began destroying the crematoria and some of the camp buildings before retreating, but they did not have enough time to destroy the gas chambers. The camp was liberated by the Red Army in 1945. In 1947 Auschwitz-Birkenau was established as the **Memorial and Museum Auschwitz-Birkenau** (Miejsce Pamięci i Muzeum Auschwitz-Birkenau; ul Więźniów Oświęcimia 20; www.auschwitz.org.pl; daily Dec–Feb 8am–3pm, Mar, Nov 8am–4pm, Apr, Oct 8am–5pm, May, Sept 8am–6pm, June–Aug 8am–7pm). Visitors are taken on a guided tour of the camp – children under the age of 13 are not admitted. One of the films shown was taken by troops who liberated the camp in 1945. Other film footage and photos from the camp's archives can also be seen, while the museum depicts the struggle and martyrdom of daily life, with heart-breaking exhibits such as piles of spectacles and shoes belonging to the victims. A monument to the Victims of Auschwitz was unveiled in the grounds of the camp in Birkenau.

Around Bielsko-Biała

Situated by the River Skawa on the way to Wadowice (see page 211) is the town of **Zator**, which until 1494 was ruled by Silesian princes and subsequently became part of the Polish Republic. Places of interest are the Old Town walls, the Gothic Church of St George and a palace in an eclectic style but with numerous neo-Gothic features. An important place of pilgrimage in southern Poland is the small town of Kalwaria Zebrzydowska. Up in the Wadowice Hills is the historic and renowned 'Way of the Cross' (Road to Calvary). The route culminates at the Bernardine Monastery's Baroque Church of Our Lady of the Angels. This hill is a setting for performances of a Passion play in Holy Week, leading up to Easter.

The West Beskid Mountains, in the Polish Carpathians, form the southern boundary of Upper Silesia, which includes the towns of Beskid Śląski, Beskid Mały, Beskid Żywiecki and Beskid Makowski. The capital of the region is **Bielsko-Biała**, where the most impressive buildings are the 14th-century Gothic St Stanislaus' Church (Kościół Św Stanisława Biskupa Męczennika), and the 17th-century wooden church St Barbara's Church (Kościół Św Barbary). Dom Tkacza (Weaver's House; Sobieskiego 51; Tue, Sun 9am–3pm, Wed–Sat 9am–4pm) is a reconstructed weaver's house furnished in a 17th-century manner; the Old Factory (Stara Fabryka; Tue, Sat–Sun 9am–3pm, Wed–Fri 9am–4pm) reflects the town's traditional status within the Polish textile industry.

South of Bielsko-Biała is **Szczyrk**, Poland's second most popular ski resort after Zakopane (see page 239). Located at the foot of the Skrzyczne (1,257 metres/4,122ft), this is the destination for some 30,000 winter sports enthusiasts every year. The sources

of the Czarna and the Biała Wisełka meet in Czarne and continue as the longest river in Poland, the Vistula. Wisła and Ustroń, two other popular holiday resorts, can be reached via the Salmopolska Pass (934 metres/3,063ft). An abundance of minerals in the spring water has led to the establishment of several spas in this district.

Near the border with the Czech Republic, on the banks of the Olza, is the historic town of **Cieszyn**. From 1282 to 1653 it was the capital of a duchy owned by the Silesian Piasts, which has left a rich architectural legacy, including the Piasts late 13th-century tower. The Chapel of St Nicholas is one of Poland's few remaining Romanesque rotundas, and there are several other medieval and Baroque churches to see. The Market Square features a Renaissance Town Hall and fine burghers' houses of the same period, while early 16th-century fragments of the town walls can be seen on Przykopa. Known as Cieszyn's Venice, Młynówka district by the Olza canal is a picturesque place to take a stroll and unwind.

TIP

Within easy reach of Wisła are two centres of Beskid folk arts and crafts. Koniaków and Istebna are both renowned for lacemaking, and Istebna also has a museum of sacred art, housed in an 18th-century church.

Reconstructed barracks, Auschwitz II–Birkenau.

The Silesian Lowlands

Further to the west, beside the gently flowing Odra (Oder), are the fertile Silesian Lowlands, which become hillier further south. The climate is perfect for agriculture and the area continues to attract holidaymakers keen on outdoor pursuits.

Bordering the Upper Silesian industrial area to the west are the **St Anna Mountains** (Góra Św Anny), which reach a height of 404 metres (1,325ft). Mount St Anna was the site of a fierce battle between Polish insurgents and the German army in 1921. This mountain lies at the heart of the German-speaking region and mass is usually conducted in two languages. The village of Góra Św Anny, situated on the Chelmer Ridge, has been the centre of the cult of St Anna since the beginning of the 17th century. A Franciscan monastic complex built here in the mid-18th century includes no less than 37 chapels, two devotional churches and the Basilica of St Anna. A Renaissance figure of St Anna with the Madonna and Child can be seen in the parish church.

Busy Nysa Lake.

Opole ❻ was initially a fortified settlement inhabited by the Opolanie tribe, and the town was established on the River Odra (Oder) in the 13th century; it soon became the capital of the Opole principality. Reminders of the past include the massive Piast Tower, part of the former castle of the Opole princes. Other elements of the town's fortifications include fragments of the town wall, and a bastion. The town centre, on the banks of the Młynówka Canal, has retained a delightful Renaissance atmosphere. The Town Hall in the Market Square has a distinguished Italianate character, which isn't surprising as it was intended to be a copy of the Palazzo Vecchio in Florence. The surrounding buildings combine Gothic, Renaissance and Baroque elements. However, it is the town's sacred buildings which are the most impressive. The Gothic Church of the Holy Cross (now the cathedral) dates from the 15th century, while the 14th-century Franciscan Monastery complex includes a church with the St Anna Chapel, also known as the Piast Chapel, where the Piast princes of Opole were buried. The **Śląsk Opolski Museum** (Muzeum Śląska Opolskiego; ul Św Wojciecha 13; http://muzeum.opole.pl; Tue–Fri 9am–4pm, Sat–Sun 11am–5pm; free on Sat) occupies some splendidly renovated old town houses and displays archaeological and historical exhibits, as well as 19th- and 20th-century Polish paintings. Those who prefer to stay outside may take a stroll on Bolko's island, with its network of interesting cycle paths, a kayaking club and a Zoo.

The road to Wrocław (see page 261) leads past the **Opole Open-Air Museum of Rural Architecture** (www.muzeumwsiopolskiej.pl; Apr–Oct Mon 10am–3pm, Tue–Fri 10am–5pm, Sat–Sun 10am–6pm, Nov–Mar Mon–Fri 10am–3pm), a *skansen* displaying farm buildings from the Opole region, including cottages, windmills, a forge and granaries from the 17th century.

Towards the Góry Opawskie

Nysa **❼**, to the southwest of Opole on the Nysa Kłodzka River, was the capital of Wrocław's bishops for several hundred years until 1820, with its most prosperous period during the 16th and 17th centuries, when it was a centre of handicrafts. When the Red Army 'liberated' the town in March 1945, around 80 percent of it was destroyed in the process. The town's original fortifications, comprising 28 bastions and four towers, were reduced to a couple of 14th- and 15th-century town gates and a fragment of the town wall. The postwar expansion followed the opening of a factory producing pick-up trucks. The town's sacred buildings are well worth seeing, with the **Church of St Jacob** in the town centre a great example of Gothic architecture, with Gothic, Renaissance and Baroque sculptures. Comprising three naves, 19 chapels, three porches and a belfry (added in the 16th century), the monumental proportions are impressive considering it was built in the 13th century. The Church of SS Peter and Paul, built in the 1720s, contains one of finest Baroque interiors in Silesia. The man-made Nysa Lake to the west of town provides opportunities for various water sports.

A few miles further west, at the foot of the Gold Mountains, is **Paczków ❽**, a town popularly known as 'Poland's Carcassonne' because of its perfectly preserved medieval fortifications, comprising stone defensive walls, 18 turrets and four city gates. In the market square is the fortified Church of St John, a massive triple-naved Gothic church with a carved portal adorning the west wall and an ornamental Renaissance attic. The Renaissance altar is a work of art, with the interiors also featuring Gothic sculptures. The surrounding burghers' houses provide fine examples of various architectural genres. Up in the Góry Opawskie hills beside the border are some picturesque little towns such as the historic spa **Głuchołazy**. In the market square stands a linden tree said to be more than 400 years old, surrounded by burghers' houses. The town's other impressive features are the Baroque twin-towered Church of St Lawrence and the Lower Gate Tower, part of the original defensive system.

Map on page 248

TIP

In June Opole is flooded with visitors who come here to enjoy the Festival of Polish Songs.

Market Square, Opole.

POLAND'S LIQUID ASSETS

Spa towns throughout Poland specialise in treating specific illnesses and provide a wide range of reviving and relaxing treatments.

The earliest Polish health spas were established in the 12th century and entered a golden age during the 18th and 19th centuries, when it was fashionable for high society from France, Germany, Austria and the United States to 'take the waters' and mingle.

Today there are more than 40 spas in Poland, offering a range of treatments including mud baths, inhalations, hydrotherapy, kinetic therapy and, of course, drinking mineral water, with each spa's water having its own mineral profile. Individual spas specialising in treating specific illnesses include Połczyn Zdrój, renowned for treating rheumatism, and Ciechocinek, the first choice for curative baths in the treatment of respiratory illnesses. The range of resort locations also means that spas can be chosen on the basis of their setting and surrounding attractions, as well as their range of facilities. On the Baltic Coast, for example, there is a clinic in Sopot, while the largest spa on the coast is in Kołobrzeg.

There are a few spas in central Poland, such as Inowrocław and Nałęczów, while the greatest concentration of spas is in the south, along the Carpathian mountain range.

Ciechocinek's amazing salt-filtering graduation towers exten to a total of 1,750 metres (5,741ft), with the earliest tower dating from 1824.

A vintage illustration of Bad Alt-Schmecks, a spa resort in the High Tatras.

The spa in Kudowa Zdrój. Mineral waters smell worse than they taste. The traditional way to "take the waters" is to drink from a porcelain tankard while walking slowly.

The clinic at the delightful 19th-century seaside town of Sopot is perfectly located right by the sandy beach and the pier.

HEALTH FROM A BOTTLE

Each spa resort has a water source with a different mineral profile. Some spas such as Kudowa Zdrój in the south of Poland have three separate water sources, each offering variations on the theme, including hydro-carbon-calcium-soda, chalybeate and boron, which is quite a mouthful in more ways than one. Numerous spas also bottle and distribute their waters throughout Poland. Ciechocinek, for example, has been bottling the Krystynka brand since 1903, and the Kujawianka brand since 1962. Similarly, from Kołobrzeg comes Woda Jantar (Amber Water) mineral water, while Polanica Zdrój is the source of Staropolanka (Old Polish). Other spas market mineral water under their own name, such as Kryniczanka, bottled since 1808 in the spa town of Krynica.

Early 20th-century drawing of the great bath at Bad Warmbrunn.

...duation tower and reservoir of saline solution in Goldap, ...zury. In the past, the saline mist produced during the ...ation process was inhaled by respiratory patients walking ...ugh the tower for its high level of iodine.

...axing in the spa at Hotel Stary in Kraków.

Wrocław University building.

WROCŁAW AND LOWER SILESIA

Wrocław's long and turbulent history provides
a packed sightseeing itinerary which contrasts
with the relaxed scenic beauty of the
surrounding Lower Silesian countryside.

The most important city in Silesia and capital of Dolnośląskie voivodeship, Wrocław is characterised by broad thoroughfares and imposing buildings, which are handsome and robust rather than beautiful. And despite the city's varied architecture, with definitive examples of every genre, there is a distinct sense of harmony. This is not due to some master plan, but to their character: big, bold and beckoning. The buildings merit closer examination. Arriving in Wrocław by train means you get the picture straight away. The splendidly renovated railway station's late 19th-century neo-Gothic white stucco building, with various gables, turrets and castellations, houses a main hall that is 200 metres (650ft) long, built as one of the largest stations in Central and Eastern Europe. And yet, even within the city it is easy to escape, with quiet walks through parks or riverside greenery, and around the city's islets, linked by small bridges.

Changing rulers and artistic heyday

Wrocław's location, close to the borders with both Germany and the Czech Republic, is one reason why the city frequently changed hands, and nationalities, during its long history. Wrocław dates from the 9th century, with the earliest settlement established on small islands within the River Odra (Oder) by a Slavonic tribe called the Ślężanie. This settlement was already recorded in the 9th century by the so-called "Bavarian Geographer". During the 10th century this developed into a Slavic trading post, benefiting from its advantageous position on the routes between Western Europe and Russia and between the Baltic and Mediterranean. Briefly taken over by a 10th-century Bohemian prince called Wrotisłav, after whom the city takes its name, the Piast prince who

Main Attractions

Wrocław University
Wrocław's Town Hall and Market Square
Historical Museum
Centennial Hall and Discovery Centre
Zoological Garden
Trzebnica
Złotoryja
Książ Castle

Nuns visiting Wrocław.

became the Polish Duke Mieszko I incorporated Silesia into Poland in AD 990. In the year 1000 the first Silesian episcopal seat was founded in Wrocław. The town recovered quickly from the Tartar invasion in 1241, and in 1259 became the capital of a Piast dukedom. After joining the Hanseatic League, Wrocław prospered during the 14th and 15th centuries under Bohemian and then Austrian rule, developing into one of Central and Eastern Europe's largest cities.

The city's architecture reflects its varied rulers. Romanesque dominated during the Piast era, with Gothic established by the Bohemians, which includes the late-Gothic town hall. The Austrian Habsburg dynasty ruled during the Baroque, with Silesia coming under 200 years of Prussian rule during the partitions of Poland, and becoming part of Germany between the two world wars. During this period the artist Adolph von Menzel (1815–1905) and Ferdinand Lassalle (1825–64), the founder of social democracy, lived in Breslau, the German name for Wrocław.

An industrial centre

In 1939, with a population of 700,000, **Wrocław** ❶ was one of the Third Reich's largest cities. However, 75 per cent of the town, including many historic buildings and monuments, were destroyed during World War II, with a massive rebuilding programme beginning in May 1945 within days of the Polish authorities regaining control of the city. Having expelled the German population, the city was resettled by Poles from Polish territories which had, in turn, been lost to the Ukraine. With a current population of 633,000, Wrocław is now Poland's fourth-largest city, with the university one of Poland's most historic and prestigious. Together with ten further education colleges, this also ensures a high youth quota, and the inevitable accompaniment of student and alternative cultures. Meanwhile the city's cultural events include the biennial Musica Polonica Nova Polish contemporary music festival (April; www.MusicaPolonicaNova.pl), Jazz on the Odra festival (April; http://jazznadodra.pl), T-Mobile Nowe Horyzonty international film festival (July/

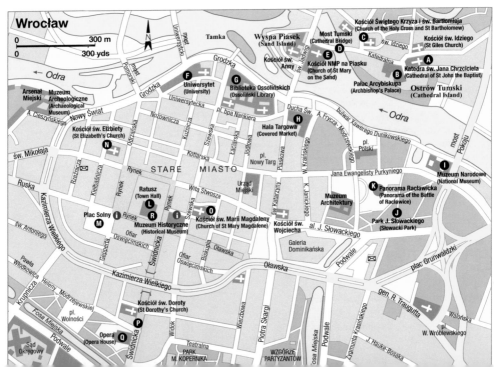

August; www.nowehoryzonty.pl), International Wratislavia Cantans Festival (classical music festival in September; http://2014.wratislaviacantans.pl) and the biennial International Theatre Festival Dialog–Wrocław (www.dialogfestival.pl). It wasn't by chance that Wrocław was chosen to be the European Capital of Culture in 2016.

Ostrów Tumski

During the 9th century, the earliest settlement was established on what is now **Cathedral Island** (Ostrów Tumski). Around 1000 the episcopal church was built here and, until the Tartar attack of 1241, this was also the site of the Piast dukes' original residence. Ostrów Tumski continues to be the city's spiritual centre, with several churches, and although it ceased technically to be an island, after a tributary of the River Odra (Oder) was filled in during the 19th century, Ostrów Tumski continues to feel isolated from the bustle of the city. An evening stroll is particularly delightful, with gas lamps still lit to illuminate the views.

The **Cathedral of St John the Baptist** Ⓐ (Katedra Św Jana Chrzciciela; Mon–Sat 10am–4.30pm, Sun 2–4pm), dating from the 13th century, is the largest and most important church on Ostrów Tumski. The three chapels in the ambulatory provide contrasting styles: the Italianate Baroque of St Elizabeth's; the Gothic chapel of Our Lady Mary; and the Duke's Chapel, designed by the Viennese master architect Fischer von Erlach. Other outstanding features include an impressive Renaissance stone portal, a triple-winged altarpiece dating from 1522, and an alabaster pulpit. A viewing deck at the cathedral offers excellent views over the city and surrounding areas.

To the right of the cathedral's main portal stands the renovated neoclassical **Archbishop's Palace** Ⓑ (Pałac Arcybiskupa; visitors allowed upon request). It is the first in a series of historic buildings along Katedralna

(Cathedral street). The second-largest church on Ostrów Tumski is the Gothic **Church of the Holy Cross and St Bartholomew** Ⓒ (Kościół Św Krzyża i Św Bartłomieja), also an architectural rarity. The building actually comprises two churches. The elegantly appointed Gothic Church of the Holy Cross (Kościół Św Krzyża) is on the ground floor. Meanwhile, the crypt houses the Greek-Catholic (Uniate) Church of St Bartholomew, which is the final resting place for two of Wrocław's most renowned bishops, Nanker and Lubusz.

The impressive **Cathedral Bridge** Ⓓ (Most Tumski) was constructed from iron in 1889. The bridge displays figures of St Hedwig and John the Baptist and links Ostrów Tumski with the **Sand Island** (Wyspa Piaskowa).

Wypsa Piaskowa is dominated by the Gothic **Church of St Mary on the Sand** Ⓔ (Kościół NMP na Piasku). Built over a 12th-century Romanesque chapel, this lofty edifice has an interesting 16th-century icon of the Blessed Virgin Mary in the north aisle, originating from eastern Poland.

Cathedral Bridge was constructed at the end of the 19th century. It joins Cathedral Island to the Old Town.

Children enjoying the fountain in Wrocław's marketplace.

The Town Hall, Wrocław.

Bustling Market Square, Wrocław.

Around the Old Town

With a monumental white Baroque façade, dating from 1811, Collegium Maximum forms the main building of the **University ⑤** (Uniwersytet). Situated on the leafy banks overlooking the River Odra (Oder), it was established on the site of a medieval castle which guarded the ford across the river. The façade's elegant Astronomical Tower is crowned by a globe, encircled by statues personifying the four academic sciences: law, theology, astronomy and medicine. The interiors are all eclipsed by the magnificent Leopoldine Hall (pl Uniwersytecki 1; Sep–Apr Thu–Tue 10am–3.30pm, May–Aug Mon, Tue, Thu 10am–4pm, Fri–Sun 10am–5pm). This is one of Poland's most beautiful Baroque halls, where the flamboyant architectural details, *trompe l'oeil* paintings, frescos and sculptures all harmonise perfectly. Other magnificent halls worth visiting include the Oratorium Marianum and the Mathematical Tower (opening hours as above), offering a superb view over the city. Nearby is the Baroque **Ossoliński Library ⑥** (Biblioteka Ossolińskich; tel: 071-344

44 71), erected on the site of a former Augustinian monastery. Its collection of illuminated manuscripts includes the Florentine publication of Dante's *Divine Comedy* of 1481 and original manuscripts of Polish writers such as Adam Mickiewicz and Henryk Sienkiewicz.

Passing the 19th-century red brick **Covered Market ⑦** (Hala Targowa), formerly a tram depot, you can head to the **National Museum ⑧** (Muzeum Narodowe; pl Powstanców Warszawy 5; tel: 071-343 88 39; www.mnwr.art.pl; Apr–Sept Wed–Fri and Sun 10am–5pm, Sat 10am–6pm, Oct–Mar Wed–Fri 10am–4pm, Sat–Sun 10am–5pm). Overlooking the River Odra (Oder) on one side and a wooded park on the other, this neo-Renaissance building dates from the 1880s. An extensive collection of Silesian art includes ultimate examples of Gothic, including a sarcophagus from the Church of the Holy Cross, bearing a Latin inscription: 'Prince Henryk IV passed away in the year 1290 after years of superb leadership in Silesia, Kraków and Sandomierz'. Reliefs on the side of the sarcophagus depict two eagles, representing the Polish

WROCŁAW IN FICTION

As a frontier town that changed hands many times, Wrocław makes for a fascinating story. The city is the focus of *Microcosm: Portrait of a Central European City*, a book by Norman Davies and Roger Moorhouse, who were praised for 'freeing [Wrocław's] history from the straitjackets of German and Polish nationalisms'. Wrocław is also the setting of the highly popular crime novels (translated into 20 languages, including English) by Marek Krajewski and featuring detective Eberhard Mock. A connoisseur of strong spirits and a fan of prostitutes, Mock solves the city's most complicated and darkest crimes against the backdrop of historic events such as Hitler's rise to power or the siege by Soviet troops in 1945.

crown and the principality of Silesia. There is also an extensive collection of Polish paintings from the 17th to 20th centuries, including plenty of modern, conceptual and avant garde Polish art.

A stroll across the **Słowacki Park** ❶ (Park J. Słowackiego) leads to an ugly modern building resembling a giant circus tent. Nevertheless, this purpose-built rotunda houses the city's most popular tourist attraction, the **Panorama of the Battle of Racławice** ❿ (Panorama Racławicka; Purkiniego 11; www.panoramaraclawicka. pl; mid-Apr–Sept daily 9am–5pm, Oct Tue–Sun 9am–5pm, Nov–mid-Apr Tue–Sun 9am–4pm). The exteriors are totally forgotten once you climb a circular staircase to the dome, which displays this painting in the round. Depicting the victorious battle won by Kościuszko's Polish army against Russian forces in 1793, it is 114 metres (370ft) long and 15 metres (50ft) high, and took nine months to complete. It is a truly spectacular painting: incredibly life-like and, despite the fact that you view it from a special platform, it is easy to become totally lost in the view and the historic struggle between opposing forces.

This genre of painting, hung in the round to heighten the three-dimensional qualities, was very popular during the 19th century, until overtaken by cinema. Painted in Lwów in 1893 by the artists Wojciech Kossak and Jan Styka to mark the 100th anniversary of the battle, it was first exhibited in Lwów (part of Poland between the two world wars). In 1939 it was put into storage, which is where it remained after the war – the symbolic significance of the painting being the struggle for independence. Only in 1980, when the Solidarity movement began to gain ground and could exert some pressure on the Communists, was it decided to restore the painting, which took five years to complete.

Around the Market Square

After the Tartar invasion of 1241, a new town on the left bank of the Odra (Oder) began to emerge. The **Old Town** (Stare Miasto) was laid out in a chequerboard style around the **Town Hall** ❶ (Ratusz), with the circular Kazimerza

The Aula Leopoldina of Wrocław University.

TIP

Wrocław's Market Square is the third-largest in Poland. Surrounded by 60 historic town houses, it is 213 metres (699ft) long and 178 metres (584ft) wide.

"Wrocław's dwarfs": the city is overrun by dwarfs. These whimsical statues are a visitor attraction in themselves.

Wielkiego street following the course of the town's original fortifications.

The Town Hall is one of the finest examples of Gothic in Central and Eastern Europe, while definitive of Silesian Gothic style. The flamboyant façade is decorated with tracery as well as fine carvings, with an arched roof crowned by a spire and featuring a turret on each corner. The central gable features an ornamental 16th-century astronomical clock, with clocks on each façade of the spire too. Next-door cafés allow you to marvel at the façade at leisure. In front of the town hall stands a 10 metre (33ft) sandstone pillory, which is a faithful copy of the one that had been standing in the same place since 1492 and was destroyed in February 1945. Now the pillory is one of the locals' favourite meeting points.

Equally impressive interiors feature inlaid panelling, paintings and Renaissance portals, as well as The Grand Hall and the Prince's Room. The **Museum of Bourgeois Art** (Muzeum Sztuki Mieszczańskiej; ul Sukiennice 14/15; tel: 071-347 16 90; Wed–Sat 10am–5pm, Sun 10am–6pm) is housed in the Town

Hall's upper floors, while the 15th-century cellar, **Piwnica Świdnicka**, serves local beers including the eponymous Świdnicki beer. Beer aficionados could also pay a visit to the nearby Spiż microbrewery & restaurant, which offers six types of preservative-free beer (lager, wheat, caramel, honey, strong and dark). Tanks and other brewing equipment can be observed through glass walls.

The **Market Square** (Rynek) is truly extraordinary, for the range of architectural styles and the sheer scope, number and layout of the buildings. Unusually, the Town Hall is not situated in the centre but on one edge of the Market Square. The prime location would be too much for one building, and indeed it is shared by a group of buildings arranged as an 'inner square'. One side of this inner square is taken up by the New Town Hall (Nowy Ratusz), which continues the Gothic theme but is an example of the more subtle 19th-century neo-Gothic. Moreover, there are more buildings within the inner square, with a few alleyways providing access to what were originally artisans' workshops.

The perimeter of the Market Square includes numerous burghers' houses, with Numbers 2–11 dating from the 13th century. Pod Gryfami (Under the Griffins) at Number 2 has an amazing portal with a crest bearing griffins, while a series of griffins also ascend the top five storeys of this building in a *tour-de-force* of Mannerism.

The southwest corner of the Market Square opens onto another market square, **Plac Solny** Ⓜ, which is lined with Renaissance buildings and the early 19th-century neo-Gothic New Stock Exchange (Nowa Giełda). In addition to the Market Square's civic buildings, the Gothic **St Elizabeth's Church** Ⓝ (Kościół Św Elżbiety), in the northwest corner, dates from the 14th century. The 86-metre (282ft) tower makes this the city's tallest church.

The most outstanding feature of the **Church of St Mary Magdalene** Ⓞ (Kościół Św Marii Magdaleny), in

nearby Szewska, is something older rather than taller. This triple-naved Gothic basilica has a 12th-century Romanesque portal, from a Benedictine abbey formerly in the vicinity, which was built into the south wall during the 16th century. For a change of ambience, from ecclesiastical to secular, and from Gothic to multi-period, continue to **Świdnicka ℗**. This is the city's principal thoroughfare, just as it has been since the mid-13th century. It offers prime shopping opportunities, with department stores and boutiques, while wide pavements and the mostly pedestrianised street provide plenty of space for street traders and performers. It is also one of the city's most architecturally varied streets, the oldest building being the 14th-century **Church of St Dorothy** (Kościół Św Doroty). The elegant neoclassical **Opera House ℚ** (www.opera.wroclaw. pl) was completed in 1840, while the Renoma Department Store (Świdnicka 40; www.renoma-wroclaw.pl) dates from the 1930s. Revitalised and extended in the first decade of the 21st century, it was shortlisted for the title of 'Building

of the Year' at the World Architecture Festival at Barcelona in 2010. The renovated façade features more than one hundred sculpted faces, as well as multi-coloured, shimmering tiles partially decorated with gold.

The 18th-century Royal Palace, once a residence of Prussian kings, now houses the **Historical Museum ℝ** (Muzeum Historyczne; Kazimierza Wielkiego 35; tel: 071-391 69 40; www.muzeum.miejskie. wroclaw.pl; Tue–Fri 10am–5pm, Sat–Sun 10am–6pm). Its permanent '1,000 Years of Wrocław' exhibition documents the city's history from the early Middle Ages to the present. It boasts more than 3,000 illustrative objects, audio-visuals and many other state-of-the-art technologies. Take a stroll around the Baroque museum garden or enjoy a moment of rest in its stylish café.

Across the Odra (Oder) River in the district called **Śródmieście** (Middletown) is the historic **Centennial Hall** (Hala Stulecia). Considered one of the most important pieces of 20th-century architecture in the city, it was commissioned for the Centennial Exhibition organised in Wrocław to

FACT

Ul Modrzejewska is home to one of Poland's most renowned hotels, the Monopol. Built in 1892 in the Secessionist style, it is full of exquisite original features and has welcomed many celebrity guests, including Marlene Dietrich.

The River Odra (Oder) at night.

TIP

Wrocław is a green city with lovely gardens and parks, numerous bridges, canals and a riverfront that can be explored either on foot or by bike. River cruises are also available.

commemorate the centenary of the victory over Napoleon at Leipzig. Built from 1911 to 1913, it was later used as a sports arena. In 2006 it was added to the UNESCO World Cultural Heritage List. The hall houses the cutting-edge **Discovery Centre** (Centrum Poznawcze; http://centrumpoznawcze.pl; Apr–Oct Sun–Thu 9am–6pm, Fri–Sat 9am–7pm, Nov–Mar daily 9am–5pm) with dozens of touch screens, maps, interactive games and displays, as well as more than 600 photographs documenting the history of the hall.

Not far from the hall is Wrocław's **Zoological Garden** (Wróblewskiego 1-5; www.zoo.wroclaw.pl). With 5,000 animals on 33 hectares (82 acres), it is the oldest, the largest and by far the most popular zoo in the country. It was founded in 1865 and steadily extended over the years. For several decades the zoo was run by Hanna and Antoni Gucwińscy, who would talk about their beloved animals in their popular TV show. The latest addition to the zoo is the Afrykarium, a separate pavilion dedicated to inhabitants of water environments from different parts of Africa.

North of Wrocław

One of the oldest Silesian towns, **Oleśnica** ❷ stands on a hill 30km (19 miles) northeast of Wrocław. It was the seat of the Oleśnica dukes between the 14th and 18th centuries, with the 14th-century castle one of Poland's most beautiful and best preserved Renaissance examples. In addition to an entrance gate decorated with heraldic motifs, the inner courtyard features arcaded galleries.

Trzebnica ❸ is in a shallow valley of the Trzebnickie Hills (Wzgórze Trzebnickie) north of Wrocław. The mild climate means that grapevines were cultivated here during the Middle Ages. The town is also renowned for its mineral springs, though the principal reason for visiting is the monastic complex of the former **Cistercian Abbey**. Founded in 1202 by Duke Henryk Brodaty (Henry the Bearded), the church was built around a Romanesque basilica and is now one of Poland's most precious monuments. The showpiece in the basilica is the early Gothic Chapel of St Jadwiga to the right of the chancel. It was built in 1680 in

memory of Princess Jadwiga, wife of the founder. Canonised in 1267 for contributing to the advent of Christianity and numerous charitable works, she is the patron saint of Silesia. On 15 October every year pilgrims arrive to celebrate St Jadwiga's feast day, just as they have done for centuries.

West of Wrocław

Środa Śląska ❹ is one of the most historic settlements on the trade route between Germany and Russia. Its medieval town centre has been preserved, with particular points of interest being the unusual, oval-shaped marketplace, fragments of the town walls and the Parish Church of St Andrew, which has retained its late-Gothic interiors, despite repeated alterations.

About 50km (31 miles) northwest of Wrocław is the village of **Lubiąż**, where the large Baroque monastery complex was the first Cistercian settlement in Silesia. The oldest of the monastery churches, which dates from the 13th century, was the first of its kind to be built in brick, and the largest of its kind in Europe. The main building measures 223 metres (724ft) in length, and is a fine example of Baroque. Michael Willmann, a famous painter, and a team of artists were commissioned to work on the project. The impressive Duke's Hall, considered one of the best examples of Silesian Baroque, features sculptures by Józef Mengoldt, and Christian Bentum's paintings. Another fine example of Baroque is the three-aisled St Walenty church, dating from the 1740s. The complex, which hosts concerts for the International Wratislavia Cantans Festival, has undergone vast renovation work, thanks to the efforts of the Lubiąż Society.

Further along the Odra (Oder), near the confluence with the River Kaczawa, lies **Prochowice**, where the walls of a ruined 13th-century castle have survived more or less intact. As early as the 10th century, **Głogów ❺**, about 40km (25 miles) upstream, was the seat of the Piast princes and one of Poland's strongest fortress towns. After 1745, the town played a key role in Prussia's military strategy. Destroyed during World War II, the late Baroque church and the Corpus Christi College, the

Fruit pickers on an apple farm in Trzebnica.

work of the Italian architect Simonetti, were subsequently rebuilt. So, too, was the town's most important monument, the **Piasts' Castle**, detailed in the town's Archaeological and Historical Museum (ul Brama Brzostowska 1; tel: 076-834 10 81; Wed–Sun 10am–5pm; free on Sat). Dukes of the Piast dynasty resided here from the 13th century, but the current style of the castle reflects its Baroque 17th-century incarnation, except for the cylindrical Gothic tower.

Since 1957 the area between Legnica and Głogów has been the centre of the region's copper industry, but the cost to the environment has been disastrous. Atmospheric pollution is high and this is now regarded as one of the most blighted areas in Poland. At the heart of this region lies the former trading settlement of **Lubiń**, a charming town with several examples of Gothic architecture, fragments of town wall, a fortified tower, a church and castle ruins.

The copper industry brought rapid economic expansion to **Legnica** ❻ (which can be followed in the town's Copper Museum), but the town is also renowned for producing some of the country's finest pianos, and for once having the largest garrison of the Red Army in Poland. Legnica was originally the capital of the Trzebovites, a Slavic tribe, before becoming a Polish episcopal seat and, due to its favourable location on the River Kaczawa, an important trading centre. As the capital of the Piast duchy until the 17th century, the town has some suitably grand architecture. The duke's early Gothic Castle also has Romanesque elements and a Renaissance portal by Johannes von Amberg. After a serious fire in 1835, it was refurbished according to a design by Karl-Friedrich Schinkel, the architect responsible for many of Berlin's neoclassical buildings.

The delightful Old Town includes the Academy for the Nobility and the 'herring' tenement houses, so-called because of their narrow stature. Other important buildings are the Church of SS Peter and Paul, principally Gothic with a Romanesque font, and the former presbytery of the Baroque **Church of St John**, which contains the Mausoleum of the Legnica and Brzeg Piasts.

Church of SS Peter and Paul, Legnica.

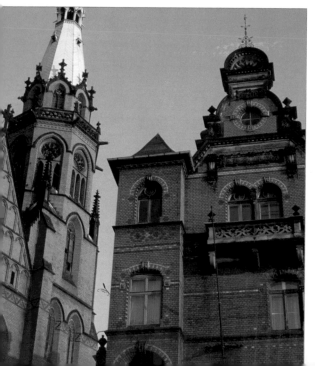

Not far from Legnica is **Legnickie Pole**. This was the scene of a fierce battle in 1241, when an army composed of Silesian knights fought bitterly against the Tartars. The mother of Henryk II the God-fearing, who led the European army and was killed in battle, founded a church in honour of her son. Subsequently, it was in her memory that the Benedictine Abbey, comprising the Church of St Jadwiga, was founded in the 18th century. The vaults of the Baroque church, the work of Kilian Ignaz Dientzenshofer, are decorated with frescos by the Bavarian master Cosmas Damian Asam.

In the town of **Chojnów** stands a Renaissance palace, built during the reign of the Prussian King Friedrich III. Subsequently extended, it now houses a museum (www.muzeum.chojnow.eu). You can also see a Gothic church and the impressive remains of medieval fortifications. From the 12th century onwards the town of Złotoryja prospered from the mining of local gold deposits. Once these had been exhausted, the inhabitants began producing textiles instead. A number of medieval buildings have survived: fragments of the original town walls, including a bastion, the Romanesque Gothic Parish Church of the Virgin Mary, the Church of St Hedwig and the Gothic-Baroque Franciscan monastery. A Museum of Gold (Muzeum Złota w Złotoryi; Tue–Sat 9am–3.45pm, also Sun May–Oct) and the former 'Aurelia' gold mine (tel: 692 019 575; May–Sept Wed–Sat 10am–4pm, Sun 9am–5pm, Oct–Dec visits upon reservation) are now open to visitors.

Świdnica-Jawor region

Jawor was the capital of the Świdnica-Jawor duchy, ruled by the Piasts for a short period during the 14th century, and the Market Square is still overlooked by imposing town residences. A Regional Museum is housed in the Franciscan Monastery (Apr–Oct Wed–Sun 10am–5pm, Nov–Mar Wed–Sun 10am–4pm; free on Wed). The **Protestant Church of Peace** is also worth seeing for its half-timbered exteriors, and wooden interiors hung with unusual paintings dating from 1710.

Perched on top of a basalt hill is the town of **Strzegom**, one of Silesia's

The wooden interior of the Evangelical Church of Peace in Świdnica.

oldest settlements. Even before the birth of Christ there was a castle here, which was subsequently used by the Poles as a fortress. The medieval **Church of SS** features elaborately carved portals with gable windows, and Mannerist interiors. Until 1456, the Church of St Barbara was a Jewish synagogue. Beyond the original town walls, with their ancient Beak Bastion, numerous historic quarries and mines were once an important source of basalt and granite.

In the centre of the medieval town of **Bolków** on the Nysa Szalona stands Poland's oldest stone castle (13th century), with a tower that provides a fine view over the surrounding region. The marketplace also occupies the highest point of a hill, where you can stroll beneath historic arcades, past the Town Hall and the Parish Church of St Jadwiga. Situated on the Bystrzyca river, **Świdnica** ❼ was originally a fishing settlement that developed into a trading centre from the 12th century, being on the key route between Kiev and Germany. Between the 13th and 14th centuries it was the capital of the Piast's Świdnica-Jawor duchy, which extended

to the suburbs of present-day Berlin, and developed into a fortified town. During the 15th and 16th centuries, under the Piast dynasty, the town was renowned for linen and brewing beer, and grapevines were also cultivated around the town.

Świdnica's **Market Square** is surrounded by 16th- to 18th-century burghers' houses, and the town walls are as decorative as they are defensive, bearing beautiful stone sculptures. The Church of SS Stanisław and Wacław, a blend of Gothic and Baroque, has the highest church tower in Silesia (103 metres/340ft), and one of the most splendid interiors, with an ornate organ and various sculptures and paintings.

In the former cemetery stands the beautiful half-timbered **Evangelical Church of Peace**. This dates from the end of the Thirty Years War in 1648, when Silesian Protestants were allowed to build three 'churches of peace' in Świdnica, Jawor and Głogów (the latter has not survived). However, this included significant restrictions: the churches had to be located outside the town, they could not be constructed

Statues of Duke George II and Barbara von Brandenburg at Brzeg Castle.

from stone or have a tower, and had to be complete within a year. Even these 'concessions' were grudgingly made by the Habsburg authorities (Silesia was then part of the Austro-Hungarian Empire). Nevertheless, this didn't result in modest churches – far from it. Gilded interiors, wooden balconies, frescos and an imposing altar create a splendid effect, within a fascinating half-timbered façade.

The scenic **Ślęża Landscape Park**, criss-crossed by mountain streams flowing into the Ślęża, which then joins the Odra (Oder) northwest of Wrocław, contains the **Góra Ślęża**, the highest peak (720 metres/2,360ft) in Poland north of the Sudety mountains. Two thousand years ago this isolated mountain rising from an immense plateau became a sacred site for the Ślężanie (an early Slav tribe), who performed pagan rites on the peak. Remains of sculptures can still be seen here, while clearly marked tourist trails lead to archaeological digs in the area, yielding stone dykes and cult statues.

Sacred objects and sculptures dating from the 3rd to 1st centuries bc can also be seen in the museum (Wed–Sun 9am–4pm) in **Sobótka**, a small town at the foot of the Góra Ślęża. The town's other attractions, such as the 14th-century churches of St Anna and St Jacob, ensure that it's a popular destination all year, particularly as a weekend break from Wrocław.

South from Wrocław

Between the rivers Odra (Oder) and Oława, to the southeast of Wrocław, lies the former episcopal town of **Oława**. By the marketplace is a 14th-century Town Hall, later converted into neo-classical style by the renowned Berlin architect Karl-Friedrich Schinkel. **Brzeg**, further south, has a superb Renaissance castle housing the Museum of the Silesian Piasts (pl Zamkowy 1; Muzeum Piastów Śląskich w Brzegu; tel: 077-416 32 57; Tue–Sun 10am–5pm). This dynasty was instrumental in the history of lower Silesia.

Resembling the Wawel in Kraków (see page 202), the castle features an arcaded courtyard. There is more Renaissance architecture to be seen in the Market Square, with a fine Town Hall, while a delightful park incorporates the medieval town walls. The foothills of the Sudeten Mountains begin around **Strzelin**, about 45km (28 miles) south of Wrocław, and these hills provide most of Poland's granite. Within the town, the **Church of St Gotthard**, a Romanesque rotunda dating from the 12th century, certainly merits a visit.

Heading southwest, **Henryków** ❽ is one of Silesia's oldest Cistercian monasteries, founded by Henryk Brodaty in the 13th century. This complex includes the Monastery Church of St Mary, with Gothic and Baroque features that include elaborately carved monks' stalls, valuable sculptures and paintings. The *Księga Henrykowska* (Henrykowska Book) manuscript, containing the earliest example of written Polish, was completed in the abbey during the 13th century. In the abbey garden is the largest yew tree

The wooden Church of Peace in Świdnicka.

FACT

The Kłodzko region provides a natural habitat for the protected yellow European globe plant, known as the "Klodzko rose", which flowers in June on mountain meadows.

in Poland – the trunk measures 12 metres (39ft) in diameter.

Ziębice, at the source of the River Oława, has retained its medieval town centre and fortifications. The Church of St George has fascinating interiors reflecting various architectural styles. Next to the former monastery hospital stands the Church of SS Peter and Paul, laid out in the shape of a Greek cross.

On the edge of the **Kłodzko Basin** (Kotlina Kłodzka) is the town of **Ząbkowice Śląskie**, renowned for its glassworks. The town's bastions and fortified towers, the Gothic Church of St Anna and the Dominican Monastery are among the historic attractions.

The former Cistercian monastery is worth visiting in **Kamieniec Ząbkowicki**, together with the ruined neo-Gothic **Hohenzollern Palace** (May–Oct 8am–4pm), poignantly set on a hill within an English-style park. Built between 1838 and 1863 by Karl-Friedrich Schinkel, this palace was one of the final but also most remarkable works by this renowned Berlin architect. The palace was destroyed by fire during World War II, but it was restored

by a Polish émigré and completed by the municipal authorities.

On the border between Silesia and Bohemia, at the foot of the mid-range Sudetens in the Nysa Kłodzka valley, lies the beautiful episcopal town of **Bardo**. In the early Middle Ages, pilgrims came to the town in large numbers to pay homage to the Virgin Mary, and the single-nave Baroque church contains a woodcarving as well as a Gothic sculpture of *Our Lady of Sorrows*.

Around Kłodzko

Adjoining the foothills of the Sudeten is the large basin through which the Nysa Kłodzka, Bystrzyca, Ścinawka and Biała Lądecka rivers flow. At the centre of this basin is **Kłodzko ❾**, founded in 1223. Its oldest feature is the Gothic stone bridge, built around 1390 and decorated with Baroque reliefs. There is also a citadel, as well as three large monasteries belonging to the Franciscans, the Order of St John and the Jesuits. The Franciscan St Mary's Church is decorated with paintings and frescos by the Prague maestro Scheffler. A feature of the twin-towered parish church is the Baroque altar designed by Tausch.

The Kłodzko region is a beautiful part of Silesia surrounded by forest-covered mountains. Other aspects of the region's natural beauty are the **Jaskinia Niedźwiedzia** (the "Bear Cave"), with almost 2km (1 mile) of tunnels, as well as the labyrinths and fascinating rock formations known as **Błędne Skały** ("Erratic Rocks"). However, this region is best known for its mineral water springs. The earliest recorded mention of these waters' medicinal benefits dates from 1272, with the earliest spas established during the 17th century in the towns of Polanica, Duszniki, Kudowa and Lądek.

The oldest of the Sudeten spas, **Lądek Zdrój**, was known for its curative mineral springs even before it was granted a town charter in 1282. The spa of Kudowa Zdrój is on the Czech border, with nearby Czerna having a macabre Baroque chapel, the floor

The Gothic stone bridge in Kłodzko.

and walls of which are covered with some 3,000 human skulls.

Chopin stayed in **Duszniki Zdrój** ⑩, one of the most beautiful spas, on his journey through Poland that eventually led to his permanent exile in Paris. To commemorate the visit the town holds an annual Chopin Festival. The 17th-century paper mill, where some fine frescos were recently discovered, is a museum devoted to the history of paper production, for which the town was once known.

Another attraction in this area is **Wambierzyce**, at the foot of Góry Stołowe. On a hill in the centre of the town, a staircase leads up to a monumental Baroque basilica and a group of Calvary chapels which has been the site of pilgrimages since 1218. Near the church is a delightful exhibition of mechanical Christmas cribs.

Westwards along the Sudetens

Wałbrzych, the largest town in the region, has little to offer tourists, being an important industrial and mining centre. However, the town does have a neoclassical Evangelical Church with an oval galleried interior, designed by K.G. Langhans, whose work includes the Brandenburg Gate in Berlin. The Museum of Industry and Technology covers mining installations, minerals, fossils and porcelain. Soon after the Communist government was ousted, several large industrial plants were closed in the area, and in parts the landscape makes a pitiful sight, though the scenery beneath the Sudetens in the west makes a marked contrast.

Not far from the outskirts of Wałbrzych is Silesia's largest castle, **Książ** ⑪ (www.ksiaz.walbrzych.pl; daily Apr–Sep 10am–5pm, Sat–Sun until 6pm, Oct–Mar 10am–3pm, Sat–Sun until 4pm). Constructed by Bolko I, the prince of Świdnica in the 13th century, the castle is in a park surrounded by multi-coloured rhododendron bushes, while a ravine with a small river isolates the castle on three sides. Until the 15th century the palace belonged to the Piasts of Świdnica, and later to the German Hochberg family, who converted the castle into a Baroque citadel. The Nazis began to convert the building into a headquarters for Adolf Hitler, and by excavating a giant bunker destroyed parts of the original building. However, remains of the medieval stone tower and the Renaissance wing have survived, while the museum's collection includes ceramic tiles and decorative glassware. An English-style garden laid out on the slopes around the palace, planted with exotic trees, is a very pleasant place for a stroll. Among various terraces in this garden is the Water Terrace, with a grand total of 27 fountains.

Of special interest in **Kamienna Góra** are the ruins of a large Renaissance palace, a row of Baroque houses with arcades on the Market Square, and an interesting exhibition detailing the history of weaving in the town's small Museum of the Silesian Textile Industry.

The Cistercian abbey of **Krzeszów** ⑫ is one of the most outstanding examples of late Baroque architecture

Looking out to the Karkonosze mountains.

in Silesia. Behind the ornamental and monumental façade, with its twin towers, the white and gold interiors are laid out in a circular manner, decorated with wall paintings, canvases and sculptures. It is thought that the renowned architect Kilian Ignaz Dientzenhofer was involved in the initial work. The neighbouring Church of St Joseph is famed for its frescos, attributed to Michael Willmann, a painter often referred to as the Silesian Rembrandt.

In nearby **Chełmsko Śląskie**, a street of centuries-old weavers' cottages has been preserved, among them the House of the Twelve Apostles. The River Bóbr and its tributaries, the Kamienna and the Łomnica, flow through the densely populated and heavily industrialised area of **Kotlina Jeleniogórska**. The former episcopal town of **Jelenia Góra ⓭**, in a low valley surrounded by mountains, is now the region's administrative and cultural centre. From the Middle Ages it was an important regional trading centre, and developed rapidly as it became industrialised. But the town has also long been a major tourist attraction, with numerous historic sights.

At the centre of Jelenia Góra is the Market Square with its imposing **Town Hall** dating from the 17th century, surrounded by colourful arcaded burghers' houses of the same period. An unusual feature of the **Grace Church** is not so much the huge 18th-century organ, but the theatrical three-storeyed gallery. The Parish Church of St Erasmus and St Pancras has a Renaissance tower, subsequently refashioned in a Baroque style, while the impressive main altar is the work of two Norwegian sculptors, Weisfeld and Kretschmer.

Beyond the fragments of the medieval town walls stands the Protestant **Church of the Holy Cross**, dating from 1718, which was designed by the Swedish architect Franz. The interior is decorated with frescos painted by the Prague master A. F. Schaffler, assisted by local artist J. F. Hoffmann. There is also a museum exhibiting 17th- and 18th-century glass, ranging from everyday functional glassware to works of art.

The spa town of **Cieplice**, one of Poland's most historic, now falls within Jelenia Góra's town boundaries. It once belonged to the Order of St John, and records from 1281 show that the monks used waters from hot sulphur springs to treat various illnesses such as skin complaints. During the 18th- and 19th-century Cieplice was established as an essential rendezvous for the fashionable and wealthy, who easily outnumbered the minority of genuine patients looking for a cure. Of special interest are the monastery, with its Church of St John the Baptist, the former Schaffgotsch Family Palace dating from the late 18th-century, and the **Museum of Natural History** (ul Cieplicka 11A; Muzeum Przyrodnicze w Jeleniej Górze; tel: 075-755 15 06; May–Sept Tue–Sun 9am–6pm, Sat–Sun until 5pm, Oct–Apr Tue–Sun 9am–4pm), with an extensive collection of birds and butterflies.

The town also has a reputation for producing excellent cut glass, as well as being a centre for manufacturing paper. The town of **Lwówek Śląski**, on the River Bóbr, dates from 1217.

The Wang wooden church, Karpacz.

The first town on Polish soil to adopt the Magdeburg laws, it was formerly a centre of gold mining. Some splendid Gothic monuments give the town its essential character, including well-preserved defensive walls and turrets, the twin-towered Church of the Assumption with superb portals, and the Town Hall, which incorporates Renaissance elements and has a vaulted vestibule.

The Karkonosze

The main mountain range, the **Karkonosze**, sometimes known by its German name, the Riesengebirge (meaning Giant Mountains), stretches for 36km (22 miles) between **Przełęcz Szklarska** (885 metres/2,900ft) in the west and **Przełęcz Kowarska** (727 metres/ 2,384ft) in the east. These mountains are known for their unusual rock formations and two lakes **Mały Staw and Duży Staw** ("Large" and "Small" lakes), which were formed in the Ice Age, as well as romantic waterfalls, alpine meadows and peat-bogs.

The highest mountain is the **Śnieżka** (1,602 metres/ 5,254ft), followed by the Szyszak and the Szrenica, with the peak of Śnieżka also the site of two man-made features: St Laurentius' Chapel dating from the 16th century and, dating from the 1960s, the saucer-shaped meteorological observatories. Reaching the top of this mountain doesn't necessarily entail a long hike, as a chairlift can do much of the work for you. Pines and mountain ash grow up to a level of 1,250 metres (4,000ft). Beneath this the vegetation consists of dwarf pines and Carpathian birches. Deer, mouflons and owls are plentiful on the hillsides. The **Karkonosze National Park** is well supplied with guesthouses for those wishing to explore it on foot. However, some of the thickly wooded mountain slopes have been affected by atmospheric pollution, largely caused by power plants in the Czech Republic and Germany.

Szklarska Poręba, at the foot of **Mount Szrenica**, occupies a picturesque spot on the banks of the Kamienna River. Skiers can reach the pistes on the nearby Szrenica via chairlifts, leading to a variety of trails. Moreover, the microclimate means that the snow stays put here until the end of April.

Another popular skiing and holiday resort is **Karpacz** , at the foot of Śnieżka mountain. It's a good starting point for excursions and skiing along the trails in the Karkonosze, with the town's cultural attractions including the Toy Museum, exhibiting dolls from all over the world. In the Karpacz Górny district is the **Wang**, a 13th-century wooden church, which was sold by the village of Wang in Norway at the beginning of the 19th century, because the congregation had become too big for the church. Dismantled, it was brought here in sections and reassembled in 1842. It is a traditional Norwegian *"stave"* church, with a vast sloping roof, a design that was typical in Norway during the 12th and 13th centuries. Two of the dragon's heads looking down from the gable were reputedly made of wood from Viking long ships. Some of the beams feature detailed carvings of mythical creatures, while carved figures on the portal narrate a Nordic saga.

Mount Śnieżka summit.

Rural landscape, Wielkopolska

WIELKOPOLSKA – GREATER POLAND

Wielkopolska isn't famous for its scenery,
but its fascinating history makes up for
anything it lacks in landscape.

Wooden windmill near Poznań.

One of Poland's largest provinces, Wielkopolska, literally "Great Poland", is also the most historic. Situated in the west of the country, along the central and lower reaches of the River Warta (the main tributary of the Odra/Oder), Wielkopolska provided the foundation for the first sovereign state of Poland.

It was the Piast dynasty who united the scattered territories of the Polanie tribe into a single dominion, which they ruled from an island on the Lednica lake, between Poznań and Gniezno.

Gniezno subsequently became the capital of this state, and also the centre of Catholicism. The archdiocese founded in the town in AD 1000 resulted in the magnificent cathedral. This is an important sacred building, exemplifying Romanesque architecture, which is also intrinsically linked with the evolution of the early state of Poland. Although Kraków and then Warsaw assumed Gniezno's role as the capital city of the country, Gniezno is still considered to be the spiritual centre of Poland.

The early Slavic settlement of Biskupin.

The region's principal city, Poznań, has always been an important trading centre, and continues this historic role by hosting the largest trade fairs in Central and Eastern Europe. An attractive city to visit, and one of Poland's greenest, Poznań also makes a good base from which to tour the surrounding countryside.

Among the attractions within easy reach of the city are the Ostrów Lednicki Piast Museum, which includes the remains of the Piast's ducal castle, the Gothic Kórnik Palace, the French Renaissance Gołuchów Palace, and the neoclassical Rogalin Palace, which are all museums set in magnificent parks. And if you want to get away from it all there are plenty of secluded villages, lakes and forests in which to enjoy tranquillity and natural beauty.

POZNAŃ

The industrial centre and trade-fair city of Poznań is one of Poland's oldest cities and the capital of the Wielkopolska (Greater Poland) region.

Poznań divides quite naturally into four equally interesting sections, that can easily be navigated on foot, and which are never far from a park or some other greenery. The most historic part of the city, Ostrów Tumski, is full of Romanesque and Gothic architecture. The Old Town is characterised by Renaissance and Baroque, while the 'New Town' district contains 19th-century neoclassical 'statement' buildings. Further west is the most modern part of town, with generic contemporary European architecture, spreading out past the main railway station to the international trade halls, which host the largest international trade fairs in Central and Eastern Europe.

This combination ensures that the city has as many business visitors as tourists, with an established infrastructure to handle both, and the town is continually being smartened up – although it is very attractive, it is not yet a 'showpiece' on the same level as Kraków. There are numerous business and tourist hotels, which tend to be outside the historic centre, but these are in great demand when the numerous trade fairs are on, so dates and accommodation need to be checked well ahead.

The history of Poznań

As the capital of the Wielkopolska (Greater Poland) region, in the centre of western Poland, Poznań is a thriving industrial and commercial hub, with a long history as a major trading centre.

One of Poland's oldest cities, Poznań dates from the 9th century, when a fortified settlement was established on an island in the River Warta. As this expanded it became the capital of the Polish state in the late 10th century, which also included Gniezno and the surrounding region (see page 295). Duke Mieszko I was baptised here in 966, converting the Slavs from pagans to Christians, and Poznań became a bishopric in 968. In 1253

The No.9 tram.

The Baroque spires on the two towers of the Cathedral of SS Peter and Paul in Poznań were reconstructed after World War II.

Poznań was granted its town charter under the Magdeburg Laws.

As trade flourished the town prospered, particularly during the 16th century, with Poznań a key transit point on numerous European trade routes: from western Europe to Russia and Lithuania, and from the Balkans to Scandinavia. However the Swedish invasion in the 17th century devastated the city, and during the partitions Wielkopolska, together with Silesia, was annexed by Prussia. In towns and villages patriotic organisations were formed to resist the 'Germanisation' policies being actively exerted on the region. Poznań played an important part in the battle for Poland's full independence, with the Wielkopolska Uprising, which began in Poznań on 27 December 1918, overthrowing the Prussians (see page 45). Wielkopolska subsequently rejoined a newly independent Poland. During World War II more than half of the city was destroyed, but a rebuilding and restructuring programme got underway immediately, and Poznań's population was soon twice its pre-war total. Since 1925 international trade

fairs have been held in Poznań, which developed from the city's medieval tradition of holding a major midsummer fair. The main event, the Industry Fair, takes place in June, with ten additional specialist fairs, such as Salmed for medical equipment, Polagra (agricultural) and Multimedia. The reason for the success of these fairs is the 'bridging' function they perform between Central and Eastern European markets, as well as their suitability for small and medium-sized companies.

In addition to the university, Poznań has ten institutes of Higher Education, a branch of the Polish Academy of Sciences and numerous scientific institutes, including the Western Institute, which provides links between Poland's industry and the European Union, particularly Germany.

As well as historic churches and civic buildings, palaces and specialised museums, this highly cultured city has several theatres, including the National Theatre (Teatr Wielki), a Philharmonic Orchestra, three well-known boys' and male-voice choirs, not to mention hosting the renowned

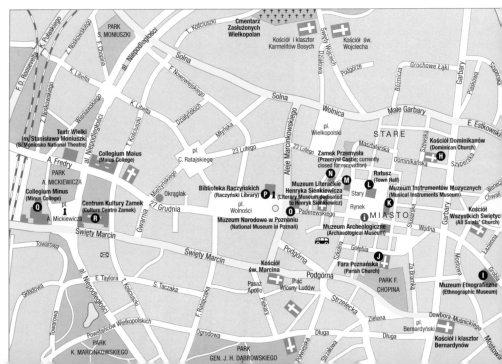

Henryk Wieniawski International Violin Competition, which takes place every five years.

Ostrów Tumski – Poznań's heart

The earliest settlement and site of Christian worship was established on Ostrów Tumski (Cathedral Island), the peninsula between the River Warta and the River Cybina, which continues to be the city's religious and spiritual centre. Just beyond the River Cybina is the late Romanesque **St John's Church**  (Kościół Św Jana; Jerozolimskiego za Murami; daily), one of the first brick-built churches in Poland. The neighbouring **St Margaret's Church**  (Kościół Św Małgorzaty; daily) stands in what was until the 18th century the independent municipality of Śródka, a district which has retained a distinct atmosphere. Near the River Cybina, at Gdańska 2, is the newest attraction of Poznań, acclaimed for its architecture: **ICHOT Gate**  (Brama Poznania ICHOT; tel: 061-647 76 34; www.bramapoznania.pl; Tue–Fri 9am–6pm, Sat–Sun 10am–7pm), an interactive centre focusing on the history of Ostrów Tumski.

Crossing the River Cybina to Ostrów Tumski, the most important of several sacred buildings is the **Cathedral of SS Peter and Paul**  (Katedra Św Apostołów Piotra i Pawła; daily). The foundations of the first Romanesque church built here in 968, and even pre-Romanesque fragments, can be seen in the crypt, with the building continually extended and refurbished until the 16th century. Reconstructed after World War II, the cathedral now resembles a Gothic basilica with three naves and radiating towers. Two Baroque towers dominate the entrance, and while it is certainly imposing, this geometric façade is no preparation for the grandeur within. The Gothic main altar with a beautiful triptych dating from 1512, crafted in a Silesian workshop, is often cited as the most outstanding feature. But there are also 12 impressive chapels, including the magnificent neo-Byzantine Golden Chapel, dating from the 19th century, containing the tombs of the nation's founder Mieszko I, as well as his

TIP

The regional tradition is to eat delicious *rogale świętomarcińskie* on 11 November, the day of St Martin. These are iced croissants filled with white poppy seeds and nuts.

St John Vianney Church, Poznań.

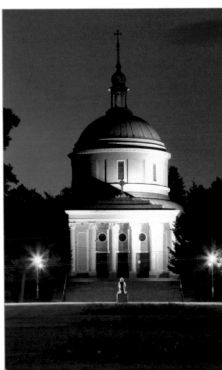

Bronze necklace, Pomeranian culture, 6th–5th century BC, Archaeological Museum.

Horse and cart in Poznań.

successor and the first king, Bolesław Chrobry. Polish rulers were buried here from the 10th to 13th centuries, which gives the cathedral immense national status. Next to the cathedral is the **Archaeological Reserve Genius Loci** **Ⓔ** (Rezerwat Archeologiczny Genius Loci; tel: 061-852 21 67; www.muzarp. poznan.pl; Apr–Sept Tue–Thu 10am–4pm, Fri noon–7pm, Sat 11am–7pm, Sun 10am–3pm, Oct–Mar Tue–Thu 10am–4pm, Fri 11am–6pm, Sat 9am–5pm, Sun 10am–3pm), which shows archaeological remains of the earliest settlements in Ostrów Tumski. Visitors first enter a pavilion with an interactive exhibition explaining the history of the area, before coming to a glass floor where they can see the archaeological remains.

Nearby are two churches, the **Church of the Blessed Virgin Mary** **Ⓕ** (Kościół Najświętszej Marii Panny; daily), dating from the 15th century, which has survived entirely in its original form, and the early 14th-century **Psałteria**, the house where cathedral choristers once lodged. Also near the cathedral on Mieszka I are the **Bishop's Palace**

(Pałac Biskupów) and canons' homes. To the north stands a building that once housed the Lubrański Academy (1518), Poznań's first university college, with an attractive arcaded courtyard. Now it's the **Archdiocesan Museum** **Ⓖ** (Muzeum Archidiecezjalne; ul J. Lubrańskiego 1; tel: 061-852 61 95; www. muzeum.poznan.pl; Tue–Fri 10am–5pm, Sat 9am–3pm), which has an interesting collection of art from the Wielkopolska region. Highlights include the Sword of St Peter (although its origin is unknown, some experts claim it was made in the first century), the monstrance of King Jagiello and a 13th-century crosier from Limoges. There are interesting collections of paintings and decorative arts – the portrait gallery is especially comprehensive.

Around the old town

In 1253 two Wielkopolska dukes, Przemysł I and Bolesław Pobożny, founded a new town on the left bank of the River Warta. This revolved around what is now the **Old Market Square** (Stary Rynek), which is one of the finest medieval urban complexes in Poland.

The **Dominican Church** ⊖ (Kościół Dominikanów; daily) in Dominikańska is one of the city's finest churches. It was the Dominicans who introduced the techniques of Gothic brick architecture to Poland, and fragments of the original monastery and Rosary Chapel can still be seen in the south wing. Retaining an impressive Gothic brick portal, dating from the 13th century, the church was subsequently rebuilt in a magnificent Baroque style.

A 19th-century former Masonic Lodge houses the **Ethnographic Museum** ❶ (Muzeum Etnograficzne; Grobla 25; tel: 061-852 30 06; www.mnp.art. pl; Tue–Thu 9am–3pm, 11am–5pm mid-June–mid-Sept, Fri noon–9pm, Sat–Sun 10am–6pm; free on Sat). It doesn't take long to see a lot here, with an extensive but compact collection of folk arts and crafts from the Wielkopolska region, as well as the paraphernalia involved in traditional celebrations such as Easter.

Now acting as the principal church in the city, as well as being one of the finest Baroque churches in Eastern Europe, the **Parish Church** ❶ (Fara Poznańska; www.fara.archpoznan.pl; daily 6am–7.30pm, except during mass), on Gołębia, was built by the Jesuits in the second half of the 17th century. Massive ornate columns lining the walls do not support the building, but are purely decorative, which is typically Baroque. Being purely aesthetic and inspirational, and together with elaborate stucco work, the effect is as palatial as it is religious. It's also possible to visit the underground part of the church on Sat at 12.45pm, just after the organ concert at noon. The neighbouring building is the Jesuit College, which currently houses the city administration.

While Ostrów Tumski and both banks of the River Warta may seem dominated by churches, the Market Square is entirely a case of civic showmanship, with the Town Hall, ornate palaces and highly individual burghers' houses with polychrome decorations creating an impressive effect, particularly stunning when floodlit at night. By one corner of the Market Square is the **Archaeological Museum** (Muzeum Archeologiczne; Wodna 27; tel: 061-852 61

Paintings in the Historical Museum of the City of Poznań.

95; Tue–Fri 10am–4pm, Sat 10am–6pm, Sun 10am–3pm). The exhibits, ranging from the Stone Age to the Middle Ages, are housed in a beautifully restored former palace (Pałac Gorków), making it also Poland's second-oldest museum. One of the city's most unusual museums is the **Musical Instruments Museum** (Muzeum Instrumentów Muzycznych; Stary Rynek 45; tel: 061-856 81 78; www.mnp.art.pl; Tue–Thu 9am–3pm,11am–5pm mid-June–mid-Sept, Fri noon–9pm, Sat–Sun 10am–6pm; free on Sat). A beautiful burgher's house, which needn't take long to negotiate, is home to more than 2,000 historic instruments from Poland and other parts of Europe, including a room dedicated to Chopin with pianos that he played. Even if you're not musical, the instruments are impressive for their craftsmanship alone, and qualify as works of art beyond their musical status.

The most outstanding building on the Market Square is the **Town Hall** (Ratusz). Built between 1550 and 1555, this is one of Europe's finest Renaissance buildings, with the façade comprising three floors of arcaded loggias surmounted by a high ornamental attic and turrets, above which extends an ornamental tower. The exquisite harmony and unmistakeably Italianate style stem from the architect being Giovanni Quadro of Lugano. Original Renaissance interiors are also exhibits in themselves, particularly the splendid Great Hall's coffered ceiling resting on two impressive pillars (concerts are held in the hall during the summer), and the Courtroom with decorative portraits; more portraits can be seen in the Royal Chamber. The Town Hall also houses the **Historical Museum of the City of Poznań** (Muzeum Historii Miasta Poznania; ul Stary Rynek 1; tel: 061-856 81 93; www.mnp.art.pl; Tue–Thu 9am–3pm,11am–5pm mid-June–mid-Sept, Fri noon–9pm, Sat–Sun 10am–6pm; free on Sat). A daily attraction at noon sees two mechanical kid goats, made from metal, emerge from above the clock on the tower and playfully lock horns to the sound of a bugle call. Locals are just as enchanted by this as tourists. In front of the Town Hall is an ornate rococo fountain of Proserpinae,

Painted houses line the Old Market Square.

and a copy of the 16th-century pillory formerly used for floggings.

The Town Hall is one of several buildings in the central area of the Market Square, with fortunately only one 'intrusion' in the form of a small 1960s-style 'concrete block' tucked among historic neighbours. A terrace of arcaded 16th-century vendors' houses, from which herrings were sold, are smaller and simpler than the ornamental burghers' houses lining the square, but equally interesting, and street traders still vie for pole positions in front of them. Behind the Town Hall is the neoclassical white stucco single-storey Guard House (Odwach) housing the **Wielkopolski Region Rising Museum** (Muzeum Powstania Wielkopolskiego 1918–1919; Stary Rynek 3; tel: 061-853 19 93; www. muzeumniepodleglosci.poznan.pl; Tue–Fri 10am–5pm, Sat–Sun 10am–3pm; free on Sat). This small museum has a new permanent, interactive exhibition presenting the moving story of local uprisings, when the Polish people of Wielkopolski region were struggling for freedom against the Prussians

during the partitions. It also provides a very personal insight into regional life, with documents, pictures and other items.

The life and works of the renowned Polish author, who won the Noble Prize for Literature in 1905 with *Quo Vadis*, are detailed in the eponymous **Henryk Sienkiewicz Literary Museum**  (Muzeum Literackie Henryka Sienkiewicza; Stary Rynek 84; tel: 061-852 89 71; www.bracz.edu. pl; Tue–Fri 9am–5pm, Sat 9am–4pm). This museum-home is worth visiting to see how this type of burgher's house was decorated at the beginning of the 20th century and to gain some idea of what life was like for its resident.

Being the heart of the Old Town, the Market Square is a key rendezvous point and a place to promenade. Burghers' houses feature smart boutiques and galleries, together with numerous restaurants and cafés ranging from expensive to fast-food outlets. Additionally, **Park F. Chopina** is only 250 metres/yds from the Market Square, and is an ideal spot for a picnic among greenery.

TIP

One of the most atmospheric restaurants in the Market Square is Ratuszova (www.ratuszova. pl) at Number 55. A *fin-de-siècle* Bohemian town house, complete with antique interiors, it serves traditional Polish food (including regional dishes).

The National Opera House and adjoining park.

Przemysł Castle to Freedom Square

While most of the city walls were pulled down at the beginning of the 19th century, medieval fragments, including a tower, have survived on Przemysław Hill to the northwest of the Market Square, in the vicinity of **Przemysł Castle**  (Zamek Przemysła; currently closed for renovation, check www.zamek-krolewski. poznan.pl for re-opening date and times). This impressive castle hosts the Museum of Decorative Arts (Muzeum Sztuk Użytkowych). Arranged over two floors, the extensive collection is concentrated without being time-consuming, providing the finest examples of Gothic and Renaissance sacred art and furniture, Gobelins rugs, Limoges porcelain and decorative enamelwork, together with crystal and glassware, and silver and gold objets d'art, many of which were formerly owned by eminent Poles. The 20th-century galleries also provide definitive examples of Secessionism and Art Deco. Beyond the square at the foot of this hill are two churches facing each other, and

both merit a visit. The façade of **St Joseph's Church** (Kościół Św Józefa) is classic early Baroque. The Gothic façade of **St Adalbert's Church** (Kościół Św Wojciecha; tel: 061-852 69 85; www.swietywojciech.archpoznan. pl) may seem to tell the whole story, but the interiors include wonderful Secessionist polychrome. Moreover, many renowned Poles have been laid to rest here, including Józef Wybicki (1747–1822), who composed the Polish national anthem. Heading for **Freedom Square** (Plac Wolności) marks a change of character, with this area dominated by 19th-century neoclassical 'statement' buildings, not to mention a modern urban buzz (from which the pedestrianised Market Square area is blissfully free). This area is also more ragged and not yet as manicured as the Old Town. Plac Wolności is actually a vast rectangle rather than a square, harbouring skateboarders as well as locals chatting on benches, overlooked by several important buildings.

The **National Museum in Poznań**  (Muzeum Narodowe w Poznaniu;

Trams are a great way to get around in Poznań.

al Marcinkowskiego 9; tel: 061-856 80 00; www.mnp.art.pl; Tue–Thu 9am–3pm, 11am–5pm mid-June–mid-Sept, Fri noon–9pm, Sat–Sun 10am–6pm; free on Sat) is housed in a neoclassical building. It contains one of the most comprehensive collections of Polish paintings, including works by Jan Matejko, Poland's greatest historical painter (see page 105). European masters such as Ribera, Bellini and Bronzino can also be seen, together with a range of folk arts and crafts. At the opposite end of the square is the neoclassical Arkadia building, currently a casino, though its provenance is more cultural, with concerts given here by Paganini in 1829 and Liszt in 1843. The **Raczyński Library** ❿ (Biblioteka Raczyńskich; www.bracz. edu.pl; Mon–Sat 9am–3pm, Thu until 6.30pm) is in an outstanding neoclassical building, dating from 1829, with the sublime colonnade featuring 24 Corinthian columns. Modelled on the Louvre in Paris, it reflects the initially peaceful Prussian regime, which changed over the following decades as the Prussians attempted to 'Germanise'

the city. Next to the old building is a modern extension, opened in 2014, that fits perfectly with the surrounding architecture.

The nearby **Hotel Bazar** (www.bazar poznanski.pl), at Marcinkowskiego 10, was a centre of the Polish Nationalist Movement against the Prussians. Dating from the 1840s, this is one of Europe's oldest hotels, with the neoclassical style being the work of renowned Berlin architect Schinkel.

Around Adam Mickiewicz Square

On **Adam Mickiewicz Square** (Plac Adama Mickiewicza) are two interesting monuments, one to the eponymous romantic poet and the other in memory of the worker's uprising of 1956, known as the 'Poznań June'. Like the Berlin Uprising of 17 June 1953, this was a spontaneous insurrection against the injustices of Communism, and one in which many people lost their lives.

This square is overlooked by the distinctive neo-Gothic architecture of **Minus College** ⓠ (Collegium Minus;

Freedom Square.

Mon–Fri 8am–8pm), the university concert hall, which is renowned for the quality of its acoustics. This is a regular venue for the city's Philharmonic Orchestra and the Poznań Ballet, while also hosting the Henryk Wieniawski International Violin Competition. Opposite Plac Adama Mickiewicza is the recently refurbished **Culture Centre Zamek** (Centrum Kultury Zamek; tel: 061-646 52 76; www.zamek.poznan.pl; daily 10am–10pm, exhibitions Tue–Sun 11am–5pm). This *fin-de-siècle* neo-Romanesque building, originally known as the Kaiserhaus, was the German Emperor Wilhelm II's former palace, and now houses various institutions. Although its appearance can seem like a grey bulk, it is worth visiting for its programme of interesting temporary exhibitions covering a wide range of subjects. It also contains the **Poznań Rising Museum – June 1956** (Muzeum Powstania Poznanskiego Czerwiec 1956; tel: 061-852 94 64; www.muzeumniepodleglosci.poznan.pl; Tue–Fri 9am–5pm, Sat–Sun 10am–4pm), which focuses on the

life of people in Poznań in the 1950s. The Culture Centre is on the prime shopping street, which has all the atmosphere of a modern, lively city. Parallel to this street is Aleksandra Fredry, which is also retail terrain and includes the extraordinary Okrąglak Dom Towarowy ('Roundabout' Department Store), a 1950s glazed rotunda. Further along Fredry is the neoclassical **Moniuszko National Theatre** (Teatr Wielki im. Stanisława Moniuszki; tel: 061-659 02 00; www.opera.poznan.pl).

Poznań's parkland

You are never far from a park in Poznań, with 20 percent of the city being green. North of the city centre lie the remains of a large citadel which was almost completely destroyed in 1945. Today, the **Park Cytadela** occupies this site, together with a cemetery for Red Army soldiers who died during World War II, and the Poznań Citadel Museum (www.muzeumniepodleglosci.poznan.pl; Tue–Sat 9am–4pm, Sun 10am–4pm; free on Fri), presenting different aspects of military history,

War tank in the Poznań Citadel Museum.

MALTA FESTIVAL

Malta Festival Poznań was created in 1991 to present fringe, independent, street and experimental theatre. Later the formula changed to include film, music and dance. The annual festival is held at the end of June and beginning of July on the Malta Lake (Lake Maltańskie) in Poznań. Since 2010 it's been organised around a topic considered essential to understanding the modern world, particularly Europe – its culture, social situation and future prospects. In 2014 the festival made the headlines as a controversial play, *Golgotha Picnic*, depicting Jesus's life 'through shocking images of contemporary consumer society', triggered protests from the Catholic Church. As a result, the staging of the play at the festival was suspended, while protests spread to other Polish cities.

including the city's wartime fate, and the history of post-war Polish aviation.

Wilson Park (daily 5am–10pm), in the Łazarz district, includes Poland's (and one of Europe's) largest palm houses (www.palmiarnia.poznan.pl; Tue–Sun 9am–5pm, Sun until 6pm in summer). A number of pavilions totalling 4,000 sq metres (4,700 sq yards) contain around 17,000 tropical plants, including 700 species from subtropical and tropical countries. An adjoining aquarium contains plenty of local and exotic fish. The city limits to the southwest of this park see the start of the **Wielkopolski National Park** (Wielkopolski Park Narodowy), with diverse landscapes, woods, hills and lakes to explore, together with *skansens* and agricultural museums.

Adjoining the northern outskirts of Poznań is a large area of park and woodland with a series of four lakes. Part of **Lake Strzeszyńskie** is an open-air swimming pool, with a motel and a campsite also on its shores. **Lake Kierskie**, which covers an area of 300 hectares (740 acres), is very popular with sailing enthusiasts, who find the

wind conditions to be near perfect.

Also within easy reach of the city centre past Ostrów Tumski is **Lake Maltańskie**, one of the finest rowing and canoeing regatta courses in Europe, created on this lake between 1985 and 1990. The world canoeing championships were held here in August 1990. In sunny weather the lakeside is very popular for a stroll, with walking and cycling trails encircling the lake, while cafés and beer gardens provide refreshments. On the eastern edge is an artificial ski slope, for practising at any time of year.

East of the lake is **Wielkopolskie Zoo** (or Poznań Zoo) **S** (Apr–Sept 9am–7pm, Oct–Mar 9am–4pm; www.zoo.poznan.pl), one of Poland's largest and most comprehensive. The animals are kept in spacious compounds under conditions that closely resemble their natural habitat. The highlight is a special compound for 10 African elephants, one of the biggest and modern in Europe. If you don't want to walk that far, a miniature railway runs along the lakeside (from Kościół Św Jana, May to September).

Statue of St John Nepomucene.

AROUND POZNAŃ

This chapter features a one-day trip that can be made from Poznań to the beautiful lakeland landscape and quiet bucolic villages that surround the city.

P oznań is in the centre of a large agricultural region, which includes forests and nature reserves, with good road and rail links making it easy to visit historic towns and villages – and to enjoy the pastoral views on the way. Nor do you have to go far to escape the city, and be in the midst of fascinating countryside. In fact, on the southern outskirts of **Poznań ❶**, only 15km (10 miles) from the city centre, lies the **Wielkopolski National Park** (see page 124), which covers an area of about 10,000 hectares (24,750 acres). This has the archetypal characteristics of the Polish lowlands: deciduous woods with many different types of vegetation, moraine hills and lakes. The most beautiful part of the park is Lake Góreckie, where the ruins of a castle remain on one of its islands.

Kórnik to Szamotuly

Two popular destinations around 20km (12 miles) south of Poznań are Kórnik and Rogalin. The small town of **Kórnik ❷**, with a three-nave Gothic church on the Market Square, is idyllically set on the shores of Lake Kórnickie. An impressive arboretum can be seen in the adjoining park (daily 10am–dusk), laid out in an English style. It contains 3,000 species of trees and shrubs from around the world, which is the most extensive collection in Poland. The centrepiece of

the park is **Kórnik Palace**. Originally built in the 16th century, it was redesigned in an English neo-Gothic style in the mid-19th century by the aristocratic owner Tytus Działyński, incorporating designs by the famous Berlin architect Karl-Friedrich Schinkel. Gothic features, which include a bridge over the moat, were intended to recall Poland's historic splendour, with the refurbishment also providing a suitable home for the owner's collection of historic books and paintings. Bestowed to the nation in 1924, the

Main Attractions
Rogalin Palace
Museum of the First Piast in Lednica
Gniezno
Biskupin
Gołuchów Palace
Międzyrzecz fortifications

Wooden windmills dot the countryside.

castle houses the library of the Polish Academy of Sciences and a museum (Polska Akademia Nauk Biblioteka Kórnicka; Zamkowa 5; tel: 061-817 00 81; www.bkpan.poznan.pl; Mar–Oct Tue–Sun 10am–4pm, May–Sept until 5pm, in winter by appointment only), including furniture, paintings, military weapons and armour. The library has one of the most valuable collections of Polish books in the country, with over 350,000 volumes, including one by Napoleon. A neighbouring building houses historic horse-drawn carriages.

The main attraction in **Rogalin** ❸, a village beside the River Warta, is the beautiful park and palace on the edge of an oak forest. Laid out in the late 18th century in a French Baroque style, with an English-style landscaped park laid out at the beginning of the 19th century, this is home to the greatest number of ancient oak trees (over 1,100) of any forest in Europe, some of which are 800 years old. The most famous are three oaks named after the legendary Slav brothers Lech, Czech and Rus, the founders of Poland, Bohemia and Russia. The late Baroque-early

neoclassical **Rogalin Palace**, formerly owned by the Raczyński family, is now a museum (Muzeum Pałac w Rogalinie; tel: 061-813 80 30; www.mnp.art. pl; due to open in June 2015). The collection includes clocks, furniture, tapestries, porcelain and 18th- and 19th-century Polish paintings. Separate pavilions house an exhibition of 20th-century Polish and European art, and horse-drawn carriages.

Superb Gothic architecture can be seen in the small town of **Szamotuły** ❹, 35km (22 miles) northwest of Poznań. The Gothic Collegiate Church has magnificent interiors, with the late 15th-century Górków Castle (Zamek Górków) now a museum (Muzeum Zamek Górków; Wroniecka 30; tel: 061-292 18 13; www.zamek.org.pl; May–Sept Tue–Sat 9am–4pm, Sun 10am–5pm, Oct–Apr Tue–Fri 9am–4pm, Sat–Sun 10am–4pm). In addition to the castle's interiors, visitors can see Poland's most comprehensive collection of icons and Russian Orthodox sacred art. The castle adjoins fragments of a moat and defensive system, with the superb three-storey

Around Poznań

late-Gothic Halszka Tower housing an exhibition of the region from ancient times to World War II. Around the Market Square are numerous late 19th- and early 20th-century burghers' houses, with another interesting 19th-century building formerly used by the mounted postal service.

An essential detour, less than 10km (6 miles) northeast of Szamotuły, brings you to **Słopanowo**, where a stunning wooden church dating from 1699 features beautiful folk interiors, 16th- and 17th-century sculptures and a late 17th-century polychrome wall.

Heading northeast of Poznań

The **Szlak Piastowski**, a road that leaves Poznań in a northeasterly direction, passes several places marking the origins of the Polish state. Consequently, this road is named after the first dynasty of Polish kings, the Piasts. The first place of interest along this route is the village of **Lednogóra** ❺, on Lake Lednica. On Ostrów Lednicki, the lake's largest island, is a fascinating archaeological site, the **Museum of the First Piasts**

in **Lednica** (Muzeum Pierwszych Piastów na Lednicy; Dziekanowice 32; tel: 061-427 50 10; www.lednicamuzeum. pl; mid-Apr–Oct Tue–Sun 10am–5pm, May–Sept until 6pm). This has the oldest architectural fragments of brickwork in Poland, and includes the remains of Palatium, the Pre-Romanesque late 10th-century residence of Mieszko I, founder of the Polish state. Massive earthworks mark the site of a castle built here in the 11th century. The island was originally connected to the shore by a series of bridges with a total length of about 700 metres (2,300ft). On the opposite shores of the lake is the **Wielkopolski Ethnographic Park** (Wielkopolski Park Etnograficzny; as above). This *skansen* (open-air museum) has plenty to see, with around 50 primarily wooden buildings, such as an 18th-century Wielkopolska farmstead, a manor house, and the oldest Polish windmill, dating from the late 16th century.

Further along this route is the hilltop town of **Gniezno** ❻, Poland's first capital. The earliest inhabitants settled here in the 7th century, with a fortified

The Rogalin Chapel, built in pink sandstone, serves as a parish church and a mausoleum for the Raczyński family.

Raczyński Palace.

TIP

There is an interesting narrow-gauge and steam engine rail link between Biskupin and nearby Wenecja. Here there is also a delightful railway museum (open Apr–Sept) from where you can take a 'historic' train ride.

The Old Fort at Biskupin.

settlement built in the 9th century and the first church founded around 970, after Poland converted to Christianity in 966. Gniezno's 14th-century **cathedral** (daily 9am–5pm, closed to tourists noon–1pm) is the grandest Gothic church in Poland, and the seat of Polish archbishops since the year 1000. A three-naved basilica with 14 chapels, featuring ornate portals and grilles, this is also the final resting place for the first Polish martyr and one of the country's most important saints, St Adalbert (Wojciech). His silver sarcophagus is in the centre of the main nave. The cathedral's magnificent pair of Romanesque bronze doors date from 1170, and illustrate the life of St Adalbert through a series of panels on each door. The saint is shown leaving the St Alexis Monastery on the Aventine, Italy and arriving in Gniezno in 996. The following year he baptised the pagan Prussians, before being killed by them. King Bolesław Chrobry is shown buying his body from the Prussians, with the final scenes showing the saint being laid to rest in the cathedral.

Collections of ancient books and works of art, some dating from the 10th century, are kept in the church archives and in the **Museum of the Archdiocese of Gniezno** (Muzeum Archidiecezji Gnieźnieńskiej; Kolegiaty 2; tel: 061-426 37 78; www.muzeummag.com; Mon–Sat 9am–5pm, Sun 9am–4pm). It doesn't take long to see the Gothic and Baroque sacred art here, together with various ecclesiastical items, and it's certainly worth it. A delightful stroll past various historic churches and buildings, past a lake surrounded by greenery, leads to the **Museum of the Origins of the Polish State** (Muzeum Początków Państwa Polskiego; Kostrzewskiego 1; tel: 061-426 46 41; www.mppp.pl; Tue–Sun 9am–5pm; free on Sun). This modern building, recently refurbished, hides a treasure trove of archaeological fragments covering the history of the Piast Dynasty. An audio-visual display and 3D films detail the town's history up to the Middle Ages. Once Kraków became the capital in the 11th century, Wielkopolska's nobility tried to reverse the town's declining status, but to no avail – the town gradually fell into provincial obscurity.

North of Gniezno is **Biskupin** ❼ (Muzeum Archeologiczne w Biskupinie; tel: 052-302 50 55; www.biskupin.pl; daily 8am–6pm, in winter till dusk), an archaeological reserve where in the 1930s an early Slavic settlement on the Biskupin Lake peninsula was discovered, with artefacts from the Bronze Age in well-preserved wooden buildings going back 2,500 years. Part of the settlement has been reconstructed, offering an insight into prehistoric Slav life. Continuing along the Szlak Piastowski from Gniezno lie the five towns of Trzemeszno, Mogilno, Strzelno, Kruszwica and Inowrocław. In **Trzemeszno** ❽ sections of the magnificent church show its 10th-century origins, although it is essentially Baroque in character. In the vicinity of Trzemeszno are several lakes, most of which have a rather unusual, elongated

shape. This is because they fill glacial channels created during the Ice Age.

One of the first Benedictine monasteries in Poland was built in **Mogilno**  during the 11th century. A Romanesque church was built at the same time, and although repeatedly refashioned, it has retained many original elements, including the crypt. Further points of interest along the Szlak Piastowski are described in the chapter on Gdańsk and the surrounding area.

East of Poznań

The eastern part of the Wielkopolska region is a flat, exclusively agricultural area with sparse woodland.

About 50km (30 miles) from Poznań is **Września** ⑩, where several monuments commemorate the local people's heroic struggle against the Prussians' attempted 'Germanisation' during the partition of Poland. The school where pupils went on strike to demand religious education in the Polish language in 1901, which led to a chain of protests throughout Wielkopolska, is now the **Children of Września Regional Museum** (Muzeum Regionalne im Dzieci Wrzesińskich; Dzieci Wrzesińskich 13; tel: 061-436 01 92; www.muzeum.wrzesnia.pl; Mon 10am–1pm, Tue–Fri 10am–4pm, every third Sun 11am–4pm), with reconstructions of the original classrooms.

The small town of **Miłosław**, 16km (10 miles) south of Września, is famous for the battles that took place here during the revolution of 1848. Its 18th-century church and neoclassical palace (now housing a school), both in the attractive setting of a large park, are well worth visiting. In the chapel in the neighbouring village of **Winna Góra** is the grave of the Polish general Jan Dąbrowski, a national hero from the time of the Napoleonic Wars (and mentioned in the Polish anthem). The palace (Muzeum Jana Henryka Dąbrowskiego w Winnej Górze; tel: 061-285 12 77; Tue–Sun) has an exhibition detailing his life.

The village of **Ląd** on the Warta River is one of the most important sites of the Cistercian order in Europe, with an extensive monastery (Pocysterskie Opactwo Najświętszej Marii Panny i św Mikołaja w Lądzie; tel:

Gniezno Cathedral at night.

063-276 33 24; www.lad.pl). Built in the 13th century and remodelled in the mid-17th century, this is now one of the most beautiful examples of Gothic and Baroque architecture in Poland. The monumental architectural style, with its splendid interiors and fine collection of 14th-century wall paintings, is an impressive sight. The Passion Plays staged at Easter attract people from across the country.

Konin ⓫, on the River Warta, has retained a medieval urban layout in the Old Town, which includes the **Old Market Square** (Stary Rynek), with numerous 19th-century buildings. There is also a late 14th-century Gothic church set in a garden that includes a 2.5-metre (8ft) high sandstone milepost dating from 1151. The post-war area of Konin contains sports and cultural centres hosting large-scale events such as the annual Children's Song and Dance Festival in June. But this is also an industrial centre, with power plants and factories (including an aluminium smelter) taking advantage of the area's deposits of brown coal. It is also rapidly expanding, and the town's

The imposing Basilica of Our Lady of Licheń.

population has increased sevenfold since 1960. A palace in the **Gosławice** district of Konin houses the **Regional Museum** (Muzeum Okręgowe w Koninie; Muzealna 6; tel: 063-242 75 99; Tue–Fri 9am–5pm, Sat 10am–2pm, Sun 10am–3pm) with a good collection of jewellery, Polish coins and 19th- and 20th-century Polish paintings. As Konin has a long history of mining, there is also a gallery of paraffin lamps. The museum also has a small *skansen* with 19th-century farm buildings and an open-air museum of mining machinery. Next door is a Gothic church dating from 1444. The countryside around Konin is popular with holidaymakers, with the area's towns also providing aesthetic sights. **Ślesin's** triumphal arch, erected in 1811 in honour of Napoleon Bonaparte, is the only monument of its kind in Poland.

Koło and Uniejów are two interesting small towns on the River Warta. **Koło** is home to an architectural rarity: a Gothic church with Art Nouveau interiors, while the resort town of **Uniejów's** main attraction is a landscape park and a Gothic castle

(www.termyuniejow.pl). This can also be experienced as a resident, having been converted into a comfortable hotel, with the surrounding park providing various walks among a variety of trees and bushes. The local museum in **Turek** (Muzeum Miasta Turku; Plac Wojska Polskiego 1; tel: 063-278 41 60; www.muzeum.turek.pl; Tue–Fri 8am–6.30pm, July–Aug until 3.30pm, Sat–Sun 10am–2pm), also worth a detour, houses works of the Polish Secessionist artist Józef Mehoffer, some archaeological artefacts from the Hallstatt D culture and an ethnographic presentation of 19th-century weavers' houses.

Towards Kalisz and beyond

Picturesquely located between moraines on the edge of the Warta valley, en route to Kalisz, are Żerków and Śmiełów. The main feature of the quiet town of **Żerków** is a delightful Baroque church. The renowned Polish poet Adam Mickiewicz stayed in the village of **Śmiełów** on a number of occasions, which helped to put the place on the map. The village and surrounding area features in Mickiewicz's

Pan Tadeusz, one of Poland's most significant poetic works. The neoclassical Śmiełów Palace, dating from 1800, is an appropriate location for the Adam Mickiewicz Museum (Muzeum Adama Mickiewicza w Śmiełowie; tel: 062-740 31 64; www.mnp.art.pl; May–Sept Tue–Fri 10am–4pm, Sat–Sun 10am–6pm, Oct–Apr Tue–Fri 9am–4pm, Sat–Sun 10am–4pm; free on Wed), detailing his life and the Romantic era.

By the village of **Gołuchów** ⑫ is the magnificent late 16th-century French Renaissance Gołuchów Palace (Muzeum Zamek w Gołuchowie; tel: 062-761 50 94; www.mnp.art.pl; May–Sept Tue–Fri 10am–4pm, Sat–Sun 10am–6pm, Oct–Apr Tue–Fri 9am–4pm, Sat–Sun 10am–4pm; free on Tue). In addition to rooms decorated with interesting furniture, porcelain and Polish and European paintings from the 16th and 17th centuries, there is an exquisite collection of Ancient Greek vases. The palace is set in Wielkopolska's largest landscaped park, which includes a Forestry Museum (www.okl.lasy.gov.pl) within an outbuilding, while the outlying areas

The organ in the Basilica of the Assumption of the Blessed Virgin Mary, Kalisz.

MONUMENTAL CHURCH

Completed in 2004 and designed by Barbara Bielecka, the monumental Basilica of Our Lady of Licheń (Bazylika Matki Bożej Bolesnej Królowej Polski; ul Klasztorna 4; tel: 063-270 81 63) in Licheń Stary near Konin, is overwhelming. At 139 metres (456ft) long and 77 metres (253ft) wide, it is the largest church in Poland and one of the biggest in the world. Steps leading to the entrance number 33, symbolising Jesus's age when he was crucified, while the 365 windows symbolise the days of the year. The church is dedicated to Our Lady of Sorrows, Queen of Poland. There is space for 250,000 people to gather outside the church, a sight intended to resemble a 'rippled field of rye'. Not everyone agrees on that. However, irrespective of diverging opinions, it is an amazing architectural achievement.

of the park are a reserve for European bison. An unusual sight worth visiting in the Gołuchów woods is the 'Erratic', a huge boulder left over from the Ice Age with a circumference of 22 metres (71ft) and a height of 3.5 metres (12ft).

Kalisz  is the second-largest town in the region and also one of Poland's oldest, retaining its medieval layout of narrow streets. The town was first mentioned 1,800 years ago in the writings of the Greek traveller Ptolemy. Formerly an important stop on the amber trade route from the Baltic, Kalisz is now an equally important centre for Polish textiles and the aircraft industry.

The Old Town's most interesting buildings include the **Cathedral of St Nicholas**, dating from 1253, with its splendid late Renaissance stucco work and Baroque altar; the late-Baroque Collegiate Church of St Joseph, as well as the Bishop's Palace and Town Hall, both neoclassical. The **Franciscan church and monastery**, dating from the 13th century, was rebuilt during the Baroque era, while fragments of the defensive walls can also be seen. The avant garde design of two modern churches in the **Asnyka** district provides an interesting contrast to the town's wealth of traditional architecture.

Idyllically located on the banks of the River Prosna is the Wojciech Bogusławski Theatre (www.teatr.kalisz. pl), a sublime confection of white stucco neoclassicism. This adjoins the Town Park, one of the country's oldest public parks, founded in 1798. Some of Poland's greatest writers, such as Adam Asnyk, Maria Konopnicka and Maria Dąbrowska, lived and wrote in Kalisz. The town's cultural calendar also includes several festivals, such as the International Jazz Pianists Festival. The **Kalisz Regional Museum** (Muzeum Okręgowe Ziemi Kaliskiej; Kościuszki 12; www.muzeum.kalisz.pl; Wed, Fri 11am–5.30pm, Tue, Thu 10am–3pm, Sat–Sun 10.30am–2.30pm; free on Sun) has a good collection of archaeological, historical and ethnographic exhibits, while also detailing the history of the town's textile trade. Another, perhaps more interesting branch of this museum is the Archaeological Reserve Zawodzie (Rezerwat Archeologiczny Zawodzie; ul Bolesława Pobożnego; Tue–Wed, Fri 10am–3pm, Thu, Sat–Sun 10am–6pm), with a partially reconstructed early Medieval settlement and a little zoo with farm animals.

Wielkopolska's southern border is formed by the Ostrzeszowskie Hills. The park in **Antonin**, a village on the busy road from Poznań to Silesia, contains many ancient oak trees and an extraordinary neoclassical wooden hunting palace of the Radziwiłł Princes (Pałac Myśliwski Książąt Radziwiłów). Odd, perhaps, but why have a mere shooting lodge if you're a distinguished aristocrat who can afford a four-storey hunting palace? Considered one of the most remarkable buildings in Europe at that time, the body of the palace is a large hexagonal tower (containing a circular galleried staircase), from which four short evenly spaced wings extend. The intention was to create an entirely new architectural

Zielona Góra.

form, and it certainly succeeded. Built at the beginning of the 19th century, it was designed by the renowned Berlin architect Karl-Friedrich Schinkel. Frédéric Chopin was a guest at the palace, which explains the frequent Chopin concerts held here, as well as a festival called Chopin in the Colours of the Autumn (every September). Now the palace belongs to the Kalisz Centre of Culture and Art (www.ckis.kalisz.pl) and houses a hotel (www.palacantonin.pl).

Southern and western Wielkopolska

The intensively cultivated agricultural region of South Wielkopolska has the highest concentration of farms of any region in Poland. The area is, however, equally rich in architectural monuments and places of historical interest.

Dating from the Middle Ages, the Market Square in **Leszno** ⓮ has numerous imposing 17th- to 19th-century burghers' houses. But they are still overshadowed by the elegant Baroque Town Hall, dating from the 1780s, with a striking colour co-ordinated façade of sienna, yellow and white. It

was designed by the Italian architect Pompeo Ferrari, who also designed the splendid Baroque parish church. The Regional Museum (Muzeum Okręgowe w Lesznie; Pl Metziga 17; tel: 065-529 61 40; www.muzeum.leszno.pl; Tue 9am–4.30pm, Wed–Fri 9am–2.30pm, Sat 10am–2pm, Sun 2–6pm) has an impressive collection of coffin portraits, which were very traditional in Poland, as well as folk art. The town is also well known for the Akwawit indoor swimming pool (www.akwawit.pl), one of the first built in Poland, which includes a 52-metre (170ft) chute.

On a hill in **Lubiń,** around 30km (19 miles) to the northeast of Leszno, stands a Benedictine monastery built in the early 18th century. The first building here was founded in the 12th century, and there are still Gothic remains (notably the tower). If you are interested in the troubled history of the monastery, it's possible to arrange a visit by booking ahead (visits are held Mon–Fri 9–11.30am, 2.30–5pm).

One of Poland's most beautiful and striking sacred buildings is the Church of the Philippians on the **Holy Mount**

Radziwiłł Princes' Hunting Palace.

TIP

In Strzyżewice, a suburb of Leszno, there is an airfield for gliders, where the world gliding championships have twice been held.

by the town of Gostyń, a replica of the Santa Maria della Salute church in Venice. Beneath a massive dome, the interiors include a painting of the Madonna dating from 1540. A view of the town forms the background of the painting – almost certainly the earliest example of its kind in Polish art. Also worth seeing in the nearby village of **Pawłowice** are the Gothic church with Renaissance interiors and the neoclassical Palace set in a beautiful park with several lakes (Pałac Mielżyńskich; Mon–Fri 3–8pm, Sat–Sun 9am–8pm). Near Leszno in the direction of Wrocław (see page 261) is the small town of **Rydzyna** , which is registered in its entirety as a historical monument of outstanding quality. The 18th-century layout includes the Market Square surrounded by burghers' houses, while the rococo monument to the Holy Trinity dates from 1760. The Baroque Rydzyna Castle (Zamek w Rydzynie; tel: 065-529 50 40; http://zamek-rydzyna.com.pl), dating from the 17th century, houses a museum, hotel and restaurant.

Some of the lakes near **Boszkowo**, a village northwest of Leszno, are

well worth exploring. The campsites, wooden bungalows and agritourism facilities by the clear waters of Lake Dominicki are a good place for holiday.

The town of **Grodzisk Wielkopolski**, lying midway between Poznań and Zielona Góra, was once renowned for brewing a strong wheat beer. This beer had a superior flavour attributed to the local spring water, whose special qualities were discovered in the 14th century. There are plans to reopen the brewery, which closed in 1994. Monuments to Grodzisk's glorious past, including a fine Renaissance church, can be seen throughout the town.

Wolsztyn, on the River Obra, is popular with water-sports enthusiasts, particularly canoeists, as the surrounding area contains many lakes. Moreover, the lakes are linked by either the river or small canals. The choice of accommodation includes a hotel located in what was once a neoclassical palace (tel: 068-346 93 58; www.palacwolsztyn. com.pl). The town was once a centre of woollen cloth production, and includes an 18th-century Baroque church, while the Regional Museum (Muzeum

Gothic cathedral, Gorzów Wielkopolski.

Regionalne w Wolsztynie; tel: 068-384 26 48; www.muzea-wolsztyn.com.pl; Tue–Sat 9am–4pm, Sun 10am–3pm; free on Sun) has three branches: a former workshop of the outstanding Polish sculptor Marcin Rożek, a museum dedicated to the microbiologist Robert Koch, and an open-air country museum.

Around Zielona Góra and Ziemia Lubuska

The western part of Wielkopolska includes a densely wooded region with many rivers and lakes, extending along the border with Germany, which follows the Odra and Nysa-Łużycka rivers. Attractively situated close to the Odra valley at the foot of a chain of hills is the region's administrative centre and the capital of Lubuskie voivodeship, **Zielona Góra** ⓰. This was traditionally a wine-growing area, with a vine-covered hill in the centre of town the only symbolic remains of this practice, where a palm house also houses a restaurant (www.palmiarnia.zgora.pl). However, this tradition is celebrated in the colourful September Days of Zielona Góra Harvest Festival, also called 'a Holiday of Vine Gathering.'

The **Lubuskie Regional Museum** (Muzeum Ziemi Lubuskiej; Niepodleglości 15; tel: 068-327 23 45; www.mzl.zgora.pl; Wed, Thu–Fri 11am–5pm, Sat 10am–3pm, Sun 10am–4pm) documents the history of wine production in the area, with a collection of tools and pots used by vine growers, as well as archaeological and ethnographic exhibits. The town also has one of Poland's most renowned distilleries, the formerly state-owned Polmos Zielona Góra, now V&S Luksusowa (owned by the Pernod Ricard group since 2008), producing a wide range of clear and flavoured vodkas.

Much of Zielona Góra's original layout dates from the town's charter, granted in 1323. The most impressive sights include the **Cathedral of St Jadwiga**, with its monumental Gothic architecture dating from the 13th century, the neoclassical Town Hall, with an elegant clock tower, and 15th-century fragments of the defensive walls. Despite the name, the **Church of the Virgin Mary of Częstochowa** is actually Evangelical, with this half-timbered building dating from the mid-18th century. There are also various early 20th-century buildings, providing a wide range of Secessionist and eclectic styles.

There are a number of interesting towns in the southern part of Ziemia Lubuska, a region which formerly belonged to Lower Silesia. In **Kożuchów**, for example, large sections of the medieval town walls have survived, while the 13th-century church with Baroque interiors is also particularly impressive.

Żagań, on the River Bóbr, was the capital of an independent Piast duchy from the 1270s, and has preserved its original medieval town structure, including fragments of the 12th- to 14th-century town ramparts. The neoclassical Town Hall is surrounded by 17th- and 18th-century burghers' houses, while the Augustinian Monastic Complex, including a 15th-century parish church, monastery and a granary,

Lake Góreckie, Wielkopolski National Park.

offers a wide range of architectural styles. The monastery houses an early 18th-century library, while another part of this complex is a hostel (Dom Turysty PTTK; tel: 068-377 34 67). The town also has the ruins of a Franciscan monastery, dating from the 13th century and refashioned in the 18th century. However, Żagań's finest architectural monument is the early 18th-century **Wallenstein Palace**, approached by a bridge over a moat, and picturesquely situated on the banks of the Bóbr, in a park with many rare species of trees (http://pkis.um.zagan.pl).

Until the end of the Communist regime the town of **Żary**, originally founded in 1260, had a long history of producing the finest cloth and linen in the country. Recalling the town's medieval heyday are the 14th-century Town Hall with a Renaissance portal, a few 13th- and 14th-century Gothic churches, and sections of the ramparts and watchtowers from the 14th century. The Dewin-Biberstein late 18th-century palace and burghers' houses by the Market Square provide prime examples of other architectural styles.

By the banks of the Warta lies **Gorzów Wielkopolski**, a town granted its municipal charter in 1257. As the principal town of this region it has a current population of 125,000 and several large textile factories. Particularly interesting is the 13th-century Gothic cathedral, with a substantial defensive tower dating from the 14th century, a 15th-century presbytery and a Renaissance altar. The town's Jan Dekert museum is in a *fin-de-siècle* Secessionist Palace (Muzeum Lubuskie im Jana Dekerta w Gorzowie Wlkp; Warszawska 35; tel: 095-732 38 14; www.muzeumlubuskie.pl; Tue–Fri 9am–4pm, Sun 10am–5pm), with a collection of decorative arts and crafts, and Polish portraits. The imposing half-timbered granary on the banks of the River Warta was built in the 1770s, and is now another branch of the museum, housing a newly opened exhibition about the history of the town and its industrial past. Every August the town sees gypsy groups converge for the annual international meeting for the Romane Dyvesa festival of gypsy musical groups.

15th-century Tower of the Oder of St John, Łagów.

South of Gorzów, surrounded by beautiful woodland and lakes, is the holiday resort of **Lubniewice**, while heading northeast brings you to **Strzelce Krajeńskie**, where the medieval fortifications, built of uneven blocks, have been preserved almost entirely intact.

The moraines and lakes of Łagów

Along the historic border between Wielkopolska and Ziemia Lubuska, to the north of the main Berlin to Poznań road, are several places worth visiting. **Łagów** is set in a particularly beautiful location, between high moraines and two lakes. Its most outstanding architectural monument is a castle, built in the 15th century for the Order of St John, with a watchtower providing a wonderful view of the surrounding area. The castle now houses a hotel and restaurant (www.zamek-lagow.com). Łagów is still protected by a medieval wall, interrupted only by two gates leading into the town. The nearby lakes offer good leisure facilities, and not surprisingly are popular in the summer months. On the western border of Wielkopolska lies the small town of **Międzyrzecz** ⓱, a good base from which to tour the area. Dating from the 10th century, the town is perched on a small hill above the River Obra. The carefully preserved 14th-century Gothic castle is worth seeing, with the grounds including the 18th-century House of the Starostas (town governors). This is now a regional museum (Muzeum Ziemi Międzyrzeckiej im Alfa Kowalskiego; tel: 095-742 18 50; www.muzeum-miedzyrzecz.pl; Tue–Sat 9am–4pm, Sun 10am–4pm, Nov–Apr also open Mon, Nov–Mar closed Sat and Sun) with historical and ethnographic exhibits, including some unique 17th-century coffin portraits. The neoclassical Town Hall, built in 1813, has a neo-Gothic clock tower, while the 16th-century Gothic parish church, with a wooden spire and beautiful star vaulting, also has thoroughly modern interiors.

North of Międzyrzecz, in the hilly area close by the lakes, is **Rokitno**, the site of a Baroque church, which is the destination for countless pilgrims who

Przystanek Woodstock in full swing.

worship its image of the Virgin Mary. Surrounded by woodland, the village of **Gościkówo** is 10km (6 miles) south of Międzyrzecz. The main attraction is a Cistercian Monastery (tel: 068-381 10 21; www.paradisus.pl; July–Sept daily 9.30am–noon, 1–5pm, and a tour at 7pm, Oct–June Mon–Fri tours at 9am, 10am, 11am, noon, also Mon and Wed–Sat 2–5pm, Sun tours at 9am and 10am, 1–3pm), dating from the 13th century but with Baroque additions.

To the west and southwest of Międzyrzecz is an extensive system of **fortifications**, which the Nazis constructed from 1934 to 1938. One of the world's largest military fortifications, the complex consists of 55 individual defensive shelters, with walls of reinforced concrete up to 2.5 metres (8ft) thick. The fortifications are connected by a network of underground corridors totalling 30km (19 miles) in length, through which electric trains ran. Part of the underground area also housed armaments factories. In January 1945, the entire complex was captured by Soviet tank units and large sections were blown up. The ominous remains

Międzyrzecz's medieval castle.

can be visited (Międzyrzecki Rejon Umocniony; tel: 095-741 99 99; www.bunkry.pl; daily 8am–4pm). There are two routes to choose from – the shorter one takes 1hr 30 mins and the other takes an hour longer. The best place to enter the complex is at **Kaława**, a village 8km (5 miles) south of Międzyrzecz. If you do, you won't be alone. Some of the tunnels have become a winter shelter for huge colonies of bats, up to about 30,000 in total, which includes 10 different species of these flying mammals. Consequently, this has been declared the Nietoperek nature reserve.

The Warta lakes

One of Wielkopolska's most scenic areas, the Międzychodzko-Sierakowskie Lakes, extends northwest of Poznań beside the lower reaches of the Warta. With over 100 lakes, moraines, woods, footpaths and recreational facilities, it has become a very popular area with holidaymakers.

There is a large holiday centre on the shores of **Lake Jaroszewskie**, while Lake Lutomskie, with its steep banks and impressive beech forest,

ŁAGÓW FILM FESTIVAL

Łagów has been on the radar of Polish cinema aficionados for decades. The first Lubuskie Film Summer (Lubuskie Lato Filmowe; www.llf.pl) was held in back in 1969 – at that time it was the first feature-film festival in Poland. Since 1990 it has become an international show, presenting works from the former Communist countries. I

It is by far the most extraordinary film festival in Poland: unlike its European counterparts there are no red carpets or paparazzi. Actors, directors and film critics mingle with the public and take part in panel discussions. The screenings are held in a spectacular 700-seat open-air amphitheatre at the foot of Łagów 14th-century castle, which is a Polish national heritage site.

forms part of a nature reserve. A route called the 'black path' leads to the town of **Sieraków**, 3km (2 miles) away. By the altar of the town's Renaissance church is a painting that originated from Rubens' studio. There is a small but interesting museum in the reconstructed south aisle of Opaliński Castle (Muzeum Zamek Opalińskich; http://muzeum-sierakow.pl; Tue–Fri 8.30am–3.30pm, Sat 11am–3pm, Sun 1–5pm) presenting the sarcophagus of the Opaliński Family. Another attraction is the stud farm (www.stadoogierow. eu), which raises a horse breed unique to the region and offers riding holidays. A large holiday centre by the side of Lake Mierzyńskie also attracts many visitors during the summer.

The town of **Międzychód** ⓲, situated between the River Warta and Lake Kuchenne, has a delightful Old Town with gabled houses. Between the Warta and the Noteć lies one of the country's largest forest areas, densely covered with pines, which is the **Noteć Primeval Forest**. In the autumn mushroom-pickers from all over the country flock to this hilly area.

North Wielkopolska

North Wielkopolska is a hilly, mainly wooded region with many lakes. One of its beauty spots is the **Noteć Valley**. Nestling among the hills and between three lakes, Chodzież occupies a picturesque site. This town has three factories producing porcelain, making it one of the main centres of this industry in Poland.

On the banks of the River Gwda, a tributary of the Noteç, lies the 15th-century town of **Piła**, the administrative centre for North Wielkopolska. The centrally located Gromada Hotel (tel: 067-351 18 00; www.gromada.pl) is recommended as a base from which to make day trips to the many different points of interest in this part of Wielkopolska and Pomerania. Piła was badly damaged during World War II, but the town has an early 20th-century neo-Gothic church of

St Stanisław Kostka and the modernist 1930s church of St Anthony, with its sculpture of Christ, over 7 metres (23ft) high. The sculpture was once said to be the tallest in Europe, but now Świebodzin (near Łagów) has beaten the record with its 36-metre (118ft) monument of Christ. This is also the home town of Stanisław Staszic, a priest, scientist and politician who reformed the Polish economy at the end of the 18th and early 19th centuries. His family house is now a museum detailing his life and work (Muzeum Stanisława Stasica; ul Browarna 18; tel: 067-213 15 67; www. muzeumstaszica.pl; Mon–Fri 9am–4pm, Sat–Sun 10am–4pm). The town's lakes include beaches and recreational areas, while Lake Rudnicki is part of a nature reserve, harbouring wild boar and various species of birds and trees. North of Piła, and over the border into Pomerania, are the remains of the German-built Pomeranian Wall, a defensive line crossing an area of forests and lakes. This World War II relic is described in detail in the chapter on West Pomerania (see page 315).

A Soviet T-34 tank and lines of dragons teeth anti-tank obstacles at Międzyrzecz.

The lofty Castle of the Pomeranian Princes in Szczecin.

THE NORTH

The well-forested countryside that surrounds
the post-glacial lakes of the north is gentle
and undulating, while the city of Gdańsk
provides an urban centre for the region.

*In the dunes at Słowiński
National Park.*

The Baltic coastline, with its secluded beaches fringed by pine trees, includes many attractive resorts and spa towns, as well as major ports such as Gdańsk and Szczecin.

As the capital of Western Pomerania (Zachodnio-Pomorskie), which borders Germany, Szczecin's historic importance is demonstrated by monumental buildings such as the Castle of the Pomeranian Princes and the Pomeranian Parliament Building. The city is also a gateway to other Hanseatic towns such as Stargard Szczeciński, as well as national parks and seaside resorts. The surrounding countryside also features vast expanses of agricultural land, with potatoes the most important crop.

The tri-city of Gdańsk, Sopot and Gdynia is the largest municipal area in northern Poland. The historic centre of Gdańsk, with numerous buildings that were designed to impress, reflects its long history as the most important Polish port. Sopot has remained a delightful seaside resort, characterised by 19th-century pavilions and *fin-de-siècle* villas, while Gdynia is a modern marina and port with dockyards, essentially dating from the 1920s.

Tall ship in Gdynia.

A lasting legacy of the Teutonic Order of Knights, who dominated this region from the 13th to the 15th century, are a large number of castles. Some are now picturesque ruins on hillsides, while others are museums. The most impressive is the vast castle in the town of Malbork, south of Gdańsk, and there are well-preserved fragments of a Teutonic castle in the delightful town of Toruń, the birthplace of Copernicus. The town also has prime examples of Gothic architecture. To the east the area is bordered by Warmia i Mazury, which includes the Mazurian Lake District – with more than 1,000 lakes it's Poland's most popular holiday destination.

Wolin National Park overlooks the Baltic Sea.

WEST POMERANIA AND SZCZECIN

Western Pomerania is the top sea and sun destination in Poland, while the capital of the region, Szczecin, has all the buzz of a busy port town and a fascinating past.

West Pomerania's 200km (124-mile) stretch of coastline means a choice of secluded beaches as well as seaside resorts with various facilities. Similarly, the Pomeranian lake district provides tranquil havens, with its series of inter-connected lakes surrounded by forests, as well as attractive resorts. Among the national parks are the islands of Uznam and Wolin, while the Słowiński National Park is renowned for its 'wandering' dunes. With numerous historic towns and villages, the region provides a range of attractions.

Slavic tribes, ruled by various dukes, first settled in this part of Pomerania in the 9th and 10th centuries. At the end of the 10th century the area was unified by the Piast dynasty, the first Polish kings, though control of the region fluctuated between the early Polish state and the Brandenburg Margraves (German nobles). In the 12th century the Margraves were forced to cede territory to the Polish king, Bolesław Krzywousty, who once again united the region's leaders. However, in league with the Danes, the Margraves subsequently re-established control, with the Greifen family, originally Slavic but then 'Germanised', ruling from the early 13th–16th centuries. In the 17th century, the region was annexed by Sweden and then by Prussia in 1720, after which the

region was again 'Germanised' and not returned to Poland until after World War II. The region's post-war prosperity rests on a combination of industry, fishery, agriculture and forestry.

Szczecin

The capital of West Pomerania and Zachodniopomorskie voivodeship, **Szczecin ❶**, is near the border with Germany on the River Odra (Oder). This river, and the fact that Szczecin is only 65km (40 miles) from the Baltic, has ensured its status as the

Main Attractions
Szczecin
Stargard Szczeciński
Drawskie Lakes
Wolin
Słowiński National Park
Łeba

Szczecin.

second-largest Polish port and a junction for land traffic.

Szczecin evolved from a 9th-century Slav settlement. In 1237 the city was granted its municipal charter, and joined the Hanseatic League in 1251. Establishing the city as the capital of their duchy, the Pomeranian dukes began to build their magnificent castle in 1346. Between the 13th and 18th centuries the harbour developed into an important commercial centre, particularly for fish and grain, trading with the major Baltic ports, including Lubeck, Tallin, Stockholm and Gdańsk. Sixty percent destroyed by Allied bombing during World War II, the city was rebuilt and expanded after the war. As a cultural and educational centre, it has a university, five institutions of higher education and the Higher Maritime Academy, a Philharmonic orchestra and several theatres.

The city's attractions are concentrated in the centre, and can easily be seen on foot, with broad boulevards, riverbanks, parks and squares providing various settings for historic architecture. While Szczecin is an attractive city, sightseeing is a case of robust, handsome 'highlights', rather than continual, refined aesthetics. Those who come by train can start the visit with the Szczecin Underground Route (Szczecińskie Podziemne Trasy Turystyczne; ul Kolumba 1/6; tel: 091-434 08 01; www.schron.szczecin.pl; Mon–Fri 9.30am–4.30pm, Sat 9.30am–2.30pm). In a big anti-aircraft shelter built during World War II under the Main Railway Station, two interactive tours are available: World War II and Cold War – Communist Era.

A prime example of Pomeranian ecclesiastical architecture, located on the banks of the River Oder, is **St John the Evangelist's Church** Ⓐ (Kościół Św Jana Ewangelisty; daily). One of the few buildings to survive the war, the 14th-century façade yields simple interiors with fragments of the original wall paintings in the right-hand aisle.

Further along by the banks of the Oder is the **Old Town Hall** Ⓑ (Ratusz Staromiejski). Dating from the 17th century, it was burned down in 1944, and reconstructed in its original Gothic style. This includes an extraordinary gabled roof, while the

decorative terracotta façade is typical of Hanseatic towns around the Baltic. The building now houses the **Museum of the History of the City of Szczecin** (Muzeum Historii Miasta Szczecina; ul Mściwoja II 8; tel: 091-4315 255; www.muzeum.szczecin.pl; Tue–Wed, Sat 10am–6pm, Thu until 8pm, Sun until 4pm), with a collection of engravings that dates from the 17th and 18th centuries. Nearby are the elegant **Loitz House** ⓒ (Kamienica Loitzów), formerly the residence of a wealthy 16th-century merchant family, now a College of Fine Art, and the far more majestic **Castle of the Pomeranian Princes** ⓓ (Zamek Książąt Pomorskich). Built between the 14th and 17th centuries, it was reconstructed after World War II in a Renaissance style, retaining Gothic elements. Originally housing the dukes' valuable art collection, it comprises five wings and two inner courtyards, which are an impressive sight. In addition to a library, there is a concert hall within the former chapel, while the belfry's observation tower provides a magnificent panorama of the city and the harbour. The east wing

houses the Castle Museum (Muzeum Zamkowe; ul Korsarzy 34; tel: 091-489 16; http://zamek.szczecin.pl; Fri–Wed 10am–6pm), which details the castle's history. Among the most interesting exhibits are six sarcophagi of Pomeranian dukes from the early 17th century. At the foot of the castle are fragments of the town's medieval defences, the **Maiden's Tower** ⓔ (Baszta Panieńska; summer months 10am–6pm), also known as the Bastion of Seven Cloaks.

Walking along **Chrobry Embankments** ⓕ (Wały Chrobrego) takes you past an eclectic group of red-brick buildings. Dating from the early 20th century and built on the site of the former town walls, these buildings house the Maritime Academy (Wały Chrobrego 1-2) and the **National Museum of Szczecin** (Narodowe Muzeum w Szczecinie; Wały Chrobrego 3; tel: 091-4315 255; www.muzeum.szczecin.pl; Tue–Wed, Sat 10am–6pm, Thu until 8pm, Sun until 4pm), including maritime, ethnographic, and archaeological exhibits. Proceeding further north brings the harbour into view, from where boats leave on sightseeing tours of the

Climb the bell-tower of the Castle of the Pomeranian Princes for a great view of the city.

The view from the Castle of the Pomeranian Princes.

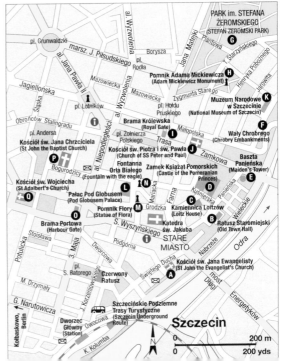

FACT

The tune that now traditionally accompanies all brides down the aisle, The Wedding March, was first played by its composer Felix Mendelssohn-Bartholdy in 1827 at Szczesin's St James's Cathedral.

river, and cruise further north to the port of Świnoujście by the Baltic (see page 369). Strolling through **Stefan Żeromski Park** (Park Żeromskiego; open daily) takes you through wooded greenery, including numerous trees and shrubs from around the world, as well as to the **Mickiewicz Monument** (Pomnik Adama Mickiewicza) honouring Poland's most romantic poet (see page 102).

The north of the city

The streets and squares of the northern part of the city are laid out in a star-shaped pattern, with the radial roads meeting at **Grunwald Square** (Plac Grunwaldzki). Unlike the city centre, which was badly damaged during World War II, the surrounding area was relatively unscathed. Although some of the area's houses are ready for refurbishment, they are, nevertheless, attractive. The ornate and ceremonial **Royal Gate** (Brama Królewska), also known as the Gate of Prussian Homage, is one of the city's landmarks. Replacing an earlier Gothic gate, this was built by the Prussians at the beginning of the 18th

The flower market.

century as a reminder of the Prussian purchase of the city from the Swedes in 1720. This highly artistic gate now houses Brama Jazz Café (www.brama.szczecin.pl). Nearby, at Małopolska 48, is the new, some say iconic, Szczecin Philharmonic Hall (Filharmonia im Mieczysława Karłowicza w Szczecinie; http://filharmonia.szczecin.pl), which opened in September 2014.

The **Church of SS Peter and Paul** (Kościół Św Piotra i Pawla; daily) is a superb example of Pomeranian Gothic sacred architecture, with an ornate façade featuring an impressive rose window. The façade is decorated with glazed terracotta mascarons (faces), while the interiors include an 18th-century wooden ceiling, buttresses and a historic portal from a monastery in Grabów.

The Baroque Parliament Building of Pomeranian States on the Square of the Polish Soldier (Plac Żołnierza Polskiego), built in the 1720s, now houses the **National Museum of Szczecin** (Muzeum Narodowe w Szczecinia; www.muzeum.szczecin.pl; Tue–Wed, Sat 10am–6pm, Thu until 8pm, Sun until 4pm). A fascinating collection encompasses medieval sculptures from eastern Pomerania, Polish paintings from the 18th to the early 20th centuries, the history of Szczecin and Pomerania, silver, folk arts and crafts. Among the sacred art are some beautiful altarpieces. Modern Polish art is displayed at the museum's annex across the road in the neoclassical Pałac pod Głowami (Palace under the Heads), named after the busts that decorate the windows. This is one of several neoclassical buildings in the immediate area.

The **Pod Globusem Palace** (Pałac Pod Globusem) was built in the 1720s for the Governor of the Province of Pomerania, and features a decorative tympanum. It houses an art academy. Opposite the 18th-century Baroque **Statue of Flora** (Posąg Flory) is one of Pomerania's largest Gothic churches, St James's Cathedral (Katedra Św Jakuba). After the war, only the

bomb-damaged tower and the choir remained, until reconstruction began in 1971. Few of the original features have survived, though the 14th-century altar triptych and Baroque epitaphs are worth seeing. The Baroque **Fountain with the Eagle**  (Fontanna Orła Białego) is indeed crowned with a majestic sandstone eagle. Erected in 1723, it also served as a well, being part of the city's newly established water system. The willows surrounding the fountain really do make this a green oasis, and the best view of the fountain is with the Pod Globusem Palace as the backdrop.

Harbour Gate  (Brama Portowa) was also built by the Prussians at the start of the 18th century, on the site of an earlier Gothic gate. Among the ornate inscriptions and carvings is a panorama of Szczecin. The late 19th-century neo-Gothic **St John the Baptist Church**  (Kościół Św Jana Chrzciciela; open daily) is arranged in the form of a cross. It is often known as the 'Polish church' as even during the Prussian regime mass was occasionally celebrated in Polish. The early 20th-century **St Adalbert's**

Church  (Kościół Św Wojciecha; open daily) pays homage to Poland's most famous saint, with stained-glass windows depicting his life. As the garrison church, there are also monuments to Polish troops who lost their lives in various uprisings and wars.

Further north is Jasne Błonia, where a monument was erected to commemorate the dramatic events of 1970, when many dockers were killed during an uprising against the Communist regime. Directly adjoining the woodland of the Wkrzańska Forest is **Jan Kasprowicz Park** (open daily).

Founded in the late 19th century, it includes an amphitheatre together with various rare trees and shrubs. The southern districts of Zdroje and Dąbie, both originally villages, border onto delightful countryside. The Emerald Lake (Jezioro Szmaragdowe), created on the site of a former chalk quarry, is named after the colour of the water. Around the lake are marked trails through the **Beech Tree Forest** (Puszcza Bukowa), with the highest hills providing a wonderful panorama of the city and surrounding lakes and forest.

A comprehensive tram service operates in Szczecin. A local map (from the tourist office) details tram routes.

Ornate façades in Szczecin's Old Town.

South and east of Szczecin

One of the most popular and interesting towns, situated by the River Ina about 35km (16 miles) to the east of Szczecin, is **Stargard Szczeciński ❷**. It provides a great day out and a leisurely stroll will take you past all the Gothic and Renaissance attractions, set amid a delightful country town atmosphere.

The Market Square includes the ornate late Gothic Town Hall, with a wonderful flourish of mascarons on the façade, neighboured by Gothic and Renaissance burghers' houses and the former police station, which houses the Regional Museum covering local history. The twin-towered **Church of the Blessed Virgin Mary** (Kościół Najświętszej Marii Panny) was designed by Henryk Brunsberg, one of the most renowned Gothic architects. Construction began in 1292, but continued until the end of the 15th century. The 15th-century Gothic **St John's Church** (Kościół Św Jana) has Pomerania's tallest tower, at almost 100 metres (328ft), not to mention an impressive vaulted nave.

The town's powerful defensive system has survived remarkably well. Dating from the 13th and 14th centuries, the city walls enclose the Old Town, with attractive parks laid out along the walls. Several gates and towers provided aesthetics as well as defence. The oldest tower is the imposing red-brick Brama Pyrzycka, dating from the 13th century, set among wooded greenery. The most striking is the 15th-century Mill Gate. The tallest is the Morze Czerwone Tower (Red Sea Tower) at 34 metres (111ft), while the Harbour Gate crosses a tributary of the River Ina, with a tower on each bank.

The village of **Chojna**, originally a 10th-century Slav settlement, is also a popular destination. The 15th-century **Church of the Blessed Virgin Mary** (Kościół Najświętszej Marii Panny) has been reconstructed, while the Augustinian Monastic complex dates from the 13th century, and the Town Hall is 15th-century. Fragments of the defensive walls and two splendid gates are 15th-century.

There are more defensive walls and impressive 15th-century gates to be

Looking out to the Baltic Sea in Wolin National Park.

seen in **Trzcińsko Zdrój**, by the picturesque Trzygłowski lake and park. Traditionally a cattle and sheep trading town, a spa was established in 1895. The church dates from the 13th century and has a vast stone tower, while the 15th-century Town Hall includes an ornamental façade and vaulted interiors.

Heading south are a number of towns which played a prominent role during the war, with forts by the Odra erected by Polish and Russian soldiers in April 1945, shortly before the capture of Berlin. A monument on a hill near Cedynia, Poland's most westerly town, recalls the battle between Mieszko I and German Margraves in 972. The town also has a 13th-century church and a reconstructed 14th-century abbey, converted into a hotel (www.klasztorcedynia.pl). The Cedyński Landscape Park, which includes a reserve for rare plants, is within easy reach of the town.

Myślibórz ❸, a small town close to a number of lakes, is encircled by the remains of a medieval wall. The walls of the late 13th-century parish church are also worth seeing, being constructed of loose stones arranged on top of one another, a building method typical of early-Gothic churches in Pomerania. The grand Town Hall is Baroque.

Among various sights in **Pyrzyce** are the well-preserved town walls with three medieval gates, and the early 16th-century Church of the Blessed Virgin Mary, with notable stained-glass windows. To the east, by the lower reaches of the River Drawa, large wooded areas extend across Drawska Forest. This countryside is perfect for outdoor pursuits, such as hiking and cycling. Meanwhile, the section of the River Drawa between Czaplinek and Krzyż is a kayaker's paradise.

The Pomeranian Lakes

West Pomerania's landscape is dominated by lakes, most of which are ringed by delightful wooded hillsides. The **Drawskie Lakes** (Pojezierze Drawskie), including the towns of Drawsko Pomorskie, Połczyn Zdrój and Szczecinek, is the most attractive region. The largest and most beautiful of the 200 lakes is Lake Drawsko, with the popular tourist town of **Czaplinek** on its southeastern edge.

The Old Town of Szczecin, beside the River Odra.

Travelling northwards through the picturesque Valley of the Five Lakes leads to **Połczyn Zdrój**. This popular spa town has been renowned for the medicinal benefits of its waters since the 14th century. Nestling between high moraine hills, the town's attractions include a castle and the Gothic Church of the Blessed Virgin Mary. The **Pomeranian Wall** (Wał Pomorski) stretches from Szczecinek through Wałcz and Tuczno to Krzyż. This defensive barrier built of reinforced concrete by the Germans in the 1930s was part of an ambitious system of fortifications. It was only in February 1945 that Polish soldiers managed to break through. Monuments in Podgaje near Jastrowie, and in Wałcz, as well as the military museum in Mirosławiec, serve as memorials to the fierce battles waged in this part of West Pomerania. The best preserved fragments of the wall can be visited near Wałcz. This town, on the shores of two lakes, also has a vast military cemetery where victims of World War II are buried. The **Bytów Lakes** (Pojezierze Bytowskie), found among wooded hills, begin east of the Drawa Lakes. **Bytów ❹**, on the edge of the Bytów Lake District, has a Gothic castle built by the Teutonic Knights which is now a Regional Museum of Western Kashubia (Muzeum Zachodnio-Kaszubskie; tel: 059-822 26 23; http://zamekbytowski.pl; daily 10am–4pm, until 6pm Tue–Sun Sept–Apr), with a collection that includes folk arts and crafts. The castle also houses a hotel and restaurant (www.hotel-wzamku.pl). The town's other attractions include the Gothic tower of St Catherine's church, the 18th-century neoclassical former post office, and a half-timbered 19th-century granary.

Along the Baltic Sea coast

Świnoujście occupies three islands: Uznam, Wolin and Karsibór. While this is a major port for cargo ships and passenger ferries to Hamburg, Copenhagen and Ystad, it is also a tourist centre. The western end of Świnoujście has long sandy beaches, with Poland's tallest lighthouse (68 metres/220ft), and being a long-established spa town there are various Secessionist spa buildings. A cross-border promenade, established in 2011, links Świnoujście with the German town of Heringsdorf; at the actual border there is a symbolic steel gate. The town of **Wolin ❺**, in the south of the island of Wolin, was one of the oldest Slav settlements, flourishing during the 9th and 10th centuries. A Slav burial mound and cemetery both date from the 9th century. However, it was also a Viking stronghold, which accounts for the annual Viking Festival. Part of the island is a national park, established to protect the unusual geological formations, cliffs and offshore rocks. The remote eastern edge of the park has several lakes which link to form a small lake district. This includes Lake Turkusowe at the southern end of the park, with Lake Gardno close to the seashore. Eagles, waterfowl and other protected species such as wild boar can be seen in the woods surrounding the lakes, with a small bison reserve at the edge of the park.

A sunny day on Międzyzdroje beach.

Having attractive sandy beaches, impressive cliffs, and dense forests on either side makes **Międzyzdroje** ⑥ one of the most popular Baltic resorts. In addition to numerous sports facilities, the spa operates from attractive wooden buildings dating from the 19th century. The Natural History Museum (Przyrodnicze Wolińskiego Parku Narodowego; www.wolinpn.pl; Tue–Sun 9am–3pm, May–Sept until 5pm) will also enable you to get the most out of visiting Wolin.

Kamień Pomorski ⑦, a town which joined the Hanseatic League in the 14th century, is situated by the Kamieński Lagoon about 10km (6 miles) from the sea. This was once an important trading centre, with a mint issuing Pomeranian coins in the late 12th century. Retaining its original medieval layout, the town's most important building is the Romanesque-Gothic cathedral. Elegant features animate the red-brick façade, while the interiors include a 12th-century baptismal font, a 17th-century wrought-iron screen and a Baroque organ, which can be heard during the town's Summer Festival of Organ

Music. The late Gothic Bishop's Palace, the 14th-century Church of St Nicholas, now housing the Regional Museum (Muzeum Ziemi Kamieńskiej; www.mhzk.eu; daily 10am–5pm, Oct–Apr till 4pm), and St Mary's Church, built in the 18th century, are also prime examples of sacred architecture. Fragments of the town walls include the 15th-century Wolin Gate, which leads into the Old Town, and the late-Gothic Town Hall. To explore the lagoon, boats can be hired by the day at the harbour.

The coast is lined with numerous holiday villages such as Dziwnów, Dziwnówek, Mrzeżyno and Dźwirzyno, which are renowned for their recreational facilities. Parts of the coast have suffered from erosion, which is particularly evident in Trzęsacz, where the ruins of a 14th-century Gothic church, originally built 2km (1 mile) from the coast, have been lapped by the sea since 1901. Its story is retold in an interactive museum on the cliff (Multimedialne Muzeum na Klifie; tel: 0504 074 780; http://muzeumtrzesacz.pl; May–Sept daily 9am–7pm, Oct–Apr Tue–Sun 9am–2pm). Founded in the 13th century,

A fun boat ride in the Kamieński Lagoon.

WALK OF FAME

Międzyzdroje, a posh seaside resort known as the 'Pearl of the Baltic', is famous for its Film Stars Festival. Founded in 1996, it attracts the crème de la crème of Polish actors, directors, artists and intellectuals, who meet in a relaxed atmosphere 'to forge their professional group identity', which usually stands for socialising, networking, image building, but above all partying and having fun. The film festival is accompanied by concerts, lectures, debates and many other cultural events, which attract tourists from all parts of Poland. There is also a local version of Hollywood's Walk of Fame, called the Alley of Stars, with more than 130 handprints of popular actors and film directors. The festival is usually held on the first week of July.

Trzebiatów, beside the River Rega, has managed to preserve its delightful medieval character. The main sights include the Gothic St Mary's Church, dominated by a stately 90-metre (295ft) steeple which is typical of West Pomeranian architecture and contains one of Poland's heaviest bells (7.2 tons). Scaled-down Gothic can be seen at the delightful Holy Ghost Chapel. Fragments of the town walls include the late-Gothic Kaszana tower. A cycling path crosses the town and another great way to see the surrounding countryside is from a narrow-gauge passenger train, which operates between Trzebiatów and other coastal towns (www.kolejwaskotorowa.wrewalu.com).

Kołobrzeg ❽, at the mouth of the River Parsęta, is both a port and a major holiday spa resort. The city dates from AD 1000, when King Bolesław Chrobry established an episcopal see, and it later prospered as a member of the Hanseatic League. A great asset was salt production, which also fostered production of salted herrings. Almost 90 percent of Kołobrzeg was destroyed in World War II, but the Old Town has

now been rebuilt. The Gothic Collegiate Church of St Mary is the town's most impressive building, with leaning columns supporting a vaulted ceiling. These pillars may give the impression that the church is about to collapse, but they have leaned at an angle since the 16th century. Gothic features include a bronze font, a vast chandelier, and beautifully carved stalls. It's an effort to climb to the top of the brick steeple, but the reward is a magnificent panorama of Kołobrzeg and its surroundings. Fragments of the medieval city wall include the **Gunpowder Tower** (Wieża Prochowa), while the Military Museum (Muzeum Oręża Polskiego w Kołobrzegu; tel: 094-352 12 88; www. muzeum.kolobrzeg.pl; May–June Sun–Fri 9am–5pm, Sat 9am–2pm, July–Aug Mon 9am–2pm, Tue–Sun 9am–6pm, Sep–Apr Tue–Sun 9am–4pm) exhibits weapons and other items salvaged in 1945. The museum also has an open-air maritime branch. The 19th-century neo-Gothic Town Hall, designed by prominent German architect Karl-Friedrich Schinkel, houses the Patria Colbergiensis Museum (tel: 0784 789 218; www.colbergiensis.eu; May–Aug daily 10am–6pm, Sept–Apr Sat–Thu 10am–7pm), showing the history of the town in a modern, interactive way. Lying beyond the dunes east of Kołobrzeg are more holiday villages, with Ustronie Morskie, Sarbinowo and Mielno popular with tourists especially during the summer. Around this area the countryside has an extraordinary beauty, combining lakes and flooded meadows.

The sleepy fishing village of **Darłowo** ❾, by the mouth of the River Wieprza, was granted its municipal charter in 1270. The Pomeranian Duke Eryk I, who also ruled Denmark, Sweden and Norway, established the 14th-century castle as the capital of his dukedom. This magnificent castle is now a museum (tel: 094-314 23 51; May–Sept daily 10am–4pm, July–Aug until 6 pm, Oct–Apr Mon–Fri 10am–6pm) with an interesting collection of folk arts and crafts, furniture, armour,

Fishing boats in Łeba.

sacred art and portraits of Pomeranian dukes. Duke Eryk also founded the Scandinavian Gothic-style St Gertrude's Chapel, which is a rarity, being twelve-sided. He is buried, together with other Pomeranian dukes, in the Gothic St Mary's Church. The Old Town has retained a medieval character, which includes the town walls and one of the Gothic town gates. A Baroque Town Hall overlooks the market square, with its Fisherman Fountain.

The neighbouring village of **Darłówko** is another popular seaside resort, as is the small town of **Sławno**, 20km (12 miles) from Darłówko, which has several monuments that are well worth a detour, including the medieval town wall, the huge Gothic St Mary's Church, and various burghers' houses.

Jarosławiec ❿ is one of Poland's most attractive seaside resorts, partly due to its proximity to Lake Wicko. The traditional fishermen's cottages and half-timbered houses surrounding the lake, and the 17th-century lighthouse, create a delightful atmosphere. At the mouth of the River Słupia is **Ustka**, a small port and popular resort. The harbour was built to serve **Słupsk** ⓫, a busy town situated some 20km (12 miles) inland. One of the largest coastal resorts, Słupsk's attractions include the 14th-century Gothic Parish Church and the Renaissance Castle of the Pomeranian Dukes. This houses the **Museum of Central Pomerania** (Muzeum Pomorza Środkowego; tel: 059-842 40 81; www.muzeum.slupsk.pl; Wed–Sun 10am–4pm), as well as a gallery devoted to the works of Witkacy (see page 238). The castle's grounds also include the Dominican Church of St Jacek, with its ducal tombs and Baroque organ.

The **Słowiński National Park** (see page 121) encloses four lakes: Łebsko (the third largest in Poland), Gardno, Dołgie Wielkie and Dołgie Małe. Separated from the sea by a small beach, the lakes are a refuge for numerous birds. However, the park is most renowned for its unusual 'wandering' sand dunes, along the coastline between Rowy and Łeba. In some areas the dunes are moved up to 10 metres (30ft) per year by the wind. The tallest dune is just over 40 metres (130ft) high, and the largest extends to around 300 hectares (740 acres). In the western part of the park are the remains of V-2 rocket launch pads, abandoned by the Nazis at the end of World War II, which now attract a lot of visitors (Muzeum Wyrzutnia Rakiet w Rąbce; near the Dune Łącka).

Kluki, a remote fishing village on the edge of Lake Łebsko, has some fine half-timbered houses and a *skansen* (open-air museum) (Muzeum Wsi Słowińskiej w Klukach; tel: 059-846 30 20; www.muzeumkluki.pl; May–Aug Mon 11am–3pm, Tue–Sun 10am–6pm, Sept–Apr Mon 11am–3pm, Tue–Sun 9am–4pm) with a collection of historic regional buildings. Most of the local inhabitants are descended from the Slavic Slovincian tribe. The coastal village of **Łeba** is an attractive seaside destination and a fishing port, and is a good base from which to explore the Słowiński National Park.

The shifting dunes at Łeba.

Gdańsk's historic centre at dusk.

GDAŃSK

Gdańsk was reduced to rubble during World War II, but it has been reconstructed and today looks much the same as in the Hanseatic era when it was built by rich ship-owners and merchants.

The most important city along the Baltic Coast is actually a "Tri-City", comprising Gdańsk, Sopot and Gdynia, which together extend along the Bay of Gdańsk for 20km (12 miles). Originally separate towns, the suburbs of each have linked to create a conurbation inhabited by almost 800,000 people, which is well connected by road, rail, ferry, bus and tram links.

These three cities have nevertheless retained their own distinct characters. Gdańsk is the historic and cultural centre, with outstanding examples of Gothic, Renaissance and Baroque architecture. Sopot is a traditional seaside resort, which developed in the 19th and early 20th centuries, and is characterised by Art Nouveau villas, while the maritime character of Gdynia dates from the 1920s, when the city was 'purpose-built' to provide a modern harbour and docks.

Historic pearl of the Baltic

Gdańsk has long been an important port and trading centre. Originating as a Slavic fishing village, a defensive settlement was established in the Gdańsk area during the 9th century. From the 10th century this was a seat of the Pomeranian dukes, with Poland's most important saint,

Adalbert, baptising the local inhabitants in AD 997. The earliest recorded mention was in 999, in *The Life of Saint Adalbert*, written by a Benedictine monk. Being a river port on the Vistula also meant that Gdańsk was an important link in the early Middle Ages with the historic capital of Kraków (see page 193), with grains, furs, leather and amber among the most important commodities.

The region's evolution was also dictated by Polish-Prussian rivalry. In 1226 the Mazovian Duke Konrad

Main Attractions
Town Hall and Długi Targ
Mariacka Street
St Mary's Church
National Maritime Museum
Tower Clock Museum
European Centre of Solidarity
Gdańsk Shakespeare Theatre

The Neptune Fountain, symbol of the city of Gdańsk.

TIP

On the first weekend of July Gdańsk welcomes participants of the International Baltic Sail Festival, which aims to revive the marine traditions of the Baltic Sea. Tourists are invited to visit yachts and cutters moored alongside Wełtawa wharf and take part in concerts and cruises on Gdańsk Bay.

Mazowiecki asked the Teutonic Order of Knights (see page 30) to help in his struggle against the heathen Prussians, in order to control the area around Toruń in East Pomerania. The Teutonic Knights agreed, but it soon created another problem, as the Knights used this as an opportunity to strengthen their presence in East Pomerania. Gdańsk and East Pomerania came under the control of the Teutonic Knights in 1308, the same year in which the Main Town district received its town charter. The Knights also founded the New Town (Nowe Miasto) in 1380, which subsequently merged with the Main Town, while also incorporating the neighbouring East Pomeranian town, now known as the Old Town district. The Knights also transferred their capital from Venice to nearby Malbork.

As a member of the Hanseatic League, Gdańsk developed into a prosperous town during the 14th century, and the town's burghers set about constructing major civic buildings, with St Mary's Church intended to be the largest brick-built church in the world.

The princes of East Pomerania and Greater Poland (Wielkopolska) attempted to resist the growing dominance of the Teutonic Knights, and a Polish triumph in 1454 brought Gdańsk and East Pomerania under Polish rule. This was further ratified by the Teutonic Knights agreeing to the Second Peace of Toruń in 1466. Being granted exclusive rights to Poland's maritime trade in the 15th century resulted in Gdańsk enjoying even greater prosperity, with two-thirds of Poland's external trade passing through the town. Gdańsk continued to have the status of an independent town until the partitions of Poland brought it under Prussian control in 1792, regaining its original status as a free town during the Napoleonic era. Between the two World Wars, Gdańsk was under the protection of the League of Nations.

It was in the Westerplatte region of Gdańsk that the first shots of World War II were fired (the military post that was attacked is open to visitors in summer; see www.mhmg.pl for details), and Gdańsk remained in the active

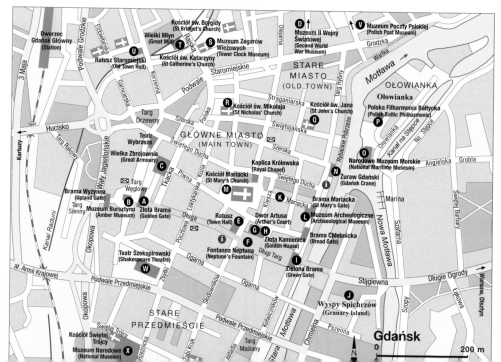

war zone for longer than any other region, with the occupation lasting until the Nazis surrendered on the Hel peninsula in May 1945. By the end of the war Gdańsk was reduced to rubble, though much of this was inflicted by the 'liberating' Red Army, who thought of Gdańsk as 'Danzig', in other words German.

Following the end of World War II, Gdańsk became part of Poland and, despite the town's devastation and Poland's precarious economic situation, there was never any question that the city would be reconstructed. The question was how this should be done. It was suggested that a new, modern city be built on this site, but it was eventually decided to reconstruct the city in its historic style. This presented a huge challenge for architects and planners. Although some fragments of the original buildings, such as church walls, towers and gates, could be retrieved from the rubble, many of the landmarks were totally destroyed. It was a massive undertaking, and it wasn't until 1975 that the main reconstruction programme was completed. Indeed, St John's Church was only finished in the 1990s. The historic granaries are still waiting their turn.

In 1997, Gdańsk, now with a population of nearly 500,000, commemorated its millennium, and the city continues to be Poland's largest port as well as an important industrial, scientific and cultural centre, not to mention a major tourist attraction. Among the city's varied cultural repertoire is the Baltic Philharmonic, with annual events including the Festival of Organ Music, the Film Festival and the Dominican Fair in August. First established during the mid-13th century and revived in 1972, this market offers numerous folk arts and crafts, antiques and bric-a-brac, amber jewellery and other local specialities, with various concerts and events organised to coincide with this fair.

Gdańsk's historic centre

Much of the historic centre was originally constructed as a showcase of the city's prosperity. The buildings were designed to impress. From grand and imposing to flamboyant and ornamental, the city is beautiful but never ostentatious. The burghers had that rare combination: wealth and style. As much of the historic centre is pedestrianised, a walking tour is the best way to explore, with the numerous cafés, boutiques and galleries providing plenty of refreshing stops en route. Nine principal thoroughfares each link to a waterside gate that provides access to the harbour, so you are never far from a sea view.

The principal thoroughfare, Długa (literally 'Long street'), is best approached through the **Golden Gate** Ⓐ (Złota Brama). Designed by Abraham van den Blocke between 1612 and 1614 in a Renaissance style, it was inspired by a triumphal Roman arch, and the view along Długa is equally triumphant. As this was the route along which Polish kings paraded when attending events in the city, it's hardly

FACT

The most famous chronicle of the wartime years is *The Tin Drum*, by the German writer Günter Grass. Born in Gdańsk (or Danzig as it is known in German) in 1927, he describes this period through the eyes of a child.

Gdańsk Shipyard Monument.

surprising that Długa features numerous impressive buildings. An immediate example is the neighbouring Court of the Fraternity of St George (Dwór Bractwa Św Jerzego). This Gothic mansion was built in the late 15th century, as the seat of this fraternity. Across Długa is the 14th-century Fore Gate complex (Gdańsk Barbican), with the **Amber Museum** (Muzeum Bursztynu; www.mhmg.pl; Tue 10am–1pm, Wed–Sun 10am–4pm, Thu until 6pm; free on Tue) presenting the role of amber in the regional culture.

The statues on the Golden Gate are copies of the originals made in 1648.

Before continuing along Długa, turn left into Tkacka to see the **Great Armoury** (Wielka Zbrojownia). A magnificent example of Renaissance architecture, the intricate symmetry of its four-gabled façade was designed by Dutch architect Anthonis van Opbergen. He was highly regarded in Gdańsk, and also built the Kronborg ('Hamlet's Castle') in Helsingør, Denmark. The armoury now houses the Academy of Fine Arts (Państwowa Wyższa Szkoła Sztuk Plastycznych; www.asp-gda.pl), with a great exhibition space.

Gdańsk street life.

Continuing along Długa, at 81/83, is the **Second World War Museum** (Muzeum II Wojny Światowej; tel: 058-323 75 20; www.muzeum1939.pl; due to open in 2015), in a modern glass building. It presents the story of the war as experienced by the Polish people. Further on, at Długa 12, Uphagen House (www.mhmg.pl; Tue 10am–1pm, Wed–Sun 10am–4pm, Thu until 6pm; free on Tue) shows the typical interiors of an 18th-century merchant's town house.

The **Town Hall** (Ratusz) is unusual in not occupying a central position in a square, but forming part of a terrace of buildings at the far end of Długa. Nevertheless, this red-brick 14th-century Gothic building stands out as the largest building in the street, with its elegant Renaissance tower crowned by a gilded statue of King Zygmunt August, dating from 1561. Needless to say, the view from the top of the tower is magnificent. The interiors are equally impressive, and the Red Room, originally the setting for the Town Council's debates, is truly a showpiece. Set against a vivid

red and gilded background, this room has a wealth of sculptures and ornamental carvings, and numerous paintings – 25 on the ceiling alone, while a series of seven allegorical paintings are the work of Hans Vredeman de Vries. Many of the furnishings are original, having been shipped from Gdańsk prior to the outbreak of war for safekeeping. Housed amid these sumptuous interiors is a stylish restaurant and the **Historical Museum of the City of Gdańsk** (Muzeum Historii Miasta Gdańska, Długa 46/47; tel: 058-767 91 00; www.mhmg.pl; Tue 10am–1pm, Wed–Sun 10am–4pm, Thu until 6pm; free on Tue). At this point Długa broadens out to form **Długi Targ** ('Long Marketplace'). The architectural magnificence is also heightened, as this is where the very wealthiest merchants and shipowners built their residences. The beginning of this street is marked by the decorative **Neptune's Fountain** ❺ (Fontanna Neptuna). Enclosed by its original wrought-iron railings, this statue of Neptune, symbolising the city's maritime links, dates from 1613.

Another impressive building is **Arthur's Court** ❻ (Dwór Artusa), the traditional seat of the Gdańsk Merchants' Guild and Poland's first stock exchange. The highly individual Mannerist architecture includes windows that dominate the main façade (equal to three storeys of the neighbouring houses). The vaulted entrance hall contains various historic features, including an ornate tiled stove. One of the few buildings not to be totally destroyed during World War II, this is now part of the Historical Museum of the City of Gdańsk (www.mhmg.pl; Tue 10am–1pm, Wed–Sun 10am–4pm, Thu until 6pm; free on Tue).

Façades of neighbouring buildings are equally definitive of other architectural genres. Baroque *in extremis* is the only way to describe the **Golden House** ❽ (Złota Kamiennica). Dating from the early 17th century, this

four-storey house was built for the Mayor of Gdańsk and was named after its gilded bas-reliefs, comprising mythological figures including Achilles and Cleopatra. Home to the Cunard Line between the world wars, this is now the Maritime Institute.

The marketplace culminates in another gateway, the ornate quadruple arched **Green Gate** ❶ (Zielona Brama). Designed in a Flemish Renaissance style, this was also an official residence of Polish kings when visiting the city. Now it's a temporary exhibition space of the National Museum of Gdańsk.

Gdańsk's waterfront

The Green Gate opens onto the wharf by the Motława estuary, formerly the site of the town's harbour. Boats leave from here for trips along the coast to Sopot, Gdynia and Westerplatte, or across the Bay of Gdańsk to the popular holiday resort of Hel on the Gdańsk peninsula (see page 341). Across the estuary on **Granary Island** ❿ (Wyspa Spichrzów) are numerous historic granaries. This

CRADLE OF SOLIDARITY

Gdańsk is now best known as the birthplace of the trade union movement Solidarity (Solidarność), which challenged the Communist regime and shaped Polish history during the 1980s. Lech Wałęsa, the union's leader and President of Poland (1990–95), wrote:

'Visitors… have no trouble finding their way to the monument… outside the Gdańsk shipyard. Striking workers were murdered here in December 1970, in a hail of fire from the militia. They sacrificed their lives for more than Gdańsk – even at a time when nobody had foreseen what far-reaching effects their struggle would have on the future of all of Europe. Their resistance and deaths were experiences from which we learned lessons…

'The resounding slogan of 1980 was "good bread for good work". Of course, the call for freedom was within everyone's heart all over Poland, but it was also clear to every one of us that such a cry at that time could have triggered off a swift Soviet intervention.

'And yet 10 years later, we have attained our goal – in a revolution without force and without bloodshed, a revolution which overthrew the Communist regime and set an example for democratic freedom initiatives throughout central and eastern Europe.'

FACT

Mariacka Street provided a location for the film version of Thomas Mann's novel *Buddenbrooks* – as no such street could be found in post-war Lubeck, where the novel is set.

area is being redeveloped as the city's modern commercial and banking centre; the newly constructed wharfs are good for walking and offer views of Gdańsk's Old Town. The Green Bridge leading to the island is a popular spot for tourists to stop to take a photo.

Turning left leads to the Bread Gate (Brama Chlebnicka), with the waterfront featuring numerous galleries selling souvenirs, antiques and, above all, 'Baltic Gold' or amber, alongside cafés and bars. Amber is almost the only thing you can buy, together with antiques, in the boutiques and galleries along the street **Mariacka** Ⓚ, entered through St Mary's Gate (Brama Mariacka). One of the city's most beautiful streets, with its original granite cobblestones, it is also one of the most individual, characterised by '*perrons*'. A feature of grander houses in numerous Baltic cities, this comprises a small but ornate flight of steps from the pavement to a terrace by the entrance to each building (rather like a box at the theatre). This was a prime place for the residents

to sit and watch passers-by, as well as being seen themselves. Mariacka was totally rebuilt after World War II. The **Archaeological Museum** Ⓛ (Muzeum Archeologiczne; Mariacka 25; www.archeologia.pl; Tue–Sun 9am–7pm; Mon for observation deck only) has 27,000 archaeological artefacts and offers a sweeping view of Gdańsk from the observation deck.

At the end of Mariacka is the transcendent **St Mary's Church** Ⓜ (Kościół Mariacki; www.bazylikamariacka.pl; Mon–Sat 9am–5pm, summer until 6.30pm, Sun from 1pm; visits to the Royal Chapel by request only, tel: 058-301 39 82). This monumental red-brick Gothic building is thought to be the world's sixth-largest church, able to accommodate a congregation of 25,000 (or crowds of tourists). Not surprisingly, it took more than 150 years to complete, from 1343 to 1502. Austere through its simplicity, but undoubtedly beautiful, the initial impact is provided by the scale and height of the three-naved arrangement. It is certainly worth looking up at the Baroque organ, and the magnificent vaulting, much of which was reconstructed following a fire in 1945.

While many original treasures were looted by the Nazis (or ended up in Polish museums), this still leaves plenty to see: 13 Gothic altars, over 30 Renaissance and Baroque epitaphs and a stunning sculpture of the so-called Beautiful Madonna. An astronomical clock, the work of Hans Duringer in 1470, is one of the world's largest medieval clocks, revealing the phases of the moon as well as the positions of the sun and the moon. Another outstanding feature is a triptych by Hans Memling entitled *The Last Judgement*, dating from 1466–73. This painting was actually en route to a church in Tuscany when intercepted by the citizens of Gdańsk. A copy now hangs in the church, with the original in the National Museum. If you feel like climbing the lofty tower, a wonderful

TRAILBLAZING FESTIVAL

What do Pearl Jam, Björk, Coldplay, New Order, Rihanna, Black Keys, Prince, Snoop Dogg and Nick Cave have in common? Well for one they have all taken part in the Open'er Festival, which is held every year in July at Babie Doły near Gdańsk. Considered by many to be the best summer festival in Europe, Open'er also features the best theatre (with plays staged in the most unusual setting), art installations, a Kids' Zone, Silent Disco and many other attractions. In the end, however, it is the great atmosphere that prevails overall. As one past reveller puts it, it's 'a beautiful, loved-up affair'.

It's well organised, too. Free shuttle buses transport the hordes of music fans from Gdańsk main railway station to Babie Doły, where they duly exchange their tickets for wristbands, another original solution pioneered at Open'er. From its foundation in 2002, the festival has expanded from 3 to 75 hectares (7 to 185 acres) and it is the only event that starts selling tickets even before the name of the first artist is announced. In a record year as many as 80,000 revellers made the trip to Babie Doły. With several stages, a dizzying mix of genres and an impressive array of talent, from Poland and abroad, Open'er is a must-do experience for all music lovers. So better book those tickets in advance (http://opener.pl)...

view across the historic centre is your reward.

Neighbouring the church is the elegant **Royal Chapel**, built in 1678–81. Founded by King Jan III Sobieski, it is thought to be the work of Tylman of Gameren, the Dutch architect responsible for many of Poland's most beautiful Baroque buildings; sculptures decorating the façade are by Andreas Schluter. In front of the chapel is a new fountain surrounded by four lions, symbols of Gdańsk, beautifully lit at night.

Returning to the riverfront, the 15th-century **Gdańsk Crane N** (Żuraw Gdański) was meticulously restored after World War II. Housed in the largest double-towered gate on the waterfront, it handled cargos as well as raising ships' masts. Capable of lifting up to 2,000kg (2 tonnes), it is one of the largest industrial constructions to have survived from the Middle Ages, and seeing the crane in action is a major attraction. This building now houses a branch of the National Maritime Museum (Szeroka 67/8; Narodowe Muzeum Morskie w Gdańsku;

tel: 058-301 69 38; Tue–Sun 10am–3pm; tickets are sold in other branches of the museum). Next to the Crane is another branch of the museum, the **Centre of Maritime Culture** (Tue–Fri 10am–4pm, Sat–Sun 10am–5pm), in an impressive brick and glass building. Its main highlight is the interactive exhibition 'People – Ships – Harbours'. The main branch of the **National Maritime Museum O** (Narodowe Muzeum Morskie; tel: 058-301 86 11; www.nmm.pl; Tue–Sun 10am–3pm) is in three historic granaries on the island of Ołowianka. The ship *Sołdek* on the waterfront is also part of the museum. The principal exhibition presents the maritime history of Poland – especially interesting is the collection of artefacts salvaged from shipwrecks lying on the Baltic Sea bed. There are ferry shuttles between the crane and the granaries (Tue–Sun 10am–3pm; 3PLN return ticket). Also on the island of Ołowianka is the **Polish Baltic Philharmonic P** (Polska Filharmonia Bałtycka; www.filharmonia. gda.pl), based in a converted power station, constructed at the end of the

Green Gate.

19th century, and the royal granary. The beautiful red-brick building is equipped with a state-of-the-art sound and light system.

There are two prime examples of sacred Gothic architecture on Świętojańska. **St John's Church** ⓠ (Kościół Św Jana), which has only recently been reconstructed after its wartime devastation, has an impressive altar and various tombs of city dignitaries. **St Nicholas' Church** ⓡ (Kościół Św Mikołaja) was one of the few buildings to survive the war intact. The Gothic façade gives way to highly gilded Baroque interiors, with a beautiful altar where a central painting is surrounded by gilded figures.

The Old Town

Although the **Old Town** (Stare Miasto) district was not rebuilt to the same extent as the Główne Miasto, there are numerous historic buildings and architectural styles. It has a different character: less densely built up, and providing greater variety, with broader streets and more open spaces interlaced with greenery. The

Detail of St Mary's Church Astronomical clock. It is claimed that the clock has only lost three minutes in the first hundred years of service.

parish church **St Catherine's Church** (Kościół Św Katarzyny) on Wielkie Młyny has a magnificent Gothic tower with unusual ornamentation soaring above the façade, and the interiors feature late Gothic vaulted ceilings and Baroque details and monuments. This includes the tomb of the renowned Gdańsk astronomer, Jan Heweliusz, also known as Johannes Hevelius (1611–87), who published one of the first detailed maps of the moon and a catalogue of stars. However, earning little money from astronomy, he was also a successful brewer, with profits from the brewery providing funds to establish an observatory (the Hevelius beer brand continues to be very popular). In 2006 the church was badly damaged by fire. After seven years of restoration, the **Tower Clock Museum** ⓢ (Muzeum Zegarów Wieżowych; daily 10am–3pm), in the church's Gothic tower, opened to the public. Its main highlights include the carillon composed of 50 bells, with the biggest weighing 17 tons, and a unique pulsar clock that counts time using signals from pulsars (neutron stars emitting electromagnetic radiation); arguably it is the most accurate clock in the world.

Immediately behind this church is **St Bridget's Church** (Kościół Św Brygidy), which played a significant role in Poland's recent history, being known as the 'Solidarity church'. During martial law in 1981–3, anti-Communist groups met here to worship, which was then considered an act of political opposition. This church is also unusual in not having recreated period interiors. Instead a modern layout, in a form of 'sacred minimalism' creates a poignant setting for contemporary works of art, including a monument to Father Jerzy Popiełuszko, the outspoken supporter of Solidarity who was murdered by members of the Communist security intelligence service (SB).

Both St Brigitte's and St Catherine's Church are part of a cluster of buildings around the **Radunia Canal** (Kanał Raduni), at the heart of the Old Town. The combination of a small park and other stretches of greenery, canals and cascades gives this area a relaxed identity. The **Great Mill** ❶ (The Wielki Młyn) completed in 1595, and the Small Mill (Mały Młyn) are both prime examples of medieval architecture. The former is a terrific structure with a sloping tiled roof, now housing an elegant shopping centre (daily 10am–7pm). Next to it is a fountain featuring a cascade and three big loops, inaugurated in 2014. The 16th-century **Old Town Hall** ⓤ (Ratusz Starego Miasta; tel: 058-301 10 51; www.nck.org.pl; daily 10am–6pm), with its Dutch appearance, has splendid interiors; although not on the same scale as the main Town Hall it is worth seeing, with some beautiful paintings and fine examples of the Gdańsk chests. Now it's a branch of the Baltic Sea Cultural Centre. The 14th-century bridge over Radunia Canal at the end of Korzenna is now called the Bridge of Love. Continuing along Podwale

and Tartaczna streets you get to the **Polish Post Museum** ⓥ (Muzeum Poczty Polskiej; www.mhmg.pl; Tue 10am–1pm, Wed–Sun 10am–4pm, Thu until 6pm; free on Tue). Even if the history of telecommunications is not your cup of tea, it's worth visiting as it commemorates the heroic defence of the Polish Post Office in the Free City of Gdańsk by its employees in September 1939.

Heading further north in the direction of the shipyards is the poignant **Monument to the Shipyard Workers** (Pomnik Poległych Stoczniowców). Three huge crosses, on which much smaller anchors are attached, soar above Gate 2 of the entrance to the Gdańsk shipyards, commemorating the 28 people who died when the December 1970 strike was suppressed. The crosses symbolise Faith and the anchors Hope, while metal figures of dockyard workers feature at the base of the crosses. The monument was unveiled by the Solidarity movement in 1980, the year in which the trade union movement was legally recognised by the government. The

Amber shop on Mariacka Street.

Communists did not dare touch the monument because of its powerful significance. In 2014 the **European Centre of Solidarity** (Europejskie Centrum Solidarności; tel: 0 506 195 673; www.ecs.gda.pl; daily Oct–Apr 10am–6pm, May–Sept 10am–8pm; entry to the building free of charge, fee for seeing the permanent exhibition) opened nearby, in a striking building in a rusty metallic colour. It tells the history of the Solidarity movement and the defeat of the Communist regime. From the shipyard it's worth going to the Góra Gradowa (Gradowa Hill), crowned with a cross. From the top you can see a sweeping panorama of the historic areas of Gdańsk, as well as the shipyards and even the **PGE Arena Gdańsk** (www.pgearena.gdansk.pl), the football stadium built for Euro 2012 in a beautiful amber colour. The former fortress on the hill is now the **Hewelianum Centre** (tel: 058-742 33 52; www.hewelianum.pl; Tue–Sun 10am–5pm, some exhibitions until 8pm, winter 9am–4pm), full of interactive exhibitions offering an insight into the world of physics and astronomy.

South of Długi Targ is **the Old Suburb** (Stare Przedmieście). Near Podwale Przedmiejskie is the imposing **Gdańsk Shakespeare Theatre** Ⓦ (Teatr Szekspirowski; tel: 058-351 0151; www.teatrszekspirowski.pl), which opened in 2014. Its black bricks contrast with the illuminated interiors, and the roof is retractable, making the theatre open-air just like a typical Elizabethan playhouse. Every year it holds the annual Gdańsk Shakespeare Festival (www.festiwal szekspirowski.pl).

Among the area's most important buildings are the Church of the Holy Trinity (Kościół Św Trójcy), built at the beginning of the 16th century, with a former Franciscan monastery housing a branch of the **National Museum** Ⓧ (Muzeum Narodowe; Toruńska 1; tel: 058-301 70 61; www.mng.gda.pl; May–Sept Tue–Sun 10am–5pm, Thu noon–7pm July–Aug, Oct–Apr Tue–Fri 9am–4pm, Sat–Sun 10am–5pm; free on Fri). The extensive collection includes Polish paintings, *objets d'art* and furniture, such as the renowned Gdańsk chests.

The riverfront with the Gdańsk Crane.

Amber

Fondly referred to as 'Baltic Gold', amber is Poland's national stone.

Whether it's in the form of rings, earrings, necklaces, bracelets or cuff-links, not to mention various decorative items for the home such as lampshades and jewellery boxes, amber is a visible element of daily life.

Amber varies enormously in terms of shape and size, while the colour ranges beyond amber from yellow to white, red and green. Being transparent, amber is usually streaked with various colours, while the inherent flaws add character.

Artificial amber can be convincing and inexpensive (if sold honestly), prepared from substances such as camphor. The genuine article is actually fossilised resin that seeped from deciduous and coniferous trees and has solidified and matured over thousands of years. The resin frequently trapped insects and flora, resulting in numerous pieces of amber containing perfectly preserved specimens of prehistoric life. Polish amber has even included fragments of date trees and tea bushes from the primeval forest that originally occupied the Baltic coastline.

A gift from the gods

Beyond the technical explanation, various legends define amber as the solidified tears of the passing of time, and more specifically as the tears of the Heliades, the sisters of Phaeton, who couldn't stop weeping after his death. Phaeton's father was Helios, god of the sun, who drove the chariot that dragged the sun across the sky from sunrise to sunset. One day Phaeton drove the chariot, but brought the sun too close to the earth: mountains burned and seas evaporated into deserts. Phaeton's punishment was to be struck by a fatal thunderbolt by Zeus. To stop his sisters from weeping the gods turned them into willows on the banks of the River Edrin, into which their tears continued to flow. En route to the Baltic the teardrops turned into amber. Locals who collected the amber on the beach assumed it was a gift from the gods.

Amber continues to be collected from beaches as the sea washes it up from beneath the surface of the sand. The best time to go amber hunting is after a storm. The region between Chlapowo and the Sambian peninsula yields the largest amounts.

Amber was prized by the Ancient Egyptians, who called it the 'stone of life and health' as it was thought to promote youthfulness and longevity. In fact, the world would be a far healthier place if amber fulfilled all the claims made for it.

Where to buy amber

There is no shortage of amber boutiques throughout Poland. Gdańsk is the historic centre, with a guild of amber craftsmen established in the 15th century. The city still has hundreds of shops selling amber jewellery and decorative items. It's best not to buy amber on the street as it is likely to be fake. Look for a sign of the Amber Association of Poland in shop windows as a guarantee of quality and authenticity. Some of the finest are along Motława Quay and Mariacka; it's also worth visiting the Amber Museum (see page 330). Outside the city is the Bakowo Forest, which includes an amber mine. The most extensive collection of historic amber can be seen at the castle in Malbork.

Amber in all its guises.

AROUND GDAŃSK

To follow the route around Gdańsk to the historic towns of Toruń, Frombork and Chełmno is to journey through the 1,000-year history and culture of the country.

At the entrance to the harbour, about 5km (3 miles) from the city centre, is the Westerplatte peninsula. It was here, at 4.45am on 1 September 1939, that 210 Polish soldiers and officers came under fire from the *Schleswig-Holstein*, a German battleship. The garrison held out for seven days before surrendering, after 3,000 Nazi soldiers landed here. The site has become a memorial, with some of the ruins left exactly as they were after the bombardment, and there is a modernistic monument commemorating the bravery of the garrison.

Oliwa is one of **Gdańsk**'s ❶ most attractive suburbs, with a large Cistercian monastery complex including the Oliwa Cathedral (www.archikatedraoliwa.pl; museum: summer Mon–Fri 10am–5pm, Sat 10am–3pm). The incredibly slender, twin-towered façade actually houses the longest church in Poland. The Romanesque-Gothic style, dating from the first half of the 13th century, was partly remodelled in the 18th century, adding rococo elements. The 23 side altars date from the 16th and 17th centuries, with a marble tomb of Gdańsk princes who were buried here in the 13th century. Many famous musicians have performed on the cathedral's rococo Oliwa organ. The work of J. Wulf at the end of the 18th century, the organ has an amazing 1,876 pipes and 110 voices. Organ concerts are a regular attraction at the cathedral, and the adjoining park is a delightful place for a stroll.

Sopot ❷ is full of greenery, open perspectives along tree-lined streets, boulevards and parks. As there was little damage to the town during World War II, many buildings are original 19th-century Secessionist, with wooden villas providing a bourgeois character in contrast to the 'showcase' architecture of Gdańsk.

The original settlement of Sopot was established by Oliwa's Cistercian

Sopot's beachside Grand Hotel.

monks. During the 16th century the Gdańsk burghers decided that sea air was beneficial to their health and began turning the village into a spa. This received a much greater impetus at the beginning of the 19th century, mainly due to the fact that Napoleon's former doctor, Jean Haffner, erected bathing pavilions by the sea in 1823. The evolution of Sopot can be seen in the **Sopot Museum** (Muzeum Sopotu, ul Poniatowskiego 8; tel: 058-551 22 66; www.muzeumsopotu.pl; Tue–Wed, Fri 10am–4pm, Thu, Sat–Sun 11am–5pm).

It's easy to see why Sopot became so popular: a park runs the length of its wide, sandy beaches, which provide an ideal setting for sunbathing. Some highly eclectic spa buildings can still be seen around the seafront. The

pier (Molo; www.molo.sopot.pl; daily Apr–June 8am–9pm, July–Aug 8am–11pm, Sept 8am–8pm, freely accessible the rest of the year) is the longest in Poland, extending 516 metres (1,693ft) into the sea, which is a favourite place to promenade while also providing an embarkation point for boat trips to Gdańsk, Gdynia and the Hel peninsula. Another favourite place to promenade is the adjacent main thoroughfare, Bohaterów Monte Cassino (Heroes of Monte Cassino street): lined with pavement cafés, trendy boutiques and galleries, it encapsulates Sopot's relaxed spirit. The Grand Hotel (www.accorhotels.com) is a reminder of Sopot's traditional grandeur. Built in an Art Deco style in 1926 and renovated in 1990, the hotel offers a beachside terrace, tea

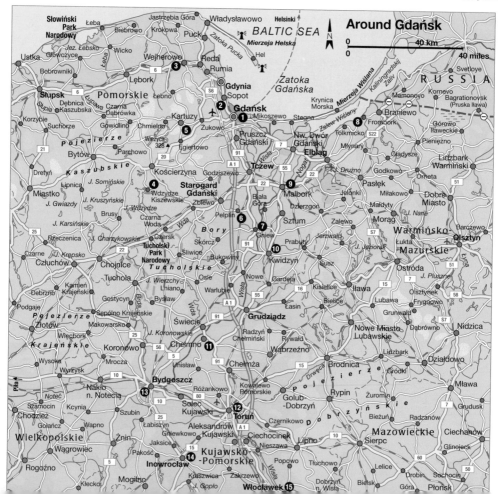

dances, gourmet meals and Poland's most elegant, not to mention most historic, casino.

Gdynia, 9km (6 miles) north of Sopot, is Poland's second-largest port. A small fishing village until 1921, it was transformed into a purpose-built port to ensure that Poland would not be entirely dependent on Gdańsk. Tourist attractions reflect the maritime character. The museum ships *Błyskawica*, a World War II destroyer, and *Dar Pomorza*, a three-masted frigate (both Tue–Sat 10am–4pm), are moored at the dockyard and have exhibits tracing the history of the Polish navy. They form part of a Naval Museum (Muzeum Marynarki Wojennej; ul Zawiszy Czarnego 1B; tel 058-620 13 81; www.muzeummmw. pl; Wed–Sun 10am–5pm). The city also has an excellent Oceanographic Museum and Aquarium (Zjednocze-nia 1; tel: 058-621 70 21; www.akwarium. gdynia.pl; daily May–Aug 9am–7pm, Sept–Apr 10am–5pm). Climbing the 50-metre (165ft) Stone Hill (Kamienna Góra) provides a great view of the harbour.

The Bay of Gdańsk and Kashubian Lakes

Curving almost 35km (20 miles) across the Bay of Gdańsk is the narrow **Hel Peninsula** (Mierzeja Helska). This is an idyllic area, with fishing villages Chał-upy, Kuźnica, Jastarnia, Jurata and, on the tip of the peninsula, the old village of Hel, whose fascinating history is documented in the local fishing museum.

Beautifully situated on the Bay of Puck is the quiet port of **Puck**, which developed from a Slavic settlement into a naval base for the Polish fleet in the 16th and 17th centuries. The town's buildings are mainly 16th to 18th century, with an 18th-century half-timbered former hospital housing the Museum of the Puck region (Muzeum Ziemi Puckiej; http://muzeumpuck.pl). Southwest of Puck, **Wejherowo** ❸ has a distinctly religious character, with the 16th-century governor establishing the *Kalwaria Wejherowska* (the Wejherowo 'Road to Calvary') over the nearby hills. It includes some 26 17th-to 19th-century chapels in total. To the west of the tri-city is the **Pojezierze Kaszubskie**, an extraordinarily scenic

Windsurfing in Puck Bay.

CYCLING IN HEL

Cycling is one of the best ways to explore an area, and Hel Peninsula is no exception. A 78km (47-mile) cycle path leads from Gdynia's main railway station to Hel town at the tip of the headland. Although the first section, from Gdynia to Puck, might be a bit disappointing, what comes next is a feast for the eyes. Along the way, there are superb views over the beautiful Puck Bay, full of kite- and windsurfers, as well as many signposted short detours leading to peat bogs, small nature reserves, lookouts or isolated beaches. The path winds past small villages, pretty fishing ports, smart resorts, evocative World War II bunkers and perfect picnic spots. It is a one-day excursion but the railway line is always within reach so you can get on a train at any time. Look out for people walking near campsites, who often block the path.

TIP

The Opera Leśna (Opera in the Woods), in Sopot, is a delightful al fresco auditorium set in a wood (daily 11am–3pm). It hosts various annual events, including the Opera Festival in July and the Polsat Sopot Festival in August.

Malbork Castle on the River Nogat.

combination of lakes and hills, the highest point of which is the Wieżyca at 329 metres (1,080ft). These uplands are also the source of the rivers Radunia, Wierzyca, Wda, Słupia and Łeba, all of which flow into the Baltic Sea.

The largest lake is the Wdzydze, and around it is **Wdzydze Kiszewskie** ❹, (see page 108), a superb *skansen* (open-air ethnographic museum; Muzeum – Kaszubski Park Etnograficzny im Teodory i Izydora Gulgowskich; tel: 058-686 12 88; www.muzeum-wdzydze. gda.pl; Apr, Sept Tue–Sun 9am–4pm, May–June Tue–Fri 9am–4pm, Sat–Sun 10am–6pm, July–Aug Tue–Sun 10am–6pm, Oct, Feb–Mar Mon–Fri 10am–3pm), which extends over an area of 21 hectares (52 acres). This collection of traditional buildings from the Kashubian region, including an exquisite wooden church painted with rustic motifs, provides a wonderful insight into the region's heritage. **Kartuzy** ❺, surrounded by lakes and woods, is the capital of Kashubia. The Carthusian abbey complex has a fascinating 14th-century Gothic church, with a roof shaped like a coffin. The Kashubian

Museum (Muzeum Kaszubskie im Franciszka Tredera; tel: 058-681 14 42; www. muzeum-kaszubskie.gda.pl; May–June, Sept Tue–Fri 8am–4pm, Sat till 3pm, Sun 10am–4pm, July–Aug Tue–Fri 8am–6pm, Sat–Sun 9am–5pm, Oct–May Tue–Fri 8am–4pm, Sat 8am–3pm) has a rich collection of folk arts and crafts, and also details the history and lifestyle of this historic West Slavic tribe.

A little further southwest is the 1,000-year-old city of **Kościerzyna**, the main centre of Kashubian culture. It has a nice open-air railway museum (Muzeum Kolejnictwa; ul Towarowa 7; tel: 058-721 86 31; http://muzeum kolejnictwa.com.pl; Mon 10am–4pm, Tue–Sun 10am–6pm). In June the popular Kashubian tradition of floating wreaths on the lake is followed by a procession around other lakes in the region. With numerous sporting facilities to hand, this makes an ideal base from which to explore the region's towns, such as Chmielno. A popular holiday destination and one of the most historic Kashubian settlements, it is located on the banks of three lakes, the Białe, Kodno and

Rekowskie. Traditionally a pottery centre, the renowned Necel workshop can be seen on request. The Kashubian Country Park was established at the centre of this lake district in 1983.

Further south on the River Wierzyca is **Pelplin ❻**, where you can see one of Poland's most beautiful Gothic cathedrals. Originally the church of a Cistercian abbey, this vast triple-naved basilica includes Gothic stalls, as well as Renaissance, Baroque and rococo works of art by Herman Han and Bartlomej Strobel. The Diocesan Museum (Muzeum Diecezjalne w Pelplinie; ks Biskupa Dominika 11; tel: 058-536 12 21; www.muzeum.diecezja.org; Tue–Fri 10am–4pm, Sat 10am– 5pm, in summer also Sun) has a collection of sacred art, a Gutenberg Bible printed in 1453, and an amazing collection of musical manuscripts.

Gniew ❼ is situated on a steep cliff at the confluence of the Wierzyca and Vistula rivers. Originally settled by the Cistercians, it was subsequently controlled by the Teutonic Knights – the knights' Gothic castle, perched on a hilltop near the town, is now a hotel (www.zamek-gniew.pl). The original medieval layout includes churches and town walls, some dating from the 16th century, while the arcaded burghers' houses are the finest in Pomerania. South of Gniew, and also on the Vistula, is Nowe. Now a centre of the furniture industry, the outline of this medieval town, with its small castle and two Gothic churches, rises high above the river.

The **Świecka Uplands** (Wysoczyzna Świecka) run to the south of the Starogard Lakes, with the main town being **Świecie**. From 1309 to 1466, Świecie was the headquarters for a local commander of the Teutonic Knights, with the ruins of the knight's castle, together with a Gothic church, standing above the fork of the Wda and Vistula. One of Poland's largest forests, the **Tuchola Forest** (Bory Tucholskie), lies to the north and northwest of Świecie beside the rivers Wda and Brda, which are popular for water sports. Distinctive features in this landscape are the narrow 'channel' lakes, with countless man-made lakes, such as Lake Kornowskie near Koronowo. In an isolated and wooded area in Wierzchlas, about 32km (20 miles) southeast of Tuchola, is the **Cisy Staropolskie Larch Reserve** (guided tours only). In Odry, north of Czersk, the Stone Circles (Kręgi Kamienne) archaeological and biological reserve, a megalithic site dated to the first or second century BC, is also of particular interest. At the western tip of the forest lies **Tuchola**, the area's main tourist centre, with medieval buildings and remnants of the town's fortified walls drawing visitors.

On the right bank of the Vistula

Poland's most northerly holiday region lies east of the Vistula estuary, where resorts are typically separated from the beach by narrow strips of dunes and woodland. However, resorts such as Mikoszewo, Jantar and Stegna are close to the beaches of the Mierzeja Wiślana spit. The nearby town of Sztutowo was the site of a concentration

Frombork Cathedral.

Tombstone detail, Frombork Cathedral.

camp in which 85,000 people of various nationalities died. Near the Russian border, overlooking the Vistula lagoon, is the fishing town of **Frombork** , which has an outstanding 14th-century Gothic cathedral (http://katedra-frombork.pl; daily 9am–5pm, until 4pm Oct–May). This fortified complex includes defensive walls, and a bastion where the famous astronomer Nicholas Copernicus lived from 1512 to 1543, while writing his celebrated work *De Revolutionibus Orbitium Coelestium* (*On the Revolutions of the Celestial Spheres*). The bastion now houses the Copernicus Museum (Muzeum Mikołaja Kopernika; tel: 055-244 00 70; http://frombork.art.pl; Tue–Sun 9am–4pm; free on Fri), with his early treatises and scientific instruments.

A chain of hills covered with beech and oak forests runs alongside the Vistula Lagoon (Zalew Wiślany). To the south lies **Elbląg**, the region's second-largest city after Gdańsk, and an important centre for industry, culture and tourism. Established in the 9th century, it developed into a flourishing port during the 16th and 17th centuries.

Toruń Old Town.

Despite devastating losses in World War II, a number of interesting monuments have survived. The Market Gate (1319) includes fragments of the town wall, the Dominican St Mary's Church from the 13th to 14th centuries (now an art gallery; www.galeria-el.pl) and the Gothic Church of St Nicholas, with its 95-metre (312ft) tower are the main highlights, along with the city museum (Muzeum Historyczne w Ełku; tel: 087-732 02 83; www.mhe-elk.pl; Mon–Fri 7.30am–3.30pm). Just below Elbląg lies Jezioro Drużno, a nature reserve that harbours around 150 species of waterfowl.

The town of **Malbork** , on the Nogat river southwest of Elbląg, is dominated by the monumental Malbork Castle (Muzeum Zamkowe w Malborku; tel: 055-647 09 78; www.zamek.malbork.pl; daily May–Sept 9am–7pm, Oct–Apr 10am–3pm; free entry on Mon, night visits by request), the largest fortification in Europe. Built by the Great Masters of the Teutonic Knights in the late 13th century, it is actually a castle within a castle, with various chapels, churches and refectories. This museum has Poland's finest collection of amber

There is another Teutonic castle, with an attractive courtyard, further south in **Kwidzyń**  , also now a museum (Muzeum w Kwidzynie; http://zamek.kwidzyn.pl; Tue–Sun 9am–5pm). This is part of a Gothic complex including a two-tier chancel, a tower and a triple-naved fortified cathedral. Massive columns support the cathedral, which also has fine 14th-century frescos.

At the northwestern edge of the triangle formed by the rivers Vistula, Osa and Drwęca lies the small but significant town of **Chełmno** . The medieval city walls, including several bastions and the Grudziądz Gate, enclose about 200 monuments of historic interest within the Old Town, perched high up on the banks of the Vistula. Among the most impressive are the 16th-century Italian Renaissance Town Hall with ornamental attics. The design also turns conventional proportions upside down, with the largest windows at the top of the building, diminishing in size as they reach the ground floor. The Town Hall now houses the Regional Museum (Muzeum Ziemi Chelmińskiej; tel: 056-686 16 41; www.muzeumchelmno.pl; Apr–Sept Tue–Sat 10am–4pm, Sun 11am–3pm, Oct–Mar Tue–Fri 10am–4pm, Sat 10am–3pm), as well as a bizarre little exhibition dedicated to Ludwig Reideiger, Poland's most celebrated surgeon. The Gothic parish church of St Mary's, also on the Market Square, features beautiful frescos in the choir and the apostles on pillars. Chełmno claims to be the Polish capital of love and it has its reasons – in the parish church there are relics of St Valentine and the reliquary is displayed on 14 February.

About 30km (19 miles) to the north of Chełmno lies Grudziądz, with its medieval town centre. The Gothic parish church, several Baroque Jesuit churches and a group of granaries joined by a complex system of defensive walls on the banks of the Vistula deserve special attention, especially the reconstructed Water Gate. Near Grudziądz is Radzyń Chełmiński,

noted for its 14th-century Teutonic Knights' Castle, an architectural masterpiece for this era (summer daily 10am–6pm). About 6km (4 miles) to the east is Rywałd, where a 15th-century sculpture of the Virgin Mary in the Capuchin monastery draws numerous pilgrims. In the Drwęca Valley at the eastern edge of the Chełmno region, about 35km (22 miles) east of Toruń, lies the town of Golub-Dobrzyń. At the top of the steep valley walls is a Gothic castle originally built by the Teutonic Knights, though its present appearance reflects Baroque additions. Every July the castle (http://zamekgolub.pl), now a museum and a hotel, hosts the International Knights' Tournament, re-enacting medieval jousting. By the river's upper reaches is Brodnica, a gateway to Brodnicki Krajobrazowy country park. Parts of the town's medieval fortifications, including the Mazurian Tower and Chełminski Gate, have survived, while overlooking the Drwęca are the ruins of a Teutonic castle with an 85 metre (278ft) tower. The remains of medieval architecture can also be seen in nearby Nowe Miasto Lubawskie.

Szerova Street, Toruń Old Town.

Toruń – a Gothic haven

Toruń ⑫ is one of Poland's most interesting cities, and outstanding restoration work has also turned it into one of the most attractive. Numerous buildings that largely survived the Nazis intact provide variations on a historic theme: Renaissance and neo-Renaissance, Gothic and neo-Gothic, not to mention some splendid Baroque and the occasional Secessionist flourish. In fact, the city is full of delightful architectural surprises: a decorative frieze here, a stained glass window there. You have to keep looking, but you'll be rewarded. Comprehensive and compact, Toruń is easily covered on foot, with a day's walking tour taking in all the sights, though you obviously need longer to visit the museums.

As the largest city in the Chełmno region, with a population of almost 200,000, Toruń was founded on the right bank of the River Vistula in 1233 by the Teutonic Knights. This order effectively ruled the town for the next 260 years, as it developed into an important trading centre within the Hanseatic League. In the 17th century Toruń became a centre

for the Protestant movement, and subsequently for the Polish nationalist movement against Prussia after the partitions of Poland. Becoming part of an independent Poland in 1920, Toruń is now an educational and cultural centre, with the Mikołaj Kopernik University one of Poland's finest institutions.

The Old Town and New Town have retained their medieval layout, with the 14th-century **Town Hall** ④ (Ratusz) at the centre of the Old Town Market Square (Rynek Staromiejski). One of Europe's finest Gothic civic buildings, it houses the Regional Museum (Muzeum Okręgowe; Rynek Staromiejski 1; tel: 056-660 56 12; www.muzeum.torun.pl; Tue–Sun 10am–6pm, Oct–Mar until 4pm, in summer the tower is open until 8pm; free on Wed), with a superb collection of Gothic sacred art, exhibited amid Gothic interiors with vaulted ceilings, a portrait gallery of Polish monarchs and impressive 18th- and 19th-century Polish paintings. Climbing the Town Hall Tower is an experience in itself, and the observation terrace at a height of 42 metres (140ft) provides great views

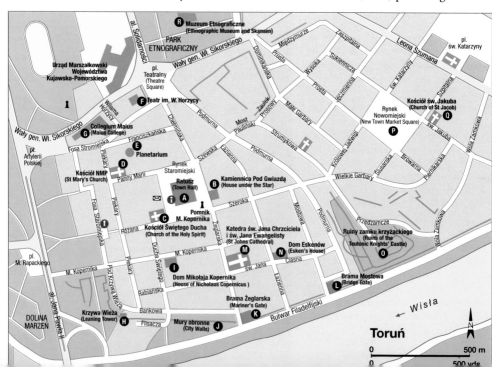

of the Old Town. To the side of the town hall, the Nicholas Copernicus (Mikołaj Kopernik) Monument bears the inscription, '*ruszył ziemię, zatrzymał słońce i niebo*' ('*he put the earth in motion and stopped the sun and sky*'). Every 19 February the University Rector places a bouquet here, honouring his status as the university's patron.

Among the surrounding buildings are Arthur's Court (Dwór Artusa; www.artus.torun.pl), a late 19th-century neo-Renaissance building, formerly the seat of the town's burghers and now a cultural centre, while one of the most extravagant is the **House under the Star** ❸ (Kamiennica Pod Gwiazdą; tel: 056-622 11 33; www.muzeum.torun.pl; Tue–Sun 10am–4pm, Apr–Sept until 6pm). Its Baroque architecture, featuring a flourish of fruit and floral motifs culminating in a wonderful gabled roof crowned with a star, dates from 1697. This is now a museum exhibiting the arts and crafts of the Far East (Rynek Staromiejski 35), its highlight, besides the exhibition, is the small oriental garden on the patio. The neo-Baroque, late-18th century **Church of the Holy**

Spirit ❸ (Kościół Św Ducha; open daily) is next door to the late 19th-century neo-Renaissance main post office. By the edge of the Market Square is the vast **St Mary's Church** ❹ (Kościół Najświętszej Marii Panny; daily). Built in 1351, it incorporates fragments of two earlier churches and is approached through a cloistered courtyard. In addition to the Baroque altar, the church has an amazing vaulted ceiling, while the walls bear poignant frescos of Christ.

The city's other attractions include Poland's most modern **Planetarium** ❺ (Franciszkańska 19; tel: 056-622 50 66; www.planetarium.torun.pl; Mon–Sat 9am–5pm), with an interactive exhibition, Geodium, showing a model of the Earth. The most impressive of several theatres is the neo-Baroque **W. Horzyca Theatre** ❻ (**Teatr im W. Horzycy**; www.teatr.torun.pl). It was built in 1904 by the renowned Viennese architects Ferdinand Fellner and Hermann Helmer, who specialised in theatres and concert halls. Meanwhile, the most historic part of the university is **Maius College** ❼ (Collegium Maius; not open to the public), dating from 1594.

Old Town Hall, Toruń.

Local explanations for how the **Leaning Tower**  (Krzywa Wieża) acquired its 1.5-metre (5ft) tilt vary. It may have resulted from a Teutonic Knight caught fraternising with a townswoman. As this monastic order stipulated celibacy, his penance was to build a leaning tower, to remind him of having 'deviated' from the rules. A more technical (and probable) explanation is that the foundations are on clay soil. Now it houses a café and a souvenir shop. The **House of Nicholas Copernicus** (Dom Mikołaja Kopernika; M. Kopernika 15-17; www.muzeum.torun.pl; tel: 056-622 67 48; Tue–Sun 10am–4pm, Apr–Sept until 6pm) is a fine red-brick Gothic house, documenting the life and work of this great astronomer, born here in 1473. It also has a small exhibition, The World of Toruń Gingerbread, presenting some important facts about this delicious Toruń speciality. You can find more information at the Gingerbread Museum (Muzeum Piernika; Rabiańska 9; tel: 056-663 66 17; www.muzeumpiernika.pl; daily 10am–6pm). There are baking demonstrations in the reconstructed 16th-century gingerbread factory.

The well-preserved **City Walls** (Mury Obronne), dating from the late 13th century, have been preserved virtually in their entirety along the river, with four bastions and three gates including the **Mariner's Gate** (Brama Żeglarska), built in 1432, and **Bridge Gate** (Brama Mostowa). Formerly the parish church of the Old Town, the **Cathedral of St John** (Katedra Św Janów; www.katedratorun.pl; Mon–Sat 9am–4.30pm, Sun 2–4.30pm) dates from the 15th century, built on the site of a church dating from 1250. A combination of restraint and extravagance, Gothic murals and a chapel in which Copernicus was baptised are among the features, together with Baroque and rococo elements. The cathedral bell, Tuba Dei, is the oldest in Poland and one of the biggest in this part of Europe (7.3 tonnes). It can be heard only a few times each year, including when it announces the new year. The Renaissance palace **Esken's House** (Dom Eskenów; Łazienna 16; www.muzeum.torun.pl; Tue–Sun 10am–4pm, Apr–Sept until 6pm) includes 20th-century Polish paintings and military effects from the 15th to 19th centuries.

Loathed as a symbol of oppression, the Teutonic castle was pulled down by the town's inhabitants in 1454. However the **ruins of the Teutonic Knights' Castle** (Ruiny Zamku Krzyżackiego) still show what an important building this was. Constructed between 1250 and 1450, it is now a picturesque, romantic spot. The castle's Centre of Culture organises numerous festivals (Centrum Kultury Zamek Krzyżacki; tel: 056-621 08 89; http://ckzamek.torun.pl; daily 9am–7pm).

New Town Market Square (Rynek Nowomiejski) includes a delightful café, Pod Modrym Fartuchem (Under the Bright Blue Apron), first established in 1489 and still going strong. The original Baroque interiors once hosted Polish kings such as Jan Olbracht and Kazimierz Jagiellończyk. The

Leisure boat on the River Vistula.

neighbouring 19th-century **Church of St Jacob Q** (Kościół Św Jakuba; daily) includes beautiful arches, together with Gothic sacred art, including crucifixes.

The **Ethnographic Museum and Skansen R** (**Muzeum Etnograficzne**; Wały Gen Sikorskiego 19; tel: 056-622 80 91; www.etnomuzeum.pl; mid-Apr–Sept Tue–Fri 9am–4pm, July–Sept Tue and Thu until 6pm, Oct–mid-Apr Tue–Fri 9am–4pm, Sat–Sun 10am–4pm) comprises two museums. One is housed within the former Arsenal, built in 1824, and has an incredible collection of fishing items, a traditional occupation in the city. In the *skansen*, you forget the city-centre location as this enchanting village enclave transports you back to 18th- and 19th-century village life. Various farmsteads and households are furnished with period furniture and effects.

Bydgoszcz and surroundings

Nearby **Bydgoszcz ⑬** has always had a sense of rivalry with Toruń, and the inhabitants of both typically deride each others' city. Toruń is infinitely more attractive to visit, although Bydgoszcz has its moments. An administrative centre with a population of almost 400,000, it was founded by Casimir the Great in 1346. The city's heyday was in the 15th and 16th centuries, when its warehouses and breweries supplied the entire region, with barges being the mode of transport along the River Vistula to Gdańsk. Destroyed during the Swedish invasion, Bydgoszcz flourished under Prussian rule, but paid the price of being thoroughly 'Germanised'. Nevertheless, the Nazis were met by fierce resistance from the inhabitants and when the city surrendered, mass executions were carried out – some 50,000 by the end of the war.

Known for a time both as Little Venice and as Little Berlin, the heart of the city is Old Town, and the main market square, **Stary Rynek**. This large open space is surrounded by brightly painted houses, of which the pick is the former **Jesuit College**, today the city's Town Hall. The square packs out with terraces during the summer months, as does much of **ulica Długa**, old Bydgoszcz's main street, today fully pedestrianised. While the joy of old Bydgoszcz is simply walking around its streets and many embankments (two rivers and a canal converge here), you should make a point of visiting **The Granary** (Spichrze nad Brdą; ul Grodzka 7-11; tel: 052-585 99 74; http://muzeum.bydgoszcz.pl; Apr–Sept Tue–Wed, Fri 10am–6pm, Thu 10am–7pm, Sat–Sun 11am–6pm, Oct–Mar Tue–Wed, Fri 9am–4pm, Thu 9am–6pm, Sat–Sun 10am–4pm), where three separate exhibitions outline the city's somewhat exotic history. The **Exploseum – DAG Fabrik Bromberg War Technology Centre** (www.exploseum.pl; Apr–Sept Tue–Sun 9am–5pm, Thu until 7pm, Oct–Mar Tue–Sun 8am–4pm) is also worth seeing. It's an open-air museum of German industrial architecture located in what was once the biggest Nazi armament factory, Dynamit Nobel AG, hidden in Puszcza Bydgoska (Bydgoska Forest). Also recommended is the Opera Nova (www.

The three roofs of the Cathedral of St John date from the 14th century. The Beautiful Madonna statue on the north wall of the apse is a copy of the original statue which disappeared during World War II.

The River Vistula.

Nicholas Copernicus

One of the most influential astronomers, Nicholas Copernicus (Mikołaj Kopernik) was born in Toruń in 1473, the son of a prosperous merchant.

The house in which Copernicus was born is now a museum detailing his life and works (see page 348). The collection includes the original edition of *De Revolutionibus Orbium Coelestium*, Copernicus's revolutionary theory that the sun and not the earth was the centre of the universe, and that the earth and planets revolved around the sun.

Formative years

Copernicus was a student at the Jagiellonian University in Kraków from 1491 to 1495. As central and eastern Europe's second-oldest university (after Prague), it was already renowned for its astronomy and mathematics faculties. Collegium Maius, the oldest college, now includes a Copernicus Room, with a collection of astronomical instruments from the 1480s including astrolabes

Copernicus monument in Toruń.

and handwritten sections of the *De Revolutionibus* manuscript.

In 1497 Copernicus went to Italy, studying under renowned Italian astronomers including Domenico Maria Novara. It was after arriving there that he witnessed a lunar eclipse, which first led him to question whether the earth was the centre of the universe. Meanwhile, he studied cannon law at Bologna and lectured on astronomy in Rome, before studying medicine at Padua and becoming a doctor of cannon law at Ferrara in 1503.

Returning to Poland in 1503, he was appointed administrator and physician at the Bishop's Castle of Lidzbark Warminski in the Mazurian lake district, where his uncle was Bishop of Warmia. This Gothic castle, built between 1350 and 1401, is now a museum with part of the collection devoted to Copernicus and his work. From 1510 he was based in Frombork, where he was appointed cannon, although between 1510 and 1519 he spent regular periods of time in Olsztyn.

Revolutionary theory

It was in Olsztyn's Gothic Cathedral Chapter and Castle that he created an astronomical table on the walls of the cloisters, where he recorded his findings. Olsztyn's Copernicus Planetarium now provides the opportunity to 'experience' outer space from the perspective of an astronaut. Continuing to study astronomy, it was here that he wrote a treatise questioning the belief that the earth was the centre of the universe. This was the foundation of his famous book, completed in 1530. Popular phraseology in Poland (which every schoolchild learns) sums this up as: 'He stopped the sun, and set the earth in motion.' However, the book was not published until 1543 in Nuremberg. Copernicus only saw a copy as he lay dying in Frombork, having suffered a brain haemorrhage. He was buried in Frombork cathedral.

Legacy

Copernicus dedicated the book to Pope Paul III, but the Roman Catholic Church still considered his theories to be 'subversive' and the work was banned until 1757. Yet it provided a basis for subsequent theories by distinguished astronomers including Galileo.

The Copernicus Museum in Frombork exhibits astronomical instruments and an edition of his book inscribed by the 17th-century astronomer Jan Hevelius, who lived in Gdańsk.

opera.bydgoszcz.pl), a majestic white building in the form of a three-leaf clover, constructed from 1973 to 2006. The **Bydgoszcz Canal** is itself worthy of note. The 24.7km (15-mile) stretch of water has six locks and links up with the Noteć River, making it possible to travel from Bydgoszcz to Berlin by water. West of Bydgoszcz stretch the Pojezierze Krajeńskie (Krajna Lakes), where deep gorges cutting through the moraine hills provide attractive views, with Sępólno Krajeńskie and Więcbork especially popular holiday destinations.

Kujawy Region

Always one of Poland's wealthiest regions, **Kujawy** became part of the Polanie State at the beginning of the 10th century.

The spa town of **Inowrocław** , the administrative centre for West Kujawy, has a few interesting buildings, including the triple-naved, Romanesque St Mary's Church, built from stone, and the Gothic-Baroque Church of St Nicholas.

To the south, on the large Lake Gołpo, is the town of **Kruszwica**. Among the ruins of the 14th-century castle is an ornate Romanesque collegiate church in the form of a basilica, and the Mysza Wieża (Mouse Tower), with a fantastic view over the lake and the Nadgoplański Park Tysiąclecia. A wide variety of waterfowl is protected by this nature reserve. The banks of the lakes provide excellent breeding grounds for the birds.

Nearby **Strzelno** has an interesting monastery. The village church here is a combination of the circular, early-Romanesque Church of St Procopius, dating from around 1160, and the interesting Church of the Holy Trinity (1133–1216) (http://parafiastrzelno.pl; Tue–Sat 9am–5pm, Sun 1.30–5pm), where you can see highly artistic 12th-century sculpted pillars and a tympana.

In the eastern part of Kujawy, on the left bank of the Vistula, is the former episcopal see of **Włocławek** . Now an industrial town with a population of 115,000, the highlight here is the brick

Church of the Assumption, dating from 1411. Baroque elements and chapels were subsequently added around the church. This includes the Chapel of the Mother of God, with late-Gothic carvings by the renowned Wit Stwosz dating from 1493. Soft light from a magnificent window designed in an Art Nouveau style by Józef Mehoffer illuminates the chancel. Try to make it to the Gothic Church of St Vitalis (dating from 1330), with its famous 1493 triptych depicting the coronation of the Virgin Mary. The 14th-century Church of St John dominates the historic Market Square. The city was famous for its faïence products, available for purchase in local shops. The impressive collection of Włocławek faïence is displayed in a local museum (Muzeum Ziemi Dobrzyńskiej i Kujawskiej; www.muzeum.wloclawek.pl; Apr–Oct Tue–Sun 10am–3pm, Tue and Thu until 6pm, Nov–Mar Tue–Fri 10am–3pm.

Stretching between the towns of Włocławek and Płock is the vast Gostynińsko-Włocławski Country Park. The pretty Dobrzyński lakes are located to the north of Włocławek, between the Vistula, Drwęca and Skrwa rivers.

Along the Bydgoszcz embankment.

Fishing in the Mazurian Lakes district.

Węgorzewo marina.

THE NORTHEAST

One of the best ways to explore the
'Land of the Great Mazurian Lakes' is by
a locally hired yacht, canoe or kayak.

Out on the yacht in Wegorzewo.

An area of outstanding natural beauty, the Mazurian Lake District includes more than 1,000 lakes, many of which are linked by rivers and canals, and surrounded by several national parks that shelter various rare species of flora and fauna. Extending across three separate regions of northeastern Poland – Warmia, Mazury and Suwalszczyzna – this area is also known as the 'green lungs' of Poland, reflecting the absence of any industrial development. With numerous lakeside resorts in the area, this is the most popular holiday destination for Poles.

Warmia is named after the ancient Prussian tribe known as the Warms, with Mazury also originally part of East Prussia. It was the constant threat to Polish territories posed by the Prussians that led Duke Konrad Mazowiecki to seek help from the Teutonic Order of Knights in the mid-13th century. However, this resulted in the Order establishing its own territories in the process. Being extremely well-organised and industrious, the Teutonic Knights built a chain of heavily fortified castles to consolidate their presence, and continued to extend their territory through military conquests.

It was only in 1410, during one of the greatest European battles of medieval times, that a combined Polish and Lithuanian army succeeded in defeating the Teutonic Knights, around the village of Grunwald. Consequently, part of this northeastern region was returned to Poland, and the remainder of the knights' territory became a Polish fiefdom.

Following the Swedish invasion of the 17th century, the region came under Swedish rule, and under the partitions of Poland, these regions were annexed by Prussia. Suwalszczyzna was returned to Poland after World War I, and Warmia and Mazury after World War II.

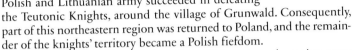

Sunset over Wielki Szelag Lake near Olsztyn.

Tranquil lake scene.

THE MAZURIAN LAKES

The 'Land of a Thousand Lakes' is the ideal place for water-sports enthusiasts, anglers and hikers, or visitors who just want to get away from it all.

A region of outstanding natural beauty, the Mazurian landscape is characterised by countless lakes, gentle hills, deep valleys and flat depressions, as well as sandy plains, wooded areas and extensive forests, formed after the Ice Age. Popularly referred to as the 'Land of a Thousand Lakes', this is in fact Europe's largest complex of wetlands, with a series of national parks and primeval forests providing a sanctuary for an amazing range of flora and fauna. Many of the region's lakes are linked by rivers and canals, which means you can travel for days entirely on water. Almost the entire region is fully protected, with no industrial development allowed, and even agriculture is strictly monitored to be eco-friendly. Nevertheless, a range of hotels, guesthouses and campsites offer leisure facilities, while organic farms provide a novel and inexpensive option, with board and lodging partly paid by helping out with the work. Moreover, many historic towns throughout the region provide an interesting contrast to 'nature's architecture'.

Olsztyn

Olsztyn ❶, on the banks of the River Łyna, is an ideal base with 11 lakes and several parks spread across the town (notably a new Central Park). There is also plenty to see in this engaging town – although renovation is ongoing, the important buildings are well maintained.

The Old Town, granted its municipal charter in 1353, was largely destroyed by the Red Army in 1945. The key sights are the neo-Renaissance New Town Hall, which is early 20th-century, while several impressive churches include the Gothic St James's Cathedral (Katedra Św Jakuba). A monumental tower sets the tone of this grand building, and the interior features vaulted ceilings, the altar of the Holy Cross, with its mid-16th-century

Main Attractions

Interactive Museum of the Teutonic State, Działdowo
Elbląg-Ostróda Canal
Święta Lipka
Wolf's Lair and Mamerki
Mikołajki
River Krutynia
Wigry National Park
River Biebrza

Leisure boat in Mikołajki.

Learning to windsurf.

Renaissance triptych depicting the crucifixion, and the neo-Gothic altar to the Madonna of Ostrobrama, which is late 19th-century. One monument that survived the war intact is the High Gate (Wysoka Brama), a handsome brick construction that continues to provide an 'official' entrance into the Old Town. Beyond the Old Town there are wonderful examples of Prussian, Secessionist and eclectic early 20th-century architecture.

However, Olsztyn's most important historical building is the 14th-century Gothic **Castle of the Cathedral Chapter**, a fortified residence of the Bishops of Warmia. Between 1516 and 1521, the astronomer Nicholas Copernicus was in residence here, in his capacity as the town administrator. Fragments of an astronomical chart drawn by him can be seen in the courtyard, and his study has been re-created complete with astronomical instruments.

The castle is now the Warmia and Mazurian Regional Museum (www. muzeum.olsztyn.pl; Tue–Sun June–Aug 10am–6pm, May and Sept 9am–5pm, Oct–Apr 10am–4pm, Sun always closes one hour later). Atmospheric interiors provide a setting for a fine collection of regional art and furniture, as well as folk arts and crafts, the earliest dating from the 17th century. Archaeological finds from ancient burial sites in the area can also be seen here.

Several idyllic lakes heighten the appeal of the nearby landscape. The largest, Lake Ukiel, has a good beach, as do lakes Skanda and Kortowskie. There are cruises, or you can hire a boat and travel independently. The Copernicus Planetarium (al Zwycięstwa; www.planetarium.olsztyn.pl; daily; a time slot must be booked on the website) and the Observatory at Żołnierska 13 are another aspect of the city's astrological heritage.

West of Olsztyn

The delightful lakeside scenery in the Ostróda and Iława regions is very popular with holidaymakers from Warsaw, Gdańsk and Germany. The peak summer months, July and August, see the most popular beaches crowded, the campsites often full and boat-hire companies booked up.

In addition to aqua- and eco-pursuits, the region's sightseeing options include the delightful town of **Morąg** ❷. Key sights include a Gothic Town Hall, fragments of the town walls and the Baroque Dohn Palace where the German philosopher and writer Johann Gottfried von Herder was born in 1744; a museum exhibits details of his life and works (www.olsztynmuzeum. pl; Tue–Sun 9am–4pm, till 5pm in summer). The nearby Narie Lake (Jezioro Narie), with almost 20 islands, is a beautiful sight.

A principal attraction of **Olsztynek**, located on the northeastern edge of town, is the open-air Ethnographic Museum (skansen; www.muzeum olsztynek.pl; daily May–July 9am–5pm, July until 6pm, Aug 10am–6pm, Tue–Sun Apr and Sep–Oct 9am–5pm, Oct until 4pm; free entrance two days a month). Set in prime countryside, the traditional timber cottages and farmsteads exemplify the Warmia and Mazurian style, together with buildings from the Vistula Valley and Lithuania. The most interesting include a watermill, a Mazurian farmyard, a wooden church and three windmills. To the east of Olsztynek is an attractive forest with numerous small lakes.

The **Elbląg-Ostróda Canal**, linking Elbląg and Ostróda, is a fascinating feat of engineering, completed in 1860. A journey along this almost 130km (80-mile) stretch is a major tourist attraction and takes around 12 hours. Comprising a network of lakes, canals and locks, there are also special platforms on wheels used to transport ships of up to 50 tonnes across tracts of land with major height differentials of up to 100 metres (330ft) onto the next stretch of water. This is the only operational system of its kind in the world. The views are also spectacular, with the large and shallow Lake Drużno, outside Elbląg, an ornithological reserve, and numerous lakes and forests between Iława, Ostróda and Morąg.

Being a Baltic port meant that Elbląg was always a priority for invading armies, with each invasion, including World War II, reducing the town to rubble. Now known chiefly as a brewing centre, a limited area of the original Old Town is being recreated in its

Reenacting the Battle of Grunwald.

historic style, with the surrounding area rebuilt using ultra-modern designs. It's worth visiting the modern art gallery Galeria EL (www.galeria-el.pl), located in a 13th-century church, and the archaeological museum (www.muzeum.elblag.pl; Tue–Sun 9am–4pm, longer in summer), with artefacts from the Viking settlement Truso. Elbląg is still the key departure point for the nearby Russian territory of Kaliningrad.

The great Mazurian lakes

The Mazurski Landscape Park embraces the central Mazurian Lake District. The park has the largest number of lakes in the region, with almost a third of its 50,000 hectares (124,000 acres) accounted for by water, including Lake Śniardwy, surrounded by the primeval Piska forest (Puszcza Piska). The peaceful town of **Mrągowo** ❸ is an ideal base, with 18th- and 19th-century buildings including the Town Hall, Evangelical Church and the Bismarck Tower. The latest attraction is a theme park, Mrongoville (ul Młynowa 50; tel: 089-743 3350; www.mrongoville. pl) recreating the Wild West. Sorkwity

has one of Mazuria's few Protestant churches, an attractive brick and white-washed building with a carved baptismal angel suspended above the congregation in the nave. The angel can be lowered at christenings, and the head of the child anointed with holy water from the silver dish it holds. Another neighbouring attraction is the impressive Sorkwity Palace (tel: 089-742 81 89; www.palacsorkwity.pl), a 19th-century neo-Renaissance confection in a landscaped, wooded park near Lake Lampackie. It is currently a hotel.

Near Mrągowo, on the edge of Lake Dejnowa, is **Święta Lipka** ❹, where the church is an important shrine for Roman Catholic pilgrims (tel: 089-755 14 81; www.swlipka.org.pl). This dates from the 13th century, when a roadside wooden statue of the Madonna appeared to have miraculous powers and was moved to a nearby church. During the 16th century the statue and chapel were destroyed by the Protestants who ruled this region, which was then part of Prussia. However, at the beginning of the 17th century the Polish king was allowed to build a Catholic church on the site where the statue had originally stood. The present Italianate Baroque church (1687–93) was designed by Georg Ertly, a native of South Tyrol, who spent nearly all his working life in Vilnius. Ertly also used his skills as an illusionist: painting frescos to simulate a dome, and the wood chancel to resemble marble. When the organ plays, small gilded figures depicting saints and angels are activated. Organ demonstrations are held here during the summer (daily, almost every hour). Parish festivals take place on the last Sunday of May and on 15 August.

The ruins of the **Wolf's Lair** ❺ (Wilczy Szaniec; tel: 089-752 4429; http:// wolfsschanze.pl; daily 8am till dusk), Adolf Hitler's former headquarters in the Gierłoż Forest near Kętrzyn, are a chilling reminder of the Nazi occupation. Around 70 buildings were constructed here, including seven massive

---

GRUNWALD BATTLE

Grunwald, 20km (12.5 miles) southwest of Olsztynek, is chiefly known as the site of one of Poland's most famous battles and one of the greatest battles of the Middle Ages, fought by almost 80,000 men. On 15 July 1410, a combined army of Polish and Lithuanian troops defeated the Teutonic Knights (see page 362). A monument erected in the town in 1960 commemorates this victory, which effectively broke the knights' dominance in Poland, while an amphitheatre houses a museum detailing the battle and presenting medieval weaponry (www.grunwald.waria.mazury.pl; 10 Apr–Oct daily 9.30am–6.30pm; free on Mon). Every year in July around 2,000 knights from many European countries participate in a re-enactment of the battle.

About 30km (19 miles) to the south, in Działdowo, is the fabulous **Interactive Museum of the Teutonic State** (Interaktywne Muzeum Państwa Krzyżackiego; ul Mickiewicza 43; http://muzeum.dzialdowo.pl; Tue–Fri 10am–5pm, Sat 10am–4pm; free). By means of highly entertaining interactive displays, touch screens and 3D animations, it tells the fascinating story of the Teutonic Knights. Five rooms on the first floor are dedicated to the history and expansion of the Teutonic state, everyday life, military techniques and the Battle of Grunwald. The fifth room contains audio-visual materials including games, battle animations, jigsaw puzzles and much more.

bunkers with walls up to 8 metres (25ft) thick. With only a few short intervals, Hitler directed much of his military strategy from here between 1941 and 1944, particularly the eastern front. On 20 July 1944, Count Claus von Stauffenberg made his courageous, though unsuccessful, assassination attempt on Hitler. Although the bomb exploded, Hitler was not close enough for it to harm him. The hotel (and restaurant) in the former SS hotel makes a good base for visiting other fortifications. Near Mamry Lake, in **Mamerki** ❻ (Mauerwald), you can visit the former field headquarters of the supreme high command of the German army (tel: 089-7524429; www. mamerki.eu; summer daily 10am–6pm, winter by request only). Its 29 bunkers form the largest complex of military architecture from World War II.

A major centre for various water sports, **Giżycko** ❼ is on the edge of Lake Niegocin. The town has a church designed by the German architect Karl-Friedrich Schinkel, and a water tower (www.wieza-gizycko.pl; summer daily 9am–11pm), with sweeping panoramic views from the terrace and café. A castle built by the Teutonic Knights is now St Bruno Hotel (www. hotelstbruno.pl). An interesting attraction is the Boyen Fortress (tel: 087-428 83 93; www.boyen.gizycko.pl; daily July–Aug 9am–7pm, Apr until 4pm, May–June and Sept until 6pm, Oct until 5pm, Nov–Mar only by request), a well-preserved example of 19th-century Prussian fortifications in the shape of a hexagram.

The delightful town of **Mikołajki** ❽ is on the edge of Poland's largest lake, Śniardwy – so large that it's also referred to as the Mazurian Sea, while the town is frequently described as the 'Venice of Mazuria'. This may be an exaggeration, but the small 19th-century houses, fountain and long quayside with pleasure cruisers and sailing boats create an inviting atmosphere. Lake Łuknajno, near Mikołajki, is listed as a World Biosphere Reserve, and is a nesting ground for mute swans among other rare breeds. Only marked trails can be followed in this protected area. In **Kadzidłowo** ❾, 17km (10.5 miles) from Mikołajki, is a safari park (tel: 087-425 73 65; www.kadzidlowo.pl) where you can see endangered animal species (lynx, wolf, black and wood grouse).

Boat excursions

As many of the smaller lakes surrounding Augustów, Ostróda and Iława, not to mention the Great Mazurian Lakes, are linked by a network of canals, an ideal way of seeing them is by taking a pleasure cruise. A popular cruise covers the main lakes in five separate stages. A passenger service operates between Giżycko and Węgorzewo (25km/16 miles), between Giżycko and Mikołajki (40km/25 miles), between Mikołajki and Ruciane-Nida (20km/12 miles) and between Mikołajki and Pisz (25km/16 miles). Sightseeing trips via Ruciane-Nida can be booked in Giżycko and Mikołajki (see page 369). One of the most attractive sections of the canal network connects Mikołajki

see page 369

FACT

It is sometimes possible to spot a tarpan from the zoological station in Popielno, near Mikołajki. Europe's only wild horse, the tarpan became extinct in the wild in the 18th century. However, some farmers continued using them as work-horses, which provided a means of breeding.

The castle of the Teutonic Knights in Olsztyn.

Teutonic Knights

The Teutonic Order of Knights was a medieval religious order which established a state spanning the modern countries of Estonia, Latvia, Lithuania, Poland and Russia.

The Order of St Mary of the Germans in Jerusalem (to give it its full name) was the last of the religious-military orders. It was founded in 1198 as part of the Hohenstaufen emperors' crusades and employed as an auxiliary force against infidel armies. It won territory in Palestine, Greece, Italy and Germany.

Expanding eastwards

The order greatly stretched its power base under the fourth Grand Master, Hermann von Salza, when the Teutonic Knights began expanding in central Europe with the backing of German overlords.

In 1211, the knights defeated the Cumans, a Turkic nomadic people, in Transylvania, but when they became too powerful for the Hungarian king they were expelled.

The Battle of Grunwald.

The Knights in Poland

In 1226 Duke Konrad Mazowiecki employed the knights in his struggles with the Prussians, a pagan tribe that repeatedly invaded and laid waste to the north of the dukedom. Konrad gave the knights land north of Toruń in exchange for their protection and the conversion to Christianity of the Prussians.

The duke wanted to retain sovereignty over the land he entrusted to the knights, but the agreement turned sour. The conflict between Germans and Poles would continue for 250 years. Instead of being converted, the native Prussians were simply wiped out. Bismarck's Prussians were in fact descendants of the people who had eliminated the original tribe and whose ethnic origin was quite different.

One important element was the signing of the 'Golden Bull of Rimini', ratified in 1226, which allowed Emperor Friedrich II to call upon the knights in any lands that he had conquered. This papal edict encouraged him to extend his empire further, and the knights captured regions around the Baltic. In 1308, the order won control of the region around Gdańsk and moved its headquarters to the castle at Marienburg, now Malbork.

At the head of the knights' hierarchy was a Grand Master, elected for life, who had five regional commanders-in-chief. The dioceses were led by knight-priests. Knights and priests had equal status, but they were all sworn to obedience, poverty and chastity. The white cloak with the black cross became the knights' uniform. The achievements of the Teutonic Order can be attributed to their expansionist policies, cultivation of farmland and the resettlement of Germans. This was underpinned by an efficient bureaucracy and wealth from the Hanseatic League cities under its control, such as Gdańsk, Toruń and Königsberg, which traded cereals, timber and amber. This wealth encouraged architects and craftsmen – Pomerania and Mazuria have magnificent castles and churches from this period.

After the unification of Poland and Lithuania the order started to decline and the rivalry came to a head in the Battle of Grunwald in 1410. The order's Grand Master, Ulrich von Jungingen, died in the battle. Under the Second Peace of Toruń of 1466 the knights ceded Gdańsk and Malbork to the Poles. Marienburg Castle was captured in 1457 and their headquarters moved to Königsberg.

The order was finally dissolved in Germany by Napoleon. The surviving branch of the order has its headquarters in Vienna.

and Ruciane-Nida, with the woodland of the Puszcza Piska lining almost the entire route. The lock in Guzianki compensates for the difference in water levels between the Bełdany and Guzianka lakes.

If you'd rather explore in your own boat, an interesting route that extends for 90km (55 miles) begins in Sorkwity between Biskupiec and Mrągowo, and ends in Lake Bełdany. The **River Krutynia** changes its name between the various lakes, with a large section running through the untamed woodland of the Puszcza Piska, past several camping and rest areas, and close to nature reserves. It's the most popular and one of the most picturesque kayaking routes in Poland. Another beautiful route is the River Dajna trail from Mrągowo to Święta Lipka (see page 387).

The eastern region

The route along the Czarna Hańcza River (97km/60 miles) is one of the most attractive and popular in Poland, particularly for kayak enthusiasts (see page 387). Beginning on the eastern bank of Lake Wigry in Stary Folwark, the river meanders through the beautiful Augustów forest.

The Augustów Canal is also a popular route for boat trips. Engineered in the first half of the 19th century, it linked the Vistula and Niemen rivers in order to transport Polish goods to Baltic ports. Constructed between 1822 and 1839, the Augustów Canal begins in Biebrza and extends through the lakes of the Augustów forest for 100km (60 miles), reaching Hrodna in Byelarus. A total of 18 sluice gates regulate different water levels. The engineers were led by the Polish general Ignacy Prądzyński, and the canal is now considered a historic monument, as well as a great tourist attraction, with canoes and boats cruising the waters (see page 369).

The Suwałki lake district includes the **Wigry National Park** ❿ (Wigierski Park Narodowy, see page 388), of which almost two-thirds is forest, mainly fir and pine, with some trees more than 200 years old. It's a natural habitat for rare species including the mute swan, wild boar, wolf, elk and the white-tailed eagle.

Lake Wigry, Poland's second-deepest lake, is outstandingly beautiful – if you feel like strolling all the way around it's a 70km (45-mile) hike. The park also has Poland's deepest lake, Hańcza, at 110 metres (360ft), while Lake Jaczno is renowned for its amazing malachite coloured water. In the village of **Wigry** ⓫ is a Camaldolese priory (www.wigry.pro; daily 9am–5pm), partially reconstructed as it was destroyed during World War II.

The **River Biebrza** flows into the narrow valley around Sztabin, where it twists and divides to create a stunning vista.

Overflowing during the spring, the river floods the surrounding bogs and meadows supporting a community of beavers, though the area is best known for rare birds, including ruffs, the spotted eagle, whooper swans and the double snipe.

Sunset over Lake Jaczno.

Morning light in the Mazurian Lakes district.

INSIGHT GUIDES TRAVEL TIPS
POLAND

TRANSPORT

EATING OUT

ACTIVITIES

A – Z

LANGUAGE

TRANSPORT

GETTING THERE AND GETTING AROUND

GETTING THERE

By Air

The flight time from the UK to Poland is approximately two-and-a-half hours; from New York, just under 10 hours. Poland has regular connections to almost all capital cities of Europe.

Warsaw Chopin Airport (www.lotnisko-chopina.pl; tel: 022-650 4220) is the hub of most Polish National Airlines' worldwide services. There are daily flights to and from London, New York (except Mon), Chicago and Toronto (except Wed and Fri). Warsaw has regular direct flights to the main cites of former republics of the Soviet Union, such as Minsk, Riga and Vilnius. From the UK, the two scheduled carriers are Polskie Linie Lotnicze lot and British Airways, with Norwegian Air Shuttle

and Wizz Air also offering low-cost flights from Gatwick and Luton. You will find airline offices, banks, post offices and car rental companies in the terminal.

Travel to and from the Airport

Warsaw Chopin Airport is only 6km (4 miles) from the centre of Warsaw. To reach the city, you could take buses 175 or 188, which take you to the centre. Buy a ticket at the newsstands, from a bus driver or from a ticket machine (at the bus stop in front of Terminal A and in some buses) and validate it immediately on entering the bus. Always watch your luggage, as these routes are more exposed to theft than other regular lines. For large luggage you need to purchase an extra ticket. The SKM (Szybka Kolej Miejska) trains S2 and S3 take 25 minutes to get to the stations in the city centre: Warsaw Śródmieście and

Warsaw Centrum; they run every 15 minutes from 6am to 11pm. The same ticket as for a bus is needed. Another possibility is to get a taxi. The best way is to phone for one of the three companies recommended by the airport: Ele Sky Taxi (www.ele taxi.pl; tel: 022-811 11 11), Super Taxi (www.supertaxi.pl; tel: 022-578 98 00) or Sawa taxi (www.sawataxi. com.pl; tel: 022-644 44 44). It should cost around 40PLN (€10).

Warsaw Modlin Airport (www.modlinairport.pl; tel: 022-315 18 80), 35km (22 miles) from the Polish capital, serves Ryanair flights to the UK (London, Glasgow, Liverpool, Bristol, Manchester and East Midlands) and Ireland (Dublin), as well as to other European countries. The cheapest way to get to Warsaw is by bus (www.modlinbus. pl); tickets (from 9PLN/€2) can be purchased online, at the airport or from the driver paying by credit card or cash (złotys or euros). Koleje Mazowieckie trains run from Modlin to Warsaw, and some even to the Chopin Airport. The ticket costs around 15PLN/€3.75 and can be purchased at the airport, ticket machines, on a train or by mobile phone (SkyCash system). A special Koleje Mazowieckie shuttle (5PLN/€1.25) runs every 20 minutes between the airport and the railway station. A taxi ride to Warsaw is expensive (about 200PLN/€50).

There are also low-cost flights from the UK and Ireland to Kraków (www.krakowairport.pl), Gdańsk (www.airport.gdansk.pl), Katowice (www.katowice-airport.com), Poznań (www.airport-poznan.com.pl), Wrocław (http://airport.wroclaw.pl), Łódź (www.airport.lodz.pl), Rzeszów (www.rzeszowairport.pl), Lublin

Chopin Airport, Kraków.

(www.airport.lublin.pl), Bydgoszcz (www.plb.pl) and Szczecin (www.airport.com.pl).

By Train

Travelling to Poland by train is relatively easy and comfortable. The Polish train operator, Polskie Koleje Państwowe (PKP; www.pkp.com.pl), offers several direct international connections (www.intercity.pl): Eurocity trains (EC) from Warsaw to Vienna, Villach, Prague (all three via Ostrava) and Berlin (via Frankfurt on the Oder); from Wrocław to Hamburg and Berlin, from Gdansk to Berlin. EuroNight trains run from Warsaw, Katowice and Kraków to Prague, Vienna, Bratislava and Budapest, from Warsaw also to Moscow and Kiev. The EuroNight Jan Kiepura train goes from Warsaw to Amsterdam via Utrecht, Arnhem, Düsseldorf, Cologne, Hannover and Berlin. Trains have first- and second-class carriages, berths, sleepers and restaurant cars. Almost all international trains arrive at Warsaw Central Station (Warszawa Centralna), in the heart of the city centre.

The easiest way to get to Warsaw from London by train is to take the Eurostar to Brussels, then a high-speed train to Cologne, followed by the direct air-conditioned sleeper Jan Kiepura from Cologne to Warsaw. Alternatively you can take an Intercity Express train to Berlin from Cologne (www.bahn.de) and then the Berlin-Warszawa Express. For timetables of Polish trains check http://rozklad-pkp.pl. The fare can be as cheap as €88, but prices vary and it's better to buy your tickets early (booking opens 92 days ahead for German trains and 60 days for Polish international ones). Tickets are available online (www.eurostar.com; www.bahn.de and www.intercity.pl) or at the railway stations. You can also use ticket agencies: European Rail (www.europeanrail.com; tel: 0207-619 1083) and Rail Bookers (www.railbookers.com; tel: 0203-327 0761) in the UK and Polrail (www.polrail.com; tel: 052-332 57 81) in Poland.

By Sea

Passenger ferry services – Polferries (www.polferries.pl), Unity Line (www.unityline.pl), TT Line (www.ttline.com) and Stena Line (www.stenaline.pl) – link the Polish ports of Świnoujście, Gdynia and Gdańsk with Denmark and Sweden.

Hop on a tram to get around.

By Road

Coach Services

Regular services run most of the year, with air-conditioned coaches, some with a bar and toilet facilities. Since Poland joined the EU, the UK and Ireland have become very popular destinations among Poles, who travel there to work and study, so it's possible to find a coach connection from almost everywhere in Poland to almost everywhere in UK, as well as to Dublin and some other cities in Ireland. There are many coach operators, the biggest are: Sindbad (www.sindbad.pl; tel: 077-443 44 44), Eurolines (www.eurolines.pl; tel: 014-657 17 77), Polonia Transport (www.poloniatransport.pl; tel: 084-638 93 96) and Almabus (www.almabus.pl; tel: 071-343 09 90). The journey time is almost 30 hours, with fare reductions for students, senior citizens and children. Tickets can be purchased in travel agencies or at bus stations (Victoria Coach Station in London), but the most convenient way is to book them online.

By Car

It is possible to drive from the UK to Poland. The first stage is to get to Continental Europe. For those travelling from the north the most convenient way, although not the cheapest nor the quickest, is the ferry from Harwich to the Hook of Holland, for example with Stena Line (www.stenaline.com). Those travelling from the south could choose a ferry from Dover to Calais or Dunkirk (P&O ferries, www.poferries.com;

DFDS Seaways, www.dfdsseaways.co.uk). The crossing lasts around two hours. The quickest but more expensive way is via the Channel Tunnel (www.eurotunnel.com). The driving time from Calais or the Hook of Holland to the Polish border is about 10 hours.

A driver entering Poland should have a valid passport or identity card, an international driving licence (or national licence for EU citizens), the vehicle registration certificate with a valid MOT certificate and third-party insurance. Fully comprehensive insurance is recommended. All vehicles should be equipped with a fire-extinguisher, a warning triangle and a first aid kit.

GETTING AROUND

By Air

The Polish airline LOT (www.lot.com and www.eurolot.com) operates flights from Warsaw to Gdańsk, Katowice, Kraków, Poznań, Szczecin, Rzeszów, Lublin, Bydgoszcz and Wrocław. While LOT will happily sell you tickets from one regional Polish city to another (Gdansk to Kraków, or Wrocław to Katowice for example), note that there are in fact no direct flights: in all cases you will have to change in Warsaw. Also Ryanair (www.ryanair.com) offers some domestic connections from Warsaw Modlin Airport to Gdansk and Wrocław as well as direct flights between Gdansk, Wrocław and Kraków.

By Train

The Polish railway network covers the whole country. The Polish train operator Polskie Koleje Państwowe (PKP; www.pkp.com.pl; tel: 022 19 757) offers several types of trains. The fastest are Express InterCity Premium (high-speed Pendolino trains) that runs between Warsaw and Gdynia, Kraków, Katowice and Wrocław. The Express InterCity services are also fast, always have a restaurant or bar car and connect the major Polish cities. For these trains you have to book a seat. The InterCity trains run between Szczecin and Przemyśl and between Gdynia and Wrocław. The cheapest category are TLK trains, but seats can't be reserved, and they may be overcrowded. For timetables visit www.intercity.pl. Tickets can be purchased at the railway stations, in travel agencies and online.

Przewozy Regionalne (www.przewozyregionalne.pl; tel: 0 703 202 020) offers regional and local connections and it's cheaper than InterCity. In Mazovian, Warmian-Mazurian and Kujavian-Pomeranian regions another option is Arriva RP (www.arriva.pl; tel: 022 481 39 48), providing regional and local trains.

Getting Around Towns

Buses and trams are the main forms of public transport in the larger towns (although in Warsaw it is the metro). They usually operate between 5.30am and 11pm (Warsaw's metro closes around midnight, Fri and Sat at 2.30am). In some cities there is a night service, but fares are more expensive.

Tickets *(bilety)* can be purchased at newsstands, from ticket machines (at bus and metro stations, also on some buses) or from the bus drivers (only at the bus stops). Tickets must be validated immediately on entering the vehicle in the metal boxes on the bus or tram wall.

In Warsaw there are many types of tickets, some are valid for a single journey, others for 20, 75 or 90 minutes from the ticket's validation (you can change vehicles without punching a new ticket). All-day tickets and weekend tickets (from 7pm Fri till 8am Mon) are available at newsstands with a ZTM sticker on the door or at the ZTM-Transport Authority (www.ztm.waw.pl; tel: 022-19 115). It's also possible to buy tickets using mobile phones (moBilet system). Route maps are usually displayed inside buses and at

stops. The ZTM website is also very comprehensive.

By Coach

There are many possibilities. The most popular is Polski Bus (www.polskibus.pl; tel: 022-417 62 27). The company offers a wide choice of connections, with several shuttle services between major cities in Poland. Standards are relatively high, with buses having air-conditioning, free Wi-Fi, a toilet, seat belts and facilities for travellers with a disability. Prices may vary, but if booked in advance can be really cheap (from as little as 1PLN). Tickets can be purchased online on the company's website, at bus stations and in some travel agencies (the full list is available on the website.

The companies PKS and PPKS offer cheap, local bus connections, although the standard can be rather basic, so they are not recommended for longer distances. The timetables for all lines are available at www.rozklady.com.pl. Tickets can be bought at the bus stations or from the driver.

In Warsaw coach service is offered by PKS Polonus (www.pkspolonus.pl; tel: 0708 208 888). The bus station, Warszawa Zachodnia, is at Al Jerozolimskie 144.

By Taxi

When available for hire taxis display an illuminated sign. The best places to find one is at taxi ranks in city centres and outside hotels, railway

stations and airports. It is also possible to phone for a radio taxi. This usually works out cheaper, as independent drivers, who are not linked to companies, are more likely to overcharge. At night, and for journeys into the outlying countryside, fares are usually 50 percent higher.

In all cases drivers must display their fares (however exorbitant) in the window of their cabs. All taxis are metered, and journeys are charged per km, plus a small starting fee (usually around 8PLN). Check that the taxi meter is switched on as soon as your journey starts.

Taxi contacts

Warsaw
Ele Sky Taxi: www.eletaxi.pl; tel: 022-811 11 11
Sawa Taxi: www.sawataxi.com.pl; tel: 022-644 44 44
Super Taxi: www.supertaxi.pl; tel: 022-578 98 00

Kraków
Barbakan: www.barbakan.krakow.pl; tel: 012-196 61
Kraków Airport Taxi: www.krktaxi.pl; tel: 012-258 0 258
Krak Taxi: www.kraktaxi.pl; tel: 012-267 267

Hitchhiking

The normal method of signalling to drivers that you are looking for a lift in Poland is to wave the whole arm, but the thumbs-up signal is also understood by drivers. Sometimes, a small contribution is expected. Hitchhiking is considered a perfectly acceptable way of travelling in Poland. However, as with anywhere in the world, safety can never be guaranteed, and this mode of transport is, on the whole, not recommended.

Driving

The road network in Poland covers over 420,000km (262,500 miles) and even remote tourist attractions are relatively easy to reach. Roads have internationally recognised signs. There is a toll system on motorways A1, A2, A4 and A8.

In main towns during peak hours you will find traffic jams and slow traffic. You may also experience heavy traffic during summer and on holiday weekends. At night on country roads it is often difficult to spot pedestrians. There are a lot

Taxis are useful for journeys beyond the city centre.

of car accidents in Poland and the most dangerous places are marked with signs.

Petrol Stations

The majority of petrol stations along highways and main routes are open 24 hours a day. They offer similar services to those in western Europe, including small shops and tea and coffee facilities. In small towns, however, you can expect petrol stations to be open from 6am to 6pm. Credit cards are widely accepted. The most popular types of petrol are: 95-octane, 98-octane and diesel, and generally they are lead-free. There are also LPG gas stations.

Breakdown Services

In the case of a breakdown contact your car rental company or, if you are in your own car, your own breakdown services provider if you have arranged cover.

The Polish Motoring Association (PZM; www.pzm.pl), the main breakdown service, is very efficient, but there are many other roadside assistance stations. In an emergency you can call SOS PZMOT (tel: 19637). The cost varies depending on your situation.

Rules of the Road

If you break Polish driving laws, expect to be charged and to pay on-the-spot fines in cash.

Drive on the right-hand side of the road. Seat belts must be worn by the driver and front-seat passenger at all times. If belts are fitted on rear seats, they must be worn as well. Children can travel in the car only in special child-seats.

Maximum speed limits are: in built-up areas 50 kmh (31 mph); motorways 130 kmh (80 mph); express roads (specially signed) 110 kmh (68 mph); outside built-up areas 90 kmh (56 mph). Motorists caught exceeding speed limits (radar traps are very frequent) can expect a large fine. The maximum fine for speeding is 500PLN.

From 1 November to 1 March, it is necessary to keep dipped headlights on throughout the day. Motorcyclists should leave their headlights on throughout the year.

Many traffic lights have green arrows, which permit filtering to the right on a red light as long as there are no pedestrians crossing the road. However, it's necessary to stop before the lights, and to turn right only after checking that the road is clear. Vehicles on roundabouts have priority over joining traffic. Where priority is not clearly stated, trams always have priority over other road users. Stopping within 100 metres (330ft) of a level crossing is not permitted. Many of the main trunk roads have slow lanes to allow faster traffic to pass.

The permitted blood alcohol level is virtually zero, so do not drink at all when driving or you could face a prison sentence.

Using mobile phones when driving is not permitted.

Parking

Parking is a major problem in any of the big cities, especially where historic centres are pedestrian-only. In many cities and towns, you must pay to park in the centre on weekdays (in Warsaw Mon–Fri 8am–6pm, in Kraków till 8pm). Before leaving your car, pay at the parking meter and leave the ticket where it can be seen through the windscreen. Parking is not expensive, but normally the machines accept only cash. It's worth checking whether your hotel has parking facilities. A car parked in a prohibited zone will be towed away. It's better to use guarded car parks and make sure nothing of value is visible to passers-by.

Car Hire

Branches of the main car rental companies are to be found at airports, stations, leading hotels and in the major cities. Many are open seven days a week and 24 hours a day. The following conditions apply: drivers should be at least 21 years old, have a valid passport and a full driving licence. In addition, they must either pay a substantial deposit or leave security in the form of a credit card imprint. Daily rates are similar to those in western Europe.

Cruises

In the summer season (Jun–Aug daily; May and June weekends only) there are water trams going several times a day to the Hel Peninsula (to the town of Hel and Jastarnia) from Gdynia and Sopot. The same operator offers cruises around the port of Gdynia and Gdańsk. For more information check the website of Żegluga Gdańska (www.zegluga.pl; tel: 058-620 26 42).

Pomerania is a great place for cruising. In Szczecin two passenger cruisers, Odra Queen and Peene

Drive on the right-hand side.

Queen, sail daily from Chrobry Embankment (www.statki.net.pl; tel: 091-434 57 00; May–Aug at 11am, 1pm, 3pm and 5pm, Apr, Sept and Oct at noon and 3pm). MS Dziewanna also offers interesting cruises, around the port and lakes (www.statek.pl; tel: 091-460 14 37).

The great attraction is the cruise on the Elbląg-Ostróda Canal, because of the different water levels the boats need to overcome. The system of inclined planes is a real hydraulic engineering achievement. For more information check the website of Żegluga Ostródzko-Elbląska (www.zegluga.com.pl; Ostróda tel: 089-646 38 71, Elbląg tel: 055-232 43 07). There are also cruises on the Augustów Canal, offered by Żegluga Augustowska (www.zeglugaaugustowska.pl; tel: 087-643 28 81), including a trip to Rospuda Valley. Netlink (www.kanal-augustowski.pl; 087-643 24 30) organises barge trips and offers houseboats for holiday rental.

There are many companies offering cruises on the Mazurian Lakes in summer, including Bosman (http://statki.mazury.info.pl; tel: 087-428 57 86) and Hotel Robert's Port (www.hotel-port.pl; tel: 0503 018 600). Another good option is Żegluga Mazurska (www.zeglugamazurska.com; tel: 087-428 25 78), offering cruises from the ports of Giżycko and Mikołajki. The Port U Faryja (www.faryj.pl; tel: 087-423 10 06) in Ruciane-Nida operates several different cruises daily, including to the lock of Guzianka. One-hour cruises begin every hour 9am–7pm; the longer ones (lasting 3 or 5 hours) are offered once a day.

TRANSPORT

EATING OUT

ACTIVITIES

A – Z

LANGUAGE

EATING OUT

RECOMMENDED RESTAURANTS, CAFES & BARS

WHAT TO EAT

Polish cuisine ranges from rich and substantial to light and elegant. Poles allow themselves a generous amount of time in order to enjoy their meals.

A classic lunch is usually composed of two courses, starting with a soup, such as *barszcz* (beetroot), *żurek* (sour rye), *rosół* (chicken broth) or *pomidorowa* (tomato). These are the most popular, but Polish cooks have an unlimited imagination as far as soups are concerned. For the main course you may want to try the national dish, *schabowy z kapustą* (breaded pork chops with sauerkraut), mielone (fried meatballs), bigos (sauerkraut with pieces of meat and sausage) or Kiev chicken. Finish on a sweet note with ice-cream or a piece of *makowiec* (poppy-seed cake) or *drożdżówka* (a type of yeast cake). Other Polish specialities include *chłodnik* (a chilled beetroot soup), *golonka* (pork knuckles cooked with vegetables), *kołduny* (meat dumplings), *zrazy* (slices of beef served with buckwheat) and *flaki* (tripe), plus the ubiquitous *pierogi* (dumplings) in all varieties. Roast duck and goose are also highly appreciated by foreigners. At the seaside or near lakes fresh fish is often served fried or grilled with mushrooms and sauce.

Traditional Polish cuisine is undergoing revolutionary changes as young chefs start experimenting with lighter dishes made with locally produced or freshly picked ingredients. Vegetarian and vegan options abound, as healthy living is encouraged. Gluten-free restaurants are also fashionable. Even fast foods have experienced a transformation,

with the old *zapiekankas* (grilled baguettes with cheese, mushrooms and lots of ketchup) superseded by oriental kebabs, falafels and wonderful Italian pizzas, often prepared by immigrant Italian chefs.

WHAT TO DRINK

Coffee or lemon tea *(herbata)* are favourite drinks and usually follow a meal. Poles prefer to drink vodka or *piwo* (beer) with their meals. Among the best-known brands are: Żywiec, Lech, Okocim and Warka. Most restaurants offer a selection of German and Czech beers. Stronger alcoholic drinks, usually brands of vodka such as Żubrówka, Wyborowa, Premium and Żytnia, are invariably present on every festive table. Finding good wine is easy.

WHERE TO EAT

It is common that good, smart, well-managed restaurants are located in

A table with a view at Café Camelot, Kraków.

the Old Town of major cities. More and more restaurants are also serving foreign specialities, particularly Italian, Chinese, Japanese, Vietnamese and French cuisine. A few restaurants serve traditional Jewish kosher fare. Most hotels have details of nearby restaurants.

A service charge is usually included in the price at restaurants, but it is customary to pay a figure rounded up by 5–10 percent in recognition of good service.

Milk bars *(bar mleczny)* are now almost a thing of the past but if you can find one, they make a good alternative to restaurants and are excellent value for money. Mainly self-service, cafeteria-style, they occupy simple premises and have a limited choice of basic dishes. Often you get a home-cooked and filling plate for very little. There are also a number of popular Oriental food bars (usually Chinese or Vietnamese) in the city centres. During the summer season in the tourist resorts along the Baltic Sea coast, stalls sell freshly caught baked or smoked fish.

WARSAW

Restaurants

A Nuż Widelec
Ul Dobra 14/16
Tel: 507 367 520
Open: daily noon–10pm, Fri–Sat until midnight.
Owned by brothers who came to Warsaw from Mazuria district, this cosy bar in the Powiśle district is chiefly known for tasty soups and wonderful freshly smoked fish (trout). The owner says it comes from his private smokehouse, which explains its extraordinary taste. €€€

Atelier Amaro
Ul Afrykola 1
Tel: 022-628 57 47
www.atelieramaro.pl
Open: Tue–Fri noon–2.30pm and 6–10.30pm, Mon and Sat 6–10.30pm (last order).
Easily Warsaw's best restaurant and the first Michelin star in Poland. Chef Modest Amaro creates the innovative Polish cuisine from the freshest ingredients including sometimes forgotten traditional Polish products. Booking is essential. €€€€

Belvedere
Ul Agrykoli 1
Tel: 022-55 86 701
www.belvedere.com.pl
Open: noon–11pm, Sat–Sun until 8pm.
Located in Łazienki Park's New Orangery, the Belvedere has a short but impressive French and Polish menu that includes barszcz (beetroot soup), smoked catfish, fried sturgeon and pheasant with foie gras. In the summer there is an open-air café where you can order a coffee and cake. €€€€

Bistro de Paris
Pl Piłsudskiego 9
Tel: 022-826 01 07
www.restaurantbistrodeparis.com
Open: Mon–Fri noon–midnight, Sat 1pm–midnight.
Run by French-born chef Michel Moran, this restaurant offers the best French cuisine in town, including fabulous fresh scallops, warm duck foie gras and Bourgogne snails. Excellent for dinner before or after an evening at the adjacent National Opera. €€€€

Butchery & Wine
Ul Żurawia 22
Tel: 022-502 31 18
www.butcheryandwine.pl
Open: Mon–Sat noon–10pm.
This restaurant has an airy, simple and smart interior. It serves arguably the best steaks in Warsaw. The

Eating alfresco in Warsaw.

wine list is very extensive – you can even sample Polish wine from the Lubuskie region. The prices are not low, but you won't regret it. €€€–€€€€

Concept 13
Al Bracka 9 (Vitkac)
Tel: 022-310 73 73
www.likusrestauracje.pl
Open: 11am–11pm, Sun until 6pm.
This elegant restaurant is on the top floor of the exclusive VITKAC department store. From the terrace there are wonderful views across Warsaw and the Old Town. The five-course lunchtime set menu costs PLN55. €€€–€€€€

Czerwony Wieprz
Ul Żelazna 68
Tel: 022-850 31 44
www.czerwonywieprz.pl
Open: noon–midnight.
A theme restaurant, 'Red Pig' tries to recreate the atmosphere of Communist Poland with special dishes for the working class and for prominent members of the Communist Party. Besides the extravagant decor and names, it´s a really good example of the traditional Polish cooking that was popular 50 years ago. The menu includes beef tartare, pig trotters in aspic and Warsaw-style tripe soup. €€€

Der Elefant Fishmarket
Pl Bankowy 1
Tel: 022-890 00 10
http://derelefant.com
Open: daily noon–midnight.
Located in a superbly converted townhouse with inner courtyard designed by Hollywood set decorator Allan Starski, this casual fish and seafood bar offers excellent grilled octopus, whole dorado with fennel, and traditional herring. A more formal part of the restaurant serves

international dishes, grilled meats and Polish pierogi. €€€

Krowarzywa
Ul Hoża 42
Tel: (0) 516 894 767
Open: noon–11pm, Fri–Sat till midnight.
The vegan burgers served here are popular not only among vegetarians. It's a great place for a quick break, although queues can be very long. Cash only. €

Mąka i Woda
Ul Chmielna 13A
Tel: 022-505 91 87
Open: noon–10pm, Fri–Sat until 11pm, Sun until 8pm.
In one of the courtyards off Chmielna Street, this is a perfect place to relax far from the noise. The decor is modern and simple. It claims to serve the best Italian-style pizza in Warsaw and has a state-of-the art pizza oven. The ravioli con uovo is delicious. Good place for a lunch. €€

Momu Gastrobar
Ul Wierzbowa 9/11
Tel: (0) 506 100 001
www.momu.pl
Open: daily 11am–1am.
Conveniently situated near the National Opera, this funky eatery serves street-food type fare from all around the world. On the menu are burgers, spicy Thai seafood, salads, ceviche and beef udon. It's famous for its lunchtime set menus (different every day) for 19 or 25 PLN. The list of cocktails is long. €–€€€

PRICE CATEGORIES

Prices are for a two-course meal for two:
€€€€ = over 200PLN
€€€ = 100–200PLN
€€ = 50–100PLN
€ = below 50PLN

TRANSPORT

EATING OUT

ACTIVITIES

A – Z

LANGUAGE

Nolita
Ul Wilcza 46
Tel: 022-292 04 24
www.nolita.pl
Open: Mon–Fri noon–3pm,
6–10.30pm, Sat 1–11pm.
One of the best restaurants in
Warsaw offers creative international
cuisine. You can choose dishes à
la carte or opt for the degustation
menu (slightly over 200PLN). The
menu changes constantly, but is
always well presented and top
quality. The service is impeccable.
€€€–€€€€

Norma
Ul Wierzbowa 19/11
Tel: 022-828 01 30
The inspirational fusion cuisine
by chef Kuba Korczak, an active
supporter of the famous Slow Food Poland,
features Polish, Italian and Asian
dishes prepared in an original,
innovative way. Simply decorated with
huge, colourful paintings by Walton
Ford, the restaurant is spacious,
and service is helpful and attentive.
€€–€€€

Opasły Tom
Ul Foksal 17
Tel: 022-621 18 81
www.kregliccy.pl
This small place is in a former
bookstore of the famous Polish
publishing house PIN. The menu
is short and seasonal and all the
ingredients are fresh. The salad with
tomato, raspberry and goat's cheese
is delicious. It´s also one of the few
places where you can sample Polish
wines. €€€–€€€€

Pierogarnia
Ul Bednarska 28/30
Tel: 022-828 03 92
www.pierogarnianabednarskiej.pl
Open: daily 11am–9pm.
For cheap eats in Warsaw you can
do no better. Come here to feast
on meat or vegetarian *pierogi* filled
with cottage cheese, potatoes,
mushrooms or fruits, sold by weight
and eaten at canteen-style tables. €

Prasowy bar mleczny
Ul Marszałkowska 10-16
Tel: 0 666 353 776 (there´s no booking)
Open: daily 9pm–8pm.
This is a modern incarnation of a
former *mleczny Prasowy* (milk bar).
Milk bars were very common in
Communist Poland, providing the
working classes with cheap and
healthy food. The first thing you see is
a long queue, which is not surprising
in a place where you can eat a bowl
of soup for 3PLN or pierogi (Polish
dumplings) for 6PLN. It's not just a
bar – there are also lots of cultural
events going on. €

There are plenty of excellent cafés in Poland.

Restauracja Polska Różana
Ul Chocimska 7
Tel: 022-848 12 25
www.restauracjarozana.com.pl
Open: daily noon–until last
customer.
In this airy, full-of-flowers restaurant
situated just off Plac Unii Lubelskiej
you can sample good Polish cooking,
from tasty *zurek* (sour soup) with
sausage to baked farmhouse duck
and deer saddle. The desserts are
delicious, especially meringue with
cream and home-made cheesecake.
The beautiful garden, open in
summer, is another asset. €€€

Salto
Ul Wilcza 73
Tel: 022-584 87 71
www.saltorestauracja.pl
Open: daily noon–10pm.
In a renovated 1920s building, Salto
is run by South American chef Martin
Gimenez Castro, who successfully
blends his homeland flavours
with modern cooking techniques.
Highlights include fish and seafood
(ceviche) as well as exquisite (though
pricey) Argentinian beef tenderloin
with white truffle sauce and baked
Jerusalem artichokes. Impressive
interior and fantastic atmosphere.
€€€–€€€€

Warszawa Wschodnia
Ul Mińska 25
Tel: 022-870 29 18
http://gessler.sohofactory.pl
Open: daily, 24 hours.
This smart restaurant with modern
minimal interiors serves a mix of
traditional Polish cooking and French
cuisine by Mateusz Gessler. The
degustation menu of eight different
plates is highly recommended. At
the bar around an open kitchen you
can watch the chefs work. It´s a
good reason to visit Soho Factory,
an industrial area now colonised by

artists, designers and local activists,
and its Neon Museum. €€€

Zielony Niedźwiedź
Ul Smolna 4
Tel: (0) 795 794 784
www.kafezn.pl
Open: Tue–Sat 10am–11pm, Sun
until 10pm, Mon dinner only.
The menu of this beautifully located
restaurant is seasonal and features
modern variations of Polish cuisine,
with some international influences.
The priority for the chef is to use the
highest quality ingredients. Besides
some national staples such as
goose or local fish, there are always
some vegetarian dishes, including
dumplings. €€€

Cafés

Batida
Ul Marszałkowska 53 (Konstutycji Square)
Tel: 022-621 53 15
www.batida.pl
Open: Mon–Fri 8am–10pm, Sat–Sun
9am–10pm.
French-style café, suitable for
breakfast or lunch. Variety of salads
and freshly baked croissants.
Delicious cakes and tarts with
fruit. Excellent coffee. It has more
branches in Warsaw, at Królewska
2 (Krakowskie Przedmieście) and
Klimczaka 17 (Wilanów).

Blikle
Nowy Świat 33
Tel: 022-826 64 50
www.blikle.pl
Open: daily 9am–10pm.
This elegant café, one of Warsaw's
most popular meeting places, is
famous for its delicious *pączki*
(doughnuts) – arguably it´s the best
place to sample them. Next door is
a pastry shop where you can buy
more sweet treats. There are several
branches around Warsaw, mostly in
shopping centres.

Café Bristol
Bristol Hotel, Ul Krakowskie Przedmieście 42/44
Tel: 022-551 18 28
www.cafebristol.pl
Open: daily 8am–8pm.
Elegant Viennese-style café that serves delicious desserts and coffees, especially tempting is the wide selection of mousses. There is also a special lunch menu with sandwiches, salads and some light dishes like salmon or pasta.

Coffee Karma
Ul Mokotowska 17 (enter at Pl Zbawiciela 3/5)
Tel: 022-875 87 09
www.coffeekarma.pl
Open: Mon–Fri 7.30am–11pm, Sat 8.30am–11pm, Sun 9.30am–11pm.
Great coffee is served at this otherwise nondescript place overlooking bustling Plac Zbawiciela, famous for being Warsaw's hipsters' meeting point. Besides coffee, it serves salads, sandwiches and breakfasts.

E. Wedel Pijalnia Czekolady
Ul Szpitalna 8
Tel: 022-827 29 16
www.wedelpijalnie.pl
Open: Mon–Fri 8am–10pm, Sat 9am–10pm, Sun 9am–9pm.
This long-established and stylish café serves arguably the best hot chocolate in Poland, as well as sweets and cakes. The first branch of this famous Polish confectionary opened here in 1894. Wedel has more outlets in other Polish cities (notably at Old Town Square in Kraków).

THROUGH MAZOVIA

Białowieża

Carska
Ul Stacja Towarowa 4
Tel: 085-6812119
www.carska.pl
Open: daily 10am–last customer.
The restaurant (and a hotel) is located in an old railway station built in 1903 for the Russian Tsar Nicholas II. The main wooden building is beautiful and restored to evoke tsarist times. The menu includes traditional Polish dishes based on forest products such as mushrooms, juniper, blueberries and staples of Russian cuisine, including bliny (pancakes) or pelmeni (dumplings). The prices are high, but the surroundings and atmosphere are unbeatable. €€€–€€€€

Stoczek 1929
Ul Waszkiewicza 74
Tel: 085-730 32 09
www.stoczek1929.pl
Open: daily noon–10pm.
In a villa built in 1929, this small, charming restaurant has stylish, carefully designed interiors. The speciality is the eastern European cuisine, mixing Ukrainian, Russian, Byelarusian, Lithuanian, Polish and Jewish influences and reflecting the multicultural character of the region. The menu is seasonal but try the excellent pelmeni (dumplings), bliny (pancakes) with caviar, wild boar pierogi (Polish dumplings) and dishes made of bison meat. Make sure you leave space for a dessert – the meringue cake is a must. Also offers nice accommodation. €€€

Białystok

Centrum Astoria
Ul Sienkiewicza 4
Tel: 085-665 21 50
www.astoriacentrum.pl
Open: Mon–Fri 1–10pm, Sat 1pm–2am, Sun noon–10pm, café from noon, Sun from 10am.

A classy restaurant, pub and cafeteria. The latter is especially popular because the prices are lower and the food quality equally good; also, there is a panoramic view over the old town through the big window. The menu has mostly traditional Polish dishes. Good desserts. €–€€€

Czarna Owca Trattoria
Ul Lipowa 24
Tel: 085-744 55 45
http://trattoriaczarnaowca.pl
Open: Mon–Sat 9am–10pm, Sun from noon.
The menu of this simple, clean restaurant includes mostly Italian fare; there is a large selection of pasta, salads and pizzas. The pizza with the local Koryciński cheese is definitely worth a try. The seasonal dishes are listed on the chalkboard menu. €€

Sztuka Mięsa
Ul Krakowska 11
Tel: 085-742 07 40
www.sztukamiesa.com.pl
Open: Mon–Fri 9am–10pm, Sat 11am–last customer, Sun 11am–8pm.
The decor of this small but airy restaurant is a blend of romantic (flower wallpaper) and rustic (wooden chairs) features. The specialities are the meat dishes, as the name ('Art of Meat') suggests. Steaks and ribs are particularly recommended. For a dessert, the cheesecake of Mrs K is a must. €€

Łódź

Restaurants
Anatewka
Ul 6 Sierpnia 2/4
Tel: 042-630 36 35
www.anatewka.pl
Open: noon–last customer.
A very atmospheric restaurant, with interiors recreating a traditional

Jewish house and a menu that includes herrings, goose broth, goose liver and duck with cherries. It's worth trying some of the liquor (nalewka) made by the owner. There's another branch in the Manufaktura building (Karskiego 5). €€€

Bistro Tari Bari
Ul Piotrkowska 138/140
Tel: (0) 728-50 73 23
http://offpiotrkowska.com
Open: Mon–Thu 1–10pm, Fri 1–11pm, Sat noon–11pm, Sun noon–8pm.
An airy, unpretentious, modern bistro located in an old factory at Off Piotrowska. The chef is Italian and so is the menu, which changes every day. The panna cotta is amazing. It's also good for families, so it can get crowded. €€–€€€

Drukarnia Skład Wina i Chleba
Ul Piotrowska 138/140
Tel: 042-672 80 01
www.drukarniaoff.pl
Open: Mon–Wed 7am–10pm, Thu–Fri 7am–midnight, Sat 11am–last customer, Sun until 10pm.
In a chic contemporary post-industrial setting (also at Off Piotrowska), imaginative cuisine is served. You can choose between mouthwatering burgers and pasta, curry or fish dishes. Good place for weekday breakfast as it opens at 7am, which is unusual. €€–€€€

Lokal
Al Leona Schillera
Tel: (0) 666-03 40 06
Open: noon–7pm.

The airy space, relaxed atmosphere and central location make this a perfect stop for lunch. The menu offers creative versions of Polish and French dishes. 'Little plates' (a lot of them are gluten free) for 3 or 4 PLN and the board of Polish cheeses make good starters. Don't forget the desserts! €€–€€€

Cafés

Café Verte
Ul Piotrkowska 113/115
Tel: 042-639 91 29
Open: daily 11am–10pm, Fri–Sat until midnight.
This small, charming café serves arguably the best apple pie in Poland. Other options are also amazing.
Dekadencja
Ul Piotrowska 35
Tel: (0) 690-504 435
Open: noon–10pm.
Charming and very romantic, this café on the main street serves great cakes and coffees, plus pancakes for those with a bigger appetite.
E. Wedel Pijalnia Czekolady
Al Karskiego 5
Tel: 042-631 00 36

www.wedelpijalnie.pl
Open: daily 10am–10pm.
Another branch of the famous Wedel cafés, this one has a nice location in Manufaktura, a factory converted into a shopping and entertainment centre.

Kazimierz Dolny

Galeria U Dziwisza
Ul Krakowska 6
Tel: (0) 509-599 429
www.herbaciarniaudziwisza.pl
The cosy teashop and café also doubles as an art gallery. Good cakes, even some gluten-free choices, and the meringue is highly recommended.
Kuchnia i Wino
Ul Krakowska 13
Tel: 081-881 08 76
www.restauracjakuchniaiwino.pl
Open: daily 8am–9pm, Fri–Sat till 10pm.
The interior is simple, modern and rustic, in contrast to the refined menu created by the renowned Polish chef Wojciech Amaro. The dishes are creative interpretations of Polish cuisine and are prepared with local ingredients. The set lunch costs 29PLN. €€–€€€

U Fryzjera
Ul Jana Koszczyca Witkiewicza 2
Tel: 081-888 55 13
http://restauracja-ufryzjera.pl
Open: daily 9am–midnight, Fri–Sun until 2am.
Not far from the main square, this cosy restaurant, in a lovely wooden villa, is the only place in Kazimierz serving Jewish cuisine. The mixture of sweetness and saltiness typical in Jewish cooking can be an interesting experience: fish soup, goose liver and lamb are all accompanied by almonds and raisins. There are also some vegetarian options based on mushrooms. €€€
Zielona Tawerna
Ul Nadwiślańska 4
Tel: 081-881 03 08
Open: daily 10am–10pm.
This small restaurant is in a typical wooden villa surrounded by a lovely garden – dining in the evening under the trees is magical. *Ruskie pierogi* (dumplings with cottage cheese and potatoes) and sirloin steak with pumpkin are the specialities. In high season it gets crowded and they don't take reservations. €€€

KRAKÓW

Restaurants

Bal
Ul Ślusarska 9
Tel: (0) 604-814 484
www.facebook.com/balnazablociu
Open: daily 8.30am–10pm.
A self-service cafeteria located conveniently near the Museum of Contemporary Art (MOCAK), with a long table in the middle and smaller tables around. The menu changes constantly and there are breakfast buffets. €–€€
Bon Appétit
Ul Dajwor 2a
Tel: 012-422 67 86
www.bonappetitkrakow.com.pl
Open: Tue–Sun noon–10pm.
This welcoming restaurant, in Kazimierz, offers dishes from all regions of France: lamb, duck, onion soup and foie gras. The interior is all white with simple tables and wooden chairs, although still very cosy. A glass ceiling over part of the restaurant allows in plenty of light. Be sure to leave some space for desserts. €€€
Cyrano de Bergerac
Ul Sławkowska 26
Tel: 012-411 72 88
www.cyranodebergerac.pl
Open: daily noon–11pm.

French cuisine, with an emphasis on fish. In the heart of the Old Town in vaulted cellars. The lamb foie gras is particularly recommended, as is the duck curry with apples. €€€€
Klimaty Południa
Ul Św Gertrudy 5
Tel: 012-422 03 57
http://klimatypoludnia.pl
Open: daily 1pm–midnight.
In a tranquil courtyard, a little bit off the busy street, this small restaurant

Arka Noego in Kazimierz.

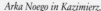

serves a mix of Mediterranean and Polish cuisine. The nice garden is a good option on sunny days. €€–€€€
Konfederacka 4
Ul Konfederacka 4
Tel: 012-341 40 94/0 535 10 60 04
www.facebook.com/konfederacka4
Open: 10am–10pm.
Far from the city centre in Dębniki, this curious industrial place, in an old bakery, serves tasty lunch dishes, pasta and salads. €€

Mamma Mia
Ul Karmelicka 14
Tel: 012-422 28 68
http://mammamia.net.pl
Open: Mon–Fri 8am–11pm, Sat–Sun 9am–11pm.
This busy Italian trattoria near the old market square serves good breakfasts. Later in the day, the speciality is wholemeal pasta with prawns, and cod with squid ink risotto. Booking is essential. €€€

Marchewka z Groszkiem
Ul Mostowa 2
Tel: 012-430 07 95
Open: daily 9am–10pm.
Perfectly located on Mostowa Street, this restaurant serves the most traditional Polish food you can imagine: there are pierogi (dumplings), gołąbki (stuffed cabbage leaves) and pea and carrot soup. A good selection of lemonades and beers. €–€€

Milkbar Tomasza
Ul Św Tomasza 24
Tel: 012-422 17 06
Open: daily 8am–10pm.
This stylish eatery, on one of Kraków's most picturesque streets, is a mix of traditional Polish bar mleczny ('milk bar') and American diner. The food is simple: pierogi (dumplings), pancakes, salads, sandwiches. Good lunch menus. €€

Moaburger
Ul Mikołajska 3
Tel: 012-421 21 44
www.moaburger.pl
Open: Mon–Sat 11am–11pm.
Great selection of huge, tasty burgers served in a simply decorated, pleasant interior. There are also vegetarian burgers made from goat's cheese and beans. The milkshakes are also recommended. €€

Pod Aniołami
Ul Grodzka 35
Tel: 012-421 39 99
www.podaniolami.pl
Open: daily 1pm–midnight.
Enjoy excellent Polish and regional cuisine in a large, atmospheric cellar. The meat dishes are the speciality, but vegetarians also can find some delicious food, such as cabbage rolls filled with mushrooms or pierogi ruskie (Polish dumplings with cottage cheese, potatoes and onion). €€€

Pod Baranem
Ul Św Gertrudy 21
Tel: 012-429 40 22
http://podbaranem.com
Open: daily noon–10pm.
Highly recommended restaurant just 200 metres (220 yards) from Wawel Castle. It's a good place to

sample typical Polish starters such as beefsteak tartare, herrings or venison pâté, as well as other traditional Polish food. There's a large selection of gluten-free dishes. €€€

Starka
Ul Józefa 14
Tel: 012-430 65 38
www.starka-restauracja.pl
Open: daily noon–11pm.
The interior is certainly very cosy: wooden ceiling beams, leather sofas and drawings on the red walls. This restaurant in the Jewish quarter serves tasty meat and fish dishes. The wild mushroom soup is delicious. It's a good place to sample home-made vodkas with selected appetisers. Booking is essential. €€€

Trzy Rybki
Ul Szczepanska 5
Tel: 012-384 08 06
http://stary.hotel.com.pl
Open: daily noon–11pm.
This smart, top-notch restaurant, on the ground floor of the Stary Hotel, has high vaulted ceilings, white tablecloths and impeccable service. The international cuisine of chef Krzysztof Żurek is exquisite. Great wine list. €€€€

U Romana
Ul Św Tomasza 43 (6th floor)
Tel: 012-423 20 81 ext. 166
http://uromano.com.pl
Open: Mon–Fri 9am–5pm, Sat 9am–3pm.
Cheap cafeteria located in the Kraków Music Academy. The food is simple and traditional, and there is a wonderful view over the city skyline. €€€

Wierzynek
Rynek Główny 15
Tel: 012-424 96 00
www.wierzynek.com.pl
Open: daily 1–11pm, café from 10am.
Polish royal cuisine based on authentic old recipes with a modern twist. There is also a vegetarian menu. The historic restaurant is where kings, dukes and princes dined in the 14th century. Nowadays everybody can eat here, if their wallet can bear it. €€€€

Zazie Bistro
Ul Józefa 34
Tel: (0) 500-410 829
www.zaziebistro.pl
Open: Sun–Thu noon–midnight, Fri–Sat noon–11pm.
This small French bistro serves good soups, salads and sandwiches. A stylish place for lunch. Booking is recommended. €€

Zielona Kuchnia
Ul Grabowskiego 8

Tel: 012-634 55 22
http://zielonakuchnia.eu
Open: daily 1–10pm.
Claiming to serve the healthiest dishes based on organic and natural ingredients, this is a really nice place and the food is very tasty and beautifully presented. Smoked duck is really worth a try. The steaks are also amazing. €€€

Cafés

Bunkier Café
Pl Szczepański 3a
Tel: 012-431 05 85
http://bunkiercafe.pl
Open: daily 9am–1am
Next door to the modern art gallery Bunkier Sztuki, this café has a nice garden in the Planty park, open all year round, and is one of Kraków's classics. It serves the best lemonade in the city and good tank beer. Lunch dishes such as pasta, burgers and salads are available from 1pm.

Café Camelot
Ul Św Tomasza 17
Tel: 012-421 01 23
www.lochcamelot.art.pl
Hot cherry wine and apple pie are some of the favourites here. Loch Camelot cabaret and jazz are in the basement.

Café Magia
Pl Mariacki 3
Tel: 012-426 47 73
http://cafebarmagia.pl
Open: daily 8am–2am.
This café, in the Oskar Schindler's Factory museum in the heart of Kraków, has beautiful and atmospheric interiors. The home-made cakes are delicious, but there are also sandwiches or salads for more hungry visitors.

Café Szafé
Ul Felicjanek 10
Tel: (0) 663-905 652
www.cafeszafe.com
Open: 10am–last customer.
This is more than just a café, it offers many cultural activities, especially meetings with writers and poets. The name means 'wardrobe' because customers have the rare opportunity to drink coffee sitting in a blue wardrobe!

Jama Michalika
Ul Floriańska 45

PRICE CATEGORIES

Prices are for a two-course meal for two:
€€€€ = over 200PLN
€€€ = 100–200PLN
€€ = 50–100PLN
€ = below 50PLN

TRANSPORT

EATING OUT

ACTIVITIES

A–Z

LANGUAGE

Tel: 012-422 15 61
www.jamamichalika.pl
Open: daily 9am–10pm, Fri–Sat until 11pm.
In the heart of the Old Town, the Secessionist-era Jama Michalika (founded 1895) is the best-known café in Poland. It also serves lunches.
Kawiarnia Noworolski
Rynek Główny 1/3
Tel: 012-422 47 71
www.noworolski.com.pl
Open: 8am–last customer.

A tourists' favourite in the arcade of the Cloth Hall, this is a good place to have a coffee and observe the main square. Stylish 19th-century interior and good service.
Massolit Books & Café
Ul Felicjanek 4
Tel: 012-432 41 50
www.massolit.com
Open: daily 10am–8pm.
English-language bookstore and café with delicious cakes. In winter it also serves soups.

Pijalnia Czekolady Wedla
Rynek Główny 46
Tel: 012-429 40 85
www.wedelpijalnie.pl
Open: Mon–Thu 9am–10pm, Fri–Sun 9am–midnight.
A great place for a coffee break, or rather a chocolate break, on the main square. Just like the Warsaw branch, it serves delicious chocolate cakes, chocolate sweets and drinking chocolates.

LITTLE POLAND

Łańcut

Pub Kamienica
Ul Rzeźnicza 8
Tel: 017-225 25 70.
www.pubkamienica.pl
Open: 11am–last customer.
Good international cuisine served in a modern, smart interior just 15 minutes away from the castle. Also has a children's menu and a selection of pizzas. It's possible to taste rosolis, liquors from local spirits manufacturer Polmos Łańcut. €€
Zamkowa
Ul Zamkowa 1
Tel: 017-225 28 05
Traditional Polish cuisine in the castle. The setting is exceptional but the food is just ok. *Żurek* (sour soup) and Counts' roulade are specialities. €€

Lublin

Insomia
Ul M. Curie-Skłodowskiej 12
Tel: (0) 512-393 511
http://insomnia-restauracja.pl
Open: daily 11am–10.30pm.
There is something romantic about this small restaurant serving international cuisine with Italian and Mediterranean touches, mostly pasta and seafood dishes. The owners are very friendly and the desserts exceptional. The lunch menu (soup and main course) is good value. €€
Kardamon
Ul Krakowskie Przedmieście 41
Tel: 081-448 02 57
www.kardamon.eu
Open: Mon–Sat noon–11pm, Sun noon–10pm.

The decor here is smart but inconspicuous. The restaurant is famous for its beefsteak tartare prepared by the chef in front of the customer, but other Polish and international dishes are also recommended. A small glass of liquor served with the bill is a nice touch. €€€
Madragora
Rynek 9
Tel: 081-536 20 20
www.mandragora.lublin.pl
Open: Sun–Thu noon–10pm, Fri–Sat noon–midnight.
This nice Jewish restaurant on the old market square even has a special menu for the Shabbat (Sabbath). The liver in honey and wine, and the 'Jewish caviar' (liver with walnuts) are superb starters. It also has a kosher food shop. €€–€€€

KARPATY

Bieszczady

Kawiarnia w Młynie
Ul Fabryczna 12, Ustrzyki Dolne
Tel: (0) 607 477 110 / 013-461 13 12
Open: daily 10am–7pm.
Cosy place in an old mill, in the Museum of Milling, where you can sample traditional regional cuisine, and dishes typical of the Lemkos ethnic group. Sometimes there are jazz or folk music concerts. €€
Oberża pod Kudłatym Aniołem
Ul Cisna 130, Cisna
Tel: (0) 664 390 898
www.kudlatyaniol.pl
Open: daily 11am–8pm.
Wooden furniture, a big red rug, stained-glass door and good regional food. Garlic soup and *pierogi* with local cheese *bryndza* are really worth a try. There is a good selection of beers from the local brewery Ursa Maior (http://ursamaior.pl). €€

Zakopane

Casa Mia
Ul Krupówki 69
Tel: (0) 516 645 313
Open: daily 9am–10pm.
Very smart, unexpected place on Zakopane's main pedestrian street, perfect for those tired of heavy regional cuisine. The menu includes salmon and beef Carpaccio, tiger prawns and some French and Italian dishes. The breakfasts are delicious. €€€
Dobra Kasza Nasza
Ul Krupówki 48
Tel: (0) 791 523 245
www.dobrakaszanasza.pl
Open: daily 10am–10pm.
The main product served in this restaurant, situated in a nicely decorated stylish villa, is *kasha* (pearl barley and buckwheat), prepared in the traditional way (baked in an oven) or in more modern internationally-influenced dishes. €€

Gazdówka
Ul Jagiellońska 18
Tel: 018-206 43 27
www.restauracja-gazdowka.pl
Open: daily noon–11pm.
The rustic interior of this beautiful wooden villa, built at the beginning of the 20th century, is bright and spacious. The menu is a mix of traditional cuisine from Podhale with some modern flavours. The specialities are beef Carpaccio, *pierogi* and chocolate parfait. €€€
Samanta Café and cake shop
Ul Witkiewicza 2
Tel: 018-201 45 72
www.samanta.zakopane.pl
Open: daily 8am–8pm.
The desserts at this family chain of cake shops are delicious, especially the cream pie and poppy-seed cakes. There are more branches at Krupówki 4a and Słoneczna 1a.

UPPER SILESIA AND KATOWICE

Bielsko-Biała

Restaurants
Klimczok Zajazd
Ul Bystrzańska 94
Tel: 033-814 15 67
www.klimczok.beskidy.pl
Open: daily 10am–10pm or until last customer.
Polish regional cuisine, homely atmosphere in a wooden house with fireplace. On the road to Szczyrk. €€

Nowy Świat
Ul 11 Listopada 25-23
Tel: 033-816 66 90
www.nowy-swiat.com
Open: Mon–Sat 10am–last customer, Sun from noon.
This smart restaurant is full of plants and flowers. The menu is mainly international, but also includes some traditional Polish dishes. The less hungry can have *pierogi* or salads. €€€

Ristorante Al Caminetto
Pl Św Mikołaja 2 / Cieszyńska 11
Tel: 033-822 21 00
www.alcaminetto.pl
A real Italian restaurant run by an Italian chef. There are good pizzas and perfect pasta dishes on the menu. It's a little bit expensive, but certainly worth paying for. €€€

Cafés
Aquarium Café and Club
Ul 3 Maja 11 (in the BWA Gallery)
Tel: 033-812 31 63
www.galeriabielska.pl
Open: Mon–Fri 8am–6pm.
A nice place in a local art gallery with a lot of events going on. The menu is short, mostly coffees, teas and cakes.

Blekota & Mlekota
Ul Cieszyńska 1
Open: Mon–Sat 10am–8pm.
This pleasant café with pastel decor serves the best ice-creams in town. The rose ice-cream is really worth a try.

Farma Café
Pl Franciszka Smolki 7
Tel: 033-812 31 63
www.farmacafe.pl
Open: Mon–Sat 8.30am–10pm.
An unpretentious place serving toasted sandwiches, cakes and ice-creams.

Oscar Café
Rynek 16
Tel: 033-816 98 19
Open: daily 10am–11pm.
A nice little café with retro decor, perfect for a romantic date. Great selection of coffees.

Częstochowa

Dobry Rok
Al Najświętszej Maryi Panny 79
Tel: (0) 533 950 533
http://dobry-rok.pl
Open: Mon–Thu 8am–10pm, Fri 8am–midnight, Sat 9am–midnight, Sun 10am–10pm.
This restaurant on the main street has black and white tiles on the floor, white armchairs and high ceilings. The menu is inspired by French Provençal cuisine, with great garlic soup and duck dishes. The coconut ice-cream is extraordinary. €€–€€€

U Braci
Ul 7 Kamienic 17
Tel: (0) 515 314 190
www.ubraci.czest.pl
Open: Tue–Sun noon–10pm, Fri and Sat until 11pm.
At this restaurant opposite the Jasna Góra Monastery the menu is a mix of Italian, Polish and international cuisine. The meat dishes are good, and the liver with rocket salad is highly recommended. The chocolate cake is a must. €€€

Katowice

Little Hanoi... and More
Ul Staromiejska 4
Tel: (0) 886-623-388
http://littlehanoi.pl
Open: Tue–Sat 12.30–11pm, Sun and Mon 1.30–11pm.
This popular Vietnamese restaurant offers unpretentious interiors, pleasant service and a good selection of well-prepared Vietnamese dishes. The food is delicious, but sometimes you have to wait. The dumplings and soups are exceptional. €€€

Tatiana
Ul Staromiejska 5
Tel: 032-203 74 13
www.restauracjatatiana.pl
Open: Mon–Sat 11.30am–11pm, Sun noon–10pm.
Although the name suggests Russian cuisine, this long-established restaurant on the main pedestrianised street serves mostly traditional Polish dishes such as *żurek* (sour soup), *barszcz* (beetroot soup), *pierogi* (dumplings) and roasted goose and duck. The desserts are also recommended. €€€

Via Toscana
Ul Uniwersytecka 13
Tel: 032-603 01 91
www.viatoscana.pl

Open: daily 11.30am–last customer.
The best Italian restaurant in town. Grilled tuna steak is a must. Located on the first floor of the Altus Shopping Centre. €€€–€€€€

Złoty Osioł
Ul Mariacka 1
Tel: 032-253 01 13
http://wegebar.com
Open: Mon–Sat 10am–10pm, Sun noon–10pm.
A cheerful vegetarian restaurant in the city centre. The food is as colourful as the interiors and the menu changes every day. There's another branch in Gliwice at Kłodnicka 2. €€

Szczyrk

Gościniec Salmopolski
Ul Wiślańska 56 A
Tel: 033-487 66 82
www.gosciniec-szczyrk.pl
Open: daily noon–11pm.
A smart restaurant with a wooden ceiling in a guesthouse far from the town centre. The fresh fish from its own farm is the speciality here, served in a traditional way, grilled, baked or smoked. It's also a good place to sample regional vodkas and buy wooden folk sculptures. €€€

Pierogarnia & Café
Ul Myśliwska 34
Tel: (0) 504 613 265
Open: daily 10am–8pm.
The perfect place to satisfy even the biggest appetite. The menu of this atmospheric restaurant includes *pierogi* (dumplings) with meat, potatoes, vegetables and even fruits. The cherry ones, served with fresh sour cream, are a must. €€€

Stara Karczma
Ul Myśliwska 2
Tel: 033-817 86 53
www.karczma.szczyrk.pl
Open: daily 10am–last customer.
A typical wooden inn serving local cuisine from Podhale, with dishes such as *żur* (sour soup), *kwaśnica* (sauerkraut soup) and roasted mutton leg. Often you can listen to traditional folk music as you eat. €€

PRICE CATEGORIES
Prices are for a two-course meal for two:
€€€€ = over 200PLN
€€€ = 100–200PLN
€€ = 50–100PLN
€ = below 50PLN

WROCŁAW AND LOWER SILESIA

Jelenia Góra

Kuźnia Smaku
Pl Ratuszowy 34/35
Tel: 075-752 69 68
www.kuznia-smaku.com
Open: daily 9am–10pm.
It's a good and cosy place to try traditional Polish and Silesian cuisine: *żur* (sour soup), borsch, *bigos* (meat and cabbage stew) and *pierogi* (dumplings) are all very good. The food is freshly prepared so expect to wait at least 30 minutes. €€

Mazurkowa Chata
Ul Sudecka 72
Tel: 075-225 00 00
www.mazurkowachata.pl
Open: daily 10am–10pm.
Traditional Polish cuisine served in a country inn atmosphere. The portions are really generous and the service kind and efficient. On sunny days it is a good idea to sit outdoors with an excellent view over Śnieżka mountain. A perfect stop on the way to Karpacz. €€

Soari
Ul Górna 9
Tel: 075-616 26 66
Open: daily noon–9pm.
It may seem a little out of place but this Japanese noodle bar with a minimalist interior (long, wooden tables, dark walls) is a good option

if you want a change from Polish cuisine. The portions are big. Great cheesecake for dessert. €€–€€€

Wrocław

Bernard
Rynek 35
Tel: 071-344 10 54
http://bernard.wroclaw.pl
Open: daily from 10.30am.
This restaurant and beer hall, in a historic town house on the old market square, is a good place for lunch. The Bernard beer is from the small family brewery Humpolec, in the Czech Moravia region. Also serves breakfasts. €€–€€€

Central Café
Ul Św Antoniego 10
Tel: 071-794 96 23
http://centralcafe.pl
Open: Mon–Sat 9am–9pm, Sun 9am–4pm.
This popular, always busy place in central Wrocław is good for a quick lunch or breakfast. It offers the biggest selection of bagels in Poland. The cakes are also fresh and tasty; cheesecake and carrot cake are especially recommended. €–€€

Novocaina
Rynek 13
Tel: 071-343 69 15
www.novocaina.com

Open: daily 11am–last customer. Modern European and Italian cuisine at its best in a classy setting on the main market square. The interior may be a little bit overloaded. Good pizzas are a decent option if the budget is a bit tight. €€€

Od Koochni
Ul Oleśnicka 7
Tel: (0) 603 886 398
http://odkoochni.pl
Open: Mon–Sat noon–7pm.
Cheap-and-cheerful doesn't mean bad at this modern hipster bistro with an open kitchen. On the contrary, the food is freshly prepared and the menu changes every day. Good soups and quiches. It's small (two big tables and two small), so gets crowded quickly. €–€€

Steinhaus Café & Restaurant
Włodkowica 11
Tel: (0) 512 931 071
www.steinhaus.pl
Open: daily from 11am.
The interior is smart and there is a modern feel to it: wooden floors, black chalkboard, dimmed lights. Jewish, Polish and Lviv cuisine is the speciality. There is no pork on the menu, but you can choose from duck, turkey, beef and fish. Goose served with red cabbage and potato dumplings is delicious. Great selection of wines. €€€

WIELKOPOLSKA

Poznań

Bazar 1838
Ul Paderewskiego 8
Tel: 061-222 68 64
www.bazar1838.pl
Open: Mon–Sat 9am–10pm, Sun 9am–8pm.
This place has smart interiors and a really nice patio. Goose and duck are well represented on the menu, which offers regional Poznań cuisine with some international additions. The restaurant is quite expensive – if you're on a budget it's worth trying the good-value lunch menu. €€€–€€€€

Brovaria
Stary Rynek 73
Tel: 061-858 68 68
www.brovaria.pl
Open: daily 7am–1am.
A hotel, restaurant and small brewery all in one, on the Old Market Square. Dishes prepared with beer are the speciality: pork shank stewed

in local beer, or beer ice-cream, but other dishes are also tasty. The interior is elegant and the service efficient. Good terrace in summer. €€€

Jadalnia
Ul Grunwaldzka 182
Tel: (0) 883 031 313
www.jadalnia.com
Open: Mon–Tue 8am–6pm, Wed 8am–9pm, Thu–Fri 8am–midnight, Sat 10am–midnight, Sun 10am–6pm.
Spacious, modern interior, with funny lampshades and long tables with different-style chairs. Through the glass door you can peer into the kitchen. The simple and tasty dishes change every day – the menu is available on the website. €€

Kwadrat Vegan Bistro & Café
Ul Woźna 18
Tel: (0) 609 314 717
Open: Mon–Thu 1–9pm, Fri–Sat 1–10pm, Sun 1–8pm.

Delicious vegan dishes will impress even the non-veggies. Although soups, *pierogi* and vegetarian *shawarma* (doner kebabs) are all very tasty, the home-made cakes are best. The menu changes every day. €€

Ratuszova
Stary Rynek 55
Tel: 061-851 05 13
www.ratuszova.com
Open: daily 11am–last customer.
This long-established, smart restaurant with a garden, in the southern part of the Old Market Square, is great for outdoor dining, but the cellar area is especially welcoming. Traditional *żur* (sour soup) is nicely served with bread, but also worth a try is *czernina* (soup made with broth and duck blood), not that common nowadays. Although the place is famous for its steaks, it also has good vegetarian options based on mushrooms. €€€–€€€€

TRANSPORT

GDAŃSK

Fellini
Targ Rybny 6
Tel: (0) 888 01 02 03
http://restauracjafellini.pl/
Open: daily noon–midnight.
In the old town not far from the waterfront, this smart restaurant offers great pasta dishes, especially the home-made *garganelli* in creamy truffle sauce. The menu is short, but should impress all Italian-cuisine lovers. Don't forget about the desserts. €€€–€€€€

Kubicki
Ul Wartka 5
Tel: 058-301 00 50
http://restauracjakubicki.pl
Open: daily noon–11pm.
One of the oldest restaurants in Gdańsk, in the Old Town on the banks of the Motława River. The cosy interiors are smart and modern, with brick walls. Pork knuckle, smoked eel and duck are recommended. It's also a good

place to try typical Polish aspic dishes. €€€

Metamorfoza
Ul Szeroka 22/23 – 24/26
Tel: 058-320 30 30
www.restauracjametamorfoza.pl
Open: Thu–Sun 1pm–last customer.
This gourmet restaurant clearly stands out and offers a real culinary adventure. The menu changes every season and it's worth a try. The tasting menu is available in 3, 5, 7 and 9 sets. The cuisine is a creative interpretation of Polish and international cooking and a set lunch menu costs only PLN45. Service is impeccable. €€–€€€€

Nova Pierogova
Ul Szafarnia 6
Tel: (0) 516 414 200
Open: daily 11am–9pm.
This lovely little place with a great view over Moltava River serves all kinds of home-made *pierogi* (dumplings). The portions are large but you can pick different flavours:

meat, salmon, mushroom, fish and even sweet ones. €–€€

Retro Café
Ul Piwna 5/6
Tel: (0) 665 217 965
http://retro.gda.pl
Open: daily 10am–11pm, Fri–Sat till midnight.
This café with stylish, vintage decor serves more than 40 varieties of tea and coffee. The desserts are supreme, especially the Pecan turtle (warm chocolate cake, vanilla ice-cream, nuts, cream and cherries). There's also a branch in Malbork.

Targ Rybny Fischmarkt
Ul Targ Rybny 6c
Tel: 058-320 90 11
www.targrybny.pl
Open: daily 11am–11pm.
The name means fish market, and the menu is an excellent selection of fish dishes. Brilliant decor makes it feel like you're dining in your grandmother's kitchen. €€€

EATING OUT

WESTERN POMERANIA AND SZCZECIN

ACTIVITIES

Kołobrzeg

Café Czarna Mamba
Ul Mariacka 16b
Tel: 094-354 43 75
Open: daily 11am–9pm.
It's not easy to find this small, cosy café, tucked away behind the cathedral. There's a nice aroma of coffee in the air and chocolate in every imaginable form is served. Highly recommended.

Domek Kata
Ul Ratuszowa 1
Tel: 094-354 66 35
www.winogrona.pl
Open: daily 10am–midnight.
In the heart of the old town, this stylish restaurant with high ceilings and overloaded decor serves a mixture of Polish and international cuisine. All the dishes are freshly prepared with local ingredients. Pork tenderloin with chanterelles is delicious. Also offers good breakfasts. Booking is advisable. €€€

Gruba Ryba
Ul W. Reymonta 3 a-b lok. 13
Tel: (0) 509 474 204
Open: daily 11am–6.30pm.
One of the best fish restaurants in town, located on the main pedestrianised street. The baked fish are especially recommended and the salmon tartare is exquisite. Only eight

tables. The service is helpful and efficient. €€€

Łeba

Koga
Ul Wróblewskiego 13
Tel: 059-866 24 88
Open: daily 9am–last customer.
Simple fish restaurant with a nice interior full of flowers and empty bottles (as the lampshades!).
The Bosman hot fish soup and famous 'diabolic' cod are highly recommended. The dishes are freshly prepared, so expect to wait at least 30 minutes. €€

Słupsk

Atmosphere
Ul Norwida 12
Tel: 059-844 40 44
http://atmosphere-slupsk.pl
Open: Tue–Sat 1–10pm, Sun noon–6pm.
This restaurant, located far from the town centre, is arguably the best local choice. Crayfish soup is highly recommended. For dessert try a chocolate soufflé. €€€

Herbaciarnia w Spichlerzu Richtera
Rynek Rybacki
Tel: 059-842 40 81 ext. 331
Open: daily 10.30am–9pm.
This lovely tearoom is in an old

granary beside the castle. There is a large selection of teas (literally hundreds), coffees and home-made cakes. Although everything is delicious, what counts more is the atmosphere of this place. A must!

Szczecin

Hotel Park
Ul Plantowa 1
Tel: 091-434 00 50
www.parkhotel.szczecin.pl
Open: daily 1–11pm.
Arguably the best restaurant in Szczecin. You can choose between the smart indoor area and a nice green terrace. Besides regional dishes such as *żur* (sour soup) or roasted duck with apples, there is a special molecular cuisine menu. It's a fashionable place and the menu changes every season. €€€–€€€€

Kroopnik
Ul Monte Cassino 36
Tel: (0) 608 802 707
http://kroopnik.skubacz.pl

PRICE CATEGORIES

Prices are for a two-course meal for two:
€€€€ = over 200PLN
€€€ = 100–200PLN
€€ = 50–100PLN
€ = below 50PLN

A – Z

LANGUAGE

Open: Mon–Fri noon–8pm, Sat–Sun 24hrs.
This eatery may be not the most stylish, but the interior is simple and clean. It's a good place to eat tasty home-made Polish food for really low prices. The menu includes all typical dishes: *pierogi* (dumplings), breaded pork chops and pancakes. €€€
Nowy Chief
Ul Rayskiego 16
Tel: 091-488 14 17

www.chief.com.pl
Open: daily 11am–11pm.
The restaurant has been refurbished, and now has new aquariums. It offers Polish cuisine, and is reportedly the best fish restaurant in Poland. Dishes include perfect shark goulash, zander three ways and salmon tartare. Besides refined seafood dishes, there is a more reasonably priced lunch menu. €€€
Popularna Café
Ul Panieńska 20

Tel: 091-695 565 525
http://cafepopularna.pl
Open: Mon–Fri 9am–midnight, Sat–Sun from 11am.
This popular café (as the name suggests), in the heart of the old town, is good for all occasions. The slightly vintage decor is quite original and the terrace perfect on sunny days. The menu features a mix of international cuisine, as well as good breakfasts. €€

AROUND GDAŃSK

Bydgoszcz

Katarynka
Ul Niedzwiedzia 3
Tel: 052-320 30 95
www.katarynkabydgoszcz.pl
Open: Mon–Sat 9am–11pm, Sun 11am–10pm.
Situated right in the Old Town, this unpretentious bistro has something for everyone: Polish cuisine staples, pasta dishes and salads. The good wine list and home-made ice-creams are certainly big assets. Fix-priced lunch menu for just 18PLN. It gets crowded sometimes, so booking is advisable. €€
Kuchnia Bar & Restauracja
Ul Grodzka 4
Tel: 052-321 22 22
http://restauracjakuchnia.com.pl
Open: Tue–Sat noon–10pm, Sun noon–6pm.
The menu changes constantly – generally you'll find Italian and Polish dishes with some modern twists. On the last Friday of the month it offers a great selection of seafood. You can call the restaurant a day before to order the meal you want. There are only six tables (in summer more outside), so book in advance. €€€
Stary Port 13
Ul Stary Port 13
Tel: 052-321 62 08
www.staryport13.pl
Open: Mon–Sat noon–11pm, Sun noon–10pm.
Beautifully situated in an old granary, with a working waterwheel adding to the atmosphere. On the menu you'll find traditional Polish food, including arguably the best *smalec* (pork dripping) in Poland, flavoured with mushrooms; the borsch, *żur* (sour soup) and *pierogi* (dumplings) are also very tasty. Also offers several fish dishes and a children's menu. €€–€€€
Strefa Café

Ul Długa 11
Tel: (0) 665 522 755
www.strefabydgoszcz.com.pl
Open: Mon–Thu noon–10pm, Fri–Sat noon–midnight, Sun 3–10pm
If you are looking for a trendy place in Bydgoszcz, this is definitely the one. Coffees, cakes, salads and sandwiches are all good, but the best is the atmosphere.

Elbląg

Pod Kogutem
Ul Wigilijna 8/9
Tel: 055-641 28 82
Open: daily noon–10pm.
This restaurant, in an old town house, claims to be the only one that serves local cuisine based on old Prussian and Polish recipes. The specialities are herring tartare, wild mushroom soup and slices of beef served with buckwheat. The owners are very friendly and keen to talk about the local history. €€€
Mamma Mia
Ul Krótka 4
Tel: 055-611 47 02
www.mammamia.elblag.pl
Open: daily noon–11pm.
The nice, airy interior at this Italian restaurant fits the delicious menu. The *bucatini con gamberetti* (shrimp pasta) and *saltimbocca alla Romana* (veal chops) are excellent . The seasonal dishes are always worth a try. €€–€€€€
Pizzeria Strzecha
Ul Studzienna 4-5
http://strzecha.elblag.pl
Tel: 055-237 11 77
Open: Mon–Thu 9am–11pm, Fri–Sat 9am–midnight, Sun noon–11pm.
Situated near the Old Town's main street, this unpretentious restaurant with slightly rustic decor offers a good selection of pizzas, pastas and salads. It also has typical Polish staples such as pork chops and *żur* (sour soup). The fish dishes are fresh

and tasty. €€–€€€

Gdynia

Sztuczka
Ul Władysława IV
Tel: 058-622 24 94
www.sztuczka.com
Open: Mon–Thu noon–9pm, Fri–Sat 1–10pm, Sun 1–8pm.
Arguably the best restaurant in Gdynia, created by the Wałęsa brothers (relatives of Lech Wałęsa). Despite the fine dining, the atmosphere is relaxed. The menu, changing constantly, features interesting interpretations of traditional Polish and international cuisine. The three-course lunch menu (listed on the website) costs PLN45 and it's a good opportunity to try this creative cooking. The desserts are delicious. €€€

Hel

Maszoperia
Ul Wiejska 110
Tel: 058-675 02 97
www.maszoperia.net/
Open: daily noon–10pm.
On Hel's main street, in a traditional fisherman's house, this restaurant specialises in fish and Kashubian cuisine. Fish soup, herrings and other fish (grilled, cooked or fried) are all delicious. It's a good place to have a break when visiting Hel. €€€

Malbork

Gothic Restaurant & Café
Ul Starościńska 1

PRICE CATEGORIES
Prices are for a two-course meal for two:
€€€€ = over 200PLN
€€€ = 100–200PLN
€€ = 50–100PLN
€ = below 50PLN

Tel: 055-647 08 89
www.gothic.com.pl
Open: daily 9am–8pm.
The restaurant is inside the Teutonic Castle, in the eastern wing of the Middle Castle (there is no need to buy tickets to enter). The Gothic architecture creates an amazing setting for a lunch or a simple cup of coffee after a long visit in the museum. The speciality is Polish cuisine with a modern twist. The set menu costs around €10. The staff are very helpful and the chef loves to chat with the customers. €€€

Lancelot
Ul Ceglana 9
Tel: (0) 693 073 085
www.lancelot.malbork.pl
Open: Tue–Sun from noon.
The photo wallpaper featuring the Teutonic Castle in this smart, modern interior reminds you that you are in Malbork. The menu is not very long but there are fish and meat dishes. The less hungry may go for *pierogi* and/or salads. The menu changes seasonally. They also have seven guest rooms. €€–€€€

Przystanek Patrzałkowie
Ul Kościuszki 25
Tel: 055-272 39 91
www.patrzalkowie.pl
Open: daily 10am–10pm.
This nice family restaurant offers a menu that changes with every season, based on local products from regional farmers. Besides some traditional Polish dishes, there is a good selection of salads and pizzas. The café serves over 40 varieties of teas and coffees and a very tasty version of the American

dessert Pecan turtle (warm chocolate cake, vanilla ice-cream, nuts, cream and cherries). Nice summer terrace. €€

Sopot

Café Zaścianek
Ul Haffnera 3/1a
Tel: 058-550 05 43
www.cafezascianek.pl
Open: Tue–Thu 11am–10pm, Fri–Mon 11am–9pm.
This small, old-fashioned café, situated a little bit off the main street, is heaven for all dessert addicts. The cheesecake is unbeatable, but the apple pie is equally tasty. There's a large range of chocolates, teas and coffees.

E. Wedel Pijalnia Czekolady
Ul Bohaterów Monte Cassino 36
Tel: 058-550 03 35
www.wedelpijalnie.pl
Open: daily 9am–10pm.
This stylish café serves the best drinking chocolate in Poland. It's a branch of the long-established and famous Polish chocolate factory located in Warsaw.

Toruń

Karrotka
Ul Łazienna 9
Tel: (0) 663 723 893
Open: daily noon–7pm.
Small, cheap and cheerful, this vegetarian bar has a constantly changing menu. Good cakes and milkshakes for dessert. €

Kawiarnia Lenkiewicz
Ul Wielkie Garbary 14
Tel: 056-622 56 35
www.lenkiewicz.net
This long-established family café offers arguably the best

ice-cream in Toruń, some say even in Poland. A perfect place for a coffee break.

Kuranty
Ul Rynek Staromiejski 29
Tel: 056-662 52 52
http://gotujemy.pl
Open: daily 10am–midnight.
A bohemian atmosphere with Polish and international dishes. *Żur* (sour soup) served in bread is delicious, followed by Pavlova for dessert. A terrace on the Old Market Square, near the Town Hall, is an asset. €€–€€€

Luizjana
Ul Mostowa 10/1
Tel: 056-692 66 78
http://restauracjaluizjana.pl
Open: daily noon–10pm, Fri–Sat until 11pm.
This smart, vintage restaurant in Toruń serves surprisingly good Cajun cuisine. The owners, after spending seven years in the US, decided to recreate the atmosphere of old New Orleans. The chowder lives up to expectations, as do the fish soup Bouillabaisse and the Creole chicken. Sometimes there's live jazz music. €€–€€€

Pierogarnia Stary Młyn
Ul Łazienna 28/1
Tel: 056-621 03 09
www.pierogarnie.com
Open: daily 11am–11pm.
It's a chain restaurant, but each branch is different and offers regional versions of traditional Polish *pierogi* (dumplings). These can be baked or fried, salty or sweet. The portions are big and tasty. Through the glass window in the floor you can see how the *pierogi* are being prepared. €–€€

MAZURIAN LAKES

Olsztyn

Karczma Jana
Ul Kołłątaja 11
Tel: 089-522 29 46
www.karczmajana.pl
Open: daily noon–10pm.
Traditional Polish cuisine served in a rustic inn with a terrace, in the Old Town near the bridge. The extensive menu features Polish staples such as chicken broth with dumplings, crayfish soup, *pierogi* (dumplings), goose liver and roasted duck. €€€

Na Rogu Czasu
Ul Wilczyńskiego 6c

Tel: 089-612 99 90
http://naroguczasu.com
Open: daily 1–10pm, café from 11am.
The restaurant is far from the city centre but it's worth a trip. The interior is a little old-fashioned, but the food, made from fresh ingredients, is amazingly good and the service impeccable. The cold tomato soup and chicken broth are really tasty. For dessert try home-made cheesecake. €€

Przystań
Ul Żeglarska 3

Tel: 089-535 01 81
www.przystanolsztyn.pl
Open: daily 10am–10pm.
Beautifully situated on the lakeshore in a tranquil part of the city. The large wooden terrace offers the possibility of eating almost on the water; the views are delightful. The menu has mostly international cuisine – best are the fish dishes, especially the freshwater zander baked in cream, typical of the Mazuria region. There is also a hotel and a spa (www.hotelprzystan.com). €€€

ACTIVITIES

THE ARTS, NIGHTLIFE, SPORTS, TOURS, ACTIVITIES AND FESTIVALS

THE ARTS

Theatre

Poles are stalwart supporters of the performing arts. Theatre is very popular in Poland. In Warsaw alone there are over 40 theatres to choose from. The most famous are the Teatr Wielki in Warsaw and the Teatr Stary and Teatr Słowackiego in Kraków, with a predominantly classic repertoire.

Polish drama ranges from productions of classical works by both Polish and international dramatists to contemporary experimental plays. The latter have a strong representation in Poland, with directors Krystian Lupa, Krzysztof Warlikowski and Grzegorz Jarzyna proudly following in the footsteps of the great innovator Jerzy Gorotowski. They often take part in international theatre festivals and are well known beyond Poland's borders. Plays staged at Jarzyna's TR Warszawa and Warlikowski's Nowy Teatr have English subtitles. Also in Warsaw, the Jewish Theatre (Teatr Żydowski) performs Jewish popular drama in Yiddish with the audience able to follow the action with the aid of a translation played on headphones. No words are necessary at the Warszawski Teatr Pantomimy and in Wrocław's Teatr Polski, where Henryk Tomaszewski's world-famous mime group once played. The International Shakespeare Festival is organised every year in the first week of August in Gdańsk and Trójmiasto, while the Elizabethan-style Gdański Teatr Szekspirowski (Gdańsk Shakespeare Theatre), which opened in 2014, stages the plays of the English master, as well as Polish and foreign classics. It is the only theatre with an opening roof that allows actors to perform in daylight, just as it was done in the Renaissance. Children and adults are fascinated by the puppet theatres: Baj (www.teatrbaj.waw.pl) and Lalka (www.teatrlalka.waw.pl) in Warsaw, Wrocławski Teatr Lalek (www.teatrlalek.wroclaw.pl) in Wrocław and Teatr Baj Pomorski (www.baj pomorski.art.pl) in Toruń.

Cabaret is also very popular in Poland, with numerous troupes performing across the country. The most famous and with the longest tradition is Kraków's Piwnica pod Baranami (www.piwnicapodbaranami. pl). It is advisable to book tickets well ahead, particularly for the most popular performances.

Theatres and Concert Halls

Gdańsk
Baltic State Opera (Opera Bałtycka)
15 Aleja Zwycięstwa
Tel: 058-763 49 12/13 ext. 342
www.operabaltycka.pl
Gdansk Shakespeare Theatre (Gdański Teatr Szekspirowski)
Ul Bogusławkiego 1
Tel: 058-351 01 01
www.teatrszekspirowski.pl
Miniature Puppet and Actor Theatre (Miejski Teatr Miniatura)
Ul Grunwaldzka 16
Tel: 058-341 94 83
www.teatrminiatura.pl
Polish Baltic State Philharmonic (Polska Filharmonia Bałtycka)
Ołowianka 1
Tel: 058-58 320 62 69
www.filharmonia.gda.pl
Wybrzeże Theatre (Teatr Wybrzeże)
Ul Św Ducha 2
Tel: 058-301 13 28
www.teatrwybrzeze.pl

Kraków
Helena Modrzejewska Stary Theatre (Teatr Stary im Heleny Modrzejewskiej)
Ul Jagiellońska 5
Tel: 012-422 40 40
www.stary-teatr.pl
Karol Szymanowski State Philharmonic
Ul Zwierzyniecka 1
Tel: 012-619 87 21
www.filharmonia.krakow.pl
Juliusz Słowacki Theatre (Teatr im Juliusza Słowackiego)
Plac Św Ducha 1
Tel: 012-422 45 44
www.slowacki.krakow.pl

Poznań
Music Theatre (Teatr Muzyczny w Poznaniu)
Ul Niezłomnych 1e
Tel: 061-852 29 27

Juliusz Slowacki Theatre.

www.teatr-muzyczny.poznan
Polish Dance Theatre (Polski Teatr Tańca)
4 Kozia
Tel: 061-852 42 41
www.ptt-poznan.pl/
Poznań State Philharmonic (Filiharmonia Poznańska)
Ul Św Marcin 81
Tel: 061-852 47 08
www.filiharmoniapoznanska.pl
Stanislaw Moniuszko Grand Theatre (Teatr Wielki im Stanisława Moniuszki)
Ul Aleksandra Fredry 9
Tel: 061-659 02 00
www.opera.poznan.pl

Warsaw
Ateneum Theatre (Teatr Ateneum)
2 Jaracza
Tel: 022-502 81 51
www.teatrateneum.pl
Dramatyczny Theatre, Palace of Science and Culture (Teatr Dramatyczny, PKiN)
Pl Defilad 1
Tel: 022-656 68 44
http://teatrdramatyczny.pl
Grand Theatre of Opera and Ballet (Teatr Wielki Opera Narodowa)
Plac Teatralny 1
Tel: 022-692 02 00
www.teatrwielki.pl
Jewish Theatre (Teatr Żydowski im Estery Rachel i Idy)
Plac Grzybowski 12/16
Tel: 022-620 62 81
www.teatr-zydowski.art.pl
National Philharmonic Hall (Filiharmonia Narodowa)
Ul Jasna 5
Tel: 022-551 71 11
http://filharmonia.pl
Nowy Theatre (Nowy Teatr)
Ul Madalińskiego 10/16
Tel: 022-849 35 53
www.nowyteatr.org
Polonia Theatre (Teatr Polonia)
Ul Marszałkowska 56
Tel: 022-622 21 32
http://teatrpolonia.pl
Polski Theatre (Teatr Polski im Adolfa Szyfmana)
Ul Kazimierza Karasia 2
Tel: 022-826 92 71
www.teatrpolski.waw.pl
Rampa Musical Theatre (Teatr Muzyczny Rampa)
Ul Kołowa 20
Tel: 022-679 50 51/52
www.teatr-rampa.pl
Roma Musical Theatre (Teatr Muzyczny Roma)
Ul Nowogrodzka 49
Tel: 022-628 70 71
www.teatrroma.pl

TR Warszawa Theatre (Teatr Rozmaitości Warszawa)
Ul Marszałkowska 8
Tel: 022-480 80 08
http://trwarszawa.pl

Wrocław
Polski Theatre (Teatr Polski we Wrocławiu)
Ul G. Zapolskiej 3
Tel: 071-316 07 00
www.teatrpolski.wroc.pl

Classical Music

Poland's concert halls do not just offer Chopin's piano concertos, which are most people's idea of Polish classical music. Other options include experimental works by Krzysztof Penderecki or Witold Lutosławski – composers whose reputation has admittedly not spread that far afield.

Opera and ballet are performed at The Grand Theatre in Warsaw (Teatr Wielki). If the Polish National Opera is performing Halka during your stay, do try to get a ticket. Even if you cannot understand a word of Polish, you will still be able to follow this sad love story about a poor girl from the mountains.

The finest musicals in Warsaw can be enjoyed at the Roma and Rampa Musical Theatres.

There are numerous concerts of classical music in Warsaw and other big cities all year round, including the International Music Festival 'Chopin and his Europe' organised in August or at the beginning of September, which brings together the best soloists and excellent ensembles playing on contemporary and historic instruments. Every five years the best piano players come to the capital to participate in the International Fryderyk Chopin Piano Competition. The next is in October 2015, with a record number of applicants – 450 pianists from 45 countries. Other well-known events are the Mozart Festival (Warsaw), the International Henryk Wieniawski Violin Competition (Poznań, every five years, next one in October 2016) and the Wratislavia Cantans (Wrocław). Free concerts open to the public are also becoming popular, such as the Concerts under the Stars organised at Warsaw's Copernicus Science Centre every Friday at 7pm.

Information and Tickets

Information about all cultural events can be found in local newspapers. In the Gazeta Wyborcza-Co jest grane, in the Friday supplement, there is everything about the latest films, exhibitions and performances taking place in Warsaw. The WIK – Warszawski Informator Kulturalny is a good way to find out what's on if you understand Polish. Another option is the website GdzieCo? (http://gdzieco.pl), with listings of cultural and other events (sport, folk festivals, workshops etc...) taking place in major Polish cities. The following websites also give information about cultural events in English: www.culture.pl and www. warsawvoice.pl

Tickets for theatres, concerts and all cultural events can be bought at major hotels, at theatre box offices, Empik bookstores and online at:
www.ebilet.pl
www.eventim.pl
www.empik.com
www.ticketpro.pl

Cultural Centres in Warsaw

British Council
59 Jerozolimskie
Tel: 022-695 59 00
www.britishcouncil.pl
Centre for Contemporary Art Ujazdowski Castle
Ul Jazdów 2
Tel: 022-628 12 71/3
http://csw.art.pl
Centrum Łowicka
Ul Łowicka 21
Tel: 022-845 56 75
www.lowicka.pl
Fabryka Trzciny
Ul Otwocka 14
022-619 05 13
www.fabrykatrzciny.pl
The Institute of Polish for Foreigners
Ul Kopernika 3
Tel: 022-826 22 59
www.iko.com.pl

NIGHTLIFE

Where to Go

Poland is quite simply a hedonist's dream. There are pubs, bars, discos, clubs and live music venues in every major city, and finding something to do when the sun goes down will not be difficult. The big student cities of Wrocław and Poznań are particularly lively during term time, while Sopot's strip – all beach bars and open-air discos – comes to life in summer. Kraków's nightlife is perhaps more cerebral than that in the capital, but

TRANSPORT

EATING OUT

ACTIVITIES

A – Z

LANGUAGE

you can still find plenty of places to dance to the latest sounds.

High rollers are well catered for in the shape of casinos: every major city has at least one, with the most famous being in the Sofitel Grand Hotel in Sopot. Europe's richest people have been gambling here for almost a century. For live music look out for big-name concerts during the summer, with the country's former national football stadium in Chorzów, Katowice's Spodek and Warsaw's National Stadium often used to host the biggest names in rock, jazz and pop.

Warsaw Nightlife

Warsaw nightlife is exciting, edgy, expensive, and everyone loves it. Trendy cocktail bars abound. Among the most popular are those in Powiśle, Praga and the city centre, although virtually every neighbourhood usually has something to offer. The name of the game is originality, as trendy crowds quickly get bored and look for new, more exciting haunts. Many nightclubs and bars offer live music and interiors that satisfy even the most demanding revellers' tastes. Some, like the hippy **1500m2** (ul Solec 18; tel: 022-628 84 12; www.1500m2.com; Fri, Sat), are a bizarre blend of club, bar, concert venue and art gallery. Located in the former printing shop in the trendy Powiśle district, this huge post-industrial place has a rugged warehouse feel that attracts the most creative lot, including performers, artists, and musicians. World-famous DJs, singers and bands regularly have shows at 1500m2. For the tired and hungry, there is also a refuelling pit stop called Bistro sto900. Check Facebook or the website for current events.

Not far away is **Warszawa Powiśle** (ul Kruczkowskiego 3b; tel: 022-474 40 84; www.grupawarszawa.com; daily noon–midnight, until last customer at weekends), another example of a *klubokawiarnia* (club and café) that enjoys a cult-like status among Warsaw's clubbers. The interior of this former ticket hall is cheap and tatty, but it is for the drinks and the atmosphere that people come here. Try one of its original drinks, including Warsaw's mojito with vodka instead of rum. In summer, there are plenty of deck chairs outside. Another perk is an expanded menu featuring Polish dishes and street food.

Owned by the same people as Grupa Warszawa, the whisky

and cocktail bar **Syreni Śpiew** (ul Szara 10a; tel: 602 77 32 93; www.syrenispiew.pl; Tue–Sat 8pm–2am) is yet another excellent watering hole for Warsaw's jet set. Its main attraction, besides top whiskies, is the interior design, which smoothly combines elegance with features from the 1960s. During the week it is a rather low-key gathering place for posh people, while at weekends live music and DJs keep the party going into the night.

The enormous interiors of the Palace of Culture house another nightlife gem – **Cafe Kulturalna** (Plac Defilad 1; tel: 022-656 62 81; www.kulturalna.pl; noon–midnight, Fri–Sat until 4am), catering mainly for student intelligentsia. Decorated with vinyl armchairs and tatty chandeliers, Kulturalna offers DJs, shows, film screenings, readings and much more.

A Warsaw night tour has to include at least one of the trendy multi-tap bars, which serve excellent micro-brewed craft beers. The beer renaissance is a fact and Warsaw has long been in the vanguard of this trend. Beer enthusiasts should either head for **Cuda na Kiju** (ul Nowy Świat 6/12; tel: 662 00 61 06; daily noon–2am) or **Kufle i Kapsle** (ul Nowogrodzka 25; www.kufleikapsle. pl; Mon–Fri 2pm–2am, Fri–Sat 2pm–4am). Housed in the former Communist party building, Cuda na Kiju offers 16 taps pouring beers from Poland and Europe. A minimalistic unobtrusive design, knowledgeable barmen and three outdoor sitting areas make for a nice and relaxed atmosphere. Mixing traditional European bar design with Polish features such as a large tiled heater, Kufle i Kapsle offers twelve taps, bottled beers and interesting snacks including prunes wrapped in bacon. At night it is usually packed, which is why in summer the beer party spills over to the pavement in front of the bar.

If you prefer more traditional discos, head for Mazowiecka street, which has plenty of night spots including **Enklawa** (ul Mazowiecka 12; tel: 022-827 31 51; www.enklawa.com; Tue–Sat 10pm–4am). Its sleek modern interior attracts a pretty crowd and the place is vastly popular, so lads on the door tend to be picky. Wear smart clothes and ooze confidence to get past them. Old School Night (70s and 80s music) is a hit and a bit of a legend in Warsaw. However, other days see mostly current club and live music. Next to it there is

another classic venue – **Organza** (ul Mazowiecka 12; tel: 609 88 66 44; www.kluborganza.pl; daily 24 hours) with its black and purple interior and popular 'disco fever' dance parties on Wednesdays. Beware of hen and student parties, though. The no-nonsense **Tygmont** (ul Mazowiecka 6/8; tel: 022-828 34 09; www.tygmont.com.pl; Tue–Sat 9pm–5am) is a much welcome respite from the nearby posh clubs. With a dark interior, speakeasy vibe and extensive musical menu, including disco, dance, electro house and jazz, it offers an excellent atmosphere. Check the website for regular jazz concerts. If interesting and original interiors is what you're looking for then head for **Capitol** (ul Marszałkowska 115; tel: 608 08 95 04; www.clubcapitol.pl). With its post-Communist bling and theatrical decorations designed by Dorota Banasik, it offers shows of club circuit legends and VIP rooms. However, selection at the gate can be rigorous, or even rude sometimes.

Jazz lovers might be disappointed that the legendary Akwarium jazz club no longer exists but there plenty of places to make up for this loss. **Metro Jazz Bar & Bistro** (ul Marszałkowska 99a, Hotel Metropol; tel: 022-325 31 06; noon–midnight) is a classic jazz bar on the ground floor of the Metropol Hotel. Decorated with large black-and-white photos of jazz legends on the wall, it offers live music on Tuesdays and Thursdays. You can also watch your favourite games on a wide screen tuned to sports. The central location makes it a perfect base for exploring Warsaw's night attractions. At **Piękna Bistro** (ul Piękna 20; tel: 022-627 41 51; www.jazzone.pl; daily 11am–midnight), with its elegant interiors, live performances of emerging jazz stars are invariably excellent. Another jazz venue worth popping into is **Fabryka Trzciny** (ul Otwocka 14; tel: 022-619 05 13; www.fabrykatrzciny. pl), in a refurbished building of the old marmalade factory in the Praga district. Brick walls, exposed pipes and leather sofas make it an ideal setting for jazz concerts. It also organises art and photographic exhibitions, theatre plays and many other artistic activities. For details check the website. Several other venues, including **Harenda Pub** (www.harenda.pl), **Pardon, To Tu** (http://pardontotu.blogspot.com) and **Jazz Café** (www.jazzcafe.com.pl) in Łomianki near Warsaw also hold regular jazz concerts.

Cocktails for two in Kraków.

Rock and Pop

Poland has been on the radar of major international acts for some time, and the chances of you catching a concert when in the country are high. The biggest names usually play at football stadiums or other sports arenas: the National Stadium in Warsaw, the stadium in Chorzów, Katowice's sports arena (Spodek), PGE Arena in Gdańsk and many others. In Warsaw regular rock concerts are also organised in student clubs such as **Remont** (www.remont.klub.waw.pl) and **Stodoła** (www.stodola.pl). Good sources of concert info are the *In Your Pocket* guides, English-language publications published bi-monthly in eight Polish cities. Tickets for almost all events can be bought online, or at branches of the ubiquitous Empik book and music stores.

Around Poland

Every major city has its entertainment district, with music bars, nightclubs and concert venues. It's best to ask locals for the trendiest place as these tend to change rapidly.

Kraków

In Kraków head either for the Old Town or for Kazimierz, a former Jewish quarter, which comes to life after dark and has plenty to offer. Kazimierz has none of the queues, cover charges, dress codes and mainstream music ubiquitous in the Old Town haunts and dance halls. It boasts a more casual and bohemian clientele too. If you want to mingle with artists, counter-culture aficionados and expats head for the **Klub Piękny Pies** (ul Bożego Ciała 9). On weekdays it is usually all about classic rock, indie hits, post-punk and new wave, with DJs taking over during weekends. Other options in Kazimierz include **Kolektyw Dajwór** (ul Dajwór 16), a clubbing complex consisting of five distinct venues clustered around a garden where bass throbbing and dancing go on until dawn. The modern **Masada** (ul Krakowska 41; www.masadaklub. pl) has a huge main dance floor and plenty of side rooms. The highlight is a salsa night on Wednesdays. **Stara Zajezdnia** (ul Św Wawrzyńca 12; www.starazajezdniakrakow.pl; 3–11pm, Sat–Sun until midnight), a converted old tram depot, which is now Kraków's biggest brewery. A huge main hall features the longest bar in the city and a selection of on-site brewed beers, including lager, wheat and honey ale.

The Old Town is said to have more bars per square metre than any other town in the world. Regrettably, many cater for bachelor/stag/hen parties, which have become a sort of plague, particularly for people living near the Market Square and on the adjacent streets. Nevertheless, there are so many bars and nightclubs around the Old Town that everyone will be able to find something interesting. Dance clubs include the extravagantly stylish **Baccarat** (ul Stolarska 13; tel: 695 11 67 60; www.baccaratclub. pl). A lavish interior features plush upholstery, velvet-draped walls,

elegant chandeliers, ten separate rooms and one VIP saloon capable of accommodating up to 60 people. On offer are stag/hen and even proposal-of-marriage parties. **Prozac 2.0** (Pl Dominikański 6; tel: 733 704 650; daily from 8pm), with three bars and four dance floors, has an impressive line-up of DJs at weekends and gets very busy, mostly with a local crowd. High on the list is also **Rdza** (ul Bracka 3; tel: 513 188 749), with its cosy interior, three spacious rooms, ambitious music and relaxed atmosphere. Expect the cream of Polish and Europe's DJs to be playing the latest music for a lively crowd of serious clubbers.

Jazz lovers might pop in to **Drukarnia** (ul Nadwiślańska 1; tel: 012-656 65 60; www.drukarniaclub. pl; daily from 10pm till the last guest), a two-storey cosy café and jazz club also famous for its dance parties on weekends. The ground-floor café offers wonderful views over Kazimierz and the Old Town. Just across the river is yet another legendary jazz venue – **Alchemia** (ul Estery 5; tel: 012- 421 22 00; http://alchemia. com.pl), organising live concerts and the popular Kraków's Jazz Autumn festival.

Tri-city (Gdańsk-Sopot-Gdynia)

As far as nightlife is concerned, Sopot beats its neighbours hands down. With a long history of attracting an artistic crowd, Sopot caters for all tastes and satisfies the wildest revellers' dreams. Most nightclubs and bars are centred on and around the popular Monte Cassino street. Ordering a fruit cocktail (alcohol-free options are also available) at **Cocktail Bar Max Sopot** (ul Grunwaldzka 1–3; tel: 691 13 00 00; www.barmax. pl; daily 9am–5am) is a great way to start the night. The bar, with branches in Jastrzębia Góra and Warsaw, makes good use of tropical fruits, the wildest recipes and the craft of the knowledgeable bartenders, who are among the best in Poland. After a drink, head for one of the many Sopot dance dens. Fans of 1970s–90s sounds may want to try out **Atelier** (ul Mamuszki 2; tel: 058-555 89 06; www.klubatelier.pl). Its great atmosphere and splendid location on the beachfront (arguably the best spot to watch a sunrise) attract crowds, particularly on weekends. Located in the famous Crooked House, **Ego** (ul Bohaterów Monte Cassino 53; www.egoclub.pl; Wed–Sat from 10pm) is a modern club offering a nice mix of classic and modern beats, including R&B and Funky & Soul. A bit old-fashioned but still legendary, Spatif (ul Bohaterów Monte Cassino 54; www.spatif.sopot.pl), once a den of beatniks and actors, is a must-see, if only for a drink.

Wrocław

As a city with the third-largest student population in Poland, Wrocław is young at heart and certainly knows how to party. The cafés, pubs and nightclubs on the Market Square, Pasaż Niepolda and Mikołajska street offer great variety and lots of fun until small hours. One of the venues with the longest tradition is **Pod Papugami** (ul Sukiennice 9a; tel: 071-343 92 75; http://podpapugami.com.pl), a pub, cocktail bar, concert venue and disco rolled into one. There's live music on weekdays and DJ sets at weekends. Its interior resembles a classic Hollywood cinema, with film memorabilia galore. Excellent food is another attraction. Newer clubs include **Domówka** (Rynek 39; www.klubdomowka.pl; Tue–Sat from 9pm). With its elevated dance floor and edgy design, it is a first port of call for the trendy set. Beer aficionados should visit one of Wrocław's breweries. **Bierhalle** (www.bierhalle.pl) and **Spiż Brewery** (www.spiz.pl) are both conveniently located on the Market Square. Meanwhile old-fashioned **Ragtime** (Plac Solny 17; www.ragtimecafe.pl), with its Wednesday and Thursday live jazz nights, is a jazz lover's paradise. Another bright spot on the city's jazz map is **Collosseum Jazz Café** (www.jazzcaffe.com.pl).

Poznań

With its flexible opening and closing hours, Poznań's nightlife hubs concentrate around the Old Town Square area, as well as Nowowiejskiego and Taczaka streets. **Brovaria** (Stary Rynek 73-74; www.brovaria.pl) attracts crowds as much for its sleek, steel and glass design as for the superb quality of its home-brewed lagers. The atmosphere is excellent, too. Serious clubbers will certainly pay a visit to **Pacha** (ul Paderewskiego 10; http://pachapoznan.com), the world's most famous clubbing franchise, throbbing with house beats.

Łódź

Łódź is definitely a rising star among Poland's nightlife destinations, mainly thanks to the fabulous redevelopment of the Off Piotrkowska

area, with its host of bars, artistic workshops and galleries, trendy restaurants and alternative music venues. For a unique experience check out **Dom** (ul Piotrkowska 138/140), with its concrete, squat-like post-industrial space or relax over a drink at one of the artsy bars: **Spaleni Słońcem**, **Ganimedes** (a LGTB bar) or **Tari Bari Bistro**, all scattered around the courtyard at Piotrkowska 138/140.

Gay scene

Although the situation has vastly improved over the last few years, homosexuality is still regarded by the majority of Poles, especially those living outside big cities, as morally doubtful to say the least. Public demonstrations of affection between people of the same sex are rare and could attract contemptuous looks from bystanders, except in gay-friendly or strictly gay bars and clubs. Warsaw is one of the most tolerant cities, with many venues catering for gays and lesbians. Among the oldest is the men-only bar and sauna **Phantom** on ul Bracka 20b. Meanwhile **Wild Club** (closed on Mon) on Chłodna 39 is best known for its regular dress code parties. Hetero-friendly **Galeria** (Pl Mirowski 1, Hala Mirowska; www.clubgaleria.pl; closed Mon) is an underground labyrinth of dance floors which offers excellent drag shows and highly popular karaoke nights. The lesbian café/bar **Bastylia** (www.bastylia.eu) on Mokotowska 17 organises screenings of LGTB films and serves excellent crêpes with salads, milkshakes, as well as local beers. Other popular meeting points for homosexuals in Warsaw include **Le Garage** (ul Burakowska 12) and **Toro** (ul Marszałkowska 3/5). The latter frequently has disco parties and all-night shows. Several bars, including **Między Nami Café** (ul Bracka 20; www.miedzynamicafe.com), **Café Bar Szpilka** (Pl Trzech Krzyży 18; open non-stop) and **Plan B** (Aleja Wyzwolenia 18) are gay-friendly and attract a mixed crowd. More on the gay scene at:
http://gayguide.net
www.queer.pl

Cinema

In main cities in Poland you will find modern cinemas usually equipped with Dolby stereo sound system. Check in the local newspapers for titles and times. Small towns,

however, still have simple, old-fashioned cinema halls. Foreign films are shown in their original language with Polish subtitles. Multikino, Cinema City Poland and Helios are the largest cinema chains, with branches in major Polish cities.

SPORTS

Horseriding

Poland has many riding centres for holidaymakers who wish to explore on horseback. In the tourist regions, particularly Mazuria, some large hotels have their own stables.

In Kraków the options include **Decjusz** (ul Kasztanowa 1; tel: 012-425 24 21), **Krakowski Klub Jazdy Konnej** (ul Kobierzyńska 175A; tel: 012-262 14 18), **Pegaz** (ul Łowińskiego 1; tel: 012-425 80 88; www.ojkpegaz.pl) and **Stadnina Podskalany** (ul Podskalany 61; tel: (0) 606 91 50 09; www.stadnina.podskalany.pl).

The choices in Warsaw include **Podkowa**, **TKKF Horseriding Club** (ul Głogów 11, Podkowa Leśna; tel: 022-758 94 26).

For further information, contact the local tourist offices (see page 397) or the Polish Prestige office (tel: 022-620 9817), which organises auctions and transports horses in Poland.

Skiing

Krynica, Wierchomla, Zakopane and Szczyrk, to the south of Katowice, are Poland's main skiing regions. Other recently modernised resorts in southwestern Poland include Zieleniec and Szklarska Poręba. Unfortunately, during busy periods, skiers can expect long waits at the ski lifts at all the centres. In the Silesian Beskid Mountains, as well as in the Karkonosze Mountains, an alternative is a well-developed network of cross-country tracks, with Polana Jakuszycka near Szklarska Poręba (www.jakuszyce.info.pl) being the top destination for amateurs and professionals alike. Nevertheless, the downhill runs are good and overall costs are still lower when compared with the more expensive Alpine skiing regions of Europe, so it is often worth the wait. In big cities cross-country skiing has become a popular alternative to Sunday walks in winter. In Warsaw it can be practised, weather permitting, in Kabaty Forests (the equipment can be hired at Powsin's Culture Park) and Puszcza

Kampinowska. A cross-country trail also follows the right bank of the Vistula river.

Hiking

Buy a good map from one of the kiosks or bookshops and you can explore Poland along colour-marked footpaths. Walkers are well catered for in the magnificent national parks (see page 119). The routes through the High Tatras are quite demanding and hikers need to have a good head for heights and some climbing experience. The best months for a walking holiday are August and September. The PTTK (http://pttk. pl; see page 392) runs a number of hostels in walking country. It also offers basic tourist information and descriptions of trekking trails.

Water sports

Sailing and water-sports enthusiasts adore the lakes and rivers of Poland, particularly in Mazuria. These waterways are becoming increasingly popular with canoeists, rowers and amateur sailors, with many people making overnight stops at the waterside campsites. If all you want to do is swim, windsurf or paddle, then, wherever you are, you are sure to find an attractive lake close by. Meanwhile Hel Peninsula is a kiter's and surfer's paradise.

For information about the best routes and campsites, contact one of the following bodies:

Klub Mila Zegrzynek
Ul Jerzego Szaniawskiego 56
Jadwisin, 05-140 Serock
Tel: 022-782 73 02/(0) 603 565 558
www.klubmila.pl
A modern water-sports club near Warsaw. Also a hotel and restaurant.
Polish Kayaking Union (Polski Związek Kajakowy)
Ul Ciołka 17, 01–445 Warsaw
Tel: 022-837 14 70
www.pzkaj.pl
Polish Sailing Association (Polski Związek Żeglarski)
Al ks J. Poniatowskiego 1, 03–901 Warsaw
Tel: 022-541 63 63
www.pya.org.pl
Warsaw Rowing Association (Warszawskie Towarzystwo Wioślarskie)
Ul Zaruskiego 12, 00-468 Warsaw
Tel: 022-621 59 76
www.wtw.waw.pl

For more detailed information about possible cruises and tours, contact the Polish Tourist and Sightseeing Society (PTTK) branches:
PTTK Olsztyn
Ul Staromiejska 1/13 Olsztyn 10-950
Tel: 089-527 36 65
www.mazury.pttk.pl
Trekking, bicycles, kayaking tours, Nordic walking, survival.
Water sports centre PTTK Sorkwity
Ul Zamkowa 13, Sorkwity 11-731
Tel: 089-732 81 24
www.sorkity.pttk.pl
Organises kayaking tours on the River Krutynia, hires kayaks and bicycles and also offers fishing permits.

Cycling

Poland attracts many cycling enthusiasts. The northern part is particularly bike–friendly, with its quiet surfaced roads, the not-too-hilly countryside and varied scenery. Country roads often follow ancient oak-lined tracks through picturesque villages. Keep well away from the main highways at all costs. As well as a tyre repair kit, make sure you have a heavy-duty bike lock. If you don't have your own bike, don't worry. In many hotels you can rent mountain bikes. More demanding bike trails can be found in the hilly south and in the Roztocze region. Detailed information about cycling in Poland and the most interesting routes can be found at www.rowery.org.pl.

Golf

The sport has enjoyed a growing popularity among up-and-coming executives, with modern golf courses springing up across the country. Currently there are 17 18-hole courses in Poland, with Modry Las Golf Club (www.modrylas.pl), designed by Gary Player and located in West Pomerania, considered the best. Other top golf centres include the First Warsaw Golf and Country Club, which opened in 1992 in Rajszew (http://fwgcc.pl), and Kalinowe Pola (http://kalinowepola.pl) in Western Poland (Lubuskie). For details and information on golf in Poland contact the Polish Golf Union (pzgolf.pl).

Windsurfing at Puck Bay, along the Baltic Coast.

Running

If there is one sport that has captured the imagination of Poles it has to be running. The number of people running for fun and taking part in the frequent mass events (10km runs, half marathons, marathons and ultra-marathons) has increased three-fold in the last few years. Running has become a fashionable sport, with journalists, TV celebrities and politicians yielding to its charm en masse. For details check one of the many Polish websites dedicated to running such as: http://polskabiega.sport.pl; www.psb-biegi.com.pl; www.maratonypolskie.pl or http://marathons.ahotu.com.

SIGHTSEEING TOURS

Since the political upheavals of 1989, a large number of small, privately owned travel companies have emerged that run coach excursions or organise tours. We recommend using well-known and recognisable companies such as Mazurkas Travel or PTTK.

Almatur, the travel agency run by the Polish Student Association, arranges reasonably priced individual or group tours for students, including educational and cultural programmes, international student lodgings along the coast, on lakes and in the mountains. They also organise tours for film, fishing and horse-riding enthusiasts. Contact: **Almatur**, Ul Kopernika 23, 00-359 Warsaw; tel: 022-826 26 39 (www.almatur.pl).

Other useful tour operators include:
Mazurkas Travel
Al Wojska Polskiego 27, Warsaw
Tel: 022-536 46 00/389 46 00
www.mazurkas.com.pl
Polish Travel Quo Vadis Ltd
Ul Ptasia 2, Warsaw
Tel: 022-322 85 85
www.ptqv.net
Open: Mon–Fri 9am–5pm.
Specialises in business travel.
PTTK "Trakt"
Ul Kredytowa 6, Warsaw
Tel: 022-827 80 69
www.trakt.com.pl
Run by the Polish Countryside Association, PTTK offers plenty of tours for individuals and groups around Warsaw and the rest of Poland.

Suggested Tours

From Kraków to Wieliczka and the famous 13th-century **salt mine**.

Oświęcim, the World War II concentration camp, better known by its German name, Auschwitz.
Ojców National Park, by the Prądnik River. The PTTK (see page 392) organises hiking, canoeing, sailing and motorcycling tours within the park, as well as excursions on foot, on skis and in the mountains. Local tour guides are available.
From Gdańsk to Westerplatte and the **National Memorial** to 1 September 1939.
Oliwa and organ recitals in the old cathedral.
Malbork and the Castle of the Teutonic Knights.
Sztutowo, formerly Stutthof concentration camp.
Frombork, where Nicholas Copernicus (Mikołaj Kopernik) spent 28 years of his life.
From Warsaw to Żelazowa Wola, **Chopin's birthplace**.
Wilanów, the former residence of Jan III Sobieski.
Puszcza Kampinowska, with woods, marshland and dunes populated by elk, fox, boar and bird species.
Zalew Zegrzyński, a large reservoir offering leisure and water sports opportunities.

OUTDOOR ACTIVITIES

National Parks

No one should visit Poland without exploring at least one of the 23 national parks (see page 119). There is a huge variety of preserved terrains: from the rocky, alpine Tatras to the wooded Pieniny or Bieszczady ranges, from the ancient Białowieska Forest to the shifting dunes in the mini-desert on the shores of the Baltic, from the rivers and lakes hidden away among the forests of the Suwałski region to the Roztocze plateau.

All the parks are open to tourists, many accessible only on foot. The only exception is the Białowieski Park, where visitors must explore the forest in the company of a local guide. Basic overnight accommodation is available.
Babiogórski
34-223 Zawoja
Tel: 033-877 51 10
Park management:
34-223 Zawoja 1403
Tel: 033-877 51 10/51 24
www.bgpn.pl
Contains the highest portions of the Western Bieszczady Mountains, including Mount Tarnica, from 700–1,725 metres (2,300–5,560ft).

Białowieski
5 Park Palacowy, 17-230 Białowieża
Tel: 085-681 23 06/23 23
www.pl-info.net/poland/parks/
bialowieski_park.html
www.bpn.com.pl
The oldest forested park in the country (founded 1921) and the most extensive wooded area in Europe, covering 5,348 hectares (13,200 acres); a breeding centre for European bison, tarpan (wild horses), stag, roe deer and wild boar.
Bieszczady
Tel: 013-461 06 10
Park management:
38-714 Ustrzyki Górne
Tel: 090-309 156/134-610 650
www.bdpn.pl
In the Krosno area, covers 27,064 hectares (66,848 acres) and rises 660–1,346 metres (1,950–4,414ft) over the West Bieszczady Mountains and part of the Carpathians. Traces of old charcoal burning kilns and ancient sacred sites; the Bieszczadzkie Museum is in Ustrzyki Dolne.
Drawieński
Park management:
73-220 Drawno, Ul Leśnikow 2
Tel/fax: 095-768 2051/2510
www.dpn.pl
In Gorzów area, covering 9,068 hectares (22,397 acres): between the Drawa and Płociczna rivers; mud turtles, beavers, otters and many rare bird species.
Gorczański
Park management:
Poreba Wielka, 34–735 Niedzwiedz
Tel: 018-331 72 07
www.gorczanskipark.pl
In Nowy Sącz area, covering 6,763 hectares (16,700 acres): the central section of the Gorce massif (part of the West Beskid Mountains).
Kampinoski
38 Tetmajera Ul, 05-080 Izabelin
Tel: 022-722 60 01/65 59
www.kampinoski-pn.gov.pl
The largest national park in Poland covers the Vistula River Valley.
Karkonosze
Park management:
58-570 Jelenia Góra, Ul Chałubinskiego 23
Tel: 075-755 33 48/37 26
www.kpnmab.pl
In Jelenia Góra area, covering 5,562 hectares (13,738 acres): alpine park with post-glacial features in the Karkonosze Mountains.
Magurski
Krempna 59, 38-232 Krempna
Park management:
38-232 Nowy Zmigród, Ul Krampna 59
Tel: 013-441 40 99

Bieszczady Mountains hiking trail.

www.magurskipn.pl
In the Krosno area, covering 19,962 hectares (49,306 acres): it takes in part of the Beskid Niski Mountains.

Ojcowski
Park management:
32-047 Ojców, Ojców 9, Skała 39
Tel: 012-389 10 39/20 05
www.opn.pan.krakow.pl
In the Kraków area, covering 1,890 hectares (4,668 acres) and part of the Kraków-Częstochowa Upland and the Pradnik valley; numerous underground springs.

Pieniński
Park management:
34-450 Krościenko, Ul Jagiellońska 107B
Tel: 018-262 56 ½
www.pieninypn.pl
In Nowy Sącz area, covering 2,231 hectares (5,510 acres): takes in the middle section of the Pieniny mountains; very varied landscape – try a raft ride through the Dunajec valley.

Poleski
Park management:
22-234 Urszulin, Ul Lubelska 3A
Tel: 082-571 3071/2
www.poleskipn.pl
In Chełm area, covering 9,647 hectares (2,382 acres): countless lakes and marshland.

Roztoczański
Park management:
22-470 Zwierzyniec, Ul Płazowa 2
Tel: 084-687 22 86/22 07
www.roztoczanskipn.pl
In Zamość area, covering 7,886 hectares (19,478 acres): the geologically varied region in the western part of the park.

Słowiński
Park management:
Bohaterów Warszawy Ul, 76-214 Smoldzino
Tel: 059-811 72 04/73 39
www.slowinskipn.pl
Beside the Baltic, with moving sand dunes over 50m (160ft) high and desert landscape which includes a 100-metre (328ft) wide beach.

Świętokrzyski
Park management:
26-010 Bodzentyn,
Ul Suchedniowska 4
Tel: 041-311 50 25
www.swietokrzyskipn.org.pl
In Kielce area, covering 6,054 hectares (14,953 acres): covers the oldest Polish mountain range, the Gory Świętorkrzyskie. The remains of an early smelting furnace were discovered near Nowa Słupia, a village that is now home to the Museum of Ancient Metallurgy; Święty Krzyż abbey nearby.

Tatrzański
Park management:
34-500 Zakopane, Ul Chałubińskiego 42 A
Tel: 018-206 32 03
www.tpn.pl
In Nowy Sącz area, covering 21,164 hectares (52,275 acres): alpine park containing Poland's highest mountain range, the Tatras, and Mount Rysy (2,499 metres/8,196ft). Tytus Chałubiński Tatra Museum (www.muzeumtatrzanskie.pl) is at 34-500 Zakopane, Ul Krupówki 10, tel: 018-201 52 05.

Wielkopolski
Park management:
Jeziory, 62-050 Mosina
Tel: 061-813 22 06
www.wielkopolskipn.pl
In Poznań area, covering 5,337 hectares (13,182 acres): post-glacial landscape with typical geological formations.

Wigry
Park management:
16-400 Suwałki, Krzywe 82
Tel: 087-563 25 40
www.wigry.win.pl
In Suwałki area, covering 15,113 hectares (37,329 acres): surrounds one of the largest and deepest lakes in Poland, Lake Wigry; 45 other lakes and a section of the Augustówski Forest.

Wolin
Park management:
72-510 Międzyzdroje, Ul Niepodległości, 3
Tel: 091-328 07 37/27
www.wolinpn.pl
In Szczecin area covering 5,001 hectares (12,352 acres): Wolin Island and a part of Szczecin Lagoon.

Park Information
For further details of national parks and nature reserves, try:
National Parks Association
00-922 Warsaw, Ul Wawelska 52/54
Tel: 022-825 1493/5748
www.mos.gov.pl/kzpn

FESTIVALS

Poland's cultural festival calendar is brimming with interesting events taking place throughout the year. Below find our choice of the best ones:

Warsaw

Ludvig van Beethoven Easter Festival (March/April; www.beethoven.org.pl). Taking place a week before Easter, this top-notch classical music festival won the prestigious IFEA/Haass & Wilkerson Pinnacle Award in 2010 for the best art event of the year. Symphonic and chamber concerts, performed by the world's best ensembles, soloists and directors, present Beethoven's music from different perspectives, showing its sources and impact on modern performers. The director of the festival is Elżbieta Penderecka, wife of the famous Polish director and composer Krzysztof Penderecki.

Warsaw Summer Jazz Days (June; www.adamiakjazz.pl). The festival promotes contemporary jazz and hosts the most innovative artists from different cultures and contrasting backgrounds. Highlights include a free concert at Plac Zamkowy (Royal Castle Square) and the final performance of the biggest stars at Kongresowa Hall. The four-day festival is a worthy rival to Jazz Jamboree.

Międzynarodowy Festiwal Sztuka Ulicy (International Street Art Festival; end of June and beginning of July; http://sztukaulicy.pl). Dance, theatre, music and circus performances take place in city theatres, parks and public places, fostering cultural exchange in Europe. The festival attracts young people keen on avant garde and alternative art.

Jazz na Starówce (Jazz at the Old Town; July–August; www.jazznastarowce.pl). These free jazz concerts featuring established international stars as well as newcomers have enjoyed great popularity since they started more than 20 years ago. The performances take place every Saturday in July and August at the Old Town Square (at 7pm) and attract locals and tourists who listen to the music sipping their beer or wine in the numerous outdoor gardens belonging to nearby restaurants and cafés. The atmosphere is relaxed and artists are often eager to play something extra to please enthusiastic crowds.

Międzynarodowy Festiwal Chopin i jego Europa (International Music Festival Chopin and his Europe; August; http://pl.chopin.nifc.pl).

Organised in August by the Fryderyk Chopin Institute. The concerts take place in the Polish Radio Concert Hall and National Opera, among others locations, with some pieces performed on historic instruments from the 19th century.

Warszawska Jesień (Warsaw Autumn International Festival of Contemporary Music; September; www.warszawska-jesien.art.pl). Founded in 1956, Warszawska Jesień was for the entire Communist period an island of creative freedom and the only event of its kind in Central and Eastern Europe. Its character has recently changed, with the festival featuring video projections and new technologies and expanding to new venues across the city such as sports halls, old factories and modern clubs to woo the younger public. The concerts held through September present the best of new music and also take place in traditional halls such as the Warsaw Philharmonic, the Music Academy, and the city's theatres and churches.

Festival of Jewish Culture "Singer's Warsaw" (late August/ beginning of September; www.festiwalsingera.pl). Annual celebration of Jewish culture in all its forms that has been held in Warsaw since 2004. It takes place in the former Jewish quarter of the town, mainly around Grzybowski Square and Próżna Street, and features klezmer music concerts and cantor singing, but also lessons in Jewish paper-cutting and Hebrew calligraphy. Workshops allow people to try different dishes of kosher cuisine and to learn how to adapt their kitchens as required by the Jewish religion. There are also films, workshops and seminars dedicated to every aspect of the Jewish culture.

Warszawski Festiwal Filmowy (Warsaw Film Festival; October; www.wff.pl). In October cinema buffs head for the capital to immerse themselves in the week-long film feast that showcases the best world productions. The programme is varied and aims to discover new trends in world cinema – it features independent films from Russia, Romania, Iran, the US, Latin America and other places, along with Hollywood blockbusters. Besides screenings, there also workshops for film critics, journalists, directors and editors.

Jazz Jamboree (International Jazz Jamboree Festival; November/ December; www.jazz-jamboree.

pl). Conceived by the Polish writer and jazz fan Leopold Tyrmand, who coined its name, Jazz Jamboree is one of the biggest and oldest jazz festivals in Europe (first held in 1958). The main concerts take place in the lavish Sala Kongresowa, which has seen performances by the greatest jazz stars, including Miles Davis, Chick Corea, Paco de Lucia and many others.

Around Poland

Kraków

Międzynarodowy Festiwal Kina Niezależnego - Off Plus Camera (International Festival of Independent Cinema – Off Plus Camera; April; www.offpluscamera.com). As the first independent cinema festival in Poland, the event promotes Polish and international productions that set alternative standards and fulfil the creative potential of their makers. Screenings include the newest films as well as classics and take place in cosy cinemas.

Parada Lajkonika (Lajkonik Festival; June–first Thursday after Corpus Christi). A traditional parade from Zwierzyniec to Main Market Square commemorating Tartar invasions (although there are other theories about its origin). The parade features Lajkonik – a bearded man dressed like a Tartar with a wooden hobby horse around his waist. He is accompanied by a traditionally dressed group including musicians and followed by the crowd of Kraków's inhabitants. Being touched by Lajkonik is said to bring luck. The colourful procession proceeds through historic streets to the Main Square, where the mayor of the city offers Lajkonik ransom money.

Festiwal Kultury Żydowskiej (end of June, beginning of July; www.jewishfestival.pl). One of the biggest Jewish cultural festivals in the world. Every year Kraków's Kazimierz district resounds with klezmer, Chasidic and Sephardic folk music as people flock to the city from Poland and abroad to enjoy film screenings, theatre performances, seminars and workshops dedicated to traditional and modern Jewish culture. There is also the chance to taste samples of kosher delights prepared by Jewish cooks and learn how to cook them.

Sacrum Profanum Music Festival (September; www.sacrumprofanum.com). A unique blend of contemporary and experimental music, the festival draws to Kraków not only the best ensembles and icons of contemporary music, such as Steve Reich or Krzysztof Penderecki, but also stars of the alternative scene. Sacrum Profanum's aim is to blur the line between contemporary music and ambitious entertainment and experimental projects.

Krakowski Festiwal Filmowy (Kraków Film Festival; late June to beginning of July; www.krakowfilm festival.pl). A seven-day cinema feast featuring over 200 documentary, animated and short fiction films from Europe, presented in thematic, retrospective and archive sections. Being the oldest such event in Poland, it attracts hundreds of prominent guests from abroad, including directors and producers as well as thousands of cinema buffs. Its reputation is enhanced by the fact that winning productions are automatically eligible to be considered for the European Film Awards and the Oscars.

Gdańsk

Międzynarodowy Festiwal Muzyki Organowej (International Festival of Organ Music; July–August in Gdańsk-Oliwa). Classical music aficionados will certainly appreciate the organ concerts held in summer in the historic Oliwa Cathedral, dating from the 13th century and situated on the edge of the magnificent Oliwa Landscape Park, which according to the German traveller Alexander von Humboldt is the third most beautiful place on Earth.

Jarmark Dominikański (St Dominic's Fair; end of July to mid-August; http://jarmarkdominika.pl). Originating in the 13th century, St Dominic's Fair features more than 1,000 stands offering antiques, amber, arts and crafts, as well as cultural events including classical and rock concerts, culinary workshops, street performances and fireworks displays. In 2007 the three-week event was attended by a record 8.5 million visitors. Its numerous food stalls serve national dishes (dumplings, *bigos*) and regional cuisine (fried fish, smoked eel, home-made bread with pickles), as well as excellent regional beers.

Bydgoszcz

Międzynarodowy Festiwal Sztuki Autorów Zdjęć Filmowych CAMERIMAGE (The International Film Festival of the Art of Cinematography CAMERIMAGE; November;

www.camerimage.pl). This acclaimed international festival that celebrates the best cinematographers offers an interesting alternative to more traditional film competitions. The films are evaluated for their visual, aesthetic and technical values, while the festival organisers put extra effort into promoting and helping young film-makers. Accompanying events include seminars, concerts and art exhibitions.

Łańcut

Festiwal Muzyczny w Łańcucie (Łańcut Music Festival; May; www.festiwallancut.pl). Set in the amazing interiors of the 17th-century Łańcut Castle, which once belonged to the most prominent aristocratic Polish families, this is the leading chamber music festival in Poland. The week-long feast for classical music aficionados attracts the best national and international ensembles.

Łódź

Festiwal Łódź Czterech Kultur (Four Cultures Łódź Festival; June; www.4kultury.pl). Concerts, theatre plays, seminars and other events aim at restoring the Polish–German–Jewish–Russian cultural heritage of the city, which was destroyed by World War II and its aftermath. The festival is a melting pot of different traditions, including Jewish and Roma music as well as jazz, rock and electronic performances. Most events concentrate on and around Piotrowska Street.

Fashion Week Poland (twice a year; http://fashionweek.pl). Poland's largest fashion event attracts world-famous designers as well as young creators. Three main sections of the festival are dedicated to prêt-à-porter collections by the best Polish clothes designers and special guests from abroad, the avant garde and young creators. The shows, in Expo-Łódź Hall, are organised twice a year (usually in May and October) and are accompanied by photographic exhibitions, a fashion film festival and a showroom area where the best collections are displayed.

Łódź Design Festival (October; http://lodzdesign.com). The city is celebrating its long manufacturing traditions with a festival that blends traditional exhibitions with hands-on workshops, lectures, walks and shows, presenting the most relevant trends in Polish and international design. The event is organised in several places across the city,

including a beautifully converted factory. At night design buffs and their gurus may join several parties offering good music as well as a chance to meet local creators.

Opole

Krajowy Festiwal Piosenki Polskiej w Opolu (The National Festival of Polish Song in Opole; June; http://festiwalopole.tvp.pl). With a 50-year tradition, this is one of the most popular music festivals in Poland. Besides celebrating the annual achievements of Polish songwriters and performers, it also promotes young debutants. It was a springboard to stardom for such giants of Polish popular music as Ewa Demarczyk, Czesław Niemen, Ryszard Rynkowski and Anna Maria Jopek. However, in recent years it has changed into a TV show more than anything else. The years when the festival dictated what songs and artists will be on everyone's lips for the rest of the year are sadly long gone.

Sopot

Polsat Sopot Festival (late August). Along with Opole, this was a flagship song festival for decades, since its first event in 1961, which was organised by the legendary pianist and composer Władysław Szpilman. Held in Opera Leśna (Forest Opera), it once attracted world-famous artists including Charles Aznavour, Chuck Berry and Johnny Cash. However, the festival has followed in the footsteps of its main rival, the Opole song contest, losing most of its mojo.

Wrocław

Wratislavia Cantans (September; http://2014.wratislaviacantans.pl). Created almost half a century ago, Wratislavia Cantans is one of the biggest classical music festivals in Europe with human voice, the best musical instrument, at its centre. An unrivalled music experience.

Festiwal Filmowy T-Mobile Nowe Horyzonty (T-Mobile Nowe Horyzonty Film Festival; July; www.nowehoryzonty.pl). Launched in 2001 by Roman Gutek, arguably the most prominent Polish cinema promoter and director of the Warsaw Film Festival, this young and thriving arthouse festival offers retrospectives of the great film-makers, national panoramas and thematic sections, as well as the most uncompromising and unconventional contemporary films.

A – Z

A HANDY SUMMARY
OF PRACTICAL INFORMATION

A

Admission Charges

Most Polish museums, art galleries and other attractions now have at least a nominal entrance fee, though usually offer free entry one day a week. There are reductions for children, but not always for senior citizens. Some places charge fees for the use of video cameras or taking photos. Students with International Student Cards (ISIC) are eligible for discounts and benefits, including reductions in most museums; for more information see www.isic. pl. Almost all clubs and discos have admission fees, though in most cases this includes at least one free drink.

Accommodation

Hotels, private rooms and roadhouses

At the height of the season, basic hotels, youth hostels and campsites in the main tourist regions are overcrowded, so it is a good idea to reserve accommodation well in advance. However, it is not usually a problem finding a bed in the higher-price range hotels, even in mid-summer. The number of hotels is constantly growing, especially in the four-star category. The hotel chains are also expanding, especially in big cities. The biggest ones are **Orbis/ Accorn** (www.orbis.pl), **Best Western** (www.bestwestern.pl), **Louvre Hotels Group** (www.louvrehotels.com), **Qubus Hotel** (www.qubushotel.com) and **OST Gromada** (www.gromada.pl). Hotels are divided into five categories: 1-, 2-, 3-, 4- and 5-star. Hotels that target business people and tourists will offer

guests spacious rooms, translation and secretarial services, fitness suites, bars and restaurants. Prices are comparable with similar hotels in western Europe. Almost all hotels and boarding houses accept major credit cards.

If you find yourself facing a night under the stars, do not despair. Ask at the local tourist information office for a list of private houses where overnight guests are welcome. By the coast or in the Mazurian Lake District, houses with beds available show signs with the words *pokoje* (rooms) or *noclegi* (accommodation – literally 'overnight stay'). The many, often rustic-style, roadhouses *(zajazd)* on the main arterial roads offer good-quality accommodation. They do not claim to provide luxury, but, after a long car journey, they offer a comfortable overnight stay. Couch surfing is also gaining popularity.

Youth Hostels and Tourist-Class Accommodation

A list of youth hostels is available at the website of the **Polish Youth Hostel Association (PTSM)**. In summer the organisation also arranges accommodation in school buildings. The PTSM is a member of the **International Youth Hostel Federation (IYHF)**. Travellers with a valid IYHF card receive a 25 percent discount.
PTSM, ul Mokotowska 14, Warsaw 00-561; tel: 022-849 81 28; www.ptsm.org.pl.

For other youth hostels, see www.schroniskamlodziezowe.com or www.youth-hostels.co.uk.

The **Polish Tourist and Sightseeing Society (PTTK)** can arrange tourist-class accommodation in mountain chalets, hostels, campsites and motor-sport or

horseriding centres for those who are interested in activity holidays. The list is available at http://obiekty.pttk.pl. PTTK, ul Senatorska 11, Warsaw 00-075; tel: 022-826 22 51; www.pttk.pl.

Camping

Around 275 campsites are members of the **Polish Camping and Caravanning Federation (PFCC)**. The organisation grades them into four categories. All have access to running water, sanitary facilities and electricity. Standards at some reach the level of a four-star hotel. Campsites in Poland are still less expensive than elsewhere in Europe, the daily average cost for two adults, a child and a campervan is around €15–17. Many campsites also rent out modestly furnished bungalows. The camping season lasts from mid-June to mid-September, but there are also campsites open all year. A lot of campsites offers reductions with the international camping card (10 percent in high season, 40 percent out of season). The list of campsites is available at PFCC's website.
PFFC, ul Grochowska 331, 03-823; tel: 022-810 60 50; www.pfcc.eu.

A number of unsupervised sites *(miejsca biwakowe)* are located in picturesque lakeside spots or in the forests, but no sanitary amenities whatsoever are provided. Independent camping is not permitted. It is always advisable to check with the forestry office or landowner before putting up your tent. Sometimes a small fee is requested.

Some of the best campsites: Katowice

Ul Trzech Stawów 23, Katowice Tel: 032-255 53 88/256 59 39 www.camping.mosir.katowice.pl Four stars, open all year.

Malta
Ul Krańcowa 98, Poznań
Tel: 061-876 62 03/0 509 840 502
www.campingmalta.poznan.pl
Four stars, open all year. Overlooking
Malta Lake.

Pod Dębowcem
Ul Karbowa 15, Bielsko-Biała
Tel: 0 604 144 186
www.camping.org.pl
Four stars, open May–Oct.

Rafael
Ul Turystyczna 10, Łeba
Tel: 059-866 19 72/0 605 464 229
www.campingrafael.pl
Four stars, open all year, near the
Słowinski Park Narodowy and the
"moving" sand dunes.

Tumiany
Tumiany 1a, Barczewo
Tel: 0 602 757 481
www.camping-tumiany.pl
Four stars, open May–Sept, at the
beautiful Mazurian lake.

Wok
Ul Odrębna 16, Warsaw
Tel: 022-612 79 51
www.campingwok.warszawa.pl
Four stars, open all year.

Agritourism

For agritourism holidays contact:
Gospodarstwa Gościnne, Polish
Federation of Rural Tourism, Plac
Powstańców Warszawy 2, Warsaw
00-030; tel: 081-501 43 11. The list
is available at www.agroturystyka.pl.

B

Budgeting for Your Trip

While certain things remain relatively
cheap, such as public transport and
train travel, taxis, museum admission
fees and snacks, life in Poland is
becoming increasingly expensive,
especially in Warsaw and Kraków.

The biggest expense, anywhere
in the country, will always be
accommodation. Good, cheap hotels
are not hard to find, but they are often
fully booked. The mid-range hotel
sector is increasing in size, but most
new hotels are four star. Make sure
you book accommodation well in
advance, and expect to spend upwards
of 120PLN (around €30) per night for
even the most basic hotel room.

Business Travellers

Many of Poland's cities are geared well
towards business travellers, especially
Warsaw – now one of Europe's great
business cities – and Poznań, which,
at the heart of Europe, has been

hosting trade fairs for centuries.
Hotels in these cities charge far more
during the week for accommodation
than they do at weekends.

C

Children

Children have always been welcomed
in Poland, and they are increasingly well
catered for. Hotels will rarely charge for
children staying in their parents' room,
and it is now common for restaurants
to offer special children's portions and
menus. Of all Poland's destinations,
Kraków, Gdynia and Warsaw are
probably the most geared to children,
their parks and attractions all having
something to offer even the smallest
kids. Note that on public transport in
Poland children over the age of five
(over seven in Warsaw) are expected
to possess a ticket, but there are
reductions. Children do get excellent
reductions on InterCity trains and on
LOT internal flights.

Climate

Due to the country's lengthy coastline,
the climate in Poland varies between
oceanic and continental. Therefore,
weather conditions are subject to
change. From May until October Poland
enjoys beautiful weather. In March
spring begins – a little windy and rainy
and averaging -1 to 15°C (30–60°F). In
May to June temperatures rise to 21°C
(70°F) and remain as such through the
summer. August can be very warm, with
temperatures often climbing beyond
30°C (86°F). The traditional 'golden
Polish autumn' in September is usually
sunny and dry, with temperatures
around 16°C (60°F). In November
the first foggy and cold days begin,
complemented by shorter days. Winter
lasts about three months (December–
February), but can be so severe that in
many northern regions temperatures
drop to -30°C (-22°F). Snow in the
mountain regions makes for excellent
skiing. It remains in the mountains until
around Easter. To check the weather,
see www.pogodynka.pl or http://new.
meteo.pl.

What To Wear

The summer months are similar to
the UK, with less humidity. Winter,
however, is cold with heavy falls
of snow in the mountains and
temperatures falling below 0°C (32°F).
In winter bring a thick coat, boots,
a hat and gloves. In autumn it rains
often so bring a waterproof.

Crime and Security

Theft is not unusual in places
frequented by tourists. It is better to
keep any valuables and jewellery in
the hotel safe. If you are travelling by
car, it is essential to park it for longer
periods or overnight in a guarded car
park – even the smaller towns have
them. If you are the victim of a theft,
report it immediately to the reception
desk at your hotel or to the police. The
emergency police number is 997. If you
lose all your money or your passport,
you will have to seek advice from your
nearest consulate or embassy.

Customs Regulations

The following articles may be
imported into Poland duty-free from
EU countries:
Alcohol: 90 litres of wine, 110 litres of
beer, 10 litre of spirits.
Tobacco products: up to 800 cigarettes
or 200 cigars or 1kg of tobacco.
From outside the EU (for people
aged 17 and above):
Alcohol: 1 litre of spirits or 4 litres of
wine and 16 litres of beer.
Tobacco products: up to 200
cigarettes or 50 cigars or 250g of
tobacco (for transport other than by
sea or by air only 40 cigarettes, or 10
cigars or 50g of tobacco).

Dogs and cats may be imported,
but they must have been immunised
against rabies at least three weeks
before arrival at the border. The
official vaccination certificate (not
older than 12 months) must be
produced. Many hotels accept dogs,
but will make a surcharge.

Works of art bought in Poland,
such as antiques (over 50 years old),
paintings (over 50 years old and
of a value exceeding 40,000PLN),
maps (over 150 years old and over

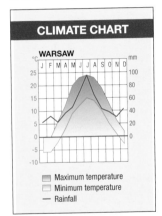

CLIMATE CHART

WARSAW

Maximum temperature
Minimum temperature
Rainfall

6,000PLN) and books (over 100 years old and over 6,000PLN), can only be exported if an authorisation from the Provincial Heritage Monuments Protection Office (www.mwkz.pl) is produced.

Warsaw Customs Headquarters: ul Świetokrzyska 12. For further information call the Customs Information Centre: tel: 801 470 477 or 33 857 62 51; info.sluzbacelna@kat.mofnet.gov.pl.

D

Disabled Travellers

This is an area, alas, where Poland still generally struggles to meet European Union standards. While legislation has been passed to make all public buildings accessible, not all of them actually are, but the situation is changing. Most forms of public transport are now accessible (about 74 percent of public transport is low floor, 100 percent in Gdynia and Zielona Góra), and while recent repairs to pavements in major cities means that getting around is easier than before, crossing the street can still be a trial. When it comes to the private sector there has been more progress, with hotels all over the country – especially those at the top end – now more than able to take disabled guests with ease. See the website www.niepelnosprawnik. eu to search for accessible hotels, restaurants and other venues.

E

Embassies and Consulates

Australia:
Ul Nowogrodzka 11, Warsaw 00-513
Tel: 022-521 34 44
www.australia.pl
Canada:
Ul Matejki 1/5, Warsaw 00-481
Tel: 022-584 31 00
www.canadanternational.gc.ca/poland-pologne
New Zealand
Al Ujazdowskie 51, Warsaw 00-536
Tel: 022-521 05 00
www.nzembassy.com/poland
South Africa
Ul Koszykowa 64, 6th floor, Warsaw 00-675
Tel: 022-622 10 05
UK
Ul Kawalerii 12, Warsaw 00-648
Tel: 022-311 00 00
http://ukinpoland.fco.gov.uk
USA
Al Ujazdowskie, 29/31, Warsaw 00-540

Electricity

220 volts. Sockets take two round pins. UK Visitors will require an adapter; travellers from North America will also need a converter.

Tel: 022-504 20 00
http://poland.usembassy.gov

Emergency Numbers

General emergency: 112
Ambulance (public): 999
Police: 997
Fire: 998
Please note: do not expect anyone at these numbers to be able to speak English.
Tourist emergency helpline (in English): 022-278 77 77 or (0) 801 888 844 (daily 8am–6pm, Jun–Sept until 10pm).

Etiquette

Poles are great hosts – especially in their own homes – but do note that they are a conservative bunch. If you can manage to get yourself invited to a Polish home (and to do so is worthwhile) always bring something; flowers go down especially well. On entering a Pole's home you should at least offer to take your shoes off. You should expect to be asked some rather personal and direct questions, which may include your views on the Catholic Church, homosexuality and Poland itself. Be diplomatic in response, even if you do not like what you hear.

When entering churches make sure you are respectfully dressed. Women should cover their shoulders, and shorts are by and large unacceptable, though increasingly tolerated, at least for men.

G

Gay and Lesbian Travellers

Poland gets a bad reputation for its attitude to gays and although the situation has improved in recent years, public demonstrations of affection between people of the same sex could attract disapproving looks. There are gay nightspots in both Warsaw and Kraków. Sopot in summer is another place gays will be more than welcome. For more information on gay nightspots see page 386 or check the specialist site www.gayguide.net.

H

Health and Medical Care

The Polish authorities do not require any special inoculations, but protection against tetanus, polio and diphtheria (the latest booster should have been carried out within the past 10 years) is recommended. If, however, you are planning to spend a lot of time in country areas, particularly those close to the Russian, Lithuanian or Byelarus border, then it is wise to see your doctor about the symptoms and treatment of Lyme Disease before leaving home.

EU and EFTA passports holders should carry with them the European Health Insurance Card (EHIC), available online at www.ehic.org.uk. Bear in mind, however, that the card doesn't replace travel insurance and doesn't cover any private healthcare or costs. In an emergency, you will be taken to a hospital where you will receive immediate treatment, but for any course of treatment or hospital stay you will be expected to pay in cash. Make sure you take out medical insurance to cover all eventualities.

Chemists

Chemists are open Mon–Fri 8am–7pm and Sat till 2pm. An emergency system operates in most towns. The address of the chemist providing out-of-hours service is usually posted in chemists' windows. To be on the safe side, it is advisable to bring a supply of any special medication you might need on your trip.

Chemists serve as the first place to ask for help in minor medical problems. There is a rota system with one chemist (Apteka) in the area staying open 24 hours for emergencies. Most standard drugs are available in Poland without a prescription, but are sometimes marketed under different names. It is always a good idea to show the chemist the empty container to ensure you get the right drug.

Doctors and Dentists

Most of the doctors and dentists in the cities speak English. Most four- and five-star hotels have a doctor on call.

Hospitals and Ambulances

Hospitals in Poland do not always meet Western standards of nursing and accommodation, but medical care is usually sufficient in an emergency. There are public and private ambulance companies operating in major cities and a public ambulance service covering the whole country. Depending on their speciality, different hospitals cover different emergencies. Patients are referred to an appropriate hospital by a doctor or ambulance crew. Self-referral is also possible via the Accident and Emergency departments (Izba przyjęć).

Warsaw Hospitals and Clinics

Centrum Medyczne Damiana (Medicover Group): Ul Wałbrzyska 46; tel: 022-566 22 22; www.damian.pl; www.medicover.pl.

Luxmed: Al Jerozolimskie 65/79 (Hotel Mariott); tel: 022-332 28 88; www.luxmed.pl. It also has other branches in Warsaw and in other cities in Poland.

FALCK: Ul Obozowa 20; tel: 022-535 91 91; www.falck.pl. Ambulance service tel: 1 96 75. It has branches in Warsaw and Gdańsk.

Klinika ProMed: Ul Uniwersytecka 5 at Pl Narutowicza; tel: 022-822 18 11; www.promed.medserwis.pl. Open: Mon–Fri 7.30am–8pm, Sat 9am–3pm.

Dental Treatment

Austria Dental Centre: Ul Zelazna 54; tel: 022-654 21 16/54 84; www.austriadent.pl. Mon–Fri 9am–8pm, Sat by appointment only. English- and German-speaking dentists.
Eurodental: tel: 022-380 70 00/666 079 420; www.eurodental.pl. Has several branches in Warsaw and English-speaking dentists. Mon–Fri 8am–8pm, some also Sat 8am–6pm.

I

Internet

Getting online in Poland is easy. Almost all hotels offer some kind of Internet connection, almost always Wi-fi, and free access is common. There are many hotspots in larger cities (also in coffee shops and fast-food restaurants). In Warsaw there are free public hotspots in the Old Town, Krakowskie Przedmieście and Nowy Świat streets, Pasaż Wiecha and near Browarna Street in Powiśle. If you want to be more independent, you can buy a pre-pay access card from one of the telecommunication providers: Orange, T-Mobile, Play or Plus (which are ubiquitous all over Poland). These provide access to the Wi-fi network for a set period of time.

M

Maps

Several words are frequently abbreviated on Polish maps. Aleja (abbreviated as Al) means avenue, Ulica (abbreviated as Ul) means street, Plac means square, and Rynek is Market Square. In addresses, house numbers usually follow the name of the street.

You can find a good selection of maps of Poland in Sklep Podróżnika (www.sp.com.pl), it has branches in Warsaw (Grójecka 46/50), Kraków (Szujskiego 2), Gdańsk (Grunwaldzka 59) and Poznań (Ślusarska 16).

Media

Newspapers

The mass media in Poland is very diverse and faces the same problems as elsewhere – tabloidisation and the growing importance of digital versions, especially those available free on the Internet. The main national daily newspapers are *Gazeta Wyborcza* (www.wyborcza.pl) and *Rzeczpospolita* (www.rp.pl), but the biggest-selling title is the tabloid-style *Fakt*. Most big cities have their own local newspapers. The most popular weekly news magazines are *Polityka*, *Newsweek Polska*, *Do Rzeczy* and *W Sieci*. There are also some papers published in English. In Warsaw there are two: the monthly magazine *Warsaw Voice* (www.thewarsawvoice.pl) and the weekly *The Warsaw Business Journal* (www.wbj.pl), both also cover current cultural events. Kraków has its *Kraków Post* (www.krakowpost.pl) monthly news magazine covering politics, business, culture and restaurant reviews. For listings look for *In Your Pocket* magazine (www.inyourpocket.com), which publishes several local issues in Warsaw, Kraków, Poznań, Katowice, Wrocław, Gdańsk, Łódź and Tarnów.

International newspapers and magazines are available from hotel kiosks, good bookshops and EMPIK (for a list of all the branches, see www.empik.com/salony). British newspapers usually arrive on the day of publication.

Radio and Television

Polish radio (www.polskieradio.pl) now offers four main stations: Jedynka (1), Dwójka (2), Trójka (3) and Czwórka (4). There is also the Radio Poland station, which broadcasts in several foreign languages; the English section provides updated daily information at www.news.pl and also offers 24-hour streaming in English. In summer, Polish Radio 1 provides a summary of the news and weather in English. Among many private radio stations, the most popular are RMF FM and Radio Zet.

Polish television (Telewizja Polska; www.tvp.pl) has two principal channels and several speciality ones, among them TV Polonia, broadcasting in Polish with English subtitles. The most popular private channels are TVN and Polsat. Most hotels provide satellite/cable channels featuring CNN, BBC and many others.

Money

Polish złoty (zł or PLN), divided into 100 groszy (gr).

Notes (for 10, 20, 50, 100 and 200 złoty) come in different sizes and are easily recognisable. The nine coins are: 1, 2, 5, 10, 20 and 50 groszy and 1, 2 and 5 złoty.

Currency and Exchange

The Polish złoty (zł) can be changed in banks and privately run bureaux de change (*kantor*). Some travel agents and hotels will change money too, although you should check the commission rate first. A *kantor* is usually the best place to exchange foreign currency, almost always offering a better rate than banks. These offices never accept travellers' cheques. Most *kantor* can be found in hotels, main railway and bus stations and in main streets. In the biggest supermarkets and in some shops it's possible to pay in euros.

Cheques are not popular in Poland, so it may be difficult to find a bank ready to cash one (some banks offer the service only to their own customers). In Warsaw you can cash cheques at the airport (Terminal A) in Currency Express and Air Tours Poland offices.

Banks (see page 393) and cash dispensers are plentiful in Poland. Cards are widely accepted and payment with a mobile phone is also possible (PayPass).

Credit Cards and Travellers' Cheques

Most hotels, petrol stations, car rental firms, restaurants, shops and supermarkets will accept payment with credit cards (check for appropriate signs at the entrance). American Express, Visa, Eurocard, MasterCard, Diners' Club and JCB credit cards are the most commonly accepted. Cash against Visa cards can be obtained in banks or in cash dispensers (*bankomat*).

Loss or theft of credit cards can be reported at the following credit card hotlines:
American Express: tel: 022-581 52 22
Diners' Club: tel: 022-826 07 66 ext. 101–106 (24 hours)

Public Holidays

January New Year's Day (1); Epiphany (6)
March/April Easter Monday (variable)
May Labour Day (1); Constitution Day (3); Pentecost Sunday (variable)
June Corpus Christi Thursday (variable)
August Feast of the Assumption (15)
November All Saints' Day (1); National Independence Day (11)
December Christmas Day (25); St Stephen's Day (26)

MasterCard: Tel: 0 800 111 1211
Visa: tel: 0 800 111 1569

Cash Dispensers

There are 24-hour cash dispensers, accepting credit and bank cards (with pin numbers) on many main streets in larger cities.
The machines usually offer a choice of three languages in which to conduct your transaction; some also issue euros (www.euronetpolska.pl).

Main Banks in Poland

Bank Pekao www.pekao.com.pl
Bank PKO PB www.pkopb.pl
BZ WBK (Santander) www.bzwbk.pl
Getin Noble Bank www/gnb.pl
ing Bank Śląski www.ingbank.pl
Mbank www.mbank.pl
Narodowy Bank Polski www.nbp.pl

Tipping

Tipping is the norm in Poland and it is usual to leave about 10 percent of the total bill as a tip in a restaurant, for hairdressers and for taxi drivers.

O

Opening Hours

Offices are generally open Monday to Friday 9am–4pm. Banks open Monday to Friday 8am–6pm (although some branches may close earlier) without a lunch break; some are open on Saturdays. Post Offices open Monday to Friday 8am–2pm in small towns, till 6pm in medium towns and till 8pm in big cities. The main post office in major cities is open 24 hours.

Shop Opening Hours

Opening times vary. Whatever the time, whatever the day, you will almost certainly find a shop open somewhere. In general, the bigger the town, the longer the opening times. Most shops open at 10am (food shops at 6am or

7am) and close at 7pm, on Saturday a little earlier. Some supermarkets open as early as 7am until 8pm or 9pm, some even later, and shopping centres are open seven days a week (10am–9pm, in big cities until 10pm; Sundays they close earlier). Most high street shops are closed on Sunday. There are plenty of small neighbourhood shops open 24 hours a day.

P

Passports and Visas

Citizens of EU countries, the US, Canada, Australia and New Zealand require only a valid passport to enter Poland for a stay of up to 90 days. Citizens of South Africa should apply for a visa to enter the Schengen area. Always check the latest regulations before you travel.

Photography

Those buildings and locations that the authorities regard as strategically important, such as stations, bridges, port installations, police and military buildings, may not be photographed. If you wish to take photographs of people, it is polite to ask permission first: 'Czy mogę zrobić zdjęcie?'

Postal Services

Post offices (poczta) are marked by a red sign with a yellow trumpet and the white letters POCZTA POLSKA, and are usually open Monday to Friday 8am–2pm in small towns, until 6pm in medium towns and until 8pm in big cities; some are also open on Saturdays. Services include sending letters, faxes, money, paying bills, etc. You can buy stamps, envelopes, prepaid calling and mobile cards and postcards.
Sending a letter within Europe costs 5PLN or more. Airmail letters to European destinations take about a week to arrive, two to three weeks elsewhere.
Main Post Office in Warsaw
Ul Świętokrzyska 31/33; tel: 022-505 33 16; daily 24hrs.

R

Religion

In Poland 88 percent of people are Catholic (Roman and Greek). The remaining population is composed of 0.41 percent Orthodox, 0.20 percent Protestant, and small pockets of

Muslims and Jews.
Throughout the country there are more than 12,500 churches.

Religious Services

A large majority of the Polish population is Roman Catholic, and Poles attend church regularly. Catholic services in English can be found at the following churches in Warsaw:
Church of the Nativity of Our Lady (Narodzenia NMP na Lesznie): Al Solidarnosci 80. Sun 12.15pm.
Chapel of the Immaculate Conception of the Virgin Mary (Kaplica Niepokalanego Poczęcia NMP): Ul Radna 14. Sun 11.30am.

S

Student Travellers

Poland has a massive student population and as such, Poland is a great place for students, not least because general living costs remain relatively low. Those in possession of recognised International Student Cards can get discounts at most attractions (at least publicly owned ones), though note that only Polish students are entitled to discounted travel (with some exceptions; see www.isic.pl). Poznań, Warsaw and Kraków are Poland's biggest university cities.

T

Telecommunications

Public Telephones

The public telephone service is provided by Orange Polska. There are two types of public telephones: silver and yellow. Both accept Orange cards and yellow ones also take Polish and euro coins. The phonecards Orange, Tele Grosik and Tele24 can be purchased at post offices, newspaper kiosks and gas stations.

Useful Numbers

Roadside Assistance: Tel: 981
International Directory Enquiries: Tel: 118 912
Inland Directory Enquiries: Tel: 118 913
Radio Taxi: Tel: 19191
Tourist emergency helpline (in English): Tel: (0) 801 888 844/022-278 77 77 (daily 8am–6pm, till 10pm June–Sept).

Mobile Phones

Mobile phones are very popular in

Dialling codes

When calling any number in Poland you need to dial both the number and the city code, even if you are in the city in question (but then you omit the initial zero).
Białystok 085
Bielski-Biała 033
Częstochowa 034
Elblag 055
Gdańsk 058
Gliwice 032
Jelenia Góra 075
Katowice 032
Kazimierz Dolny 081
Kołobrzeg 094
Kraków 012
Lublin 081
Łańcut 017
Łeba 059
Łódź 042
Malbork 055
Nowy Sącz 018
Olsztyn 089
Opole 077
Poznań 061
Rzeszów 017
Sopot 058
Szczecin 091
Toruń 056
Warsaw 022
Wrocław 071
Zakopane 018
Zamość 084

Poland – in 2013 there were 56 million active SIM cards, among a population of 38 million.
The market is divided between four GSM operators: T-Mobile (www.t-mobile.pl), Orange (www.orange.pl), Plus (www.plus.pl) and Play (www.play.pl). They all provide GSM prepaid services that you can buy in retail stores, newspapers stands and at operators' selling points. All four operators offer good coverage of GSM services (900MHz and 1800MHz) throughout Poland. They also offer third- and fourth-generation systems, UMTS and LTE, but they don't cover all the country; for more information, check the operators' websites. If you prefer to use your own service, contact your local GSM dealer for information on facilities and roaming costs.

Time Zone

Poland is on GMT plus one hour. When it is noon in Warsaw it is 6am in New York, 11am in London and 8pm in Tokyo. Daylight Saving is in effect May–October, when one hour is added.

Toilets

Decent public toilets are few and far between in Poland. Exceptions are those in railway stations (for which you may be expected to pay), shopping malls and in the metro stations in Warsaw. Some parks in Poland have portaloos, but they leave much to be desired on the hygiene front.

Tourist Offices

Local Tourist Information

Bielsko-Biała: Pl Ratuszowy 4; tel: 033-819 00 50; www.it.bielsko.pl
Częstochowa: MCIT Al Najświętszej Maryi Panny 65; tel: 034-368 22 50; www.info.czestochowa. pl
Gdańsk: ul Długi Targ 28/29; tel: 058-301 43 55. Also at the train station and the airport. Pomerania Tourist Information: ul Wały Jagiellońskie 2a; tel: 058-732 70 49; www.gdansk4u.pl; http://pomorskie.travel
Gdynia: ul 10 lutego 24; tel: 058-622 37 66; www.gdyniaturystyczna.pl
Kielce: Regional Tourist Information, ul Sienkiewicza 29; tel: 041-348 00 60; www.swietokrzyskie.travel
Kraków: InfoKraków, Rynek Główny (Main Market Sq) 1–3, Sukiennice; tel: 012-433 73 10. Also Ul Św Jana 2, Szpitalna 25, Pl Wszystkich Świętych 2 (Wyspiański Pavilion), Św Józefa 7, Powiśle 11, Balice International Airport; www.infokrakow.pl
Lublin: Ul Jezuicka 1/3; tel: 081-532 44 12; www.lrot.pl; www.lublin.eu
Nowy Sącz: ul Szwecka 2; tel: 018-444 24 22; www.cit.com.pl; http://ziemiasadecka.info
Płock: Stary Rynek 8; tel: 024-367 19 44; www.plock.eu; www.turystykaplock.eu
Poznań: Ul Ratajczaka 44 (Arkadia); tel: 061-851 96 45. Stary Rynek 59/60 (Old Market Square); tel: 061-852 61 56. Also at the railway station and the airport; www.poznan.pl
Sopot: Plac Zdrojowy 2; tel: 0790 280 884; www.sts.sopot.pl
Szczecin: Ul Korsarzy 34 (Castle); tel: 091-489 16 30; www.zamek.szczecin. pl. Ul Jana z Kolna 7; tel: 091-43 40 440; www.mosrir.szczecin.pl
Toruń: Rynek Staromiejski 25; tel: 056-621 09 30; www.it.torun.pl; www.turystyka.torun.pl
Warsaw: City Authority's Tourist Information: Pl Defilad 1 (Palace of Culture and Science); Old Town Market Square 19/21; and Arrivals Hall of Chopin Airport. Tel: 022-94 31/474 11 42; www.warsawtour. pl. Praga Information: ul Ząbkowska 27/31; tel: 022-670 01 56; www. monopolpraski.pl. Warsaw Tourist

Information Centre: Plac Zamkowy 1/13 (in front of the castle); tel: 022-831 78 53; www.wcit.waw.pl. Wrocław: 'Meeting Point' ul Rynek 14; tel: 071-3443 111. Lower Silesia Tourist Information, Sukiennice 12; tel: 071-342 28 98; www.wroclaw-info.pl

Polish Tourist Offices Abroad

UK: Polish National Tourist Office, Westgate House, West Gate, London W5 1YY; tel: 0 300 303 1812; email: london@pot.gov.pl
USA: Polish National Tourist Office, 5 Marine View Plaza, Hoboken, NY 07030; tel: (202) 420-99-10; email: newyork@pot.gov.pl

Tour Operators

UK Tour Operators
Polorbis Holidays Ltd
157/29 Abercorn Place, London NW8 9DU; tel: (020) 7624 1123; www.polorbis.co.uk

US Tour Operators
JayWay Travel
777 Pelham Road, Suite 1C, New Rochelle, NY, 10805. USA: tel: 1 (914) 500 8912; UK: tel: (020) 8133 7150. www.jaywaytravel.com

W

Websites

www.poland.pl or www.polska.pl: Poland's official website contains useful tourist information.
www.poland.travel/en: Poland's official travel website.
www.pieknywschod.pl/en: Ideas for a holiday in eastern Poland.
www.culture.pl/en: The most comprehensive website about Polish culture and current events, with listings, reviews and essays.
www.um.warszawa.pl/en and www.warsawtour.pl: Useful information about Warsaw.
www.krakow.pl/en: Useful information about Kraków.
www.polhotels.com: Hotels website, with an online reservation system.

Weights and Measures
Poland uses the metric system.

Women Travellers
Poland poses no particular threat to women travellers. Employ common sense at all times and you should have little problem.

LANGUAGE

UNDERSTANDING THE LANGUAGE

GENERAL

Polish, a Slavic language, is the mother tongue of 99 percent of the population. The most widely known foreign language is English, the second is Russian and the third German, but still 41 percent of the population doesn't speak any foreign language. In the cities English speakers are unlikely to find many problems; in the countryside, communication difficulties are to be expected.

The Polish language is extremely difficult and can be quite daunting at first, but learning even a handful of key phrases is a good idea and will prove helpful. As a general rule, the emphasis falls on the second-last syllable.

USEFUL PHRASES

Hi/bye Cześć (chesh)
Yes Tak (tack)
No Nie (nee-ar)
Thank you Dziękuje (gen-coo-yea)
Please Proszę (proshay)
Good morning /afternoon Dzień dobry (jane dobray)
Good evening Dobry wieczór (dobray vieer-chew)
Goodbye Do widzenia (do-vitzania)
Sorry/Excuse me Przepraszam (puh-shay prusham)
How much is it? Ile to kosztuje? (e-lay toe coshtu yea)
I would like... Chciałbym (men)/ Chciałabym (women) (chow bim)
Where is...? Gdzie jest? (jay yest)
How far? Jak daleko? (yak daleko)
How long? Jak długo? (yak dwugo)
OK Dobrze (dobray)
Cheap Tanio (tan-yo)
Expensive Drogo (drogo)

Hot Gorąco (gorronso)
Cold Zimno (zhim-no)
Free Wolny (volney)
Occupied Zajęty (zigh-yente)
I don't understand Nie rozumiem (nie rozumee-em)
Help! Pomocy! (po-mo-tsay)

SIGNS

Open Otwarte
Closed Zamknięte
Exit Wyjście
Pharmacy Apteka
Post Office Poczta
Avenue Aleja (al)
Street ulica (ul)
Old Town Stare Miasto
Police Station Posterunek Policji
Information Informacja
Toilets/WC Toalety
Men Panowie
Women Panie
No Smoking Palenie Wzbronione
Cash Desk Kasa

An assortment of Polish publications.

PRONUNCIATION

Polish vowels:
a = as the u in 'cut'
ą = a nasal vowel, as in the French 'Jean'
ę = as in the French 'un'
i = as in feet
ó = as the English u
u = as in book
Polish consonants:
Pronounced as in English except ć is pronounced in a much softer way than the Polish c
ch = as in the Scottish loch
cz = ch as in church
dź = as in beds
dż = j as in jam
ł = w
ń = ny (as in canyon)
rz = zh as in pleasure
ś = like s but much softer
sz = sh as in show
szcz = shch as in pushchair
w = v

FURTHER READING

GENERAL

Between East and West by Anne Applebaum. US journalist's account of her travels through Poland.
Colloquial Polish by B.W. Mazur.
Jewish Roots in Poland: Pages from the Past and Archival Inventories by Miriam Weiner. The most comprehensive guide to Polish Jewry.

HISTORY

Iron Curtain: The Crushing of Eastern Europe by Anne Applebaum.
Bloodlands: Europe Between Hitler and Stalin by Timothy Snyder.
The Jews in Poland by Chimen Abramsky, Maciej Jachimczyk and Anthony Polonsky. Comprehensive historical background to the Jewish community in Poland.
The Struggles for Poland by Neal Ascherson. Book to accompany the UK Channel 4 series. Good introduction to modern Polish history and politics.
God's Playground: A History of Poland by Norman Davies. Intelligent and entertaining history of pre-Solidarity Poland.
Heart of Europe: A Short History of Poland by Norman Davies. Balanced and entertaining history from World War II onwards.
The Polish Way by Adam Zamoyski. An accessible history of Poland going up to the 1989 elections. Books by the same author include **Poland, A History**; **The Forgotten Few: The Polish Air Force in World War II**; **Warsaw 1920**; **Chopin**; and **The Last King of Poland**.
The Holocaust by Martin Gilbert. Most-read account of the Polish role in the Holocaust.
Rising '44 by Norman Davies. Gripping account of the Warsaw uprising.
Warsaw 1944: Hitler, Himmler and the Crushing of a City by Alexandra Richie.
Winter in the Morning by Janina Bauman. A survivor's moving account of life in the Warsaw Ghetto.
Neighbours: The Destruction of the

Jewish Community in Jedwabne Poland by Tomasz Gross.
Nice Promises by Tim Sebastian. Accessible account of Poland in the early 1980s by a former BBC correspondent in Warsaw.
The Poles by Stewart Stevens. Personal journalistic account of Poland in the 1980s.
A Path of Hope by Lech Wałęsa. Autobiography of the Solidarity leader's pre-presidential days.

LITERATURE

Selected Poems by Zbigniew Herbert (1977). One of the best Polish poets. Political, contemporary observations.
Insatiability by Stanisław Ignacy Witkiewicz. In-depth 12th-century account of an artistic lifestyle, not an easy read, but worth it.

Send Us Your Thoughts

We do our best to ensure the information in our books is as accurate and up-to-date as possible. The books are updated on a regular basis using local contacts, who painstakingly add, amend and correct as required. However, some details (such as telephone numbers and opening times) are liable to change, and we are ultimately reliant on our readers to put us in the picture.

We welcome your feedback, especially your experience of using the book "on the road". Maybe we recommended a hotel that you liked (or another that you didn't), or you came across a great bar or new attraction we missed.

We will acknowledge all contributions, and we'll offer an Insight Guide to the best letters received.

Please write to us at:
Insight Guides
PO Box 7910
London SE1 1WE
Or email us at:
hello@insightguides.com

A Minor Apocalypse by Tadeusz Konwicki. Highly political novel narrating a day in the life of a political activist.
The History of Polish Literature by Czesław Miłosz. Written in the 1960s, this is still the most comprehensive book on Polish literature.
The Issa Valley by Czesław Miłosz. Semi-autobiographical account of childhood in a Lithuanian rural community.

CULTURE, ART AND ARCHITECTURE

Atlas of Warsaw's Architecture by J.A. Chróscicki and A. Rottermund. Interesting and informative atlas of Warsaw's architectural treasures.
Kraków: City of Museums by Jerzy Banach (ed). Book detailing Kraków's many museums.
Book of Warsaw Palaces by T.S. Jaroszewski.
Double Vision: My Life in Film by Andrzej Wajda. Autobiography of Poland's greatest director.

POLISH CUISINE

In My Polish Country House Kitchen by Anne Applebaum. An interesting take on Polish cuisine by a Pulitzer Prize-winning journalist and wife of the former Polish Foreign Minister Radosław Sikorski.

OTHER INSIGHT GUIDES

More than 120 **Insight Guides** and **Insight City Guides** cover every continent, providing information on culture and all the top sights, as well as superb photography and detailed maps. Other **Insight Guides** to this region include: **Estonia, Latvia & Lithuania**, **Germany** and **Russia**.
Insight Guides **Explore Kraków** brings you the very best of the city with a selection of self-guided routes and a handy pull-out map.

CREDITS

Insight Guide Credits

Distribution
UK
Dorling Kindersley Ltd
A Penguin Group company
80 Strand, London, WC2R 0RL
sales@uk.dk.com

United States
Ingram Publisher Services
1 Ingram Boulevard, PO Box 3006,
La Vergne, TN 37086-1986
ips@ingramcontent.com

Australia and New Zealand
Woodslane
10 Apollo St, Warriewood,
NSW 2102, Australia
info@woodslane.com.au

Worldwide
Apa Publications GmbH & Co. Verlag
KG (Singapore branch)
7030 Ang Mo Kio Avenue 5
08-65 Northstar @ AMK
Singapore 569880
apasin@singnet.com.sg

Printing
CTPS-China
© 2015 Apa Publications (UK) Ltd
All Rights Reserved

First Edition 1991
Third Edition 2015

No part of this book may be
reproduced, stored in a retrieval
system or transmitted in any form or
means electronic, mechanical,
photocopying, recording or otherwise,
without prior written permission of
Apa Publications. Brief text
quotations with use of photographs
are exempted for book review
purposes only. Information has been
obtained from sources believed to be
reliable, but its accuracy and
completeness, and the opinions
based thereon, are not guaranteed.

www.insightguides.com

Project Editor
Carine Tracanelli
Author
Maciej Zglinicki
Update Production
AM Services
Picture Editor
Tom Smyth
Map Production
Original cartography Colourmap
Scanning Ltd, updated by Carte
Production
Rebeka Davies

Contributors

Maciej Zglinicki is a freelance
journalist, editor and translator
based in Poland. For many years
he worked for the BBC World
Service in Warsaw and London. He
loves to travel off the beaten track
in search of unique experiences
and people.

About Insight Guides

Insight Guides have more than
40 years' experience of publishing
high-quality, visual travel guides. We
produce 400 full-colour titles, in both
print and digital form, covering more
than 200 destinations across the
globe, in a variety of formats to meet
your different needs.
   Insight Guides are written by
local authors, whose expertise is
evident in the extensive historical
and cultural background features.

Each destination is carefully
researched by regional experts to
ensure our guides provide the very
latest information. All the reviews
in **Insight Guides** are independent;
we strive to maintain an impartial
view. Our reviews are carefully
selected to guide you to the best
places to eat, go out and shop, so
you can be confident that when
we say a place is special, we really
mean it.

Legend

City maps
Freeway/Highway/Motorway
Divided Highway
Main Roads
Minor Roads
Pedestrian Roads
Steps
Footpath
Railway
Funicular Railway
Cable Car
Tunnel
City Wall
Important Building
Built Up Area
Other Land
Transport Hub
Park
Pedestrian Area
Bus Station
Tourist Information
Main Post Office
Cathedral/Church
Mosque
Synagogue
Statue/Monument
Beach
Airport

Regional maps
Freeway/Highway/Motorway
(with junction)
Freeway/Highway/Motorway
(under construction)
Divided Highway
Main Road
Secondary Road
Minor Road
Track
Footpath
International Boundary
State/Province Boundary
National Park/Reserve
Marine Park
Ferry Route
Marshland/Swamp
Glacier   Salt Lake
Airport/Airfield
Ancient Site
Border Control
Cable Car
Castle/Castle Ruins
Cave
Chateau/Stately Home
Church/Church Ruins
Crater
Lighthouse
Mountain Peak
Place of Interest
Viewpoint

INDEX

Main references are in bold type

INSIGHT GUIDES

¡ YOUR NEXT **ADVENTURE**

Insight Guides offers you a range of travel guides
to match your needs. Whether you are looking for
inspiration for planning a trip, cultural information,
walks and tours, great listings, or practical advice, we
have a product to suit you.